Nicholas Hagger has written more than 20 books on history, literature and philosophy, including a study of the founding, rise and fall of civilizations. He has lectured at universities in Baghdad, Iraq; Tokyo, Japan (where he was a Professor); and Tripoli, Libya. He has followed a career in education, and travelled widely. For seven years he owned the house in Suffolk in which the Jamestown settlement is thought to have been planned, and he was involved in the discovery of a skeleton which was thought to be that of Bartholomew Gosnold. He has appeared many times on radio and television, and has written articles in newspapers on the subject of the founding of America.

By the Same Author

The Fire and the Stones

Selected Poems: A Metaphysical's Way of Fire

The Universe and the Light: A New View of the Universe and Reality

Collected Poems: A White Radiance 1958-1993

A Mystic Way: A Spiritual Autobiography

Awakening to the Light: Diaries, Volume 1, 1958-1967

A Spade Fresh with Mud: Collected Stories, Volume 1

A Smell of Leaves and Summer: Collected Stories, Volume 2

The Warlords: From D-Day to Berlin, A Verse Drama

Overlord: The Triumph of Light, An Epic Poem in 4 volumes

The Tragedy of Prince Tudor

The One and the Many

Wheeling Bats and a Harvest Moon: Collected Stories, Volume 3

The Warm Glow of the Monastery Courtyard: Collected Stories, Volume 4

The Syndicate: The Story of the Coming World Government

The Secret History of the West: The Influence of Secret Organisations on Western History from the Renaissance to the 20th Century

The Light of Civilization

Collected Poems 1958–2005

Classical Odes

Overlord: one-volume edition

Collected Verse Plays

Collected Short Stories: 1,001 Very Short Stories or Verbal Paintings, 1966–2006

The Endless Rise and Fall of Civilizations

THE SECRET
FOUNDING
OF AMERICA

*The Real Story of Freemasons, Puritans
and the Battle for the New World*

NICHOLAS HAGGER

WATKINS PUBLISHING

LONDON

Distributed in the USA and Canada by Sterling Publishing Co., Inc.
387 Park Avenue South, New York, NY 10016

This edition first published in the UK and USA 2007 by
Watkins Publishing, Sixth Floor, Castle House,
75–76 Wells Street, London W1T 3QH

1 3 5 7 9 10 8 6 4 2

Designed by Jerry Goldie
Typeset by Dorchester Typesetting Group

Manufactured in the United States of America

Library of Congress Cataloging-in-Publication Data Available

ISBN 13: 978-1-84293-140-0
ISBN 10: 1-84293-140-7

www.watkinspublishing.com

For information about custom editions, special sales, premium and
corporate purchases, please contact Sterling Special Sales
Department at 800-805-5489 or specialsales@sterlingpub.com

For the people of East Anglia and Virginia who heard me on the planting of America and wanted to know more, including Bill Kelso; for Michael Mann, who entrusted me with an idea he had long had in mind, and for Duncan Baird, who saw it through; and for Ann, who walked with me in Gosnold's footsteps.

'Not only were many of the founders of the United States Government Masons, but they received aid from a secret and august body existing in Europe, which helped them to establish this country for a peculiar and particular purpose known only to the initiated few.'

Professor Charles Eliot Norton of Harvard, 'a century after 1776'[1]

CONTENTS

Picture Acknowledgements   viii
Introduction: Skeleton of a Planting Father   ix

Part One: The Planters: Who *Apparently* Founded America?
    Chapter 1: English Separatists in Plymouth, Puritans in
          Massachusetts   2
    Chapter 2: English Anglicans in Virginia and Chesapeake Bay   27
    Chapter 3: Spanish Catholics in Florida   63

Part Two: Who *Really* Founded America?
    Chapter 4: Freemasons in Virginia and Massachusetts   84
    Chapter 5: Enlightenment Deists in New England   107
    Chapter 6: German Illuminati   128

Part Three: Consequences of the Founders' Vision
    Chapter 7: A Freemasonic State   146
    Chapter 8: Freemasonry's Battle for America   171
    Chapter 9: The Freemasonic State Today   187

Appendices: Constitutional Documents
    I: John Winthrop, *A Modell of Christian Charitie*, 1630   205
    II: Fundamental Orders of 1639   220
    III: Anderson's *Constitutions*, 1723   225
    IV: Albany Plan of Union, 1754   231
    V: Declaration of Independence, 4 July 1776   235
    VI: The Articles of Confederation, 1781   242
    VII: The Federal Constitution, 1787   253
    VIII: The Bill of Rights, 15 December 1791   267
    IX: George Washington's Masonic Record, 1752–99   278

Chart: History of Freemansory/Secret Organizations   282
Notes and Sources   284
Bibliography   307
Index   313

PICTURE ACKNOWLEDGEMENTS

The author and publisher would like to thank the following people, museums and photographic libraries for permission to reproduce their material. Every care has been taken to trace copyright holders. However, if we have omitted anyone we apologize and will, if informed, make corrections to any future edition.

BAL = Bridgeman Art Library, London

Plate 1 Hernando de Soto (c.1496–1542), from *The Narrative and Critical History of America*, edited by Justin Winsor, London 1886. Engraving.
Private Collection/BAL

Plate 2 René Goulaine de Laudonnière (c.1529–82) and Chief Athore in front of Ribault's Column, from *Brevis Narratio*. Engraving by Theodore de Bry (1528–98), published 1591.
Service Historique de la Marine, Vincennes/BAL

Plate 3 Fort Caroline, from *Brevis Narratio*. Engraving by Theodore de Bry, published 1591.
Service Historique de la Marine, Vincennes/BAL

Plate 4 Map depicting the destruction of the Spanish colony of St Augustine in Florida, 7 July 1586, by the English fleet commanded by Sir Francis Drake (1540–96). Engraving, 16th century.
Private Collection/BAL

Plate 5 The arrival of the English in Virginia, from *Admiranda Narratio* (1585–88). Engraving by Theodore de Bry.
Service Historique de la Marine, Vincennes/BAL

Plate 6 Sir Thomas Smythe (c.1558–1625), from *Memoirs of the Court of Queen Elizabeth*, published in 1825. Watercolour.
Private Collection/BAL

Plate 7 Landing of the first settlers at Cape Henry, Jamestown. Painting by Sidney King, 1956.
Courtesy of the National Park Service, Colonial National Historical Park, Jamestown

Plate 8 Landing at Jamestown: the founding of the colony of Jamestown, Virginia, by Captain Christopher Newport and 105 of his followers, 1607. Lithograph.
Private Collection/BAL

Plate 9 The first settlers from England giving thanks for their safe arrival at Jamestown, Virginia, in 1607. Pen and ink drawing with wash by Elmo Jones (20th century).
Private Collection/BAL

Plate 10 The first day at Jamestown, 14 May 1607, from *The Romance and Tragedy of Pioneer Life* by Augustus L. Mason, 1883. Engraving by William Ludlow Sheppard. *Library of Congress, Washington DC/BAL*

Plate 11 The Indian village of Secoton, by John White, (fl. 1570–93). *British Museum, London/BAL*

Plate 12 Trading with the Indians at Jamestown. Painting by Sidney King, 1956. *Courtesy of the National Park Service, Colonial National Historical Park, Jamestown*

Plate 13 Jamestown c.1614. Painting by Sidney King, 1956. *Courtesy of the National Park Service, Colonial National Historical Park, Jamestown*

Plate 14 1622 map of Virginia, showing (upper left) a picture of Chief Powhatan by John Smith (1580–1631). *British Library London/BAL*

Plate 15 Map of the coast of New England, observed and described by Captain John Smith. Engraving, 1614, by Simon de Passe (1595–1647). *Library of Congress, Washington DC/BAL*

Plate 16 Captain John Smith. Engraving by Simon de Passe. *Private Collection, Peter Newark American Pictures/BAL*

Plate 17 A description of part of the adventures of Captain John Smith in Virginia. Illustration from Smith's *Generall Historie of Virginia, New England & the Summer Isles*. *Private Collection/BAL*

Plate 18 Arrival of Lord De La Warr at Jamestown. Painting by Sidney King, 1956. *Courtesy of the National Park Service, Colonial National Historical Park, Jamestown*

Plate 19 Pocahontas (1595–1617), a native American princess, saves Captain John Smith from execution. From Smith's *Generall Historie of Virginia, New England & the Summer Isles*. Engraving, 1624. *Private Collection/BAL*

Plate 20 Pocahontas, who was baptised Rebecca in 1613 and married Thomas Rolfe in the same year. Engraving by Simon de Passe, 1616. *Private Collection/BAL*

Plate 21 Map of Plymouth, Massachusetts, English School, 17th century. *Private Collection/BAL*

Plate 22 William Penn (1644–1718) receiving the Charter of Pennsylvania from King Charles II of England, by Allan Stewart (1865–1951). *Private Collection/BAL*

Plate 23 Portrait of Benjamin Franklin (1706–90) by George Healy (1808–94).
Château de Versailles, France /BAL

Plate 24 The Boston Tea Party, 1773. Engraving.
Private Collection/BAL

Plate 25 George Washington (1732–99) as a Freemason. Lithograph, 19th century.
Private Collection/BAL

Plate 26 Thomas Jefferson (1743–1826) writing the Declaration of Independence.
Oil on canvas by Howard Pyle, 1898.
Delaware Art Museum, Wilmington/BAL

Plate 27 Adam Weishaupt (1748–1830), founder of the Order of the Illuminati, from
Historia General de la Masoneria (General History of Freemasonry) by G. Danton, published
in Spain in 1882.
Archivo Iconografico, SA/Corbis

Plate 28 Great Seal of the US, *obverse*. Lithograph, c.1850, by Andrew B. Graham.
Library of Congress, Washington DC/BAL

Plate 29 Great Seal of the US, *reverse*. From a militia propaganda poster. The seal with
its 'All-Seeing Eye' is on the back of the $1 bill.
Corbis

Plate 30 The signing of the Constitution of the United States in 1787. Painted in 1940
by Howard Chandler Christy (1873–1952).
Hall of Representatives, Washington DC/BAL

Plate 31 The inauguration of President George Washington on 30 April 1789 at the
Old City Hall, New York. Lithograph published in 1876 by N. Currier (1813–88) and
J. M. Ives (1824–95).
Private Collection/BAL

Plate 32 Map of Washington (originally drawn 1790–2). Washington was designed by
Pierre Charles l'Enfant and laid out in 1795, the streets forming Masonic symbols.
Alan Butler

Plate 33 Abraham Lincoln (1809–65), 16th President of the United States. Photograph,
19th century.
Private Collection/BAL

Plate 34 The fall of Richmond, Virginia, 2 April 1865. Lithograph by N. Currier and
J. M. Ives.
Private Collection/BAL

Plate 35 The 300th anniversary celebration of the founding of Jamestown, 1907.
Watercolour by Edward Biedermann (b.1864).
Private Collection, © Christie's Images/BAL

SKELETON OF A

PLANTING FATHER

The United States of America boasts the most advanced civilization the world has ever known. Its technology is awesome. It has reached the moon, sent spacecraft to the far reaches of our solar system and produced images of our galaxy. Its satellites transmit instant pictures from across the world on our television screens. Its computers send instant messages round the globe via the internet. Its precision bombing has raised war to a new level, enabling surgical strikes to be made while limiting damage. Its skyscrapers, aircraft, cars, housing and potential for wealth are unrivalled, and it has opened its doors to the tired, the poor, the homeless 'huddled masses yearning to breathe free' and admitted refugees from all corners of the world. It stands for liberty and democracy and is a beacon of freedom to the rest of the world, which is apprehensive, fearing US domination and world hegemony.

All this technological inventiveness and administrative genius has developed very rapidly in a country that only 400 years ago was an empty landscape occupied only by native Americans, a place of great scenic beauty but also a terrifying wilderness. Into this vast, seemingly sparsely populated tract came Europeans – from England, Spain and France – at a time when navigators were exploring the limits of the Earth. The prevailing view was still that the Earth was the centre of the universe and the planets travelled round it in spherical orbits. New heresies were asserting that the Earth revolved around the sun and that its movement caused the stars to appear to move. But it was only a theory that the world was round and that a ship sailing west might reach the Indies of the East. Rumour had it that beyond the mariners' horizon there was a huge waterfall that ships would plunge over and be lost forever more.

In this bewildering time European voyagers set sail in small-masted ships that leaked like old tubs to unknown destinations, knowing they would be absent for a year or two and unsure whether they would ever return home. What drove them? Some, like Vasco da Gama, were in quest of knowledge. Some, gentlemen adventurers, were seeking their fortune and hoping to bring back cargos of gold and diamonds, or at least precious wood, that they could sell for commercial gain. Some hoped to own land, an impossibility for the poor under the medieval feudal system. Some were fleeing religious persecution and yearned for the freedom to worship in the way they wanted without being penalized by the State.

When they reached America after their heroic voyages, they planted settlements, and a backwoods life of great primitiveness, of hand-hewn wooden huts, shacks and fences, grew up along the eastern coast. As more colonists arrived, the lands that were settled grew more extensive. For more than 150 years there were English colonies in the north. Eventually these threw off their colonial yoke, became independent and wrote themselves a constitution, which enabled the United States to grow into the superpower it is today.

This book is about the founding of the United States from the planting of the first settlements to the constitutional founding of 1787. It shows that while religion was behind the first plantings, circumstantial evidence indicates that Freemasonry was also present and that a secret Deistic Freemasonry, subscribing to a non-Christian concept of God and hiding behind a religious façade, inspired the constitutional arrangements that prepared the way for today's superpower. Indeed, the first United States was a Masonic State. As we shall see, Freemasonry remained strong during the Civil War and is still a very powerful force behind the apparently Christian United States today. We shall see that today Freemasonry has an agenda for a new world order, a federal-continental United States of the World in which nation-states are subsumed as states within regional blocs.

All was not as it seems in the early planting of America. The story that schoolchildren learn is that Separatists came over on the *Mayflower* in 1620 and settled at New Plymouth. But they were not the first. Before this there is a real story involving Jamestown, which was settled in 1607. That is what America has chosen to base its 400th anniversary on in 2007. But, as we shall discover, even that is not the true start of America....

I first became interested in the founding of America when I did research for my study of the origin, growth, rise and fall of 25 civilizations, which became *The Fire and the Stones* (Element Books, 1991). My view has recently been updated and is appearing in two volumes, *The Light of Civilization* (O Books, 2006) and *The Endless Rise and Fall of Civilizations* (forthcoming). In these works I have identified North American civilization as separate from European civilization, though the two together form Western civilization. I have found that it is the most recent civilization and has now arguably reached the same stage that the Roman civilization reached while Rome was still a republic. I became further interested in the founding of America when I acquired Otley Hall in Suffolk, eastern England, in 1997. Otley Hall is a Tudor moated house where the Jamestown settlement of 1607 is thought to have been planned. There Bartholomew Gosnold is thought to have interviewed and recruited the crews and passengers for his two voyages, first in 1602, when he named Cape Cod and Martha's Vineyard, and then in 1606–7, when he was 'prime mover' in the founding of the Jamestown settlement. We shall see that Gosnold inspired this second voyage. He organized it and his wife's cousin funded it. John Smith, who later awarded himself much of the credit, was very much an underling who took no part during the first six months of the voyage.

I conducted research into Bartholomew Gosnold for a year and wrote an illustrated guidebook to Otley Hall – indeed, I also wrote a filmscript about Gosnold's life – and by October 1998, when I visited Jamestown, I was steeped in Gosnold. I gave a lecture on him to the English-Speaking Union in Richmond, Virginia, and showed slides. (One Virginian correspondent[1] described it as 'the Hagger gospel of Gosnold'.) There were some 200 in the audience. When I told them, 'You've got the wrong man. You've erected a statue to John Smith, but there should be a statue to Bartholomew Gosnold, who did more to establish Jamestown than John Smith,' some were shocked and several shook their heads. But many were extremely interested in the alternative pedigree I was proposing for

Virginia – one which, as we shall see, stems from the politics of the Elizabethan and early Jacobean court rather than the disreputable, semi-piratical Smith. Indeed, I was told by several prominent Virginians, 'We would rather see ourselves descended from Gosnold than from Smith.'

In the audience was the deputy of the chief archaeologist at Jamestown, Dr William Kelso. He had discovered the Jamestown Fort in 1994, thereby proving it was not a myth, in the same way that Heinrich Schliemann proved Troy was not a myth. Between April and December 1994 APVA Jamestown Rediscovery archaeologists recovered 30,000 artefacts of the early 1600s, at least half of which dated back to the earliest years of the Jamestown settlement. Dr Kelso has since uncovered some 350,000 artefacts which had lain buried within the Jamestown Fort.

I had met Bill Kelso during a visit to Jamestown before my lecture. The morning after my lecture he rang me up and said he wanted to see me. I went to Jamestown and met him again, a white-haired man of great bearing and dignity whom I now think of as America's Schliemann. We sat on a wooden seat by the river James, which lapped near our feet, the statue of John Smith towering above us, behind and to our right.

Bill said to me, 'I've been trying to figure out how three English ships arrived here in front of us in 1607 and led the way for others to come, which all brought with them the stuff we've been finding under the ground here. Who was behind it? Who organized it?'

I said without hesitation, 'Bartholomew Gosnold,' and talked Bill through the main points I had made in my lecture. I explained that Gosnold had died in the fort in August 1607 and had been buried there. I said to Bill, 'Please dig for him.'

He said, 'The ground's severely impacted, it's like concrete, and sub-ground radar won't work here. We have a triangle 140 yards by 140 yards by 140 yards. It's like looking for a needle in a haystack. It'll take decades to find him.'

I replied without hesitation, 'He'll be in the centre of the fort. There were cannons in each of the three corners, and all the ordnance was shot off during his funeral, so all three cannons were fired. Out of courtesy to the dead leader they'd have laid him in the centre of the cannons, not in one of the corners where he could only hear one. The fort was a palisaded stockade, as you know, and there were hostile Indians outside with bows and arrows. They wouldn't have stood outside the palisade with their eyes closed in prayer during the interment. They'd have buried him in conditions of relative safety, where they would not have been at risk of being shot.'

Bill was interested. 'I'm going to work with that theory,' he said. 'The trouble is, I don't know where all the corners of the fort are. One, I know, is under the river James out there somewhere. If I can find the other two I might be able to calculate the centre.'

Bill visited me at Otley Hall three or four times during the next few years and I took him round some of the villages adjoining Otley, including to Letheringham and Wetheringsett, so he could see where Gosnold's crew and passengers had come from. Forty of the 108 passengers had lived in the nearby villages. One Sunday he rang saying that he was in Lavenham with the Virginian crime novelist Patricia Cornwell and others, could he come straight along? I gave them all lunch and we talked the whole afternoon. He came again when the First Lady of Virginia, Roxane Gilmore, came to Ipswich.

This was a highly publicized visit. At a civic reception held in Ipswich's Christ Church Mansion, the First Lady of Virginia formally requested that in view of the Gosnold connection as outlined in my lecture Jamestown and Ipswich should become 'sister cities'. Governor Gilmore of Virginia had earlier sent a representative and delegation to meet the Mayor, Leader and Chief Executive of Ipswich Borough Council to discuss the requested visit. I had been present at the meeting before hosting a lunch for the Americans, and had been dismayed that in their formal statements the Leader of the Council and Mayor had been unenthusiastic about the request. The Leader had said that the Council might be accused of 'junketing on the rates'. I had made a speech about the importance of the connection, but the Americans had been rebuffed. Roxane's formal approach now was therefore deliberately low-key, but set the request on record – her speech was filmed, as were the Mayor's speech and mine – and at the time of writing, five years later, it is being taken up again by the Council. So the thunder of my lecture is still reverberating today.

On the morning of Roxane's visit I gave a long television interview in Otley Hall to the American History Channel. She later told me it had been 'broadcast to schools all over the US and the world'.

Bill came once more and we toured every local house associated with Gosnold. We also spoke regularly over the phone. Each time I would ask him, 'Have you found him yet?' and Bill would say, 'No, but....' One year he told me he had found one corner of the fort and the next year he said he had found a second corner.

Then, in January 2003, when I asked, 'Have you found him yet?', he said, 'Yes, I think so.' He told me he had found a remarkably well-preserved skeleton of a man in his thirties with a staff that indicated he was the leader of the colony. There was also a decorative captain's staff on the lid of the coffin (coffins at that time were reserved for people of higher status). 'I'm sure we've got Bartholomew,' he said. 'He was only 50 feet away from where we were sitting that day.'

Bill held a press conference in Virginia to announce the find and I had to sit by my phone in England that day and give interviews to various US newspapers. There was considerable interest in the skeleton in the USA and it was displayed in the Smithsonian for a while.

Verification then became the problem. Bill wanted to locate a relative or descendant in the female line so that he could do a DNA test. He trawled the historical records and came up with Bartholomew Gosnold's sister, Elizabeth Gosnold Tilney, who died in 1646 and was buried inside All Saints' church, Shelley, Suffolk, and his niece Katherine Blackerby who, it is believed, was buried at St Peter and St Mary church, Stowmarket, Suffolk, where a tombstone bears the name of her husband. He applied for permission to dig up the floor of Shelley church. Edward Martin, an archaeologist who had at my request dug up the Otley Hall rose-garden lawn to find the old Tudor courtyard, lent the application weight and, for the first time ever, the Church of England agreed to an exhumation for purely historical reasons.

I attended the beginning of the exhumation on 13 June 2005. The church was in a deeply rural area and cars were parked in an adjoining field. Some 20 press, radio and television employees were milling before the altar, together with about eight people like myself who were either experts or associated with the project. Bill was of course present, looking very spruce. *National Geographic* magazine had exclusive rights to the project, having funded it in return for the rights to make a film and, under the deal, as soon as a workman began hammer-and-chiselling the tiles of the ancient floor, we were all ushered out.

The verdict was leaked in October 2005 and confirmed when the television programme was shown in the UK at the end of March 2006: there was no DNA match. It was, however, claimed that the woman dug up was not Gosnold's sister. She was supposed to have died at around 70, whereas the woman exhumed is thought to have died in 1690, plus or minus 50 years, in her fifties. Edward Martin maintained that the right skeleton was exhumed.

The ancient tiled floor had been broken up and the identification of Gosnold was no further forward. At his request I sent Bill my slides of Bartholomew Gosnold's relatives Robert Gosnold III and V. During Otley Hall open days I had been approached by getting on for 30 people who claimed to be descendants of the Gosnolds. I used to stand claimants between the portraits of these two relatives and do my 'nose test'. The Gosnold nose was distinctively hooked. I would appoint a panel of visitors to adjudicate as to whether the claimant was a true Gosnold or not in terms of how hooked the particular nose appeared to be in relation to the portraits. I suggested that Bill should compare facial measurements in the slides and his skeleton.

At the time of writing Bill is focusing in greater detail on the skeleton. He is doing a DNA test on one of its teeth in the belief that it will give a more accurate reading than the previous test, which was based on an area of bone. Minerals from drinking water are deposited in teeth as they form during infancy and leave a chemical signature that can be co-related to ground water. Tests on the tooth sample may therefore prove that the skeleton is of a man who did not grow up in Suffolk, as Gosnold did.[2] The bone-sample test has confirmed that the Jamestown skeleton was an immigrant to America who had had a diet rich in wheat, as opposed to an American corn diet.

That is where we are at the time of writing. Bill is convinced that he has Bartholomew Gosnold, but it will take a bit more time to establish this. There is still another skeleton, that of Bartholomew Gosnold's niece, to try – if it can be located.

I no longer own Otley Hall. Some 40,000 people passed through during the seven years I owned it, most of whom our staff and six guides coped with, but eventually I found that running it was too time-consuming and I sold it to concentrate on my literary activities.

But the experience of the skeleton had whetted my appetite for getting to the bottom of the founding of America. I renewed my research while preparing other books. And having shed Otley Hall, I found I was researching much more impartially. Bartholomew Gosnold was just one of those involved in the founding of settlements and I was keen to be objective about him, to place him in the pattern of settlement without distorting or exaggerating his achievement. I began looking further…

PART ONE

The Planters:
Who *Apparently*
Founded America?

CHAPTER 1

ENGLISH SEPARATISTS IN PLYMOUTH, PURITANS IN MASSACHUSETTS

The generally accepted story of the founding of America is that Puritan exiles came over on the *Mayflower* from Plymouth, England, to the New World and established the first permanent New England colony at Plymouth, Massachusetts, in 1620. To 'found' is to 'establish, originate, be the original builder'. The term 'Founding Fathers' is mostly used of the eighteenth-century independence-seekers and constitutional unifiers who created the United States of America, but it is also frequently used of the early planters who first settled in America. This chapter tells the story of the New England colony.

Flight to the Netherlands

What were the colonists leaving behind? The Reformation of Luther and Calvin had sought to purify the corrupt Church of Rome. Henry VIII had separated the Church of England from Rome and his daughter Elizabeth I had overseen the fending-off of the Spanish Armada, which was supposed to reunite Europe under the Pope and the King of Spain. But the Church of England's episcopal organization had been left untouched, and bishops wearing mitres and carrying croziers still resembled Catholic prelates and smacked of Papism. Puritans wanted further purification and joined

Separatist groups who could not accept compromise. In 1593 three Separatist clerical leaders had been hanged: John Greenwood, Henry Barrow and John Penry.[1] Other leaders had been imprisoned and many Puritans had despaired of reforming the Church and added their support for separation, withdrawing from the self-seeking Anglican society to live apart in groups of other like-minded Puritans, forming congregations of their own in seclusion.

In 1593 a group of Separatists had left England for Amsterdam in the Netherlands. They had been a congregation in Scrooby, Nottinghamshire, in the East Midlands. One of the exiles, William Bradford, had been 17 years old at the time.[2] Christendom was corrupt and these Puritans had regarded themselves as pilgrims trudging through mire on their way to Heaven.

The succession to the English throne of James VI of Scotland as James I of England in 1603 had raised Puritan hopes. Eighteen years earlier, while in Scotland, James, a Calvinist, had signed the Negative Confession which favoured the Puritan position. When he had arrived in London, the Puritans had immediately presented their grievances in a petition that contained 1,000 signatures (the Millenary Petition), but at the Hampton Court conference of 1604 James had supported the Church of England's structure of bishops ('no bishop, no king') and he had encouraged the convocation of 1604 to draw up the *Constitutions and Canons* against Non-conformists. The Act of Supremacy, which had been devised to exclude the authority of the Pope, was now being used against English subjects who were not Catholic – and not Anglican. All Non-conformists now had to conform.

In view of this, in 1607 a group of Puritans withdrew from England, crossed the Channel to the Netherlands and met up with the 1593 exiles. The Netherlands had been part of Catholic Spain, but had stood up to the Spanish Habsburgs and regained its independence from Philip II's armies. Many Dutch had become Calvinists at the beginning of the Reformation and, in throwing off the yoke of Spain, had compared themselves to the Hebrews whose exodus freed them from bondage to the Egyptians. They too had covenanted with God and had been rewarded with freedom and independence. The Netherlands were thus a natural destination for

Puritans separating from unreformed England.

All nations traded with the Dutch, who exported tulips to Turkey where they were in vogue and who were fast becoming a major maritime power with a mercantile empire which by the 1650s embraced the Spice Islands (now Indonesia), the Cape (South Africa) and settlements in North and South America (New Amsterdam and Dutch Brazil). Employment was therefore not difficult to find. Capital was flowing into Dutch banks and it seemed that God was rewarding the Dutch with material plenty. One Dutchman wrote of Amsterdam:

> 'The whole world stands amazed at its riches, from east and west, north and south they come to behold it. The Great and Almighty Lord has raised this city above all others.'[3]

Furthermore, there was complete toleration for all faiths. The new arrivals felt like Hebrews entering Jerusalem. However, they were soon disillusioned. Amsterdam's population had grown from 30,000 to 100,000 between 1567 and 1600.[4] Its harbour was full of masts hung with sails and round the docks there were 500 ale-houses where prostitution was rife. To the newly arrived Puritans, the city came to resemble not the city of Moses but the corrupt Jerusalem that Hosea and Amos condemned.[5] Ironically, the religious tolerance in the Netherlands did not stimulate their faith as much as English persecution and soon they found they were blending with the corrupt society and becoming 'Amsterdamnified'.[6]

Just over a year afterwards, the new arrivals who would become the 1620 Pilgrims left Amsterdam and its worldly commerce and moved to Leiden (English Leyden), a centre for the cloth trade. From 1609 to 1620 they lived there, following varied occupations. They were used to hard work from dawn to dusk and did not expect to earn wealth. William Brewster taught English at the University of Leiden and published some books. Edward Winslow was a printer, Robert Cushman a wool-carder. Samuel Fuller was a silk maker, William Bradford a fustian (cotton cloth) maker.[7] Some of the Pilgrims undertook apprenticeships. For more than ten years the community lived at peace. The Pilgrims were on their guard against the corrupt society around them but open-minded in measuring their spiritual growth. During that time, however, the community aged: those of working age on the arrival in Leiden became tired and their children began to struggle in work.

Arminianism now posed a threat. The followers of Jacobus Arminius, who had been a professor at the University of Leiden, denied that God had chosen a separate people to be predestined for salvation. They asserted that through Jesus *all* human beings were saved, non-Christians as well as Christians. The Pilgrims' pastor, John Robinson, disputed with the Arminians, emphasizing God's Providence. The Pilgrims believed they were chosen for salvation as English Israelites, like the Chosen People leaving Egypt. They were confident that they had resisted the Arminian threat, but felt that the Dutch had been corrupted by the Arminian outlook. Arminianism was all round them.[8] It was therefore proposed that they should leave Leiden. But where should they go this time? There was no more tolerant society in Europe than the Netherlands. There was talk of the New World, but the high seas and the rumours of Indians, wild beasts and a wilderness awaiting them filled all with foreboding, even terror. But as Pilgrims they were living according to God's will, and if God willed that they should leave their Dutch habitat now that it had been polluted with Arminianism, then they must trust that God would steer them through all perils.

Dutch merchants were willing to invest in a voyage to the New World, as it could establish a trading post to their commercial advantage. Dutch investors had employed the explorer Henry Hudson, who had discovered a river, the Hudson, between the areas of French and English control, and they now wanted the Pilgrims to plant the Dutch flag on Manhattan, an island at the mouth of the Hudson river.

A British merchant, Thomas Weston, brought together English backers called the London Adventurers for the Pilgrims' colony. The Pilgrims signed an agreement with them. John Carver, the leader of the Separatist congregation at Leiden, was to lead the expedition, and the Pilgrims' council was to include William Bradford, now in his early forties. A grant of territory in Virginia was made by the Council for New England.[9]

The Pilgrims from Leiden, or 'Saints', were to be joined by a group of 'Strangers' from England, entrepreneurially-minded non-Separatists who had been sold tickets on the *Mayflower* by Weston and who planned to settle on land in the new colony. (The word 'pilgrim' comes from the Middle English *pelegrim* and Old French *pelegrin*, which both derive from the Latin *peregrinus*, 'stranger'.)[10]

Weston proposed that all the accumulated wealth of the colony be divided between the investors and colonists after seven years. Thinking only of the investors' profit, he insisted that the colonists' houses and gardens should be included in this division, arguing that the Pilgrims' greatest labours might be devoted to aggrandizing their own homes. They felt that Weston was questioning their integrity by doubting that their main labours would be to the benefit of the colony and argued for their homes to be excluded. The Strangers insisted on this condition, however, and the Saints finally agreed to it, though later they came to realize they had been too trusting.

Weston provided the *Mayflower* with part-owner Captain Christopher Jones to transport the Pilgrims to the New World. The ship was waiting for them back in England, at Southampton. Out of their savings the Pilgrims bought the *Speedwell* in Holland to accompany her.[11] She would first carry them to England and the idea was that later she would remain in the New World and be used for fishing trips.

Most of the Leiden community came on board the *Speedwell* to say goodbye. Those who were going to the New World faced great dangers. Those staying faced poverty. This was the last time they would all be together in this world. They would next meet in Heaven. They all knelt and their pastor commended those leaving to the Lord. Then there were many tearful embraces and those who stayed stood on the dock and watched the *Speedwell* recede.[12]

On board, William Bradford thought of the *Epistle to the Hebrews* 11:13–16, an exhortation of faith:

> '…They were strangers and pilgrims on the earth… They seek a country…. But now they desire a better country, that is, an heavenly: wherefore God is not ashamed to be called their God: for he hath prepared for them a city.'

He wrote that they had just left a 'goodly city that had been their resting place for twelve years, but they knew they were Pilgrims, and looked not on those things but lifted up their eyes to the heavens, their dearest country, and quieted their spirits'.[13]

The two ships left Southampton 'about the five of August' 1620, or 15 August.[14] As expected, the *Mayflower* was under the command of Captain Christopher Jones.[15]

Almost immediately the *Speedwell* leaked and both ships put in to Dartmouth. The Pilgrims realized that the *Speedwell* was unseaworthy and spent further funds on repairs. Both ships set out again, but again the *Speedwell* leaked and both ships put in to Plymouth. The Pilgrims spent further funds on repairing her. Slowly they realized they had been swindled by the ship's vendors in Holland.

The Pilgrims had to sell provisions to pay their repair bill and did not have enough to last the first winter. Fearing famine, they appealed to Weston via Jones[16] to advance funds. Bradford reports that Weston refused:

> 'And whereas there wanted well near 100 pounds to clear things at their going away, he would not take order to disburse a penny but let them shift as they could. So they were forced to sell off some of their provisions to stop this gap, which was some three or four score firkins [small casks] of butter, which commodity they might best spare, having provided too large a quantity of that kind. [The *Speedwell*] would not prove sufficient for the voyage. Upon which it was resolved to dismiss her and part of the company, and proceed with the other ship. The which (though it was grievous, and caused great discouragement) was put into execution.'[17]

The Pilgrims had been sucked into worldly concerns and now urged each other to submit to God's will. Supplies were transferred from the *Speedwell* to the *Mayflower*, which would now be very overcrowded. If a storm sank her, the Pilgrims said that God would save them, just as He had provided a whale to save Jonah. However, many of them now concluded that they were too old or weak to withstand the hardships of settling. Bradford decided that his only child should remain behind. The pastor John Robinson would stay too. Several others made their excuses and dropped out.

All those not going went aboard the *Mayflower* on the eve of her departure so that those of the Leiden community who had travelled to England could be together for the last time.[18]

The Pilgrims had turned their back on first England, then the Netherlands and now faced a wilderness.

Journey to the New World

On 6 September in the 1620 Julian calendar (16 September in our calendar), the *Mayflower* set off alone, a month after the first departure. Of 102 passengers, only about 40 were Saints. The remainder were Strangers, mostly recruited in England.[19] Saints and Strangers were forced to make common cause, but from the outset the Pilgrims would be in a minority in their own colony.

The crossing was rough. The weather was stormy. The Pilgrims crowded on deck and prayed while around them the sailors cursed. Bradford reports:

'The ship was shrewdly shaken, and her upper works made very leaky; and one of the main beams in the midship was bowed and cracked.'[20]

The beam was made safe by an iron screw the passengers had brought from Holland; this was supported by a post. Sometimes the storms were so severe that the Pilgrims had to drift with sails down for days on end.

They sighted land on 9 November (Julian calendar) or 19 November (our calendar): 'After long beating at sea they fell with that land which is called Cape Cod.'[21] There was great joy. They were not quite safe yet, as they 'fell among dangerous shoals and roaring breakers',[22] but on 11 November (Julian calendar) or 21 November (our calendar) 1620, they entered the harbour at what is now Provincetown on the tip of the Cape.

They dropped anchor and agreed to land there, rather than in the mouth of the Hudson river, where they had the land grant from the Council for New England, but there was concern that the Strangers would defy the Saints if they landed in a place other than where the grant permitted. Accordingly, 41 male passengers signed what is now known as the *Mayflower* Compact, an agreement to establish a 'Civil Body Politic' (i.e. temporary government) and to be bound by its laws. They would enact 'just and equal laws for the good of the colony'. (170 years later the writers of the United States constitution adopted the same theme of 'just and equal laws'.) This binding agreement was modelled on a Separatist church covenant and became the basis of government in the colony.[23] It prevented the Strangers from peeling off and setting up their own non-Separatist settlement. After the Compact was signed, the Pilgrims elected John Carver as their first Governor.

The shallop (a light boat for rowing in shallow water) that the Pilgrims had brought had been damaged during the crossing, so 16 of them went ashore in the ship's boat or longboat, led by Captain Miles Standish. They advanced a mile and encountered 'five or six persons with a dog coming toward them, who were savages'.[24] They fled into woods, and the English party followed their tracks for several miles to check that there was no ambush. Night fell, and they slept, taking turns to be 'sentinels'. The next morning they followed the footprints until they lost them in thickets. They found the Parnet river and, further on, a freshwater pond and corn-stubble, indicating that the native Americans had planted corn earlier that year, also the remains of a house and a kettle and, buried in nearby sand, baskets filled with corn. They took some of the corn, reburied the rest and returned to the ship. The corn meant they could plant seed that would become a crop next year.

By now the shallop had been repaired, so 30 Pilgrims set out under the captain on a second expedition. The ground was frozen and covered with snow. Nevertheless they found two native-American houses covered with mats, more corn and beans.

The weather was bad for the rest of November. On 6 December 1620 (Julian calendar), 16 December (our calendar), the shallop went out again with 10 men to explore the bay of Cape Cod. It was so cold that spray froze on their coats. They spotted a dozen or so native Americans, landed 'a league or two' (three to six miles) from them, made a barricade of logs and branches and posted lookouts. They could see smoke from the native Americans' fires.

Next morning they marched off to see if there was a location where they could build houses. They reached where the native Americans had been and found the remains of a large fish 'like a grampus' (dolphin-like cetacean). Not finding a possible site for their base, they signalled the shallop to come to a nearby creek and built another barricade with logs, pine branches and stakes. They made a fire in the centre and lay round it. During the night they heard a strange cry they thought to be wolves and fired a couple of muskets to frighten them away.

They got up at 5 a.m. and 'after prayer' carried some arms to the shallop. As they did so, they heard the same strange cry that had woken them during the night. A lookout ran in, shouting 'Indians! Indians!' And then arrows thudded round them.

While several settlers, wearing coats of mail and carrying cutlasses, ran to the shallop for their arms, a couple of muskets were fired. One native American, from the cover of a tree, fired three arrows and only fled with a shriek when a musket sent bark and tree splinters flying round his head.

Having driven off the native Americans, the settlers gave thanks to God for vanquishing their enemies and delivering them. They rounded up the arrows, which were eventually sent back to England.

The shallop, sail up, resumed its journey along Cape Cod Bay. After a few hours there was snow and sleet, and the sea grew rough and broke the rudder. The Pilgrims now had to steer by rowing with oars. The pilot had seen a possible harbour and they headed for it. The storm grew worse and broke their mast. The sail fell overboard. They rowed to the shelter of a small island and rode out the night there. Some, fearful of native Americans, preferred to stay on board. Others, cold and weak in the freezing temperature, went ashore on the island – Plymouth Rock – and lit a fire.

The next morning, a Sunday, the storm had been replaced by brilliant sunshine and the Pilgrims found that the island was without native Americans. They dried their clothes and thanked God for their deliverance.

The next day they dropped a plumb line to measure the depth of the harbour and found it suitable for the *Mayflower*. They went inland and found cornfields and running brooks. This was the so-called 'historic landing' of 11 December (Julian calendar), 21 December (our calendar), a term that disregarded the landing at Provincetown.

New Plymouth

The Pilgrims had now found their base and erected a storehouse and a few cottages in what came to be called New Plymouth. The winter was severe and scurvy was rife. Half of the 102 who had landed died in the course of January and February. (Of the initial 102 who had embarked, two had died, but there had been two births.) They may have been killed by the epidemic that wiped out 95,000 native Americans between 1615 and 1617, leaving only 5,000 along the coast.

Bradford recorded: 'As there died sometimes two or three of a day in the foresaid time, that of 100 and odd persons scarce fifty remained.'[25] Of these there were 'but six or seven sound persons' who did all the work, fetching wood, making fires, washing filthy clothes and so on. All the time the native Americans 'came skulking about them'.

In January Bradford's wife Dorothy fell over the side of the *Mayflower* and drowned. The weather was calm and apart from one brief mention, the event is not referred to. Had she been appalled by the place and the epidemic to which her husband had brought her, and thrown herself over the side in despair?[26]

On 16 March 1621 a nearly naked native American named Samoset, a Pemaquid from Monhegan Island, Maine, where 'some English ships came to fish', approached the Pilgrims and spoke to them in broken English learned from the ships' crews: 'Much welcome, English men! Much welcome, English men!'

He introduced his friend Massasoit, chief of the Wampanoags, and other native Americans, among whom was one called Tisquantum, who had been sold into slavery in Spain and had later lived in the home of an Englishman. Having been removed by a ship's captain, Captain Hunt, he had been brought back to the New World as an interpreter by Captain Dermer. The Pilgrims called him Squanto, and he taught them how to plant corn which, he said, would not grow unless it was buried with herring-like fish from the brook.

Squanto helped the Pilgrims negotiate peace with Chief Massasoit, who made a formal visit. Edward Winslow and Stephen Hoskins returned the visit, accompanied by Squanto, to Sowams, now Warren, Rhode Island, where they gave the Massasoit clothes. The Pilgrims now signed a peace treaty with Massasoit.[27]

On 15 April the *Mayflower* left New Plymouth and returned to England, leaving many graves on Cole's Hill which the settlers obscured with planted seed. Also in April, Governor John Carver died. William Bradford was elected as his successor. In May New Plymouth saw its first marriage when Edward Winslow married Susannah White. Her husband had died in February, his wife in March.

In July the Pilgrims compensated the native Americans of Nauset for the corn they had taken when they were at Cape Cod by inviting the native Americans to celebrate their first harvest, an event that gave rise to the annual celebration of Thanksgiving Day.

Now more settlers arrived by ship. They had been selected by Weston, and not for their consciences. The *Fortune* came first, on 10 November 1621, with 35 settlers. On Christmas Day most of the newcomers said it was 'against their consciences to work on that day', so Governor Bradford let them off work and led the rest to their labours. When they returned, they found those who would not work playing in the street, 'some pitching the bar and some at a stool-ball'. Bradford 'took away their implements', saying it 'was against his conscience that they should play and others work; if they made the keeping of it a matter of devotion, let them keep their houses, but there should be no gaming or revelling in the streets'.[28]

Another group of settlers arrived on the *Annie* and *Little James* in August 1623. A further group arrived on six ships in June 1629 and landed at Naumkeag (Salem). A further group arrived on 1 June 1630. They landed at Nantasket and settled at Matapan, which they called Dorchester after the English town.

In the 1620s a series of grants was made by the English Crown and a fishing and trading settlement established in 1623 was turned into the region of New Hampshire in 1629. It was named after the English county Hampshire and covered the region between the Merrimack and Piscataqua rivers, which included the settlements of Dover, Portsmouth, Exeter and Hampton.

Meanwhile, in 1624 the Dutch arrived: Captain Cornelius May on the *Nieu Nederlandt* with 30 Walloon families on board. At the mouth of the Great North River these Walloons saw off a French ship whose captain was about to erect the arms of the King of France and take possession, and went up the river to Fort Orange, now Albany. The *Nieu Nederlandt* returned to Holland with 500 otter skins and 1,500 beaver skins.

By 1626 a Dutch New Netherland colony had been established in the Manhates (Manhattan Island) by the Dutch West India Company. In 1626 the *Wapen van Amsterdam* (Arms of Amsterdam) returned to Holland with a cargo of beaver, otter, mink and wildcat skins, oak timber and hickory. The chief commercial agent of the company, Isaak de Rasières, was also secretary of the province of New Netherland and was involved in bringing most of the Dutch from Fort Orange to strengthen a settlement on Manhattan. The Maykans (Mohicans) had asked for Fort Orange's assistance in their war with the Maquaes (Mohawks), and had had to retreat.[29]

De Rasières saw New Plymouth as a market for furs and Dutch goods. He wrote a letter to the colony on 9 March 1627. Bradford replied, asking de Rasières not to trade with the native Americans round New Plymouth, in return for which New Plymouth would not molest New Netherland. As regards trade, 'For this year we are fully supplied with all necessaries, both for clothing and other things; but hereafter it is like we shall deal with you, if your rates be reasonable.'[30]

In October 1627 de Rasières visited New Plymouth, his ship laden with sugar, linen and Dutch clothes. He stepped ashore to a flourish of trumpets and after a few days the Pilgrims went on board and bought many of his goods. During his visit de Rasières spoke of the native Americans in New Netherland and their sexual lasciviousness. Usually a gift of a salmon was sufficient to make them 'lascivious'. De Rasières was shocked that the Pilgrims had 'stringent laws and ordinances upon the subject of fornication and adultery', which they enforced 'very strictly' and applied to native-American women. Bradford reproached him for the lewdness of the Dutch at New Netherland.[31]

While he was in New Plymouth, de Rasières wrote a description of the town:

> 'It was on a hill slope stretching east towards the sea, about a thousand feet long. The houses were constructed of hewn planks, with gardens also enclosed behind and at the sides with hewn planks … with a stockade against a sudden attack.'[32]

There were wooden gates at either end of the street. The Governor's house was in the centre. A large square house had six cannons on its flat roof. The lower part was the church, to which the Pilgrims were called by a beating drum. Strict deportment was imposed on all, including native Americans.

Winthrop's Puritan 'Citty upon a Hill'

Now the Puritans arrived. Unlike the Pilgrims, who came to the Cape Cod wilderness to seek religious freedom or the separation of Church from State, they wanted their Church to *be* the State ('true religion'). This introduced a theocratic political thread into the emerging America. Though it was not to succeed, it left its mark on the body politic and is today reflected in the values of some right-wing Christians.

In Merrie England Puritans were mocked (like Malvolio in Shakespeare's *Twelfth Night*) for their black dress and holier-than-thou attitudes, their hatred of jollity (especially of May Day and the maypoles' ribbons and dancing) and their odd first names (like Resolved, the name of Susanna White's second child). From 1628 to 1640 they brought their place names, their Bibles and muskets to the shoreline of Massachusetts Bay and developed a community in which they saw themselves in a covenant with God and attributed their successes and failures to God's Providence.

Not all places on a voyage could be filled by Separatist Saints, however, and a good number of landless tradesmen and victims of the Tudor/Stuart class system were drawn by the promise of land and the prospect of better livelihoods and living conditions for themselves and their families. These non-Separatist Strangers initially made common cause with the Separatists but, once established in the New World, found their rules repressive and were liable to defy them and threaten to found their own mini-settlements.

Settlement in Massachusetts Bay had taken place in a small way throughout the 1620s. Cape Ann had been settled at Stage Point by the Dorchester Company in 1623–4 and when the company had gone bankrupt around 1627 it had been superseded by the New England Company, which had received a land patent extending from the Charles to the Merrimack rivers and three miles on either side. John Endicott had led a group of

Puritan settlers to Salem and served as Governor there from their arrival on 6 September 1628.

The Massachusetts Bay Company – its full name was the Company of the Massachusetts Bay in New England – had replaced the New England Company when Puritans had converted the patent into a royal charter on 4 March 1629. This charter from Charles I empowered the Massachusetts Bay Company to trade and colonize in New England between the Charles and Merrimack rivers. The charter did not contain a clause requiring the company to hold its business meetings in England and made no mention of the location of the company's headquarters. There is a view that this was an oversight, but it is likely that it was deliberate. On 29 August the shareholders who wished to move to America reached an agreement (the Cambridge Agreement) and bought out those who wished to remain in England.[33] The Puritan stockholders were thus able to transfer control of the colony to America. This would enable them to establish a theocratic government in which the Church was the State, with the franchise limited to church members. Only the Elect could vote.

The first 400 settlers under this new charter left England in April 1629. Most of them were Puritans. They were reacting to events in the spring and summer of 1629, when Charles I had dissolved Parliament and William Laud, Bishop of London, had pressed Separatist Puritans to conform with church practice. As a result of this harassment the settlers felt they could no longer remain non-conformists in the Church of England and resolved to leave the country.

The model for the colony's church organization was John Cotton, the minister at Boston, Lincolnshire, in the East Midlands, who took a middle view between Separatism and Church of England Presbyterianism. He held the Church of England to be the true Church, though blemished, but said there could be no ecclesiastical authority between the congregation and Christ. The Church should maintain its purity by only accepting as members those who could make 'a declaration of their experience of a work of grace'.[34] This Church government would be in the hands of the Elect, those chosen by God.

Following Thomas Cartwright, John Winthrop, who sailed to the New World in March 1630, based the civil commonwealth on the Church. In his view, the Church should not govern, but prepare 'instruments both to rule and to choose rulers'.[35] The primary law for both Church and State would be biblical law.

As Winthrop sailed across the Atlantic on the *Arbella*, leading a small fleet of 700 settlers for the new colony, he composed a lay sermon, *A Modell of Christian Charitie* (*see* Appendix I). He pictured the colonists in covenant with God and with each other. They were divinely ordained to build in New England and be 'as a Citty upon a Hill. The eyes of all people are upon us.'[36] Some[37] have taken the phrase literally as suggesting that the colonists planned to settle a single site, *a* city on *a* hill. But there were too many in the fleet to establish one farming community. The phrase comes from Matthew 5.14–16:

> 'Ye are the light of the world. A city that is set on a hill cannot be hid. Neither do men light a candle and put it under a bushel, but on a candlestick, and it giveth light onto all that are in the house. Let your light so shine before men, that they see your good works, and glorify your Father who is in heaven.'

The idea was that the eyes of all people would see their example, just as all local people see a city on a hill.

The imagery of hill, light and candlestick was widely used in Winthrop's old home, the Stour Valley in East Anglia. Colchester, north-east of London, had been described as a 'town [which], for the earnest profession of the gospel, [was] like unto the city upon a hill; and as a candle upon a candlestick'.[38] The Essex clergyman Richard Rogers spoke of 'particular churches… [that] showed forth as shining lights'.[39] William Ames spoke of William Perkins as 'a burning and shining light, the sparks whereof did fly abroad into all corners of the land'.[40] Nicholas Bownde spoke of Sir Robert Jermyn, a Suffolk magistrate Winthrop knew, as 'lighting other men's candles at yours'.[41] Bezaleel Carter spoke of another Suffolk magistrate Sir Edward Lewkenor as one who 'shined like a light amongst us all'.[42] John Cotton, the minister, was spoken of similarly: 'In that Candlestick the Father of Lights placed this burning and shining light.'[43]

Nevertheless, the phrase 'citty upon a hill' shaped the colony. Theirs was to be a holy community, a Godly commonwealth. So morality, marriage and church attendance should be enforced, and education would consist of teaching the Word of God. Godly men would labour together to discern and advance God's will. All individuals and communities would lead exemplary lives and would bear witness to religious truth. The city upon a hill would be the New Jerusalem in practical, everyday life.

John Winthrop described the covenant in his sermon on board the *Arbella* before the colonists landed:

'Thus stands the cause between God and us; we are entered into covenant with Him for this work; we have taken out a commission; the Lord hath given us leave to draw our own articles.... Now if the Lord shall be pleased to hear us and bring us in peace to the place we desire, then hath He ratified this covenant and sealed our Commission, [and] will expect a strict performance of the articles contained in it.'[44]

He reminded them that the Gospel 'teacheth us to put a difference betweene Christians and others'.

According to one of the investors in the Massachusetts Bay Company, Captain Weymouth, 'One main end of all these undertakings was to plant the gospel in these dark regions of America.' Cotton Mather, writing in the early eighteenth century in *Magnalia Christi Americana*, states: 'I am now to tell mankind, that as for *one* of these English plantations, this was not only a *main end*, but the *sole end* upon which it was erected.' In other words, Massachusetts was 'the spot of *earth*, which the God of heaven *spied out* for the seat of such *evangelical*, and *ecclesiastical*, and very remarkable transactions'.[45]

On 12 June 1630, the *Arbella* led the small fleet bearing the next 700 settlers into Salem harbour. Winthrop carried the charter with him. It enabled him to replace Endicott as the colony's Governor. The leadership of the colony and headquarters of the company were now united in America, first at Charlestown, the first capital of Massachusetts Bay, but then, as water there was inadequate, across the Charles river at Boston. This demonstrated that the Puritan colony was not an official venture and established a precedent of 'home rule' that would eventually grow into independence. The colonists celebrated their first Thanksgiving Day on 8 July 1630.

The charter granted the Massachusetts General Court the authority to elect officers and make laws. It first met in America in October 1630 and was attended by only eight (Puritan) freemen, who voted that they should form a council of the Governor's assistants and handle all legislative, executive and judicial power: impose town boundaries, set taxes and elect officers. To head off unrest, presumably among the non-Puritan Strangers, 116 settlers became the court's freemen, but they were not on the council.

In 1634 a group headed by Thomas Dudley insisted on seeing the charter and discovered that the General Court should comprise all freemen, who should make the laws. They demanded that this should be implemented, but Winthrop reached a compromise with them whereby a General Court would comprise two delegates elected from each town, the Governor's council of advisers and the Governor. The court would decide taxes and 'should bind all'.

Winthrop did not grasp, however, that the election of the Governor was also binding and Dudley was elected to replace him. His election marked the beginning of the democratic tradition in what was to become the USA. The trading company had now become a representative democracy. By 1641 the council had added the first code of laws, which were written by Nathaniel Ward.[46]

By now some 1,100 Puritan refugees from England had settled in Massachusetts Bay under Winthrop. During the winter of 1631 over 200 died. When the next ships arrived, many chose to return to England despite the continued persecution of Puritan Non-conformists there. However, more fled the harassment than returned to it, and by the end of 1631 the colony had over 2,000 settlers, including ministers rejected in England, such as John Cotton, Roger Williams and Thomas Hooke.[47]

The Connecticut colony was an overflow from the Massachusetts Bay colony from 1633 to 1635. Trading posts had been established on the Connecticut river by the Dutch from New Amsterdam and the New Plymouth colony.[48] The English Crown had granted the Earl of Warwick, president of the Council for New England, the right to settle west of

Narragansett Bay, and in March 1632 the Earl had conveyed the grant to 15 Puritan English lords who were planning an American refuge if the Puritan Revolution in England failed. The patentees included William Fiennes, 1st Viscount Saye and Sele, and Lord Brooke, along with Colonel George Fenwick. In 1635 they commissioned John Winthrop Jr, the son of the Governor of Massachusetts Bay colony, as 'Governor of River Colony'.

When he arrived in Boston in October 1635, Winthrop Jr learned that the Dutch were about to occupy the mouth of the Connecticut river. He dispatched an advance party to fortify the area. They sent a small canoe to the west bank, nailed a shield to a tree to denote British possession, installed a battery of cannon and built a small fort. The Dutch ship withdrew, and Winthrop named the place 'Point Sayebrooke' after Viscount Saye and Lord Brooke.

In 1636 the first Massachusetts colonists went to Connecticut in search of greater freedom and financial opportunities. The clergyman Thomas Hooker led 100 settlers and 130 head of cattle in a trek from Newtown (now Cambridge) in the Massachusetts Bay colony to just north of the Dutch fort at Hartford.

Winthrop Sr was distressed when the colonists migrated to Connecticut. He was also annoyed when the freemen insisted on electing a representative assembly to share in the decision-making of the Massachusetts Bay colony and furthermore found himself opposed by dissidents, deeply religious dissenters who disagreed with his network of towns, each run by a church of self-professed saints.

In 1636 Anne Hutchinson gained control of the Boston church and attempted to convert the colony to a religious position Winthrop thought blasphemous: that the saved were justified by possessing the divine spark, not by their works. He counter-attacked and had her banished, and later had her tried before the General Court and excommunicated. She moved to Rhode Island and then settled on Long Island Sound. She had a stillborn baby and was murdered by native Americans, a circumstance Winthrop saw as God's judgement against heretics.

Another woman, Mary Dyer, then became troublesome. She later became a Quaker and was expelled from Massachusetts Bay but returned. She was punished and banished, but kept returning and was finally hanged.[49]

Roger Williams, meanwhile, questioned Winthrop's view that the Church and State were one, as no community could be made up only of true believers. Williams had earlier held that the patent granted by the Crown was invalid, as it had no right to grant the lands of Massachusetts, and that only purchase from the Indians gave title to American land. Now he argued that magistrates had no right to interfere in religion and could not hear the swearing of oaths of allegiance by the unregenerate, as this amounted to an act of religious communion with them. The right of magistrates to interfere in religion is constitutionally significant today. In 1636 Williams had to flee to Rhode Island, where he founded a colony.

In Connecticut the settlements of Hartford, Wethersfield and Windsor formed a combined government in 1637 to fight the Pequot War. Urged on by Puritan clergymen who regarded the Pequot Indian tribe as infidels for resisting and murdering British traders and colonists, British settlers under Captain John Mason, with the aid of Mohegans and Narragansets, burned the main Pequot fort at Mystic, Connecticut, killing 500–600 Pequots and decimating the tribe. The next year New Haven was settled.[50]

Like the Puritans of the Massachusetts Bay colony which they had left, the Connecticut Puritans were determined to plant a 'Christian Common-Wealth' in which Church and State were one. In the summer of 1638 the Connecticut Puritans of Windsor, Hartford and Wethersfield drafted a constitution affirming their faith in God and their intention to organize a Christian nation: the Fundamental Orders of Connecticut. Delegates came from the three towns, and Roger Ludlow of Windsor, who had studied law at Balliol College, Oxford,[51] drew up 11 Orders (*see* Appendix II) which made it clear that their government rested on divine authority and pursued godly purposes:

> 'For as much as it hath pleased the Almighty God by the wise disposition of his divine providence so to Order and dispose of things… [and] well knowing where a people are gathered together the word of God requires that to maintain the peace and union of such a people there should be an orderly and decent Government established according to God, to order and dispose of the affairs of the people.'

The aim of the Government was religious: 'to maintain and preserve the liberty and purity of the gospel of our Lord Jesus which we now profess, as also the discipline of the Churches, which according to the truth of the said gospel is now practised amongst us.'[52]

The Fundamental Orders were adopted by the Connecticut council on 14 January 1639. They were a civil covenant establishing how the three towns would govern themselves, creating an annual assembly of legislators and making possible the election of a Governor. This meant that the Connecticut Puritans had established their Congregational churches as the official religion of Connecticut, which from 1639 became a Christian state supported by taxes and defended by the law: blasphemy was punished with execution, and citizenship depended on religious faith. Religious freedom meant freedom from error, Church and State working together to protect true faith.

The Fundamental Orders contain some principles that were taken up by the writers of the constitution of the United States, notably the idea that government is based on the rights of an individual and that all free men take part in the election of their magistrates in a secret paper ballot. These principles were established 'according to God'.[53] Even though the Puritans were Planting Fathers rather than the Founding Fathers of the Constitution of the United States of America, they had a formative influence on the later drafting of the constitution.

By 1640, however, Winthrop was convinced that God favoured Boston, now the capital of Massachusetts. The Puritan power in the New World was now the Massachusetts Bay colony, which accepted the surrender of the Plymouth colony from Bradford (with the exception of a small reserve of three tracts of land) in 1640 and the following year absorbed the province of New Hampshire. In 1643 it joined the Plymouth colony, the Connecticut colony and the New Haven colony in the Confederation of New England. Winthrop's pragmatism had held the colony together – just. He died in 1649.

The Confederation of New England fell apart in the 1650s and after that Massachusetts Bay passed into new groupings. In 1664 the English captured New Netherland and renamed it New York after James, Duke of York, Charles II's brother and the future James II, who became its proprietor – to the extent that he never summoned the representative assembly there. In 1686 James, now the English king, unified Massachusetts Bay with the other New England colonies in the Dominion of New England, and in 1688 the province of New York, East Jersey and West Jersey were added. In 1691–2 Massachusetts Bay was unified with the Plymouth colony, Martha's Vineyard, Nantucket, the province of Maine and the present Nova Scotia to form the province of Massachusetts Bay.[54]

The Puritan settlement of New England had seen the Massachusetts Bay colony develop as a covenant community from a population of 506 in 1630 to 39,752 in 1680, when the total population of the American colonies (white and black) was 151,507. In 1680 some New England towns enjoyed a level of development that did not lie far behind that of many towns in the mother country.[55]

Penn's Quaker 'Holy Experiment'

The Quakers had now taken up the Puritan vision, their leader George Fox having undergone a religious crisis in 1647 and experienced the Inner Light. They were soon persecuted in England as much as the Puritans.

William Penn, the son of an admiral, was a pupil at Chigwell Grammar School, Essex, when 'the Lord first appeared unto me... about the 12th Year of my Age, Anno 1656'.[56] The school had been founded by the Church-of-England Archbishop Harsnett but then had a Puritan influence, being in a Puritan area. The biographer John Aubrey records what happened to Penn:

> 'The first sense of God he had when he was 11 years old at Chigwell, being retired in a chamber alone. He was suddenly surprised with an inward comfort (as he thought) and external glory in the roome that he has many times sayd that from thence he had the seal of divinity and immortality; that there was a God and that the soul of man was capable of enduring his divine communications. His schoolmaster was not of his perswasion.'[57]

The unimpressed schoolmaster was the Latin master Edward Cotton, whose mind may have been on other matters, as his two wives and six children all died during the 21 years he was at Chigwell (1638–59).

Penn's father was briefly imprisoned in the Tower of London as a punishment for a naval defeat by the Dutch in the West Indies and Penn left Chigwell and moved to Ireland. There a Quaker itinerant, Thomas Loe, preached to his family, which intensified his religious feelings.

After the Restoration, Penn's father was knighted and made commissioner of the navy. Penn went to Oxford, but refused to attend chapel and was fined and then sent down. Appalled at his son's disgrace, his father sent him to France. William read theology there, but his father brought him back to read law at Lincoln's Inn, London. Once more he went to Ireland and heard the Quaker itinerant. This time he himself became a Quaker. He preached and was imprisoned at Newgate under the Conventicle Act for preaching on a Sunday morning. He was imprisoned four times in all for his beliefs, and wrote 42 books and pamphlets including, in 1669, *No Cross, No Crown* (about his imprisonment).

So as not to provoke the government into official persecution of the Quakers, Fox reined Penn in and made him appear more moderate. He continued to write, became a Whig MP and got to know Charles II and his brother, the Duke of York (later James II), who had both known his father. Thwarted politically when the Whigs lost influence, he turned his attention to America in 1674 when he was asked to mediate between two Quakers who owned territory in West New Jersey.[58] He had always been passionate about toleration and he dreamed of a Utopia in which all Christian sects would be treated equally. This would be, he often said, 'a holy experiment'.

Admiral Penn had loaned Charles II £10,000 and William knew that the king would not repay it, so, regarding it as a purchase price, he asked for land on the Delaware river. In 1681 he secured a charter for it which made him initially king of the new colony.[59]

Penn dreamed of creating a 'Christian Common-wealth' like that in Massachusetts, but whereas Winthrop saw religious liberty as a homogeneous society of Puritans, all of whom thought the same, in which other sects (including Quakers) were not welcome, Penn saw a colony in which religious pluralism would be implemented. The 'Quaker Party' would dominate the Assembly, but Christians of any sect could live happily within the Christian State.[60] There would be no hangings for sectarian reasons, like Mary Dyer's.

Penn found his inspiration in the 'Light Within' whereas Winthrop had been inspired by the Bible. Penn's colony was to be a Utopia which would put Restoration England to shame. Liberal godliness was behind his approach: 'God will plant America and it shall have its day in the Kingdom.'[61] He wrote to James Harrison, a Quaker whom he appointed a judge in the new colony:

> 'For my country, I eyed the Lord in obtaining it; and more was I drawn inward to look to him, and to owe it to his hand and power, than to any other way; I have so obtained it, and desire to keep it; that I may not be unworthy of his love; but do that, which may answer his kind Providence and serve his truth and people: that an example may be set up to the nations: there may be room there, though not here, for such an holy experiment.'[62]

In his 'holy experiment', he wrote in his first frame of government in 1682, governors would be 'minister(s) of God to thee for good'[63] and:

> 'That all persons living in this province, who confess and acknowledge the one Almighty and eternal God to be the Creator, Upholder and Ruler of the world; and that hold themselves obliged in conscience to live peaceably and justly in a civil society, shall, in no ways, be molested or prejudiced for their religious persuasion, or practice, in matters of faith and worship.'[64]

Penn went out to what is now known as Pennsylvania in 1682. He left behind his pregnant wife and three children, one of them aged one, half-expecting not to see them again. He hoped to make the family's fortune, to turn his father's £10,000 loan to the king into a handsome profit.

All went financial awry, as Penn received no income to replace the £10,000. He had to fund the building of Philadelphia, city of brotherly love, his capital on the Delaware and Schuylkill rivers. He met the Delaware

Indians under an elm tree at a place called Shackamaxon and concluded a treaty with them. There was nothing set down in writing, suggesting that it did not reflect well on Penn's ideals of purchasing land from the Indians. However, Voltaire said it was the only treaty between the colonists and the Indians 'that was never sworn to and never broken'.[65] The elm tree was reputedly cut down in the nineteenth century.

Penn returned to England in 1684, having to sort out a boundary dispute with Maryland caused by the poor map that accompanied the charter and threatened to leave Pennsylvania landlocked. Times were changing. James II came to the throne the following year and William III's revolution followed in 1689. Quakers opposed the colonial war effort and Pennsylvania was brought under royal rule from 1692 to 1694.

Penn made a second visit there from 1699 to 1701, but was dismayed that provincial Quakers were bent on wresting powers from the executive. Quakers and non-Quakers were bickering over the appointment of judges in Philadelphia, city of brotherly love, in a collapse of religious pluralism. Penn's personal steward had defrauded him of thousands of pounds since his first visit and his son was not behaving in a Quaker manner.

Nevertheless Penn's vision was undimmed. In his 1701 revision of the *Frame of Government*, he claimed: 'Almighty God [was] the only Lord of Conscience' in the colony and no one would suffer loss of civil liberties because of his 'conscientious Persuasion or Practice'. Also:

> 'All Persons who also profess to believe in Jesus Christ, the Saviour of the World, shall be capable (notwithstanding their other Persuasions and Practices in Point of Conscience and Religion) to serve this Government in any Capacity.'[66]

In his *Fundamental Constitution of Pennsylvania*, Penn wrote that 'in reverence to God the Father of lights and spirits' everyone should be able to worship God 'in whatever way each believed was most acceptable to God'.[67]

In spite of these high ideals, the 'holy experiment' fell apart. The British government had a plan to remove Penn as the proprietor of Pennsylvania. In 1702 he began negotiations to sell it. Queen Anne's War (1702–13) complicated the sale, for Quakers were expected to provide funds for the war effort against the French. (Queen Anne detested Catholics and dissenters, including Quakers, in equal measure.) Ten years later, as a sale was about to be concluded, Penn suffered a stroke and was an invalid until his death in 1718. The province was in trusteeship because of his indebtedness. It passed to his new wife, whom he had married in 1696, two years after the death of his first wife.[68]

We have seen that by 1640, in less than 20 years, the Puritans had brought a covenant to New Plymouth, to Massachusetts and then to Connecticut. In all three, Church and State were united – the Church *was* the State – and godliness was esteemed above all else and actively pursued. The 'one true religion' was Puritanism and the New World seemed a Puritan Utopia, a New Jerusalem, Paradise in a settled wilderness. The Quaker 'holy experiment', however, ended in failure, a miserable coda to the Puritan rule. That is the accepted story of the planting.

Though a theocratic Puritan State was not to be and did not affect the later drafting of the constitution of the United States, the Puritan planting of New England proved to be rich soil in which something else was to grow.

CHAPTER 2

ENGLISH ANGLICANS IN VIRGINIA AND CHESAPEAKE BAY

T he real story of the founding of America predates the Separatist settlement and the *Mayflower*. For in 1607 there had been an expedition to Virginia which had been more officially sanctioned (or interfered with) than those of the Separatists and Puritans. Though it appeared to be religiously inspired, this expedition encountered more of a problem with discipline and moral issues than the Separatists and Puritans experienced.

Voyages of Discovery and Colonization

The fifteenth century saw European mariners exploring the globe. The Portuguese were first, voyaging to Porto Santo off West Africa in 1418. In the course of the century they sailed as far as the southern tip of Africa and set up trading stations at Arguin, Sierra Leone and El Mina. In 1497 Vasco da Gama sailed round the Cape of Good Hope and up Africa's east coast, making possible Portuguese trade with India.

Portugal was then the westernmost country in the known world and there was great interest in what lay farther to the west. The Portuguese discovered the Madeira islands in the north Atlantic, and Paolo Toscanelli, a cosmographer from Florence, suggested that the East – 'Cathay' and 'the

Indies' – could be reached by sailing west. Cardinal Pierre d'Ailly had previously asserted, in *Image of the World*, that the Earth was round and that the East Indies could be reached by sailing west, but this work was deemed heretical by the Church.

Christopher Columbus, a sailor from Genoa who had married a Portuguese woman and settled on Porto Santo in the Madeira islands, read d'Ailly in Lisbon in 1483. He also read the works of Marco Polo, who had left for the East in 1271 and returned from China in 1292. He became convinced that the Earth was round, as (he believed) had been asserted in the prophecies of Isaiah 11.10–12, and the apocryphal Second Book of Esdras 3.17–19.

After an audience with Ferdinand and Isabella of Spain in 1486, Columbus tried to reach India from the west. Having sailed for 33 days, he landed on the island of Guanahami near the Strait of Florida in October 1492. He thought he had reached the Far East. He went on to Cuba and took possession of Santa Domingo (Hispaniola) before returning to Spain in March 1493. He was received in triumph without realizing he had discovered a new world. He made two further voyages, to the West Indies, as 'India to the west' came to be called, and to South America, and died forgotten in 1506.[1]

It is possible that Columbus was not the first to reach the New World, and that talk of reaching Asia by sailing west was a cover-up to claim and officialize the 'discovery' of the New World for Spain. It has been alleged that Columbus met Portuguese people who had already been in the Caribbean and that he found out from Bristol sailors about their 1480 voyage to America, which followed the northern Viking route.

Whatever the truth of Columbus's voyage, it opened the way for more voyages to the New World. In 1500 the Portuguese explorer Pedro Álvares Cabral landed on Brazil on his way to India and in 1507 Amerigo Vespucci, a Florentine in Spanish service, sailed to Brazil and recognized that territory as belonging to a new continent. He gave his name to America. (It has also been suggested that America was named after Rickard Ameryk of Bristol, who funded John Cabot's voyage.) Soon afterwards Ferdinand Magellan, a Portuguese navigator in Spanish service, sailed round the world. He was killed in the Philippines and one of his ships returned to England to tell the tale in 1522. New explorers reached Venezuela and the Amazon and grasped that they were not in Asia. The Spanish conquered New Spain and Peru. The French reached Newfoundland and, in 1534, the Gulf of St Lawrence, and attempted to plant colonies in Florida and Brazil. Both attempts failed.

North America attracted particular attention in England, as the idea grew that there was a north-west passage to the East. An Italian in English service, John Cabot, had discovered Cape Breton Island off Nova Scotia in 1497. Trading companies followed up, starting with the Muscovy Company founded by Sir Anthony Judd in 1554. John Dee, the alchemist who is thought to have inspired Prospero in Shakespeare's *Tempest*, focused on the north-west. He laid the foundations for British imperialism by claiming that conquests by King Arthur had given Elizabeth I title to foreign lands such as Greenland, Iceland, Friesland, the northern islands towards Russia and the North Pole. He claimed that the New World was appointed by Providence for the British to influence and rule.

A number of English seamen took up the challenge. In 1576–8 Martin Frobisher made three voyages to seek the long-rumoured north-west passage. He unsuccessfully attempted to settle on Baffin Island. In 1577 Sir Francis Drake sailed round the world and plundered the western coast of South America. (Pirate raiders such as Drake and Sir John Hawkins opened up sea routes and knowledge of faraway places, but they were officially recognized only when they brought back shiploads of booty.) Sir Humphrey Gilbert tried to establish a permanent colony in North America and Newfoundland, without much success, and in 1583 he was drowned off the Azores.[2]

Gilbert's half-brother Sir Walter Raleigh then took a more southerly route across the Atlantic. In spring 1584 he sent out an exploratory expedition under Captain Philip Amadas and Captain Arthur Barlowe, which located Roanoke Island, now in North Carolina, and returned to England that autumn. Next year he sent out a military expedition under Sir Richard Grenville, which built a fort there and remained until spring 1586.

In 1587 Raleigh sent 116 men, women and children to Chesapeake Bay with their Governor, John White, and instructed them to call at Roanoke on the way. For some reason they ended their voyage at Roanoke and settled in the fort, but ran out of supplies. White returned to England, but the Spanish Armada delayed his resupplying of the colony and he could not go back to Roanoke until 1590.

When White did eventually return, the colonists had vanished. 'Cro' had been carved on a tree, suggesting that the entire colony had gone to nearby Croatoan, but no other trace was found. Years later it was reported that the missing colonists had been murdered by the Powhatan Indians. It has been suggested that Walsingham (and perhaps Essex) sabotaged the resupply of the colony to discredit Raleigh politically.[3] This was typical of the political manoeuvrings back home, which may have affected the subsequent Virginia expedition.

As a result of the disastrous Roanoke expedition, the English public was alerted to the concept of permanent colonization and the opportunities for making a commercial profit overseas. There was continuing speculation about the westward route to the Orient and the need to settle the New World to check Spanish expansion, a policy that intensified after the Spanish Armada attacked England in 1588. Some looked to the New World as an escape from religious persecution; others saw an opportunity to acquire land.

Gosnold's 1602 Voyage

An attempt to colonize the New World was made under the initial leadership of Bartholomew Gosnold in 1602. This voyage used Captain Edward Hayes' *Treatise* 'as a prospectus, or plan'.[4] This was a compilation of facts collected for Sir Humphrey Gilbert's use by Richard Hakluyt, the queen's cartographer and geographer, who was Rector of Wetheringsett, eight miles from Otley in Suffolk.

It is not clear how the leadership of the voyage devolved to the relatively unknown Gosnold. Sir Walter Raleigh may have been behind it, hoping that Gosnold would find his lost colony and counter Spanish influence in the New World. Gosnold himself, a Cambridge graduate and lawyer who had sailed with the Earl of Essex on the Azores expedition, hoped to make sufficient profit to free his father from temporary incarceration in a debtor's prison.

Gosnold is believed to have used the family seat, Otley Hall, as a recruiting base. His uncle, Robert Gosnold III, lord of the manor at Otley, had been the Earl of Essex's secretary and had been fined £40 for his role in the Essex rebellion of 1601. He was also a friend of Richard Hakluyt.

The voyage was funded by the Earl of Southampton, Shakespeare's patron. William Strachey, writing in 1611–12, reports (and in view of the importance of this passage I reflect the contemporary spelling):

> 'Henrye Earle of Southampton ... lardgly contrybuted to the furnishing out of a shippe to be Commaunded by Captainye Bartlemew Gosnell and Capt. Bartlemew Gilbert and accompanied with divers other Gentlemen, to discover a convenient place for a new Colony to be sent thither who accordingly in March anno 1602 from Falmouth in a Bark of Dartmouth called the *Concord* sett forward holding a Course for the North-parte of Virginia.'[5]

Besides knowing the Earl of Southampton, Gosnold was a cousin twice over of Francis Bacon[6] and four times over of the 17th Earl of Oxford, who Oxfordians believe was Shakespeare.

Gosnold set sail with 20 settlers (32 passengers in all)[7] on the *Concord* in March 1602. His destination was Virginia, which then meant the land stretching from Florida to Canada, and his aim was to establish a trading post and plant a colony. The first paragraph of Hayes' *Treatise* begins: 'The voyage which we intend, is to plant Christian people and religion upon the Northwest countries of America.'[8] It should be noted that there was a strong religious emphasis from the very beginning.

The voyage is well documented as Gosnold's two Cambridge friends John Brereton and Gabriel Archer kept logs. The outward voyage took 49 days. Gosnold sailed round the headland of Providence and named it Cape Cod. He landed at an island further south and named it Martha's Vineyard after his daughter Martha, who had died in 1598, aged one. He went on and settled on 'Elizabeth Island', which has long been thought to be Cuttyhunk (where there is a memorial tower), but which may have been Naushon.

The settlement did not last. The settlers ran out of food and the native

Americans, initially friendly, turned hostile. Gosnold loaded a cargo of cedar wood, sassafras (used in the making of tea and as a remedy for syphilis) and furs, and returned in 35 days.[9]

Sir Walter Raleigh had acquired the patent for all exports from America after the death of his half-brother Sir Humphrey Gilbert and ordered that the cargo should be impounded.[10] John Brereton then wrote a report on the voyage, addressed to Raleigh. The report goes into much greater detail about the *flora* and *fauna* seen during the voyage than would be appropriate for someone merely appealing for the embargo on the cargo to be lifted, and it is possible that Raleigh owned the *Concord* and contributed to the funding of the voyage, hoping for news of his lost colony, in which case he would naturally expect to receive the cargo.

It seems that Hakluyt told Raleigh that Captain Hayes, who had accompanied Sir Humphrey Gilbert on his last voyage and witnessed the sinking of his ship, had transferred the Gilbert–Hayes patent to Gosnold. A compromise was arrived at whereby the cargo would be sold in foreign ports so as not to glut the English market and depress the price and Raleigh would receive a share of the profits.

It is likely that Raleigh gave Hakluyt his consent for a new voyage in which Gosnold could be involved. This voyage was, in fact, made under Martin Pring, who set out from Milford Haven on 10 April 1603 with the *Speedwell* (then less leaky than in 1620) and the *Discoverer* and reached Virginia – perhaps Plymouth Harbour – where the crews loaded a cargo of sassafras and returned to England. The *Speedwell* arrived last on 3 October.[11]

Gosnold made little profit on his 1602 voyage and it is likely that his father was bought out of prison by his brother, Gosnold's uncle, Robert Gosnold III.

Francis Bacon, MP for Ipswich (only a few miles from Otley) from 1597 – he was readopted in 1601 and 1610 – perhaps drew on Gosnold's experiences in his *New Atlantis*, a Utopian vision of the New World published posthumously in 1627. It is possible that Shakespeare based details of the enchanted isle in *The Tempest* on Gosnold's voyage; Everett Hale has drawn attention to the similarities between the phraseology in Brereton's and Archer's logs and the language of *The Tempest*.[12]

The Founding of the 1607 Jamestown Settlement

Gosnold now set about making a second voyage to the New World. His wife's cousin, Sir Thomas Smythe,[13] organizer of an expedition to the East Indies in the 1590s and first governor of the East India Company in 1600, had also been implicated in the Essex rebellion. As Sheriff of London, he had been expected to contribute 1,000 men and he had been put in the Tower of London with the Earl of Southampton. Both were now released. Smythe had inherited the Muscovy Company founded by his grandfather, Sir Anthony Judd, and, appointed ambassador to Russia in 1604, he now directed the company's dealings in Russia and made a fortune in furs. Overnight he became London's richest merchant.

In 1604–5 Gosnold seems to have asked him to help with a new planting voyage. It seems that Smythe undertook to provide three ships. Guy Fawkes' plot in 1605 delayed plans for a charter, as the Lord Chief Justice was busy bringing the plotters to justice and execution,[14] but in 1606, charters for two Virginia companies were organized through Smythe, who became Treasurer of the First Virginia Company. Sir Walter Raleigh's patent from the Crown, which gave him the right to all produce from America, was transferred to him on 10 April with James I's signing of the First Virginia Company's charter.[15]

James I declared in the incorporation of the Virginia Company in November 1606 that it would bring glory in propagating 'Christian religion to such people, as yet live in darkness and miserable ignorance of the true knowledge and worship of God'. He directed that the Virginia Company's President and Council should ensure that the 'true Word and Service of God … be preached, planted and used according to the rites and doctrines of the Church of England'. The gentlemen of the company, while clearly seeking profits, agreed that 'true' religion should be planted in Virginia, and ordered their colonial governors to establish the Church of England in the wilderness. The strong Anglican motivation of this voyage has been obscured, indeed overshadowed, by the voyage of the Puritan Separatists and dissenters on the *Mayflower*.[16] Anglicans were less noisy than Puritans, but still felt intensely towards their national Church.

A motivational and moral confusion surrounded the Virginia Company's expedition, however. It was not as devout or morally ordered as the (also chaotic) *Mayflower* expedition, and was subject to a level of incoherence, dissonance, policy inconsistency, élitism, control issues and sheer apparent ill-fortune which is at times baffling. It is possible that a Freemasonic faction may have been working within the Anglican ambience – James I had brought Templarism from Scotland to London in 1603 – and that clashes between Anglican and Masonic factions may go some way to explain the confusion. Without such a scenario it is hard to make sense of the many tiny confused events that comprised the settling of Virginia.

At the top of the command structure of the voyage was Sir Thomas Smythe. He headed the London-based Virginia Council from 20 November 1606[17] and acted as chief executive of the entire Virginian undertaking until 1619.

Gosnold recruited his cousin, Edward-Maria Wingfield of Letheringham, four miles from Otley, as a stockholder. He interviewed 104 men and boys and 55 crew, according to George Percy (writing in 1608). Today it is thought there were 108 settlers in all,[18] 40 of whom came from villages round Otley. They included Captain John Smith, a Norfolk farmer's boy who had been made a captain for valour when fighting as a mercenary in Hungary. It is unknown whether Gosnold promised the settlers land, which they could never aspire to in England's hierarchical landed class system.

John Smith wrote that Gosnold was the 'prime mover'[19] of the voyage:

'Captain Bartholomew Gosnoll, one of the first movers of this plantation, having many years solicited many of his friends, but found small assistance, at last prevailed with some gentlemen, as Captain John Smith, Master Edward-Maria Wingfield, Master Robert Hunt, and divers others who depended a year upon his projects.'[20]

So, Gosnold had organized the funding through his relative Smythe and chosen the crew, and Smythe's Muscovy Company had chartered the ships. (Unfortunately, the Muscovy Company's records were later destroyed in the Great Fire of 1666.)[21] Around this time the East India Company and the Virginia Company were both under Smythe's leadership.

John Stow wrote in 1614, in *The Annales of England*, of Gosnold's role in organizing this second voyage:

> 'And amongest other of worthy memory in this plantation, you shall understand that Captain Gosnoll, a brave soldier and very ingenious, spent much money and adventured his person, and drew in many others, at the beginning of this plantation.'

Gosnold had the authority to draw in many others through his journey to the New World back in 1602. In view of the unprofitability of that voyage, though, the money he now spent must have been Smythe's.

In spite of Gosnold's authority, the politics of the day made it impossible for him to lead the expedition. James I had been invited to succeed Elizabeth I by Sir Robert Cecil, the First Secretary (i.e. Prime Minister), and the Cecilites were the dominant faction in politics. The Essexites were down following the beheading of Essex in 1601 and the Raleighites were down following the imprisonment of Raleigh in 1603 for being too aggressively anti-Spanish in his colonizing skirmishes. The leader of the new expedition had to be a Cecilite, but Gosnold was seen as coming from an Essexite family.[22]

At the last minute, in mid-December 1606, the First Virginia Company, which was dominated by Robert Cecil, the principal patron of the London Virginia Council and prime mover of the establishment of the Virginia Company, chose a pro-Cecil man, Christopher Newport, to be admiral. (He wrote to Cecil, who had been made the Earl of Salisbury in 1605, on 29 July 1607 in sycophantic style, offering to show James I a sample of gold from the New World, which turned out to be worthless. Sir Thomas Smythe followed up with a letter to Lord Salisbury on 17 August 1607.) The Cecilites in the Virginia Company wanted Gosnold's relative Wingfield, who had put up money as a stockholder, to lead the settlement. Gosnold was told that he would not be leading the expedition, but would be going as no. 2. He must have been bitterly disappointed. Those he had recruited looked up to him as *de facto* leader and presumably understood that Newport had been imposed on them all.

We shall see later that at some point Francis Bacon, Gosnold's cousin, threw his group's weight behind the English plan to colonize America.

It is not clear when he did this, as Bacon was not publicly associated with the Virginia Company until the 1609 charter, where he is listed as a shareholder.

The expedition left Blackwall on the river Thames near London on 20 December 1606.[23] The fleet comprised the *Susan Constant* under Admiral Newport, the *Godspeed* under Gosnold and the *Discovery* under Captain Ratcliffe. According to Purchas's marginal notes, there were 71 aboard the first ship, 52 aboard the second and 21 aboard the third.[24] The three ships were seen off by the Poet Laureate, Michael Drayton, who declaimed verses he had written which referred to 'Virginia,/ Earth's only paradise'. He had probably been sent by James I, and if so his presence was a sign that there was royal blessing for the voyage. James was officially head of the Church of England and so, being under his protection, the expedition was also Church of England. A Church-of-England vicar was on board, the Reverend Robert Hunt.

It was a miserable voyage. There were blizzards in the mouth of the Thames and they were becalmed for six weeks, camping on the ships' open decks. It must have been perishing. There were mutterings about Newport's leadership and three of the crew were put in chains for mutiny, including John Smith, who was fortunate not to be hanged when they stopped at Nevis(whose cloud-capped peak Columbus had likened to *las nieves*, the snows) beyond Montserrat and two miles south-east of St Kitts. A pair of gallows was constructed and in a kind of trial several men gave evidence against Smith, but no sentence was enforced.[25]

The fleet arrived at the mouth of the James river on 26 April 1607 and the voyagers began looking for a suitable location where they could settle. Documents containing instructions from the First Virginia Council were opened and 'the Council in Virginia' was named. The majority were Cecilites. They elected Wingfield President of the Council.

Newport and Wingfield rejected the landing site favoured by Gosnold and his friend Archer, College Creek. In a blunder which may have been caused by a personality or factional power struggle that obscured the strategic and practical issues, they preferred the Jamestown site because it allowed mooring for the three ships. However, it was swampy and mosquito-ridden and too near a deserted Paspaheg settlement. The native

Americans were menacing and there were skirmishes as the settlers built a triangular fort with palisades like sharpened pencils, point upwards, in gruelling heat. It is possible that Newport and Wingfield were members of or influenced by a Freemasonic faction that was opposed to Gosnold and Archer and would therefore never agree with their proposals. Many of the men resented Wingfield's leadership, especially when the wrong decisions were made.

The Council was sworn in by the Reverend Robert Hunt[26] and Wingfield presumably made a speech naming the site 'James his Town', i.e. Jamestown, after the English king. There was a makeshift church. The pews were tree trunks and the pulpit was a plank nailed between two trees with an awning or sail above it suspended from three or four higher branches, which acted as a shelter from rain and shade from the sun. Here the Reverend Robert Hunt held Church-of-England services.

Up to this point, it is clear that there was no Puritan influence on the colony, as there was to be at Plymouth, and that the main influence from England was royalist ('James his Town') and Church of England from Elizabeth I's time. Circumstantial evidence suggests there was a royal Freemasonic influence, but no direct evidence exists to verify it.

Moreover, besides taking the Church of England to the New World, Gosnold had brought with him the old rural agrarian system of Elizabethan England, carving the wilderness into plots. This system was based not on aristocracy, as in England, but on land: settlers with land had descendants until after a few generations there was an *élite* of landowners and a network of the unlanded who were employed in working on the land. England moved forward to the Industrial Revolution, but Virginia remained within its agrarian system, an 'aristocracy of the landed' in which owning land gave social position rather than birth. In a sense, Elizabethan England lived on in Virginia[27] and Virginia came to represent vanished England with its emphasis on farming against the wilderness, a georgic vision (akin to that of Virgil's *Georgics*) much admired by the later founders of the American constitution.[28]

Newport took 22 men – including John Smith, temporarily released from custody – of the 150-strong force upriver and while he was away 400 native Americans, sensing that defences were depleted, attacked the fort.

Gosnold repulsed them by climbing aboard the *Godspeed* and firing the saker (heavy cannon), causing 20 native-American casualties.[29]

The defeat of the native Americans ensured the survival of the colony. However, swamp fever was rife. Food shortages meant that the settlers lacked bodily resistance. Many fell ill with a combination of dysentery, swamp fever and starvation. (It has been suggested that one faction tried to wipe out another faction by overdosing the water with arsenic, which was used in minute quantities as purification. This is conjecture and is not supported by evidence.) In August 1607 13 died, including Bartholomew Gosnold, who was given a military funeral in which all the ordnance of the fort was shot off. He was buried and, as already related, his skeleton may have been found in 2003. According to John Smith, 67 of the original settlers were dead by December 1607.

The Gosnold family was severely affected by the Jamestown settlement: Bartholomew left a widow and five surviving children, his younger brother and cousin (both named Anthony) did not return and a painting of Bartholomew's uncle Robert Gosnold III in 1610 shows a bleak man in black clasping a prayer book for comfort, displaying a ring round his thumb which may have been given him by the Earl of Essex. Or was it Bartholomew's?

The Jamestown settlement was the first English-speaking colony to survive. Its founding in 1607 will be observed on its 400th anniversary in May 2007 as the founding of the United States of America. From the vantage point we have now reached (which will soon change), whoever founded the Jamestown settlement can arguably take the credit for founding the United States of America, and John Smith, in a rare moment of honesty, said that Gosnold was 'one of the first movers of this plantation'.

Bartholomew Gosnold, acting with the financial clout of Sir Thomas Smythe, who was in effect running India and America from one London office, does appear to have as good a claim as any to be considered the founder of the North American civilization that became the United States of America. What drove him? Entrepreneurial gain? Claiming the New World for England's king, James I, before the Spanish seized it? Or was he on a Freemasonic assignment that set him apart from the faction of Newport and Wingfield?

John Smith and Jamestown's Survival

In 1606 the Virginia Company of Plymouth had received a charter from James I for colonizing the northern coast of Virginia from 38° to 45° latitude north, farther north than the Virginia Company of London's territory. At the end of May 1607 it sent two ships to New England – the *Gift of God* under Captain George Popham and the *Mary and John* under Captain Raleigh Gilbert, who had sailed with Bartholomew Gosnold in 1602.

On 29 June the two became separated. The *Mary and John* reached Sable Island off Nova Scotia, found shoals of huge cod and sent 13 men ashore. By 6 August she had reached the St George's group of islands. The next day she met up with the *Gift of God* again. Gilbert took a boat and 13 companions and found the river Pemaquid. On 16 August the two ships reached the Sagadahoc (Kennebec) and a site for a colony was chosen. A fort was built in August and September.

The winter was severe, and a number of men, including Popham, died. Then Gilbert heard that his brother had died (Sir John Gilbert, on 8 July 1608) and that he had inherited land. He announced that he had to return home and all the settlers went with him. The Plymouth branch of the Virginia Company now appeared to have little future and in London the focus was fully on the Virginia Company of London's Jamestown settlement in the south.[30]

The settlement was, however, facing difficulties. George Percy wrote, in *Observations*:

> 'After Captain Gosnold's death the Council could hardly agree by the dissension of Captain Kendall…. Our men were destroyed with cruel diseases, as swellings, fluxes, burning fevers, and by wars; and some departed suddenly, but for the most part they died of mere famine. There were never Englishmen left in a foreign country in such misery as we were in this newly discovered Virginia. We watched [stood guard] every three nights, lying on the bare, cold ground, what weather soever came; warded all the next day, which brought our men to be most feeble wretches. Our

food was but a small can of barley sod[den] in water, to five men a day; our drink, cold water taken out of the river, which was at a flood very salt, at a low tide full of slime and filth, which was the destruction of many of our men. Thus we lived for the space of five months in this miserable distress.'[31]

John Smith had been permanently released following the attack by the 400 native Americans and had resumed his place on the Council which Wingfield had blocked.[32] There had been fierce quarrels between him and Wingfield in which both Gosnold (until his death) and the Reverend Robert Hunt had been intermediaries. Smith and Wingfield were clearly in different factions, which is probably why Smith had been arrested for mutiny and held in the hold. Smith certainly blamed Wingfield for his arrest. Were these factions Freemasonic?

Smith gives a vivid and lively account, which is clearly embellished and weighted in his own favour,[33] of the development of the colony from now on. This development took place against the backdrop of many tiny events whose confusion we must try to pierce.

Smith led expeditions to explore and wheedle food from the native Americans. He went up and down the river to trade for corn and on his first journey he brought back ten bushels; on his second, 'such abundance of corn, as having laded our barge, as also I might have laded a ship'.[34]

In September 1607 the Smith–Wingfield animosity came to a head. Wingfield was deposed by Smith, Martin and Ratcliffe, who signed a warrant for him to be replaced by Ratcliffe, who, Smith tells us:

'...committed the managing of all things abroad to Captain Smith: who by his own example, good words and fair promises, set some to mow, others to bind thatch, some to build houses, others to thatch them, himself always bearing the greatest task for his own share, so that in short time he provided most of them lodgings, neglecting any for himself.'[35]

The Wingfield faction blighted the beginning of Ratcliffe's presidency through the dissension of Captain George Kendall. He had been confined aboard the *Discovery* to await trial for sowing discord between President and Council back around 28 August. He was joined by Wingfield, now facing charges ranging from concealing communion wine to stealing a tin whistle.[36]

Kendall was released but was immediately in trouble, for John Ratcliffe threatened to strike, or struck, James Read, the colony's blacksmith, in circumstances that are not clear. The blacksmith struck him back and Ratcliffe ordered that he be hanged. Standing on a ladder with a rope round his neck, Read bargained for his life by promising to reveal a plot against Ratcliffe. He said that the plotter was Kendall, who had, he alleged, planned to seize the *Discovery* and take her to England to complain about the leadership. It is not clear whether Kendall was to have gone in person or to have sent letters.

Smith tells the story:

'Having occasion to chide the smith for his misdemeanour, he not only gave him bad language but also offered to strike him with some of his tools. For which rebellious act the smith was by a jury condemned to be hanged. But being upon the ladder continuing very obstinate as hoping upon a rescue, when he saw no other way but death with him, he became penitent and declared a dangerous conspiracy. For which Captain Kendall, as principal, was by a jury condemned, and shot to death.'[37]

The execution took place on 1 December 1607.

Later it was spread about that Kendall was a Spanish spy. One of the crew, a Catholic named Francis Magnel, later reported that he was a Catholic English captain who was executed 'because they knew that he wanted to come to Spain to reveal to His Majesty what goes on in that land'.[38] Was there any truth in this accusation or was it a case of one faction blackening the name of another? It is possible that Wingfield, Kendall and Read were in the same Freemasonic grouping.

It is also possible that Kendall was a spy for English Catholics in Spain or that he was a spy for Lord Salisbury, formerly Sir Robert Cecil. It is just possible that he spied for no one, and was having his name blackened posthumously.

The Kendall–Ratcliffe animosity had another twist, for part of Kendall's defence was that John Ratcliffe had no right to pass sentence as he was in fact John Sicklemore, and after Kendall's death Ratcliffe did indeed change his name to Sicklemore. Why had he been living under a false name? Had he adopted an *alias* because *he* was one of Lord Salisbury's Cecilite spies? Or were there Freemasonic reasons for concealing his true identity?

These intrigues aside, this was a crucial time for forming good relations with the native Americans, both for the Virginia colony and the future history of America. With this end in mind, in early or mid-December the Council agreed that John Smith should search for the source of the Chickahominy river, which flows into the James. With nine companions, six of whom rowed, Smith took his boat 27 miles up the Chickahominy and, finding further progress blocked by fallen trees, rented a canoe and two native American guides to go 'duck hunting' (to continue the exploration up the river). Taking John Robinson, gentleman, and Thomas Emery, carpenter, with him, he progressed another 20 miles, and went ashore to eat. He left Robinson and Emery, armed with muskets, and one of the native Americans, and with the other native American set off to explore 'nature of the soil'.

It soon became clear that the Indians of the Chickahominy were hostile, for Smith was attacked, if we can believe his own account. First he heard 'holloing of Indians' and then he was 'struck with an arrow' on his right thigh. He spotted some native Americans and shot at them. Eventually he was surrounded by 200 native Americans, or so he tells us. He inadvertently stepped into a quagmire and was captured. The place where this happened is thought to be White Oak Swamp. Smith was brought back to the canoe and saw John Robinson lying dead 'with 20 or 30 arrows in him'. There was no sign of Emery.[39]

That night Smith was well fed with 'a quarter of venison and some ten pound of bread' and was conveyed to the dwelling-place of Powhatan, the reputedly cruel native-American chieftain. This was a bark-covered house more than 100 feet long beside the Pamunkey river. Smith gave conflicting accounts of what happened there. According to one description, Powhatan lay on a foot-high bed, a woman sitting at his head and another at his feet, his chiefs sitting on each side of a nearby fire, 'ten in a rank', and behind them as many young women. He told Smith he would be free in four days. It was rumoured that he had ordered the execution of the survivors of the Roanoke colony. He wanted the new settlement of white men to leave at once, but was wily. Smith assured Powhatan that the English had come to Virginia to escape Spanish patrols and they would leave as soon as it was safe – a blatant lie.

In *A True New Relation* (1708), Smith made no mention of Powhatan's daughter Pocahontas, who would then have been 12 or 13 years old. He first mentioned the Pocahontas story in a letter to the queen, Anne of Denmark, consort of James I, when 'Princess Pocahontas' visited the English court in 1616:

> 'Some ten years ago being in Virginia and taken prisoner by the power of Powhatan, their chief king, I received from this great savage exceeding great courtesy, especially from his son Nantaquaus, the most manliest, comeliest, boldest spirit I ever saw in a savage; and his sister Pocahontas, the king's most dear and well-beloved daughter, being but a child of twelve or thirteen years of age, whose compassionate pitiful heart of my desperate estate gave me much cause to respect her.'[40]

There is another version in *The Generall Historie* (published in 1624) in which Pocahontas saves Smith's life:

> 'Finding he was beset with 200 savages, two of them he slew, still defending himself with aid of a savage his guide, whom he bound to his arm with his garters and used him as a buckler. Yet he was shot in his thigh a little and had many arrows that stuck in his clothes, but no great hurt, till at last, slipping into a bogmire, they took him prisoner.... The savages ... followed him with 300 bowmen, conducted by the King of Pamaunkee, who in divisions searching the turnings of the river found Robinson and Emery by the fireside. Those they shot full of arrows and slew... Captain Smith was led after him by three great savages holding him fast by each arm, and on each side six went file with their arrows nocked. But arriving at the town, which was but only thirty or forty

hunting houses made of mats .... Smith they conducted to a longhouse, where thirty or forty tall fellows did guard him.... At last they brought him to ... where was Powhatan their emperor. Here more than 200 of those grim courtiers stood wondering at him as he had been a monster, till Powhatan and his train had put themselves in their greatest braveries. Before a fire upon a seat like a bedstead he sat covered with a great robe made of rarowcun [racoon] skins, and all the tails hanging by. On either side did sit a young wench of 16 or 18 years, and along on each side the house two rows of men, and behind them as many women, with all their heads and shoulders painted red, many of their heads bedecked with the white down of birds, but everyone with something, and a great chain of white beads about their necks.

'At his entrance before the king, all the people gave a great shout. The Queen of Appamatuck was appointed to bring him water to wash his hands, and another brought him a bunch of feathers instead of a towel to dry them. Having feasted him after their best barbarous manner they could, a long consultation was held, but the conclusion was two great stones were brought before Powhatan. Then as many as could laid hands on him dragged him to them, and thereon laid his head; and being ready with their clubs to beat out his brains, Pocahontas, the king's dearest daughter, when no entreaty could prevail, got his head in her arms and laid her own upon his to save him from death; whereat the emperor was contented he should live to make him hatchets, and her bells, beads and copper, for they thought him as well of all occupations as themselves.'[41]

In 1609 Richard Hakluyt had published an account of an incident in 1528, when an 18-year-old Spaniard, Juan Ortiz of Hirrihigua (i.e. Tampa Bay), Florida, had been captured by native Americans and bound to a griddle and was about to be barbecued alive when the chief's daughter, Ulalah, begged her father to give him to her as her slave. It could be that Smith embellished his account of his encounter with Powhatan by drawing on this 1528 story.[42]

Smith's experiences in the Chickahominy swamps were received with indignation at Jamestown. Men seethed at the reported deaths of Robinson and Emry and resented Smith's boasting. Within a day of his return, in another outbreak of factionalism that may have had Freemasonic origins, Gabriel Archer, as councillor and recorder, indicted him for causing the deaths of Robinson and Emry and had him deposed from the Council, tried and condemned to be hanged.

The next day – the day Smith was to be hanged, 2 January 1608 – Newport arrived back with 60 or 70 new settlers, including two women, and supplies on the *John and Francis*. His arrival saved Smith from the gallows but, in another 'mischance' – another example of the ill-starred fate of the Virginia venture which may have been due to an eruption of Freemasonic factionalism – the fort, which was still under Ratcliffe's (*alias* Sicklemore's) presidency, caught fire.

Smith wrote:

'Within five or six days [In fact 7 January, according to Wingfield] after the arrival of the ship, by a mischance our fort was burned, and the most of our apparel, lodging and private provision. Many of our old men deceased, and of our new, for want of lodging, perished.'[43]

The fire began where the new supplies were stored and spread through the town. It destroyed the Reverend Hunt's library and also the timber church which had been completed in the late summer or early autumn of 1607 and which Smith described as 'a homely thing like a barn, set upon cratchets, covered with rafts, sedge, and earth; so was also the walls'.[44] It had served as a place of worship for only a few weeks.

Following the fire, the settlers depended on the native Americans for food. Smith and Newport visited Powhatan. As, according to Smith's 1624 account, he had nearly had him clubbed to death on a stone during his last visit, he went first with 20 armed men as a security precaution. They exchanged gifts with Powhatan and came away with 40 or 50 large platters of bread.

Newport joined Smith the next morning. Powhatan gave him 20

turkeys on his departure and asked for 20 swords in return. Amazingly, in a blunder that would obviously weaken the fort's security, Newport did give them.

The colonists did not manage their relations with the native Americans well. Powhatan then sent Smith 20 turkeys and asked for another 20 swords. Smith understandably refused and Powhatan ordered his native Americans to help themselves to the weapons. Smith seized seven native Americans, whipped them and kept them as hostages inside the fort. In reply, the Paspahegh Indians seized two Englishmen. Relations between the English and the native Americans had broken down.

Pocahontas was sent to the fort to express Powhatan's displeasure and the prisoners were released between 20 April and 2 June.[45]

Having armed the native Americans against Smith's wishes, perhaps to weaken Ratcliffe's leadership, Newport left for England again on the *Phoenix* on 2 June 1608. Smith and 14 companions left with him on the barge and sailed up the east coast to explore the Potomac river, visiting native Americans on the way. Smith explored Chesapeake Bay – he claims to have sailed 3,000 miles – and constructed a map of Virginia. He returned with his barge decked with red and yellow Spanish streamers to resemble a Spanish frigate, perhaps to test the fort's preparedness.

On landing he found everyone at the fort sick, some delirious. Morale was dreadful and, concluding that the colonists were 'all unable to do any thing, but complain of the pride and unreasonable needless cruelty of their sillie president' (*Proceedings*) Smith deposed Ratcliffe and took his place as President.[46]

Now things got better, according to Smith:

'Now the building of Ratcliffe's palace stayed, as a thing needless; the church was repaired, the store-house recovered, buildings prepared for the supplies we expected, the fort reduced to a five-square form, the order of the watch renewed, the squadrons [each setting of the watch] trained, the whole company every Saturday exercised in the plain by the west bulwark … we called Smithfield.'[47]

In short, under Smith's direction the fort was expanded, military training supervised, 20 houses built and crops planted. And Ratcliffe was in custody, charged with mutiny.

The fort had been rebuilt. There were now streets of two-storey houses, some of which had attics, and there was a new primitive frame church. (No mention was made of building a church either in A True Relation, 1608, or in the Proceedings, the 1612 report, of which Smith was part-author. Smith first refers to this church building in 1631, in the last year of his life.)

Smith had been President for barely three weeks when Newport (who had presumably supported his takeover) returned with 70 new settlers on the John and Francis and the Phoenix brought 40 more. They joined a population of 120, perhaps 130, as Smith estimated in 1624.[48]

The Virginia Company in London now wanted gold. Cargoes of cedar and sassafras were not what it had had in mind when it had organized the colonization of Virginia.[49] The new arrivals included specialists in garnering pitch and tar, boiling soap ashes and glass manufacturing (for there was a shortage of window glass in London). The northern end of the causeway connecting Jamestown island to the mainland became known as the Glass House.[50]

Smith sent a letter to the Council of Virginia in London, suggesting their policy was unrealistic and stupid:

'When you send again I intreat rather send but thirty Carpenters, husbandmen, gardiners, fishermen, blacksmiths, masons and diggers up of trees, roots, well provided; [than] a thousand of such as we have.'[51]

This was another example of policy dissonance, the policy of the Council of Virginia, perhaps guided by Raleigh, being at odds with local conditions and the wishes of President John Smith. Was the Council of Virginia in London influenced by the Templar Freemasonry brought to London by James I in 1603, and had it identified Smith as leader of a different faction of Freemasonry which, as we shall see, he may have been?

The Virginia Company in London had clearly been given an account by Newport of Powhatan's request for swords and had decided to court

Powhatan by supporting his coronation before his Indian tribe. The company had sent presents, presumably under Newport's care on the *John and Francis*, for the coronation, including a bed. Newport sent Smith to Powhatan to explain that he would be wearing English clothes (i.e. become an English prince). Powhatan demanded that Newport attend in person.

Newport and his men had been waiting nearby, presumably for security reasons. They arrived the next morning and unpacked and assembled the heavy wooden bed and hangings. Powhatan reluctantly put on 'scarlet cloak and apparel'. A shot was fired to signal the moment of crowning. This caused panic among the native Americans.

After the ceremony Newport returned to the fort and set off with 120 men, including a gold refiner, William Callicut, to look for gold and corn for the new settlers. He was clearly implementing the company's policy on gold. He left Smith behind.

Not trusting Newport's ability to obtain corn from the native Americans, Smith made his own journey to the Chickahominy Indians and returned with corn.[52] Once again Newport and Smith displayed a policy that lacked clarity in their dealings with native Americans.

Newport found no gold mines or corn, and his men returned tired, hungry and disheartened. He left for England between 27 November and 3 December.

Smith wanted more corn from the Nansemond Indians. He decided to seize Powhatan's corn by force and took 38 volunteers out of the 198 colonists, including George Percy (the Earl of Northumberland's brother) and Francis West (brother of Lord De La Warr, now Delaware). The two-vessel expedition spent a month progressing up the frozen river, the barge slowly breaking ice, and they spent Christmas week sheltering from a blizzard as the guests of native Americans. They reached Werowocomoco on 12 January 1609. Powhatan sent them bread, turkey and venison. He planned to massacre Smith and 16 of his men as they ate supper, but Pocahontas went to them and warned them of her father's intention, as Smith tells us in both *Proceedings* and *The Generall Historie*.[53]

Smith had not given up his attempt to seize corn from the native Americans. He went on to the village of Powhatan's half-brother, Opechancanough. He found it deserted, but 700 warriors were lurking in nearby fields. Smith claims in *Proceedings* that as the situation became desperate he grabbed Opechancanough's pigtail hair and put a pistol to his chest. However, he had no alternative but to retreat.

While all this was happening, Powhatan had sent two Dutchmen under his control with native-American carriers to the depleted fort. They managed to steal 300 hatchets, 50 swords, eight muskets and eight pikes.

In another disaster, 11 men, including Captain Richard Waldo (in command in Smith's absence), Matthew Scrivener and Anthony Gosnold (Bartholomew Gosnold's brother), were crossing the river James to hunt for hogs, when, overloaded, the boat sank in the icy water and all were drowned. Their bodies were washed ashore.

Back in the fort, six men reluctantly volunteered to convey this news to Smith. On the way Powhatan imprisoned some of them, but Pocahontas helped one of them, Richard Wiffin, to escape and find Smith. Smith now retreated with Wiffin and 279 bushels of corn, which in his *Generall Historie* he rounded up to 479.[54]

News of Smith's failures had spread and, emboldened, Wowinchopunck, King of the Paspaheghs, was now lying in wait for him in the Glass House area near the fort. There was a skirmish and somehow Smith found himself grappling with the king. Both of them fell into the river and Smith dragged the king to the fort as his prisoner.

Smith now constructed a blockhouse at the fort and another one across the river on Hog Island to protect the stock of some 60 pigs. While working across the river, he received word that rats had eaten half the store of corn, yet another disaster. He returned to the fort and sent 20 men out to fish, but many of the settlers were demoralized by now and simply wanted to take the next boat back to England.

In July the *Mary and John* arrived. Her captain, Samuel Argall, was a cousin of Sir Thomas Smythe and also related to De La Warr. He brought news that the Virginia colony's form of government had been revoked, as the Virginia Company of London had been granted a new charter on 23 May. The new Governor would be Sir Thomas Gates and he would be bringing 600 new settlers. De La Warr would be Governor-General.[55]

The Virginia Company of London put out a pamphlet that called *Nova Britannia* an 'earthly Paradice', and assembled a fleet at Plymouth: the *Sea*

Venture (or *Sea Adventure*) under Sir George Somers, which would carry Governor Gates, the *Diamond* under the deposed President John Ratcliffe, the *Falcon* under John Martin, the *Blessing* under Gabriel Archer, who had sentenced Smith to hang, the *Unity*, the *Lion*, the *Swallow* and four smaller boats, including the *Virginia*. There were undesirables aboard the fleet – Catholics under pressure after the Guy Fawkes plot – and Smith faced the prospect of the return of his opponents Ratcliffe, Martin and Archer.

There was a great storm on 24 July and the *Sea Venture* was blown onto the reefs of the Bermudas, where it stuck, wedged between rocks, allowing the 150 passengers and crew to get ashore. William Strachey was aboard and in *True Reportory of the Wreck and Redemption of Sir Thomas Gates, Knight* he gave an eyewitness account of the disaster:

> 'There might be seen master, master's mate, boatswain, quarter master, coopers, carpenters, and who not, with candles in their hands, creeping along the ribs viewing the sides, searching every corner and listening in every place if they could hear the water run. Many a weeping leak was this way found and hastily stopped, and a length one in the gunner room made up with I know not how many pieces of beef. But all was to no purpose, the leak (if it were but one) which drunk in our greatest seas and took in our destruction fastest could not then be found, nor ever was.'[56]

This account may have been read by Shakespeare before he wrote the shipwreck scene in *The Tempest*. On Bermuda the survivors built two ships from the wreckage, the *Deliverance* and *Patience*. The wreck was discovered in 1958.

Four ships arrived at the James river on 11 August. Three more came a few days later. Many of the passengers had died: 32 bodies were thrown overboard from the *Diamond* and *Swallow*.

The James fort now had a population of 400. Of these 140 were immediately sent under Francis West to build a fort on the border between Powhatan's territory and that of the Monacans, a journey described by George Percy. West built a fort near falls, but had so little powder that it was put under pressure when it was attacked by only a dozen native

Americans. Smith was summoned and brought reinforcements. He accused West of building the fort in the wrong place.[57] Again Smith was at odds with the reinforcers and the Virginia Company in London, who were supporting the newly-crowned Powhatan.

Returning to Jamestown, in what appeared to be an accident but was later claimed to be a deliberate attempt at assassination, Smith 'was near blown to death with gun-powder'. In *The Generall Historie* he says: 'Sleeping in his boat ... accidentally, one fired his powder bag, which tore the flesh from his body and thighs, nine or ten inches square in a most pitiful manner'.[58] His clothes were on fire and he threw himself in the water to put the fire out.

Smith himself thought that he had survived an attempted assassination. In *Proceedings* he describes how Ratcliffe, Martin and Archer,

> '...their guilty consciences fearing a just reward for their deserts, seeing the President unable to stand, and near bereft of his senses by reason of his torment, they had plotted to have him murdered in his bed. But his heart did fail him that should have given fire to that merciless pistol.'[59]

Whether there was in fact a second assassination attempt as he lay in bed can only be conjectured, but once again Smith had been at the centre of dissension in the colony.

Smith returned to England with the fleet. Ratcliffe, whom he had deposed, wrote to the Secretary of State, Lord Salisbury, that he had been sent to England 'to answer some misdemeanours'[60] – probably accusations by his opponents that he had not been running the colony well. According to Henry Spelman, Smith had conspired with the Powhatan Indians at the falls to kill Francis West, Lord De La Warr's brother,[61] but this was probably said to blacken his name and make sure he did not return to Jamestown.

From now on Smith's contribution to the founding of America was through his pen. He completed his map of Virginia, which was published in 1612, and worked on his history. In 1614 he made contact with the Virginia Company of Plymouth, which still retained its charter to colonize the northern coast, and, backed by Sir Ferdinando Gorges of Plymouth, began to map from Penobscot Bay to Cape Cod, an area he named New England.

He made two more attempts to cross the Atlantic. The first ended when he was captured by a French privateer – some accounts say pirates – and spent the rest of the three-month voyage, before he was able to escape, making notes for *A Description of New England*, which was published in 1625. The second voyage was abandoned when weather conditions prevented his ships from sailing for three months.

During the last phase of the Virginia Company, when the Earl of Southampton was treasurer, Smith appeared before it on 12 April 1621 to criticize the administration of Virginia and to propose that he should write a history. As a result *The Generall Historie of North Virginia, New-England and the Summer Isles* came to be written. It was published in 1624, the year the charter for the Virginia colony was revoked, and Smith brought out *The True Travels, Adventures and Observations of Captain John Smith in Europe, Asia, Africa and America* a year before he died in 1631.

The Decline of the 'Christian Colonie'

After Smith's return to England in 1609, the colony was semi-leaderless and lapsed into near-mutiny and indiscipline. George Percy became interim leader, but Smith's opponents, Ratcliffe, Martin and Archer, were effectively in charge.

Smith's policy of satellite settlements was continued. There was one by the falls under West and one on the Nansemonds' island under Martin. Now Percy sent Ratcliffe to build a fort at Point Comfort, Fort Algernon, which was named after Percy's titled brother. Martin left his fort in the care of Michael Sicklemore (Ratcliffe) and 17 of his men mutinied in his absence. Sicklemore went after them with several men and they were found dead 'with their mouths stopped full of bread'.[62]

Percy now abandoned West's and Martin's forts and decided to send Ratcliffe as an emissary to Powhatan, who had moved to Orapakes. Ratcliffe traded for corn, but according to Henry Spelman there was a dispute, as native Americans pushed up the bottoms of the woven baskets that contained corn, cheating the English. Ratcliffe and his men gathered up the corn they had bought and set off to walk back to their boat half a mile away. Most were killed, one by one, by native Americans in the woods and fields. Ratcliffe was tied naked to a tree, a fire was lit at his feet and women scraped his flesh from his bones with sharp mussel shells and threw the bits into the fire. Unsurprisingly, he 'miserably perished'.[63] So ended the life of the President Smith deposed.

Relations between the English and Powhatan deteriorated and Powhatan attacked the English individually wherever he could find them. As a result, the settlers were trapped in the fort and starving. The native Americans killed all the pigs on Hog Island and the settlers ate all their chickens, sheep, goats, dogs, cats, rats and mice, even horses' hides. Some even dug up a buried native American and ate the remains of the flesh. Both Percy and Smith report that a settler killed his wife, pleading hunger, though 'meal, oatmeal, beans and peas' were found in his house. He was tried and burned alive.[64]

The famine at Jamestown was not as bad at Fort Algernon. Two ships had been sighted there and, fearing they were Spanish, the fort's commander had fired on them and 40 men had stood to arms. It turned out that they were the *Deliverance* and *Patience*, bearing Gates and Somers and those wrecked on the *Sea Venture*. There was great joy, and then the realization dawned that there were now 148 more mouths to feed and the newcomers had brought no food with them.

The two ships arrived at Jamestown on 23 May 1610. To the new settlers, the town looked a ruin. The fort was in part made of flimsy boards which could be kicked down and the native Americans were mounting regular attacks.[65] Food had run out – Archer is one of those believed to have starved to death at this time[66] – and it was not known when De La Warr would arrive.

The church, a dilapidated, ruined lean-to made of sail and wood, was a symbol of the colony's physical and moral decline. Governor Gates immediately gave the order that it should be rebuilt, and within two years it was. The new church was 60 feet long and 24 feet wide. The chancel and pews were of cedar so that it would be 'light within', according to Strachey. There was a sermon every Thursday and two sermons every

Sunday. The bell was rung for prayers at 10 a.m. and 4 p.m. every day. Gates imposed a discipline of three services a week and prayers twice a day to resist disease, poverty, native-American attacks and the settlers' own bickering. He saw the Church as an instrument of the State.[67]

But the famine was dreadful and eventually Gates took the decision to evacuate the fort on the four ships – the *Deliverance, Patience, Discovery* and *Virginia*. The heavy cannon and artillery were removed and buried. The flotilla set off on the evacuation voyage on 8 June – and almost immediately a lookout spotted a longboat coming upriver. In it was Governor-General De La Warr, who had brought enough provisions to last 400 men for a year.[68]

Now all saw the hand of God at work. Alexander Whitaker wrote that 'the finger of God hath been the only true worker here'.[69] In London William Crashaw wrote: 'If ever the hand of God appeared in action of man, it was here most evident: for when man had foresaken this business, God took it in hand.'[70]

De La Warr's first act was to promote morality through the Council by a series of laws regulating the practice of religion which James I had emphasized in his incorporation of the company in November 1606. There had not been much evidence of religious behaviour in Jamestown since then. In a heavy-handed attempt to restore by force the colony's religious mission, the preamble spoke of 'true' religion:

> 'Whereas his Majesty ... hath in his own realms, a principal care
> of true Religion, and reverence to God, and hath always strictly
> commanded his Generals and Governors ... to let their ways be
> like his ... for the glory of God.'[71]

God should 'be duly and daily served'.[72] Settlers were forbidden from speaking against the Trinity and were ordered to attend church twice a day and study the Bible. The young had to be taught the Ten Commandments, articles of belief and the Lord's Prayer every Sunday evening half-an-hour before the service. De La Warr 'nursed' the Church – an image going back to Elizabeth I, who was spoken of as nurse of the Church.[73]

Gates and De La Warr sought to impose religious uniformity in accordance with the Elizabethan Act of Uniformity and the 'true' Church of England. They thought religious pluralism – tolerance of Catholics and dissenters – would merely intensify quarrelling. Religious liberty must not conflict with the State's maintaining order. Virginia was, and would continue to be, a 'Christian Colonie', the words William Strachey used in his preface to the colony's *Lawes* (1612).[74]

The Council was now composed of Gates (lieutenant-general), Somers, Percy, Sir Ferdinando Wainman, Newport and Strachey. Somers volunteered to return to Bermuda in the *Patience* with Samuel Argall in the *Discovery* and bring back a supply of fish and hogs, but adverse winds forced them to delay and on 16 July they sailed to Cape Cod and the New-England fishing grounds instead.

Somers and the *Patience* went missing. He turned up in Bermuda at the beginning of November and his absence has never been explained. Where had he been? He died of eating too much pork on 9 November. His nephew ignored orders to return to Jamestown and instead sailed for England with Somers' body.[75] Somers' expedition had failed to replenish Jamestown's food store.

De La Warr had been persistently ill since his arrival and was living on one of the ships. This did not stop him from deciding to sort out the native Americans with the same heavy-handedness he had applied to religion. He sent Powhatan a message reminding him of his coronation and said he now owed allegiance to England and should return the swords and control his native Americans. Powhatan retaliated by telling the English there should be no more journeys up rivers; they should stay in Jamestown or else go back to England.

After an incident at Fort Algernon in which native Americans seized and sacrificed one of the settlers, Gates was given permission to attack the Kecoughtan Indians on the north shore. On 9 July a large force landed and seized the native-American settlement with its acres of planted corn, killing at least five native Americans. Gates then returned to Jamestown. On 20 July he sailed for England to lobby support, taking Strachey's *True Reportory* back to the London controllers of the company.[76]

After Gates' departure, sorting out the native Americans continued. Percy was told to attack the Paspahegh and Chickahominy. He burned a village, killed 15 or 16 native Americans and took the Paspahegh king Wowinchopunck's queen and her children prisoner. To Percy's disgust, some of his men killed the children by throwing them in the river and 'shooting out their brains in the water'. On the way back Percy attacked and burned more native-American settlements, including a temple, and destroyed crops. On the orders of De La Warr the queen was taken into woods and killed. (The order was that she should be burned.)[77] Wowinchopunck, seeking to avenge the murder of his wife and children, then attacked the settlers and Captain Powell ran him through with a sword, after which, according to Strachey, he died.

De La Warr now focused on searching for gold to bring a return for the Virginia Company's commercial investment. Argall, now returned from his failed attempt to reach Bermuda, led a new attack on the Warraskoyacks and De La Warr sent a boatload of men to West's abandoned fort by the falls to search for gold. The corn store at Jamestown was dwindling and, while unsuccessfully looking for gold, Argall did a deal with the Patawomekes, who supplied corn.

The sickly De La Warr left a demoralized Jamestown on 28 March 1611 for the Caribbean with 50 men, but was blown to the Azores and thence to England. He never returned – he died on the way back seven years later.[78]

Sir Thomas Dale now arrived to replace Gates, who was still in England, as acting Governor. He brought three ships, men, cattle and materials, and found a depleted James fort under Percy, with Paspahegh Indians attacking to avenge the murder of their royal family.

Dale carried on the heavy-handed approach of De La Warr, but under him, the colony's discipline improved. He carried with him the *Lawes Divine, Morall and Martiall* which had been written by Strachey under the direction of Gates and De La Warr, and he implemented them. Every person in Virginia was given a military rank and certain duties, and there were severe penalties if they were not performed: for the first offence, lying with neck and heels together all night; for the second offence, whipping; and for the third offence, a year's service in the galleys. Dale's Code, as the laws were called, introduced the discipline necessary for the colony's survival.[79]

Dale now ordered the colonists to search for native Americans and destroy their villages. Now the torching of native-American settlements' wall mats and reed roofs became commonplace, leaving the inhabitants homeless among a few smoking sticks.[80]

On 2 August 1611 Governor Gates returned with nine heavily-laden ships, according to Percy. He had come with his wife, who had died on the voyage, and daughters, who went back on the next voyage.

Gates and Dale decided to establish a town – to be called Henrico after Henry, Prince of Wales – below the falls on Farrar Island, 59 miles from the James fort, and 350 settlers set out in September to build it. It was to be 13 times larger than the James fort and to have watchtowers and permanent storehouses. Native Americans disrupted the work from time to time, but the public buildings and houses were finished within four months. Dale then occupied the territory of the Appomattoc Indians and began building Bermuda City. Soon Little England was expanding round the James and Appomattoc rivers.[81]

The Virginia Company had instructed De La Warr to procure some of the native-American children and bring them up in the English language and manners. This was presumably to address James I's assertion in his incorporation of the Virginia Company in November 1606 that the company would propagate 'Christian religion to such people as yet live in darkness and miserable ignorance of the true knowledge and worship of God'.

Now Samuel Argall, having returned to Jamestown in June 1612 and worked for Gates, discovered in April 1613 that Pocahontas had been living with the Patawomekes as a corn agent for her father. The settlers were fascinated by Pocahontas, as rumour had it that she had intervened with her father, Powhatan, to spare Smith's life. She was regarded as a pro-English native American. But it was company policy to recover the swords Newport had given her father and Pocahontas could be traded for these. Argall promised Iapazaws, a friend of Smith's, that if the king of the Patawomekes kidnapped Pocahontas, he would be protected by the English king against Powhatan and that kidnapping her would bring about peace between the native Americans and the English. Furthermore, he would give Iapazaws a kettle and some toys.

Iapazaws and his wife brought Pocahontas to dine on Argall's English ship and Argall duly apprehended her. He sent a runner to Powhatan to say that his daughter was a prisoner and would be exchanged for all English prisoners and all swords and weapons he held, and a large amount of corn. The runner returned with Powhatan's assurance that he would pay the ransom. (Powhatan probably planned to seize the ship.) Argall returned to Jamestown and handed Pocahontas over to Gates. Powhatan then sent seven prisoners, a broadaxe, a whipsaw and seven old muskets with a promise of 500 bushels of corn after Pocahontas was released.[82] But no swords.

For nine months nothing happened. Gates, Dale and Argall waited. With Gates about to return to England, in March 1614 Dale tried to force the issue by sailing to Powhatan, who was at Matchot, about 15 miles north-east of Richmond, with Pocahontas on board. He was hoping to effect either a trade-off for the swords or a battle. He wanted to negotiate a permanent peace, but the boat was hit by many arrows.

Two Englishmen were then sent as emissaries to Powhatan: Sparkes and John Rolfe, who in 1612 had cultivated tobacco, introducing varieties from Spanish South America and the Caribbean. Powhatan refused to see them. A native American pointed out that it was corn-planting time and that there would have to be a delay.[83]

Now events took a surprising turn, for one of the emissaries wanted to marry the hostage. Ralph Hamor reports:

> 'John Rolfe had been in love with Pocahuntas and she with him, which thing at the instant that we were in parley with them, my self made known to Sir Thomas Dale by a letter from him, whereby he intreated his advice and furtherance in his love, if so it seemed fit to him for the good of the Plantation, and Pocahuntas her self, acquainted her brethren therewith.'

Rolfe's letter offered to marry Pocahontas 'for the good of this plantation, for the honour of our country, for the glory of God, for my own salvation and for the converting to the true knowledge of God and Jesus Christ, an unbelieving creature, namely Pokahuntas.'[84]

Incredibly, Powhatan went along with the proposal. The wedding probably took place in mid-April 1614. Powhatan had received the news of the marriage and sent an old uncle of Pocahontas's to represent him. The ceremony seems to have taken place at the James fort with both the Reverend Alexander Whitaker and Reverend Richard Buck involved in the service. As Dale had hoped, the marriage brought the war between Powhatan and the English to an end. The native Americans had finally been sorted out.

Now the Chickahominies agreed to accept James I as their king and an agreement was made whereby the eight senior native Americans were to be given red coats each year.

Next Dale sent Hamor and Savage to Powhatan and proposed that (though married), he should take another of his daughters as a bride. Dale, the heavy-handed enforcer of morality and discipline, was in effect prepared to commit bigamy. Mercifully, Powhatan declined.[85]

Nothing is known of the relationship between Rolfe and the now Christian Pocahontas for the next 18 months. Then in April 1616 Dale visited England and took them with him as an advertisement for the Virginia Company of London – visible proof of how native Americans were being integrated into English culture. To underline the point he made sure they stayed at an appropriately named inn, the Belle Sauvage Inn on Ludgate Hill in London. John Smith wrote his letter to Queen Anne to promote his saviour Pocahontas's acceptance into British society. Pocahontas was, however, very shy in society, hid her face and did not speak. Rolfe and Pocahontas spent seven months in England and she died on the day they were to return to Virginia, having caught a chill – sometimes described as smallpox – on her way to Gravesend.[86] In the end the English climate or an infectious disease did for the Anglo-Indian assimilation of their marriage.

Gates finally left Jamestown for England at the end of 1616, and was replaced by Governor Yeardley, who found a crumbling settlement packed with native Americans and tobacco growing in all the open spaces. In 1617, Argall reported:

'...in James towne he found but five or six houses, the Church down, the Palizado's broken, the Bridge in pieces, the Well of fresh water spoiled; the Store-house they used for the Church, the market-place and streets, and all other spare places planted with Tobacco, the Salvages (Indians) as frequent in their houses as themselves, whereby they were become expert in our arms, and had a great many in their custodie and possession, the Colonie dispersed all about, planting Tobacco'.[87]

In the same year, ten years after the planting of the colony, a frame church was built outside the James fort, where the memorial church stands today. It was a place of worship until 1639, when it was levelled to make way for a more substantial church building. But the religious idealism that had inspired the first planters had gone and settlers were no longer attracted to Virginia.

Yeardley's main problem was to attract new colonists. After 1618 there were incentives: 50 acres of land for those who would pay for transportation to the colony, and 50 acres after seven years of service for those who would not.[88] Yeardley called for the election of representatives to the House of Burgesses in July 1619, but because of financial problems the company was reorganized to create the Council for New England in 1620 under the Earl of Southampton (Shakespeare's patron) and his reforms could not be implemented. We should note in passing that the reorganization of the company made possible the settlement at New Plymouth which we followed in the last chapter, for the Council for New England absorbed the Virginia Company of Plymouth and, in one of its first acts, it granted a charter for land around New Plymouth to the London Adventurers who were behind the Pilgrims of the *Mayflower*.

Jamestown now collapsed. There were epidemics and an Indian massacre in 1622 killed half of the colonists. Native Americans poured into settlers' houses and the reported death toll was put at 347.[89] Despite the Gates–De La Warr laws and Dale's Code, internal disputes split the colony and, finding the venture financially disastrous, in 1624 the company surrendered the charter to the Crown, which placed the colony under royal control. Virginia was financially and morally bankrupt.[90]

What had gone wrong with the Virginia Company? Despite the religious mission stated in the incorporation of November 1606, there was a lack of clarity in the implementing of the aims of the Virginia settlement from the outset. In both England and America there were conflicts between different factions and interests. There was an unclear policy towards native Americans, who were sometimes appeased and sometimes antagonized by some settlers' actions. Foolish decisions and mistakes were made, beginning with Wingfield's and Newport's siting of the James fort. There might have been Freemasonic factions at work. There were unclear moral and operational norms. The company's work was carried out at high cost with little return – no gold was found – during the years before tobacco plantations and the slave trade began. In fact, this work might have been a causative factor in setting a trend of slave-owning in the American South. The company set the pattern of Southern landowning, slavery and exploiting native Americans.

By the end of the 1620s, when the population of Virginia was 2,500, most of the settlers' energy was going into the export of tobacco. Tobacco planters imported slaves from Africa, who were under the direct control of their masters. The Elizabethan landed values introduced by the 1607 planters had a new form, as feudal serfs called slaves were now tied to the land. By the 1660s the number of slaves began to rise and by 1670 the population of Virginia had climbed to 35,309. A 'slave-holders' Christianity' grew up, and a 'slave-holding religion' that had nothing to do with the 'Christianity of Christ'.

Commerciality rather than morality now motivated Virginians. The 'Christian Colonie' of Chesapeake lauded by Strachey in 1612 had collapsed in much the same way as the State's representation of 'true' Puritan religion was to collapse in Massachusetts.[91] And though Freemasonry may have been present in the early factionalism and questionable decision-making of the Virginia Company's representatives, it did not take root in America until later, when urbanization spread and a more sophisticated cultural development took place.

What was the true motivation for this costly venture? The shipping back of American cargo? Making an English settlement that would block Spanish settlement of North America? Planting Anglicanism, the official English religion? James I had declared, in the incorporation of the Virginia Company in November 1606, that the company should propagate 'Christian religion', 'true religion'. There had not been much of that. Or, since James I had brought Templarism from Scotland, was there a secret Freemasonic plan to erect a New Atlantis in the New World?

As we have seen, the Jamestown settlement was already 13 years old and very developed when the *Mayflower* set sail, and it was inspired by the Church of England. Yet although the Planting Fathers of the early northern settlements in the New World were Anglicans and then Puritans, the founding of America owes as much to a third, group: the Spanish Catholics farther south.

CHAPTER 3

SPANISH CATHOLICS

IN FLORIDA

S panish Catholics preceded the Jamestown settlement and can claim to be the very first planters of America. One strategic reason for the founding of the Virginia settlement was to counter Spanish and French moves into the Americas.

Ponce de León

Florida was first visited by Spain during Columbus's second voyage in 1493. On 12 October the previous year, Columbus had left his *Santa Maria* and gone ashore at San Salvador in an armed boat together with the captains of the *Pinta* and *Niña*, watched by naked native Americans, and had planted the royal banner to take possession of the New World in the names of Ferdinand and Isabella. He thought he was at the gateway to the Golden East, the Spice Islands and Cathay, and later spoke of the north shore of Cuba as being 'the most precious jewel in the Spanish crown'.

Juan Ponce de León was with Columbus during the visit to Florida in 1493, which, at the request of Ferdinand and Isabella, emphasized the Christianization of the Indies. Having become Governor of Puerto Rico in 1510 and then having been deposed, he equipped an expedition to the north in 1513 at his own expense. Spain was now in competition for America: John Cabot had claimed North America for England in 1497 and 1498, and Amerigo Vespucci had discovered South America and claimed it for Spain in 1499.

Ponce de León had heard stories from native Americans about Bimini, an island in the north which possessed the Fountain of Youth. Whoever drank from the fountain would have his youth restored, no matter how old he was. Ponce de León was in search of the fountain and may also have been seeking gold. But principally he was stating Spain's claim to the New World.

He sighted land on 3 April 1513, during the Easter season. Easter is known in Spanish as *Pascua Florida* ('Feast of Flowers'). Ponce de León stepped ashore at what is now St Augustine, which he named *La Florida* because of the luxuriant foliage of the place. It is a measure of the intense Catholicism of the time that the first place on the continent of America to be visited should be named after a church festival.

Ponce de León is thought to have landed near the modern Fountain of Youth Archaeological Park, and spent the night in the Timucuan Indian town of Seloy, which was on the site of the Park. (The native Americans are thought to have navigated to northern Florida 4,000 years ago.) The inlet came to be known as Barra de la Florida. Following their landing, the Spanish claimed North America from Florida to Labrador.

Ponce de León did not find a harbour. He turned round and followed the coast south. On 23 May he retraced his course and on 14 June he headed for Puerto Rico, not having found Bimini.

In 1521 he returned with 200 men to find out whether Florida was an island, to establish a colony and to find the Fountain of Youth. Instead he found death – native Americans opposed his landing and drove him off, and in the course of the battle he was wounded by a native-American arrow and many of his men were killed. He returned to Cuba to die of his wound in 1522.

Hernando de Soto in Florida and the South

The next significant landing on Florida was in 1528, by Pánfilo de Narváez, a one-eyed veteran who had served in Cuba and Mexico. He sailed from Spain in 1527 to explore the 'provinces of the Main', that is, from Mexico to Florida. He was driven by a storm towards Florida and landed on 12 April 1528. He anchored two days later on the west side of Tampa Bay.

The voyagers seized four native Americans, who led them to shipwrecked packing-cases, in each of which lay a dead Spaniard from a wrecked ship, covered in deerskins.

The voyagers spent 25 days in the New World, during which they took over native-American houses and lived off native-American provisions. They were attacked by native Americans and left.

They marched towards the sea and found the mouth of the bay. Many were sick, and to save the expedition they made five boats in 15 days, each 30 feet long, from tree-trunks, deerskins, pine resin and sails made of shirts. Each boat held just under 50 men and was semi-waterlogged.

With this makeshift, leaky 'fleet' Narváez sailed on and came to the mouth of the Mississippi. One of the boats overturned and Narváez stayed on one of the others all night with his page, who was sick, and another member of the crew. Their anchor was a stone. A wind swept the boat away and it was never seen again.

Narváez's deputy, Cabeza de Vaca, had fallen behind and his boat was wrecked in a storm on the Texas coast. The occupants of another boat were all killed by native Americans on the Texas coast. Some 80 men were eventually taken into the native Americans' houses, where all but 15 died. There was a famine, and the surviving Spaniards found they were slaves. De Vaca was made to dig roots under water and his fingers became so sore and tender that they bled at the slightest touch. He escaped and spent six years wandering from tribe to tribe, trading shells. Eventually he met up with Spaniards and in 1537 he was back in Spain, singing the praises of the port in Tampa Bay, 'the best in the world'.

The Spanish Crown wanted silver and gold from a mercantile empire that already, by the 1530s, stretched from Mexico ('New Spain') to Panama, Columbia and Venezuela ('the Spanish Main'), the West Indies including Cuba, and the west coast of South America (Ecuador, Peru and soon Chile). It regarded controlling Florida as crucial to protecting the naval bullion fleets sailing back to Spain. The rising position of Spain in Europe depended on this flow of rich minerals from the New World.

Despite the hardships he had endured, de Vaca was eager to return to Florida. But in fact the next voyage had already been given to Hernando de Soto, a veteran of the conquest of Peru who had become so rich there that the Spanish king Charles V borrowed money from him. The 38-year-old de Soto tried to enlist de Vaca for his voyage, without success. De Vaca would only consider going if he were in command. But he told de Soto about Tampa Bay.

De Soto would have been a massive figure in any age. He was an 'inflexible man and dry of word, who although he liked to know what the others all thought and had to say, after he once said a thing he did not like to be opposed, and as he ever acted as he thought best, all bent to his will'.[1] He sailed in April 1538 and headed for Havana. (He had formerly been Governor of Cuba.) On 18 May 1539 he left Havana, bound for Tampa Bay, where he arrived on 25 April. The native Americans saw his fleet approaching and sent up smoke signals that the villages should be abandoned.

De Soto's men disembarked and looked for native Americans to act as guides. The next day his three squadrons of horsemen occupied a village of timber houses thatched with palm leaves. All the woods round the houses were felled to improve security and the infantry went out and captured four native Americans while the horsemen caught some more. One of them, who was naked, cried out in Spanish, 'Do not kill me, cavalier – I am a Christian! Do not slay these people – they have given me my life!'[2]

This man turned out to be a Spaniard named Juan Ortiz who had sailed with Narváez and returned to Cuba, where Narváez's wife had asked him to look for her husband. On the sand of Tampa Bay he had seen a cleft stick holding what looked like a letter. He had gone to collect it and been seized by native Americans. His hands and feet had been bound to four stakes on a scaffold. He had been saved by the chief's daughter, who had said, 'Though one Christian might do no good, certainly he could do no harm, and it would be an honour to have one for a captive.'[3] We have already seen that this episode may have influenced John Smith's story of being saved by Pocahontas.

De Soto used Ortiz as a scout, as he knew the surrounding countryside. He sent ships back to Cuba for provisions and, leaving 100 men with two years' supplies to guard the remaining ships, marched inland and began a long trek of exploration that took him away from Florida. It would lead him through what are now the states of Georgia, North and South Carolina, Tennessee, Alabama, Mississippi, Arkansas, Texas, Oklahoma,

Louisiana and the Indian territory in the Old West.

First, de Soto arrived at Cale and picked all the ripe ears of corn in the surrounding fields. The native Americans tried to prevent this and the colonists killed three and took 28 prisoners. De Soto left Cale on 11 August 1539, reached Caliquen and crossed the Suwannee river. Native Americans appeared playing flutes, a sign of peace, but Ortiz spoke to one of them who confirmed that they were about to attack.

Four hundred native Americans had assembled with bows and arrows. Ready for them, de Soto met the chief and held his hand. He ordered a trumpet to be sounded and the colonists attacked and killed 30–40 native Americans. The surviving native Americans ran off and hid in the icy waters of two lakes. The cold was unbearable and soon they gave up and were taken captive. But they soon rose up again and there was a battle. Some 200 native Americans were defeated and most of them were bound to a post in the middle of the town and shot to death with arrows. Something of particular interest to the Spaniards was that one of those spared spoke of a town called Yupaha, which was ruled by a woman, to whom gold was given as a tribute.

News of the killing spread and the infantry and cavalry went out and took 100 native-American prisoners and put them in chains. They were treated as slaves and made to grind corn and carry luggage. The Spanish pressed on and reached Apalache, which was deserted, on 26 October. They made it their winter quarters and celebrated Christmas in North America for the first time.

On 3 March 1540 de Soto set off with 600 men to find the gold at Yupaha. The native-American captives – naked and in chains in the harsh winter with little food – had all died, and the Spaniards had to carry their own rations of corn and escort 300 pigs. They reached Toalli in Creek territory. The houses had cane-and-tile roofs and mud walls, and the Spanish took prisoner a native American, who fetched the chief. De Soto told him 'he [de Soto] was the child of the Sun'. The Spanish set up a cross and explained that Christ 'was God and man'.

The chief guided the Spaniards to Ocute *en route* to Yupaha. There they found a store of dried corn and flour. They were now in the chief-tainess's territory in South Carolina by the Savannah, and her sister came and made a speech of welcome.

Then the chieftainess herself came in a canoe with an awning, sitting on cushions. She presented de Soto with a necklace of pearls, shawls and skins. She told him there were pearls in graves and the Spanish thereupon desecrated many graves and removed 350 pounds of pearls. They also raped many of the native-American women.

However, De Soto found no gold in Yupaha, and prepared to leave for a nearby province called Chiaha. He asked for guides, but the chieftainess refused to supply them because of the rapes. Taking her with him instead, de Soto then marched north-west across South Carolina. The presence of the chieftainess meant that every night they were welcomed and given food (700 turkeys in one town alone). They reached Chiaha and spent 30 days there, the exhausted men recovering their health and fattening their horses. The Spanish began to molest the native-American women and de Soto asked for 30 native-American women to join his march. The next day, all the native Americans vanished.

De Soto ordered that the native Americans should be hunted down and he destroyed the maize fields of some of the chiefs who had disappeared. He sent word via a native American the Spanish encountered that he no longer wanted the 30 women, and incredibly he was given a present of some native-American women for himself. He went on to Coça with a native-American guide. There the chief received him 'borne in a litter on the shoulders of his principal men, seated on a cushion and covered with a mantle of martin skins…. On his head he wore a diadem of plumes and he was surrounded by many attendants playing upon flutes and singing.'[4]

The native Americans were at first friendly, but then slipped away and de Soto pursued them. He stayed in Coça for 25 days. The young native American who had guided them now asked to be a Christian and had his chains struck off.

De Soto then left for Tascaluça and found the chief there. A Spaniard, pursuing a fleeing native-American captive woman, disappeared, and de Soto arrested the chief and told him he would not be released until the Spaniard was found. The chief got word out to the native Americans of nearby Mavila to prepare an attack.

Though warned of Mavila's hostility, de Soto pressed on into the town with a priest, a friar and servants carrying an altar, ornaments and vestments. The chief of the Tascaluça slipped away to a house containing armed native Americans, and de Soto and his small band were attacked by native Americans who emerged from their houses and fired arrows. All the Spanish, including de Soto, were wounded before they galloped out of town, lancing native Americans and running others down.

De Soto then returned and assaulted the town. The attack lasted a long time and 'many Christians, weary and very thirsty, went to drink at a pond near by, tinged with the blood of the killed, and returned to the combat'.[5] The Spanish set fire to the buildings and killed the native Americans as they rushed outside, finishing some off with cutlasses. Others ran back into their houses to escape the slaughter and were burned to death. In the burning of Mavila some 2,500 native Americans died and only 18 Spanish (though 150 received arrow wounds).

The native Americans then told Ortiz, who told de Soto, that Francisco Maldonado, a captain of infantry who had been on a mission for de Soto, was waiting for him at Ochuse, six days away. De Soto kept this news secret, so that he would have time to replace the store of pearls, which had been lost.

In mid-November de Soto reached the territory of the Chickasaws and, on 17 December, Chicaça, which was deserted. He made it his winter quarters. Four men went into the native-American village a mile away, helped themselves to skins and shawls and caused the native Americans to abandon their houses. De Soto condemned two of them to be punished by beheading, but just before the execution native Americans arrived with a formal complaint and Ortiz was persuaded to mistranslate the words so as to exonerate the two men, who were 'not at fault'. De Soto ordered the condemned men to be released.

In March, as de Soto was about to leave Chicaça, native Americans attacked the town from all sides, yelling and beating drums and setting fire to the houses. De Soto was able to gallop to safety, but 11 Spaniards were killed by arrows and 50 horses were burned to death in their stalls. In reprisal, de Soto marched to the native-American town a mile away and attacked it. The dead were strewn across a nearby open field.

De Soto was short of food and he moved on to Alimamu, which was too small to have much corn. He sent three captains with men to outlying towns to forage for provisions. One, Juan de Añasco, encountered 'a staked fort' with armed native Americans in war paint, wearing feathers. He withdrew and sent word to de Soto, who ordered an attack. This proved costly, as many Spanish were killed by the fleeing native Americans.

On 8 May de Soto reached Quiz-quiz, where native Americans attacked. He built barges and pressed on, killing 10 native Americans and capturing 15 *en route* by the river Mississippi.

Next he reached Casqui, where the chief brought two blind men to him, saying that 'as the Governor was the son of the Sun he begged him to restore sight to those Indians'. De Soto's Catholicism came out in his reply. He tried to convert the chief to Christianity, pointing to the sky as the home of Jesus: 'What of man there was of Him dying, what of divinity being immortal; and that, having ascended into heaven, He was there with open arms to receive all that would be converted to Him.'[6]

He pressed on to Pacaha, which had a store of dried corn, and stayed there for 40 days. He then moved on to Quiguate, where his men seized the chief and 140 native Americans, and interrogated them as to where they might find gold and silver. The mountains of Coligoa seemed the most likely location.

The Spaniards went on to Coligoa, living on fish. Now they were among the Quapaw Plains Indians. They moved on to Tulla, killing 15 native Americans and occupying the settlement. The native Americans attacked by night and many of them were killed. De Soto ordered six prisoners to have their right hands and noses cut off and sent them to their chief to demand an apology. The chief came with 80 native Americans, all weeping to signal repentance. He brought cow skins which de Soto's men used as bedcovers.

De Soto marched on over the Boston mountains to Autiamque, where there was reportedly maize and water that might be the sea. It was on the Arkansas river and was deserted. There were, however, stores of corn, beans, walnuts and persimmons, and the Spaniards snared rabbits and hares. Here the interpreter Ortiz died and was replaced by the native American who had asked to become a Christian and had been baptized Pedro. Pedro's interpreting was now found to be very inadequate.

On 6 March 1542, having by now lost 250 men and 150 horses, de Soto decided to seek the sea, build two brigantines and sail one to Cuba and the other to Mexico. From Cuba he would sail west to lands where, it was rumoured, there was gold.

In fact, he headed not for the sea but for the banks of the Mississippi, killing native Americans on the way – 100 at Nilco alone. His men encountered bogs and became feverish. De Soto, also feverish from what was perhaps typhus, lay on a pallet covered with buffalo robes and summoned his captives. He told them that they should elect a governor. The next day he died.

So as not to let the native Americans know that their leader was dead, the Spanish dug a grave inside the palisade. But when the native Americans enquired after de Soto, to prevent his body from falling into native-American hands they placed it in a canoe, weighted it with sand and sent it to the bottom of the Mississippi. Then they auctioned his property: 'two male and three female slaves, three horses and 700 swine'.[7]

So ended de Soto's restless attempt to settle Florida and the south. His journey had taken him through what would become the Southern states and inflicted the Christian faith on the native Americans with great cruelty and brutality, which was typical of Spain during the Inquisitorial age.

While de Soto was making his doomed journey, another Spanish explorer, Francisco Vázquez de Coronado, was making a pioneering journey across the American Southwest from New Mexico through Texas to Kansas, driven by reports of vast riches in seven golden cities but finding only semi-nomadic native-American villages and disillusionment. Like de Soto, he too was unsuccessful in seeking worldly gold.

Menéndez de Avilés in St Augustine

The permanent Spanish settlement of Florida was preceded by a Protestant French attempt to settle North America.

On 16 February 1562 Lutheran Jean Ribaut led an expedition of five French ships from Dieppe, allegedly to Canada. In fact they arrived off Florida's St Augustine. On 1 May they reached the St Johns river, which Ribaut called the river of May, and were greeted by friendly native Americans. Ribaut erected a stone pillar to claim the territory for France.

Sailing 60 leagues to the north, Ribaut came to a place where the French ships could harbour, which he called Port Royal. He displayed his wares and native Americans came out of the woods to trade. He asked for 26 volunteers to remain behind while he returned to France and he built a fort for them which he called Charles Fort (after Charles IX, the French king, who was 12).

On 11 June Ribaut sailed for France, leaving Captain Albert behind. The colonists soon ran out of food and there were quarrels. A drummer was hanged, a man called Lachère was banished to a nearby island and a soldier who had been beaten ran Albert through with a sword. Captain Barre now assumed command.

After six months there was no sign of Ribaut and the colonists could wait no longer. They cobbled together their own ship and gave it improvised sails largely made of shirts. One man, Guillaume Rufin, chose to remain, while the rest set sail. The leaky ship soon ran out of food and men gnawed their leather shoes and jerkins and drank seawater or their own urine. Famished, they killed Lachère and ate him. Finally, a passing English ship rescued them.

Meanwhile a Spanish frigate was sent from Cuba to destroy Charles Fort and tear down Ribaut's stone columns. When it reached Port Royal, a native American told the Spaniards about Rufin. Rufin himself then came to the ship, wearing a deerskin, and showed the Spaniards to the log house, which they burned. He also showed them the column that claimed Florida for France – the Spanish had not found the one on St Johns – and they pulled it up and put it on the frigate, along with Rufin.

Ribaut's three French ships – the *Isabella*, the *Little Breton* and the *Falcon* – did return to Florida, but without Ribaut, who had had to go to England to seek help for the Protestant French in their religious war. The fleet left Le Havre under René de Laudonnière, who had been on Ribaut's earlier expedition, on 22 April 1564. It reached the Florida coast a month later at or near what is now St Augustine. De Laudonnière went on to the St Johns river, where Ribaut had left his first column, and encountered friendly native Americans.

De Laudonnière now said that though Port Royal was a fine harbour, 'it was much more needful for us to plant in places plentiful of victual(s), than in goodly havens'.[8] All agreed that there should be a fort in or near St Johns Bluff. They built a triangular fort which anticipated the triangular fort at Jamestown 43 years later:

> 'The side toward the west, which was toward the land, was enclosed with a little trench and raised with turf made in form of a battlement of nine feet high. The other side, which was toward the river, was enclosed with a palisade of planks of timber after the manner that cabins are made. On the south side there was a kind of bastion within which I caused an house for the munition to be built.'[9]

De Laudonnière's house was inside the west wall with an escape to the river. The fort was called Fort Caroline after the boy king.

The *Isabella* sailed to France on 28 July, carrying letters to the French Council and gifts for the Queen Mother (gold and silver found by native Americans in streams, and pearls).

De Laudonnière's French garrison was rebellious. On 20 September, 13 men stole a boat in which they had secreted provisions and set off to look for treasure. They captured a Spanish ship full of gold and silver, but were themselves captured by the Spaniards. Some were sent to Spain, some were held at Havana.

In November, 66 Frenchmen seized two boats and imprisoned de Laudonnière. On 8 December they sailed off. One of the boats captured a brigantine, which they boarded and made their main ship. They then captured a caravel, but were attacked by three Spanish ships and had to surrender. The Frenchmen on the caravel were hanged as pirates. The barque returned to St Johns river and the men were overpowered by troops from Fort Caroline. Four ringleaders were shot and their bodies strung up on a gibbet.

As a result of these episodes, the French colony had shrunk. And the native Americans had turned hostile. Outina, a native-American chief, had been captured and ransomed for corn, and the Frenchmen collecting the ransom were later ambushed. Two were killed, 22 wounded.

In July de Laudonnière was about to leave for France when he saw four ships. They turned out to be English under John Hawkins. They had left Plymouth, sailed to Guinea on the African coast and loaded up with slaves, which they had sold in the West Indies for gold, silver and pearls.

Hawkins gave the French garrison 'twenty barrels of meal and four pipes of beans' in return for artillery, powder and a promissory note. On 28 July he sailed towards Newfoundland – the first English navigator to sail up the American coast – and on 23 August, when fishing for cod, ran into two French fishing vessels with 'much fish', some of which he bought with his gold and silver. (John Sparke the Younger wrote an account of this voyage which was published by Hakluyt.)

These events give an idea of the comradeship at sea at this time and also of the great dangers in being a sailor if one fell into Spanish hands.

De Laudonnière was set to return to France when a French fleet arrived at the mouth of the St Johns river, under Ribaut. He had seven ships and 300 soldiers, colonists, wives and children. Three ships crossed the harbour bar and one of them went up the river to the fort. The other four ships anchored off shore.

Ribaut brought orders that de Laudonnière should return to face charges. These involved his housekeeper, the way in which he had exercised his authority and his direct communication with the French Council when he should have gone through the Admiral of France. He defended himself so vigorously that Ribaut offered to share his command with him. De Laudonnière declined as there could be only one lieutenant, but he and Ribaut remained friendly.

On 4 September 1565 five Spanish ships approached and sounded trumpets to parley. The commander of the fleet announced himself as Pedro Menéndez de Avilés. He said:

> 'This is the armada of the king of Spain, who has sent me to this coast and country to burn and hang the Lutheran French who should be found there, and in the morning I will board your ships; and if I find any Catholics they will be well treated.'[10]

The Lutherans laughed derisively, but Avilés ordered his men to board the French ships. The French cut their cables and sailed through the Spanish fleet, three to the north, the other one to the south. Avilés pursued the French ships and then returned to his landing spot on the river of Dolphins and converted a large native-American house near the water into a fort with a moat, earthworks and faggots.

On 8 September Avilés landed to flags, cannon fire and trumpet fanfares. A priest met him, holding a cross and chanting, '*Te Deum Laudamus.*' All knelt and, watched by native Americans, Avilés took possession of the New World for Philip II of Spain. He unloaded his two galleons, the *San Pelayo* and *San Salvador.*

Avilés now pursued the French. He had heard from the native Americans that Fort Caroline could be reached by land and, having seen that Ribaut was in the area, on the night of 20 September he advanced on the fort and attacked on three sides. He overran the 200 occupants, killing 130 and taking 50 women and children prisoner. De Laudonnière, roused from his sleep and wearing a shirt, fought with his sword and shield and escaped. Not one Spaniard was killed. Avilés had taken the French colony, Fort Caroline, and massacred virtually the entire male population. He hanged the bodies on trees with an inscription: 'Not as Frenchmen, but as heretics.' So the Catholic faith crushed Lutheranism in the New World.

Avilés returned to St Augustine, leaving a garrison at Fort Caroline. On 28 September native Americans brought news of shipwrecked Frenchmen on a spit of land not far away. Avilés marched to a point of land opposite the spit. There were more than 100 armed Frenchmen, and a Frenchman swam over and asked for safe conduct to Fort Caroline. In a letter, Avilés told Philip II of his reply:

'We held their fort, having taken and put to death those who were in it for having erected it there without the leave of Your Majesty, and because they were planting their wicked Lutheran sect in Your Majesty's provinces, and that I made war with fire and blood as Governor and Captain-General of these provinces upon all who might come to these parts to settle and to plant this evil Lutheran sect, seeing that I came by Your Majesty's command to bring the gospel into these parts, to enlighten the natives thereof with that which is told and believed by the Holy Mother Church of Rome for the salvation of their souls; that there I should not give them passage, but on the contrary, should pursue them by sea and by land until I had their lives.'[11]

The Catholic anti-Lutheran nature of Avilés' outlook could not be more apparent.

The next day five Frenchmen came across in a boat offering to surrender if their lives were spared. Avilés made no promise: 'I answered that they might give up their arms and place themselves at my mercy; that I should deal with them as our Lord should command me.'[12] The French surrendered the next day.

Twenty Spaniards ferried the French over in groups of 10. They were led to a line drawn in the sand by a pike. Avilés told the first to arrive: 'Gentlemen, I have but a few soldiers with me, and you are many, and it would be an easy matter for you to overpower us and avenge yourselves upon us for your people which we killed in the fort. For this reason it is necessary that you should march to my camp four leagues from here with your hands tied behind your backs.' He told Philip II: 'I had their hands tied behind them, and put them all excepting ten to the knife.'[13] The place where the executions were performed was called Matanzas, 'Place of Slaughters'.

Nearly two weeks later Avilés learned from native Americans that some 350 Frenchmen were in the same area. Ribaut's *Trinity* had been shipwrecked and the survivors had set out for Fort Caroline and were on the same spit of land, living off roots and grass and water in brackish pools. Avilés sent troops by land and went in one of two boats by sea.

The starving French drew up in battle array. Ribaut sounded a trumpet for a parley and sent a sailor to swim across the river. He was sent back by canoe to bring an officer who could speak for the French. A sergeant-major returned in the canoe and asked for boats with which to reach Fort Caroline. Avilés told him he had captured the fort and killed the occupants and those who had been shipwrecked, whose bodies he showed them. He gave his word that Ribaut could come and talk with five or six companions.

Ribaut returned with eight companions and said to Avilés, 'What has happened to me may happen to you. Since our kings are brothers and friends, do you also play the part of a friend and give me ships with which to return to France.' In reply Avilés simply asked 'that they might give up their arms and place themselves at my mercy'.[14] Ribaut returned to the French camp on the spit and there was a debate. Finally, 150 decided to surrender, 200 refused.

The next morning Ribaut rowed over with six officers and surrendered a seal of office together with his arms. The 150 were rowed over in groups of 10 and again Avilés told them they would have to be bound. They agreed. He asked, 'Are you Catholics or Lutherans, and are there any who wish to confess?' Now Ribaut realized his fate and quoted Genesis (3.19 in the King James version): 'Dust thou art, and unto dust shalt thou return.' He also sang Psalm 132, 'Lord remember David, and all his afflictions.'

Ribaut was led to the line in the sand by Avilés' brother-in-law, Solis de Meras, and a Captain San Vincente, who asked for Ribaut's felt hat. He said, 'You know how Captains must obey their generals and execute their commands,' and stabbed Ribaut in the stomach with a dagger. Meras thrust with his pike and they cut off his head.

Avilés told Philip II by letter:

'I put Jean Ribaut and all the rest of them to the knife, judging it to be necessary to the service of the Lord our God and of Your Majesty.... The other people with Ribaut, some seventy or eighty in all, took to the forest, refusing to surrender unless I grant them their lives. These and twenty others who escaped from the fort and fifty who were captured by the Indians, from the ships that were wrecked, in all 150 persons, rather less than more, are the French alive today in Florida, dispersed and flying through the forest, and captive with the Indians. And since they are Lutherans and in order that so evil a sect shall not remain alive in these parts, I will conduct myself in such wise, and will so incite my friends, the Indians, on their part, that in five or six weeks very few if any will remain alive.'[15]

By such a ruthless anti-Lutheran policy, Avilés rid Florida of the French and delivered it to Spain. He had created the first permanent settlement in North America at La Florida, which he renamed St Augustine after the Bishop of Hippo, on whose feast day he had sighted the coast. He had also established other settlements at Fort San Mateo (Fort St Matthew) in Florida and Fort San Felipe (Fort St Philip) in South Carolina, along with blockhouses. His chaplain, Father Francisco Lopez Mendoza Grajales, became North America's first parish priest for Catholicism.

In 1602 a mission, Nombre de Dios ('Name of God'), to convert the native Americans was established where Avilés landed. He sent Jesuit missionaries to Virginia, but all were killed. More permanent missions were built in the far west and California. Eventually missions would spread from the east to west coasts of North America, from St Augustine to San Diego.

After killing the Lutherans, Avilés was shipwrecked near Cape Kennedy, but returned to St Augustine. The settlement became Spain's North American military headquarters and the capital of Florida. It was attacked by pirates on two occasions, and over a period of 25 years the Governor of Florida, Manuel de Cendoya, built the Castillo de San Marcos to defend it. In 1586 Sir Francis Drake sailed into the harbour and neutralized the fort St Johns of the Pines, which was burned to the ground on his departure. He then moved south and engaged the newly expanded St Augustine site.

St Augustine was the northernmost outpost of the Spanish colonial empire for 256 years, except for 20 years, between 1763 and 1783, when it belonged to England. The Floridans became Spanish once more from 1783 until 1821, when Florida became American under Andrew Jackson.

So the Spanish Catholics can claim to be the first planters in America, 42 years before the 1607 Jamestown settlement.

1620, 1607, 1565.... We have been going further and further back in locating the date of the first planting of a permanent settlement in America. Before we return to the seventeenth century and go forwards, we should briefly go still further back and suggest that the discovery – as distinct from the first planting or unified founding – of America may not have been in 1492 but in 1418. An old map bought by a Chinese lawyer

Liu Gang from a book dealer in Shanghai, dated 1418, shows with remarkable accuracy the two hemispheres (side by side) of the whole spherical world, with every continent in its correct shape – including America. If the date on the map is authenticated and does not turn out to be of relatively recent origin, attention will focus on Admiral Zheng He's first voyage which, it is now speculated, may have taken place between 1415 and 1418. Did Admiral Zheng He discover America in those years and return with cartographic information that would enable such a map to be made 71 years before Columbus's first voyage?[16]

In *1421: The Year China Discovered the World*, Gavin Menzies assembled evidence to suggest that on 8 March 1421 the eunuch admiral Zheng He set sail with the largest fleet the world had ever seen, including some ships nearly 500 feet long, with orders from the Chinese Emperor to 'proceed all the way to the end of the earth'. The fleet was away for two-and-a-half years and the Emperor, Zhu Di (alias Yong Le or Yung-Lo), lost control of his government during this time. His mandarins loathed his grandiose foreign policy and Zhu Di was forced to trek north with almost a million men to fight the Mongol army. While he was away, some of Zheng He's battered ships returned in October 1423. Zhu Di died on 12 August 1424 while still pursuing the Mongols, and his son and successor began a new phase in which China isolated herself from the world, ashamed of her previous expansionist policies. The new Emperor may have ordered all records of Zheng He's voyage to be destroyed.[17]

There is no evidence of such a destruction, however, and Chinese historians do not share Menzies's view, as the maps referred to in *1421* have nothing to do with Zheng He. Nevertheless, the 1418 map even shows Australia, suggesting that the Chinese circumnavigated the globe a century before Magellan, 70 years before Columbus and 350 years before Cook.

It has also been claimed[18] that America was discovered in 1396, further back than the Chinese voyage or the voyages of the early fifteenth century. In that year Henry St Clair, Earl of Orkney and Lord of Roslin (now Rosslyn) and an early Templar – the St Clairs, it is claimed, were descended from the high priests of the Temple of Jerusalem – placed his fleet under the command of two sons of the Zeno family of Venice. Henry had met Carlo Zeno in 1364 and allegedly sailed with the Zenos to America, where they explored the north-east coast of what became Canada and interacted with the Mi'kmaq people. It is claimed that evidence for the voyage can be found in stone carvings on both sides of the Atlantic and in a strong oral tradition. The voyage was essentially Templar and it is possible that Templarism took root in North America in the lands St Clair is alleged to have settled.

Be that as it may, this particular pre-Columban voyage (like the later alleged Chinese one) is lost in the mists of time and may belong to legend. We must pass on, merely indicating a possibility that Templarism reached North America through the St Clairs of Rosslyn over 200 years before the Jamestown voyage.

In a sense, the first discoverers of America – as opposed to planters or unifying founders – were not the Chinese but the Indians. They may have come from Central Asia and are thought to have travelled to America across the Bering Strait as long as 20,000 or even 30,000 years ago, when Britain, for example, was covered by glaciers and therefore empty.[19] Some claim that they found America already occupied by Aborigines from Australia.

The Hopewell (c.500 BC–AD 500) and Mississippian (c.800–1500) Indian cultures and the Aztec culture in Mexico (fifteenth–sixteenth centuries) were all quite advanced and might have defined the culture of the future North America. Going further back, there have been claims that Phoenicians, Romans, Ghanaians, Welsh (Madoc), Irish (Brendan), Vikings, Templar fleets (sailing from Brest), fishermen from Portugal and France, men of Bristol and English pirates (culminating in Hawkins and Drake) all travelled to America across the high seas, questioning the tradition that it was discovered by Columbus.

Of the European settlers, we have said that the Spanish can claim to be first. However the Catholic legacy in America was cancelled out by the Church of England and Puritan settlements further north. Indeed, it can be said that the English defeated the French and the Spanish in their struggle for the New World.

The French mariner Jacques Cartier, commissioned by Francis I of France to discover gold, spices and a passage to Asia, made three expeditions to the Gulf of St Lawrence and then to Quebec and Montreal in Canada in 1534, 1535 and 1541. Another French mariner, Samuel de Champlain, voyaged along the St Lawrence River in 1603 and eventually commanded the 1608 expedition that founded Quebec. France made a strong attempt to dominate North America and encircle the English.

Because the English saw off the French and the Spanish, the Catholic legacy influenced the Founding Fathers less than a secret society that gathered influence among the Protestants: Freemasonry. Despite the efforts of Catholics, Anglicans and Puritans, the founding of America owes more to this fourth group: the Freemasons in the Anglican-Puritan north.

PART TWO

Who *Really* Founded

America?

CHAPTER 4

FREEMASONS IN VIRGINIA AND MASSACHUSETTS

Now we are moving away from the founding or planting of the first American settlements to the founding of the United States of America. In this chapter we shall trace the early origins of Freemasonry in America. We will then be able to understand its later influence on the constitution and the politics of the USA.

From the very early planting days Freemasonry, spreading throughout the New World like a rampant strain of a new virus, presented itself as a method by which union could be achieved. For any movement to be successful it must answer a need. The English Separatist, dissident settlers had sought to escape the rigid English class system with its feudal control over land and its strict regulation of religion, and Freemasonry may have filled the void left by the relative absence of social structure in the New World. Its network of secret societies afforded hierarchies in which all could rise, find a place, participate in rituals that drew on the earliest cultures, meet influential Masons socially and express ideas behind closed doors – a useful context of confidentiality in which all who questioned British colonial rule could operate without fear of being betrayed to the colonial authorities.

Freemasonry came to have an enormous hold over early America.

English Freemasonry and Bacon

It has been claimed that Freemasonry is very ancient and goes back variously to the fifteenth-century BC Egypt of Thutmose III, to the tenth-century BC Israel of the wise ruler Solomon and, more recently, to the medieval stonemasons and cathedral builders in York in 926 and Cologne in the twelfth century.

Be that as it may, it is often held that English Freemasonry was founded by Francis Bacon who, in 1579, when he was 18, saw the need for studies to be secret among 'sworn brothers-in-arms'.

It is hard to believe that the 18-year-old Bacon just made Freemasonry up without being influenced by any preceding model. Manly Hall claims that he was initiated into a secret society in Navarre in France. His brother Anthony ran an intelligence service for the Earl of Essex there and was friendly with (to the extent of borrowing money from) the Protestant King of Navarre, the future Henri IV, King of France. From 1576 to 1579 (from the ages of 15 to 18), Bacon lived in Paris with Sir Amias Paulet, the English ambassador to France, and acquired knowledge of the French court.

At that time the French court moved about the country. One of its hosts was Navarre, a kingdom in northern Spain near the Pyrenees, which was part French and part Spanish. It had been under Muslim rule from 711 to 798 and had been Spanish until 1234. In 1512 it was divided, with the Spanish portion being annexed by the Castilian Crown. Over the course of the sixteenth century the French part had become Protestant. Henri's Navarre therefore had large Muslim and Jewish populations and strong Spanish and French influence.

Hall says:

> 'While serving his diplomatic apprenticeship at the court of Navarre, Bacon had been initiated into the new liberalism represented throughout Europe by Secret Societies of intellectuals dedicated to civil and religious freedom. He returned to England fully aware of the intentions of Philip II, the Spanish king.'[1]

Hall suggests that the secret society into which Bacon was initiated was anti-Spanish and of an intelligence-gathering nature. Given Navarre's position as a Protestant country on the border of England's greatest Catholic enemy, Spain, intelligence-gathering was undoubtedly a major activity at court. But it is likely that, at an impressionable age, Bacon was put in touch with a group whose symbolism was reflected in early English Freemasonry in 1579. This may have been a Pyrenean group of Cathar exiles who had fled from Montségur, southwest France, when the Cathars had been suppressed in 1244, or, more probably, a group of refugee Templars who had fled France in 1312 and had reacted to the burning of their leader Jacques de Molay in 1314 by forming a secret society across the border.

Jewish Kabbalist exiles had also brought Jewish mysteries from the Middle East and Muslim Jerusalem, including the Temple of Solomon, to Languedoc. It is possible that Bacon learned about the Temple of Solomon from some of these. It must also be remembered that Septimania,[2] the last region in Gaul to be held by the Spanish Visigoths, whose capital was Narbonne, was in Islamic hands from 720 to 759 and was Jewish-ruled from 768 to 812. It had been a magnet for Diaspora Jews settling in Languedoc and it had become the cradle of the Jewish Golden Age in France and Spain from the ninth to the thirteenth centuries. (It is worth remembering that the Grail legend surfaced in nearby Toledo, Spain, in the twelfth century.) It contained many Kabbalistic-Manichaean schools from which, the authors of *The Holy Blood and the Holy Grail* state, the Cathars arose (rather than from the Bulgarian Bogomils). In short, it is possible that Bacon was in touch with secret Jewish knowledge on the borders of Spain and France while still in his teens.

Bacon's time in Navarre trained him to oppose Spanish power. Hall claims that his main work later on was to prevent Spanish domination of the New World. If so, it is possible that opposition to Spanish domination was the main motive behind the founding of the Virginia colony. The Spanish Armada finally arrived off England in 1588 with 90 Spanish Inquisitors on board to set up an Inquisition in England. Ever since Mary's Catholic burnings in the 1550s, England had regarded Spain with the kind of national paranoia the West experienced in relation to the Soviet Union at the height of the Cold War. It is claimed that Bacon designed Freemasonry to keep intelligence secrets from being penetrated by Spanish spies.[3]

Freemasonry has always been linked to contemporary political events, but the sincerity of Bacon's occult ideal cannot be doubted. Distinguished people who were not builders were admitted into the fraternity and were called 'Accepted' Masons. They received secret universal knowledge – about the oneness and brotherhood of mankind – and the Secret Doctrine of the Ages. They believed that America would become a New Atlantis, creating a better, non-Catholic, non-Spanish world and restoring the drowned Golden-Age Atlantis that Plato mentions. This New Atlantis would be a paradise in which men would follow reason, become gods and work for a universal world republic that would then replicate the Utopian conditions of America throughout the known world. Secret knowledge would be passed on from generation to generation in the Freemasons' Temple, a recreation of the Temple of Solomon in which Solomon became the wisest of rulers.

In 1586 Bacon may have published Whitney's *Choice of Emblems*. On page 53 stand the two Pillars of Masonry. By now Bacon had reputedly created, and was head of, the Order of the Knights of the Helmet, which promoted the advancement of learning. Learning was symbolized by Pallas Athena, who wore a helmet which bestowed invisibility. To signify their vow of invisibility the knights all had to kiss her helmet. As we have indicated, however, Bacon may have reorganized traditional material surviving from ancient or medieval times rather than *created* his order.

Initially Bacon attracted scholarly friends to the order. They were presumably drawn by his personal magnetism, fascinated by his traditional material and pleased to be in a group of talented, free-thinking, well-connected Elizabethans who were close to the queen. By 1586 the Order of the Helmet had spawned the Fra Rosi Crosse Society, which became a degree in the Knights of the Helmet.[4]

The Rosi Crosse Society also grew out of Bacon's visit to France in 1576–9 as a member of the English ambassador's suite. It was a reorganization of the old Knights Templar Order (suggesting that Bacon *had* met refugee Templars in Navarre) and took over its nine-degree ceremonial. The new Continental 'Rosicrucian College' was to be established as an inner rite of the Freemasonic Brotherhood – one had to become a Master Mason before one could progress to it.

By the time Bacon made a second visit to France between 1580 and 1582, Freemasonry had been quietly established in England and its lodge system could thus be transplanted to France and Germany. Bacon had written a series of pamphlets on Freemasonry and Rosicrucianism, extolling ethics, philanthropic goodness, straight conduct and brotherly love. It is held by some that he took with him to the Continent the first of the Rosicrucian Manifestos, which were eventually published anonymously in Germany. These Manifestos were based on Bacon's principles, which he called *Philanthropia*.

The Rosicrucians remained invisible, operating secretly until 1613. On 14 February of that year the 17-year-old Elector Palatine of the Rhine, who had succeeded his father in 1610 as Frederick V, leader of the German Protestants, married the 17-year-old daughter of James I of England, Elizabeth Stuart, in the Royal Chapel at Whitehall, London. The Earl of Southampton, Shakespeare's patron, was probably present[5] and the wedding was celebrated with performances of Shakespeare's *Othello* and *The Tempest*. According to John Chamberlain,[6] Sir Francis Bacon was the chief composer of a masque, *The Marriage of the Thames and the Rhine* (traditionally attributed to Francis Beaumont and dedicated to Bacon), that was performed at Grays' Inn in honour of the wedding.[7]

In June Elizabeth Stuart travelled to Heidelberg in the Palatinate, a landlocked country surrounded by the Spanish Netherlands, Lorraine, Württemberg and various German states. It seems she was escorted there by the Earl of Southampton[8] and built a replica of the Globe theatre (now ruined but clearly discernible) in her wing of Heidelberg castle.[9] The court at Heidelberg was now the centre of a Rosicrucian culture and state.[10]

In 1614 two Rosicrucian books appeared, *Fama Fraternitatis* and *Confessio*, the so-called 'Rosicrucian Manifestos'. They described the life of a German, Christian Rosenkreutz, who lived between 1378 and 1484 (dying at 106) and who had studied the Kabbalah in the East. A third book appeared in 1616, *The Chemical Wedding of Christian Rosenkreutz*, which was steeped in Hermeticism. These books all appeared anonymously but were later attributed to and acknowledged by the Swabian pastor Johann Valentin

Andreae. They seem to have emanated from Frederick V's court and there are references to the Elector Palatine and Heidelberg castle's terraced gardens, whose lions and lion fountains were the work of Salomon de Caus. Rosicrucianism was thus incorporated into English Freemasonry.

English Freemasonry, then, was an occult and philosophical idea, an order whose members guarded the secret knowledge of the ages and which drew in intellectuals dedicated to liberalism and civil and religious freedom.

At some point Bacon threw his group's weight behind the English plan to colonize America. He looked back to John Dee, the Renaissance mage who had encouraged voyages to America in the belief that a Utopian commonwealth could be established in the New World. Whether Bacon was involved behind the scenes in Sir Humphrey Gilbert's 1583 voyage and Raleigh's Roanoke voyages of 1584, 1585 and 1587 – and, indeed, in his cousin Bartholomew Gosnold's voyage of 1602 and the expedition that founded the Jamestown settlement in 1607 – is not known, but he is listed in the 1609 charter as a shareholder of the Virginia Company of London and one of the 52 members of the Virginia Council (board of directors).[11] As Solicitor-General, he also prepared the Virginia Company's charters of 1609 and 1612 for the king's signature, along with Sir Henry Hobart.

Bacon's involvement in American colonization is borne out by William Strachey, who in 1618 dedicated a manuscript copy of his *Historie of Travaile into Virginia Britania* to Bacon:

> 'Your Lordship ever approving yourself a most noble fautor [favourer] of the Virginia plantation, being from the beginning (with other lords and earls) of the principal counsell applied to propagate and guide it.'[12]

It is also interesting that *The Colonial State Calendar* notes: 'A letter is mentioned from John Smith to Lord Bacon enclosing description of New England, the extraordinary profits arising from the fisheries, and great facilities for plantation.'[13] John Smith's *A Description of New England* was published in 1625 from notes made in 1616, and if he sent the finished work rather than notes, then this letter was presumably sent to Bacon in the last year of his life.

John Smith, Baconian Freemason?

Against this background John Smith went to fight in Hungary against the Turks around 1600, when he was 20. Did he encounter Bacon's Freemasonry in Germany on his way? Captured in battle, he escaped to Russia, where Smythe's Muscovy Company was operating, and returned to England in 1604. Did he come home with Smythe's help and was he introduced to Freemasonry at that time?

There is something strange about Smith's writings. He had grown up on his family's farm in Norfolk and had been apprenticed to a wealthy merchant in his teens. He had little formal education, yet his works, notably *A True Relation* and *The Generall Historie*, are written in such excellent, economical prose that their perfect style has been compared to the King James Bible.[14] His writings on colonization have been considered superior to Bacon's essay *Of Plantations*. Did he have help in writing these works from a secret society of Freemasons? Did Bacon edit his works?

In *Freemasonry Came to America with Captain John Smith in 1607*, George Tudhope states:

> 'There is an abundance of evidence to show that a secret society was the prime mover behind the colonization of Virginia, America, and the founding of the Grand Lodge of the Free-Masons in 1723.'[15]

He claims that the evidence can be found in seals regularly used in emblems and engravings from *c.*1575 to *c.*1640, beyond the initial English colonization of America, which suggest a secret society's coded signature.

Reviewing the evidence and focusing on Bacon, Tudhope draws attention to the 'AA' type of seal with ornamental scrolls, one light, one dark, which was first used in 1576 and is extensively found until 1640. The light 'A' suggests the Masonic 'lost word', which is 'Light'. The light 'A' is shown being fired at by two archers who resemble Pan, the god of hunters, suggesting 'the Fraternity of Pan' whose main goal is to hunt the Light. (This goal of achieving Light was the goal of the Freemasons in their first American Lodge in 1723.)[16] Bacon's words under seals have to be counted and the total makes a 'simple cipher'. The Roman letters in these words also have to be counted and make a 'kay cipher' (which uses the letter 'K'). Scrolls appear above portraits of Bacon and Andreae to suggest that they were members – and founders – of a secret society. In one portrait, Bacon (and a light-dark scroll) is encompassed by the words, 'For the Glory of the Creator and Relief of Man's Estate', suggesting that Bacon was the creator of the secret society. The headpiece of page 41 of Bacon's *Great Instauration* also contains light-dark scrolls. The light-dark scrolls are also shown in the 1650 edition of Bacon's *New Atlantis*.

The 'AA' legs curl into 'C's. 'C' is the Roman numeral for 100, the simple-cipher seal for Bacon. It is found in nearly all emblems connected with him. The 'AA' stands for AthenA and the Knights of the Helmet, whose main goal was to bring the world from darkness to Light.

The letter 'T' in devices in Bacon's *Great Instauration* and *Advancement of Learning* stands for 'Tudor' and shows a rose, emblem of the Tudor royal family but also of the Fra Rosi Crosse Society and Rosicrucian Society. Two 'C's are suspended from the top of the 'T'.

Similar colophons suggest that other important works of Bacon's time were assisted by Bacon's secret society. The Authorized King James Version of the Bible (1611), includes light-dark scrolls and the 'A'-type emblem, and it is claimed that Bacon was its chief editor. The colophons (headpieces and tailpieces) of Shakespeare's 1623 First Folio include one 'AA' headpiece, five archer-type 'AA' headpieces and 24 Pan-type tailpieces, each with several 'C's and a light-dark scroll seal. The headpiece to the dedication page of *Venus and Adonis*, 1593, includes a light-dark 'AA'. (Light and dark scrolls appear on the top of the pillars and bottom of the door frame of Shakespeare's monument in Westminster Abbey.)

These seals show, Tudhope claims, that the secret society that presented Bacon's works was also sponsoring Shakespeare's works, which included a reference to the 'brave' New World, after his death. His assumption is that the seals and emblems were not conventional devices to be found on all writers' books, but rather the trademark of a secret society that was promoting these works to spread Elizabethan imperialism and American colonization.

Such seals are certainly prominent on maps of colonizing voyages. A print showing the crowning of Sir Francis Drake by native Americans in San Francisco Bay in 1579 shows one of his legs light and the other dark, to suggest the light-dark seal. Light and dark scrolls are shown on the *Hondius Broadside* 1590 map showing the route Drake took when sailing round the world between 1577 and 1580. Sir Walter Raleigh's 1585 map of Virginia shows seven light-dark scroll seals and the Masonic compass and gauge, suggesting that the secret society helped Raleigh in his attempt to colonize America. The frontispiece of Raleigh's *The History of the World* (1614) also shows light and dark scroll emblems and the All-Seeing Eye (the Masonic symbol for God's omniscience) above a spherical globe and two Masonic pillars. At the time the Church was still denying that the Earth was round. Again the suggestion is that Bacon's secret society was involved in promoting this work.

Bacon visited Raleigh, a member of his circle, when he was a prisoner in the Tower of London – James I having promised Count Gondomar of Spain that he would execute him to put an end to his anti-Spanish maraudings in the New World – and was rumoured to have co-authored *The History of the World* with him. If so, that would explain Ben Jonson's remark to William Drummond, the Scottish poet: 'The best wits in England were employed in making his history.'

Captain John Smith also had links with Bacon. He refers to the Virginia colony as 'pigs of my own sow'. The sow image perhaps refers to Bacon's symbol of himself as a sow with a curly tail in an emblematic device published in 1577 by Christopher Plantin and appropriated by Whitney on his page 53. The device shows an 'AA' and two Masonic pillars with a pennant-like inscription, *Plus Ultra* ('There is more beyond'). A bridge forms a sideways 'B' and there is an 'A' in a pyramid, suggesting Bacon. Beneath is a sow symbolizing Bacon, nose to the earth, rooting out the seeds and roots of truths.

If Smith was deliberately echoing Bacon, and it has to be said this is not certain, the suggestion is that instead of expressing contempt of the kind he had for the Separatist colony at Plymouth, which he described as 'a fooles Paradise', he was perhaps hinting that Bacon was head of the secret group responsible for colonizing America and behind his own activities. In 1618 he tried successfully to enlist Bacon to support a colonization plan, and he wrote to him enclosing his *Description of New England*, perhaps in 1625. Can these late contacts be taken as evidence of an earlier relationship?

Turning to the illustrations in John Smith's *The Generall Historie* (1624), we can see that his map of New England shows the Masonic compass, gauge and light and dark scrolls. The map of Virginia shows the compass, plumb bob, two 90° squares and two light-dark scrolls above the words 'Discovered and Discribed by Captyne John Smith 1606', suggesting that John Smith was an important member of this secret society. (The date actually suggests that Smith was claiming too much. We have seen that he was in chains in 1606 and took no part in the discovery of Jamestown until the fort was built in mid-1607.) The native American in the top right-hand corner wears a Masonic apron.

Another illustration is split into sections. The centre bottom shows three light-dark scroll seals. 'Their Idoll' (top centre) sits like a worshipful master and wears an apron. On each side raised arms make two 90° squares, one hand holding a Masonic maul (a club-like hammer). Below 'The Idoll', 'C. [Captain] Smith' is shown with one hand above the other, one light, one dark. He sits with seven native Americans (four light, three dark), five of whom hold mauls, suggesting Masonic squares. All the legs in the other five illustrations are light and dark – even 'C.S.', tied to a tree, has a dark right leg and a light left leg. In the lower left and upper right sections 'C. Smith' captures two kings, each wearing a Masonic apron and each showing one leg light, one dark.

Smith's *A New and Accurat Map of the World Drawn According to ye Truest Descriptions, Latest Discoveries and Best Observations that have been Made by English or Strangers* (1626) shows two 'spherical' hemispheres with latitudes, longitudes and marginal engravings: 'A figure of the Sphere', 'A figure to prove the spherical roundness of the Sea', 'The Eclipse of the Sunne' and 'The Eclipse of the Moone'.

All this material challenged the Roman Church and was risky: following the 1588 Armada and James I's declared intention of marrying his son Charles to the daughter of Philip III of Spain in 1623, England could have become a Catholic country again, and re-Romanization would have brought extreme danger to anyone too outspoken. In 1600 Bruno had been burned at the stake for pro-Copernican views and (among other things) for proposing that matter consisted of atoms, and Galileo would be persecuted in 1632 for asserting Copernicus's view that the Earth was round and turned on its axis. In short, the anti-Roman and dangerous cosmological views being proposed in Smith's maps suggest the work of a secret society behind a lone daring individual.

The 1626 map graphically shows Smith's 'one-world' outlook that embraced the New World's indigenous population, which was symbolized in his relationship with Pocahontas and in Pocahontas's marriage to the English Rolfe.

As we have seen, the quality of Smith's prose – though his experiences seem to have been embellished – and his cartographic drawings, spherical globes and scale measurements are of such high quality that only a scholar could have produced them, yet he was an uneducated farm hand and merchant's apprentice. Did he lend his name and act as a front for invisible Masons (builders) who wrote his works? Was it because they sought to project him that he appears to award himself the prime role in creating the colony, downplaying Bartholomew Gosnold's early contribution?

Clearly Gosnold's part in the founding of the Jamestown settlement *was* played down in favour of Smith, and the question is, was this solely for political reasons, because Gosnold was an Essexite, or was it for Freemasonic reasons, because Smith was to be projected as a front for invisible Masons? It is the same question that can be asked of Shakespeare's works, which share the same emblematic devices in their colophons: did a secret society use him as a front for their own philosophical purposes? And was this secret society hostile to Puritanism? Is that why Smith referred to Plymouth as 'a fooles Paradise' and why Shakespeare ridiculed Malvolio, the first Puritan in literature?

If Bacon prepared the 1609 Virginia Company charter for the king's signature and was head of the secret society committed to the advancement of learning that, with its internationalist outlook, colonized America and liberated science from the Roman Church, then he and the secret society can take credit for passing a perfect form of the English language to America, which surfaced in the noble prose of his *New Atlantis*, the Declaration of Independence and the Constitution of the United States.

Certainly, having been Lord Chancellor from 1618 until he fell amid accusations of bribery in 1621, Bacon spent the last five years of his life writing furiously. In one view he is thought to have written *New Atlantis* in 1624 or 1625; it was published after his death in March 1626, probably in 1626–7. In another view he wrote *New Atlantis* in 1610–11, basing it on Strachey's *The True Reportory of the Wracke and Redemption of Sir Thomas Gates*, which was dated 15 July 1610, and also on the Virginia Council's 1610 *True Declaration of the State of the Colonie in Virginia, with a computation of such scandalous reports as have tended to the disgrace of so worthy an enterprise*. Strachey's account was not published until 1625, but Bacon could have seen it through his work on the Virginia Council,[17] in which case, *New Atlantis* was written at the same time as *The Tempest*, which was also based on Strachey's account.

New Atlantis was about a Utopia in the New World. It concealed the Secret Doctrine to create a New World and democracy within its Utopianism, and was a Masonic blueprint for America. With hindsight, if it was written in 1624, it can be seen as lamenting the passing of the lost Rosicrucian paradise in the Palatinate. The name 'Salomon' in *New Atlantis* recalls the designer of the gardens at Heidelberg castle, Salomon de Caus. By writing of Ben Salem or 'son of (Jeru)Salem', Bacon suggests that England could become an Israelite England. Thus, payment is offered for those who care for the sick, but is declined. The Rosicrucian brothers always healed free of charge. An official wears a white turban 'with a small red cross on top', a Rosicrucian emblem.[18] In *New Atlantis* Bacon was applying his American knowledge, reinforced by what he had gleaned from his cousin Bartholomew Gosnold and other voyagers, to the Palatinate and creating a More-like Utopia which would advance the promotion of American colonization and by which flawed contemporary England could be improved.

Rosicrucian Freemasonry may have established itself in America in 1635 when missing works by Bacon were reputedly taken to Jamestown. These may have included the sequel to *New Atlantis* Bacon is thought to have written. This is believed to have included a timetable for fulfilling the Masonic plan for America. It is claimed the works were brought there by Bacon's descendant Henry Blount who, on his arrival in America, adopted the name Nathaniel Bacon for his own protection.[19] These works, it is claimed, were buried in a vault under the first brick church in Bruton.[20] Thomas Jefferson was apparently the last to read them and is said to have resealed them and reburied them, and the vault has since escaped detection because the rebuilt church was moved to the east.

To recap, the seals used in emblems and engravings from 1575 to c.1640 seem to be connected with a secret society in England that opposed Spanish domination and aggression, the spread of Catholicism and the influence of the Roman Papacy, and stood for the advancement of learning and for establishing colonies in America. The society was invisible and its members built truths, that is, they were 'masons' who recognized each other by secret language, seals, ciphers, signs and emblems. The same scroll and seal devices were found in James Anderson's *Constitution of the Freemasons* in 1723, suggesting that this secret society fed its material into the lodges of Freemasons in 1723.[21]

One more connection needs to be made. The Rosicrucian state of Frederick V came to an end in 1620 when, after accepting the Bohemian Crown in 1619, he was driven out by an alliance of the previous Bohemian king, Ferdinand II, and the Spanish Habsburgs. Frederick V and Elizabeth Stuart fled into exile in The Hague in the Netherlands in November 1620. Rosicrucianism migrated with them. They arrived shortly after the Puritans had left Leiden to sail on the *Mayflower*, but Rosicrucianism may have migrated from the Netherlands to America with a later voyage of Puritans.

Puritanism, especially Dutch Puritanism, was strongly linked to Rosicrucianism. For example, John Wilkins, Frederick V's chaplain, was closely linked to Rosicrucianism in the Palatinate and tutored Frederick and Elizabeth's son when he was sent to England. Wilkins co-founded the Royal Society when the Invisible College met in his rooms at Wadham College, Oxford, from 1648 to 1659, and he had a deep connection with Puritanism.[22] Samuel Hartlib, Andreae's friend, was the link between Andreae and Oliver Cromwell, and was the central figure of an invisible reforming group in England in the 1630s. From at least 1641 and possibly 1628, he had Cromwell's ear. Cromwell himself frequented a Rosicrucian Masonic lodge called (bizarrely) Crown. He could only have gained admittance if he was a Rosicrucian Freemason.[23]

Puritanism had risen as early as the 1590s. It was not a theological movement but a moral consciousness and individual conscience that opposed all forms of selfishness, aiming for simplicity and plainness in all things, including religion. Hartlib's 'Invisible Rosicrucian' group used similar thinking to outline a new society. By the late 1630s the Puritan revolution dreamed of replacing existing society by revolutionary means. Separated from its religious background, it had much in common with Rosicrucianism, which had gone underground in the early 1620s and whose 'Rosicrucian College' Bacon had established as an inner rite of the Freemasonic Brotherhood. Indeed, so close were Puritanism and Rosicrucianism in essence that it can be said that the Puritan philosophy was actually Rosicrucian. So it could be that some of the post-*Mayflower* Puritans who joined the Plymouth settlement as reinforcements brought Rosicrucianism with them and over a period of time it passed into Freemasonic lodges.

English Freemasonry became formalized in America in the 1720s, the first decade in which there are reports of American-based lodges. Before that, John Skene, a Mason of an Aberdeen lodge in 1670 (i.e. a Scottish, not an English, lodge), emigrated to New Jersey in 1682 and became deputy Governor. And Jonathon Belcher, an American-based settler, became a Freemason during a visit to England in 1704. In 1719 a ship called the *Freemason* did American coastal trade.

In 1733 Rosicrucian Freemasonry formally entered America when St John's Lodge was established in Boston. It became the Masonic capital of Britain's American colonies. By 1737 there were lodges in Massachusetts, New York, Pennsylvania and South Carolina,[24] all committed to imple menting the plan for a Utopian New Atlantis.

We can now begin to see how Rosicrucian Freemasonry affected the founding of America through the Founding Fathers of the eighteenth century. Benjamin Franklin, a Boston boy who moved to Philadelphia, was set up in business by the Royal Governor of what was now a Crown colony, Sir William Keith, in 1724. Franklin was supposed to make contact with stationers and booksellers and, until 1726, he set up in business in England. He returned to Philadelphia and, after a spell as a clerk in a store, started a printing partnership, organizing the Library Company of Philadelphia. In 1729 he wrote *A Modest Enquiry into the Nature and Necessity of a Paper*

Currency and was asked to print Pennsylvania's paper currency. He now printed the *Pennsylvania Gazette*.

In February 1731 Franklin became a Rosicrucian Mason[25] and in 1734 Provincial Grand Master of Pennsylvania. He worked for Freemasonry's one-world agenda. At a native-American treaty council meeting he attended in 1744, in which representatives of Maryland, Virginia and Pennsylvania met the native-American chiefs of the Iroquois League and set up an alliance to prevent France from dominating the New World, the native-American spokesman Canassatego recommended that the British colonies should unite as the Iroquois had done. In 1751 Franklin wrote urging the uniting of the colonies.

In 1754, when the French were encroaching into English territory, the Albany Congress met at the request of the British Board of Trade and confirmed the Anglo-Iroquois alliance and Franklin's Plan of Union (*see* Appendix IV). Franklin proposed that a president-general should lead the colonies, which would have a single Grand Council, like the Iroquois Great Council, with 48 members. Each state should retain its internal sovereignty. The British rejected the proposal. It would resurface 20 years later when the Stamp Act united the colonies and eventually resulted in the Articles of Confederation of 1781.

In 1753 Franklin had become Deputy Postmaster General for the colonies, which meant he had access to all letters and communications and was in effect a spymaster. In 1756 he was admitted to the Rosicrucian Royal Society for discovering that lightning was electricity. In 1757 he went to London to represent Pennsylvania in a dispute over William Penn's lands and he spent until 1762 in England and France. He was initiated as a Rosicrucian in London during his stay there.[26] He was again in England from 1764 to 1775 and discovered Baconian English Freemasonry's Secret Doctrine to create a New World or 'philosophical Atlantis' in America, the Masonic blueprint that Bacon had concealed in his *New Atlantis*.[27]

In 1775 Tom Paine, whom Franklin had sent to America to work on the *Pennsylvania Magazine*, argued that America should not just revolt against British taxation but should also demand independence. Franklin returned to Philadelphia and printed Paine's *Common Sense*, a call for independence, in January 1776. Franklin had thus brought America to readiness for independence so that the Declaration of Independence was a natural next step. Thomas Jefferson, the writer of the Declaration of Independence, was also a Rosicrucian, and a Rosicrucian code was discovered among his papers.[28]

The federalism that finally united the 13 colonies into states was identical to the federalism of the Grand Lodge system of Masonic government which had been created in Anderson's Constitution of 1723, when the first Grand Lodge appeared in America. Also, as we shall see, Franklin convinced Jefferson and Adams that they should use a Masonic seal that had come into his possession – which is now the Great Seal of the United States. Freemasonry was therefore behind the independence movement and devised a concept of independence and the structure that would follow independence.

To sum up, as Baigent and Leigh assert in *The Temple and the Lodge*:

'According to some traditions, a form of Freemasonry or proto-Freemasonry came to the New World as early as the Jamestown settlement of 1607 and established itself in Virginia, working to promote the kind of idealised society outlined twenty years later by Francis Bacon in such works as *New Atlantis*. This possibility cannot entirely be discounted. The "Rosicrucian" thinkers of the early seventeenth century were obsessively aware of the opportunities America offered for the idealised social blueprints that figured so prominently in their work.'[29]

It may be that Smith brought English Freemasonry and spread it, acting for Bacon's secret society, and that Bacon's idealism grew into lodges soon after the beginning of the eighteenth century.

In the very early days it was not Freemasonry that planted the colonies, but Spanish Catholic colonists and dissenting refugees from the Elizabethan and Jacobean English State carrying the Anglican and Puritan Light. The Elizabethan State, however, was in favour of the anti-Spanish colonization of America, especially by non-dissenters such as Raleigh and John Smith, and influenced it behind the scenes by using a secret society, Bacon's Freemasonry, to advance knowledge of the colonizing project. It spread colonization by helping with the publication and promotion of:

Drake's voyage round the world, which challenged Spanish maritime
supremacy;

the Authorized King James Bible, which was to spread Protestantism
worldwide;

Raleigh's *History of the World*;

John Smith's informative and descriptive works about the New World;

Shakespeare's plays, which championed English sovereignty against the
implied threat of Spanish rule and which were set all over Europe
and in the brave New World;

Bacon's *New Atlantis*, which stood for an 'English Israelite' rather than
a Spanish New World.

Scottish/French Templar Freemasonry

But that is not all in the Freemasonic story, for there was another branch
of Freemasonry active in London in 1606–7. The Templars (the Poor
Knights of Christ and the Temple of Solomon), who had grown rich by
escorting pilgrims in the Holy Land and (it was rumoured) by discovering ancient treasures there, and who had become bankers to every throne
in Europe, had been suppressed by the French king on 13 October 1307
and had fled France. Their Grand Master, Jacques de Molay, had been burned
at the stake in 1314. Some Templars are thought to have taken a ship or
ships from La Rochelle to Scotland and been welcomed by Robert I (the
Bruce). They fought for the Scots at the battle of Bannockburn in the early
fourteenth century, in which the Scots defeated the English under Edward
II, regained their independence and placed the Bruce on the Scottish
throne.[30] Their descendants maintained the Templar beliefs, which passed
into a form of Scottish Freemasonry in which the Templars symbolized
the death of Jacques de Molay in the ritual murder of Hiram Abiff.

Templar Freemasonry's headquarters were at the preceptory at Rosslyn.[31]
There they founded the Order of the Knights Temple, an order of Templar
Masons into which members of the Scottish royal family, the Stuarts,
were initiated. The Scottish rulers supported Templar Freemasonry as the
Templars had fought together with the future monarch.

James VI of Scotland was a Scottish Templar Freemason and when he came to London in 1603 as James I of England, he brought with him his Scottish Templarism, or Jacobite Freemasonry – Jacobus, the Latin for James, also suggested Jacques – in memory of Jacques de Molay. Sir Robert Cecil, later Lord Salisbury, had offered James the English throne and he seems to have become a Templar in the hope of controlling James (as his father, Lord Burghley, had controlled Elizabeth I). James hid his Templarism behind Puritan attitudes, however, and adopted the England / Israel analogy and language. He maintained that the Lord had made him 'King over Israel' (the land that contained the Temple of Solomon) and while on his way to London to be crowned he asserted that he was going to the Promised Land.[32]

Templarism was not hostile to Bacon's English Rosicrucian Freemasonry – hence Bacon was allowed to take part in, and perhaps write a masque for, the wedding of James I's daughter, Elizabeth Stuart. In fact, it can now be seen that through the marriage the daughter of a Templar monarch formed an alliance with a Rosicrucian monarch (Frederick V), bringing Templarism and Rosicrucianism towards each other. Nevertheless, Templarism remained separate and the court of James I was Templar.

The king's 1606 charter to the Virginia Company of London meant that the leading figures of the Virginia Company of London would have been Templar sympathizers. It is not known if Sir Thomas Smythe or Admiral Newport had strong Templar leanings. But they could not have held their positions without being at least sympathetic to Templarism.

Bartholomew Gosnold's cousin, John Gosnold IV, was at court. He had served Elizabeth I as Gentleman Usher and was retained in the same capacity by James I. (Later he would be Gentleman of the Privy Chamber to Charles I and lie across the threshold of the king's bedroom to protect him with his own body as he slept.)[33] He was also (distantly) related to Sir Thomas Smythe. He would clearly have assisted his cousin Bartholomew in the months before the 1606 charter was signed and the three ships set sail. Was John Gosnold a Templar now, in order to progress at court? And did Bartholomew Gosnold, though being a cousin twice over of Bacon's, take on his Templarism? Was his relative Wingfield therefore Templar? Is that why Wingfield was put in charge of the Council in Jamestown ('James his Towne')?

Templar Freemasonry turned the philosophical idea of Freemasonry into a means of securing political power. Its goals were political rather than occult and philosophical (as was Baconian Rosicrucianism). It sought – and still does – to transform the world into a world government, a 'universal democracy', eventually a universal republic – a New Atlantis. It should be thought of as a kind of secret intelligence service with a large network rather than a system of closed lodges where strange rituals take place.

After the reign of James I, Templarism gathered strength under Charles I and then, after the hiatus of the Cromwellian Revolution, under Charles II and James II, whose followers were known as Jacobites. On the death of James II in 1701, French policy was to restore the Templar Stuarts to the British throne in place of the Rosicrucian line of William III and Mary. The French king Louis XIV proclaimed James II's son, Francis Edward Stuart, James, King of England. The Catholic Stuart line was excluded from succession to the throne under the 1701 Act of Succession, however. In 1708, with French ships, the Pretender tried invading Scotland, but was put to flight before he could land. When Queen Anne died in 1714, he organized another invasion of Scotland, landing in December 1715. After seven weeks, the rebellion collapsed and he returned to France and spent the rest of his life in or near Rome.

On 4 January 1717 the Scottish Stuarts were sent into permanent exile in France. Jacobite Templar Freemasonry was expelled with them. Exiled Stuart sympathizers founded the first French Templar lodge with the help of Charles Radclyffe in 1725. They used it to keep alive the Jacobite cause round the Pretender's son, Charles Edward Stuart.[34]

In July 1745 Charles Edward Stuart landed in western Scotland with a dozen men. He entered Edinburgh on 17 September with 2,000 men, defeated Sir John Cope's army, crossed the English border in November and reached Derby. Confronted by 30,000 government troops, he withdrew to Scotland and was eventually defeated at Culloden by the Duke of Cumberland. About 80 rebels were executed. Charles Edward Stuart was on the run for five months and eventually escaped by boat to France, where again he became the 'King over the Water'.[35]

In 1746 many Irish and Scottish Templar Jacobites fled to America and some brought with them the French Scottish Rite which Charles Edward

Stuart had founded.[36] In 1756 Jacobean Templarism came to Boston. Its American headquarters were at St Andrew's Lodge. It offered higher degrees than English Masonry: in 1769 it offered a new degree, the Knights Templar degree. Soon afterwards another branch of Templarism, the Grand Lodge of York, set up lodges in Virginia. The York Rite offered 13 degrees, as de Molay had died on Friday 13th – hence 13 has ever since been considered unlucky.[37]

Templarism shaped the America into which the Founding Fathers were born every bit as much as English Rosicrucian Freemasonry. All the Founding Fathers and American revolutionaries belonged to Templar lodges, socially desirable secret societies in which revolution could be fomented, and all the British colonial forces belonged to English Rosicrucian lodges, equally socially desirable secret clubs where they could discuss suppressing the revolution in secure conditions.

After the 'England-first' Elizabethan imperialism of Dee and Cecil, there was now a Freemasonic internationalism abroad that professed to seek truth irrespective of national orders. English Rosicrucianism moved between Germany, England and the New World, and Templarism moved between Scotland, France and the New World.

This was particularly apparent during the Boston Tea Party of 1773. Needing money to fund the expansion of the British Empire in North America since the end of the French and Indian War of 1763, George III's government imposed a number of taxes: on sugar (1764), the quartering of British soldiers, stamps (1765) and a threepenny tax on tea (1767). Templar Freemasonry's St Andrew's Lodge in Boston had come into conflict with Rosicrucian Freemasonry's St John's Lodge in Boston in 1761. Now the Templars of Boston (including John Hancock and Paul Revere) had the support of Templars in Virginia (including Patrick Henry and Richard Henry Lee, who in 1769 persuaded the Virginia Assembly to condemn the British government). The Boston massacre of 1770 saw the Templar St Andrew's Lodge take the side of the rioters and Rosicrucian Freemasonry take the side of the British sentries. The day after the massacre the citizens gathered at Old South Meeting House and demanded that British troops should leave Boston.

However, there was no unified movement for national resistance until the Tea Act of 1773. This was passed because the British East India Company was nearly bankrupt, and there were 17 million pounds of unsold tea in London warehouses. Under the Act, the company would receive a shilling for every pound (in weight of tea sold in America) and be allowed to ship 600 chests of tea to New York, Philadelphia and Boston. The price of tea was increased.[38]

On 27 November the first of three tea ships entered Boston Harbour. Five thousand citizens gathered in and around the Old South Meeting House, milled about for three weeks and resolved that the tea should not be landed. It could not be sent back to England by law, however, and the Governor could confiscate it if the duty was not paid within 20 days. Finally, with 7,000 people round the Meeting House, Samuel Adams declared, 'Gentlemen, this meeting can do nothing more to save the country!'

After dark on 17 December 1773 at least 120 and possibly up to 200 Templar Masons from St Andrew's, disguised as Mohawk Indians, met in the Long Room of Freemasons' Hall. Other groups at the same meeting included the Long Room Club (with Joseph Warren), the Committee of Correspondents (with Paul Revere) and the Sons of Liberty (with Samuel Adams). They went to the wharf, boarded the ship whooping like Mohawks, opened the hatches, dragged the tea chests onto deck, cut them to pieces and threw the tea overboard into the harbour. They emptied 342 chests, each weighing 360 pounds, and destroyed 60 tons of tea leaves. Some patriots shouted out, 'Boston Harbour a teapot tonight!' John Adams wrote in his diary:

> 'Depend upon it, they were no ordinary Mohawks.... This is the most magnificent moment of all! There is a dignity, a majesty, a sublimity in this last effort of the patriots that I greatly admire.'[39]

This act precipitated independence. Six months later a British ship arrived with news of British retaliation: Massachusetts's charter of 1691 was revoked and it was now a Crown colony; it was placed under a military governor, General Gage; Boston's port was closed until the townspeople paid for the tea; British soldiers could be quartered in American homes against their hosts' will; and any trial involving British officials was to take place in England.

American indignation expressed itself in the First Continental Congress of 5 September 1774. It took place under the presidency of a Templar Freemason, Peyton Randolph, and was held in Carpenters' Hall, Philadelphia. Boston delegates included Son of Liberty Samuel Adams and Templar Mason Paul Revere.

In February 1775 the Massachusetts Provincial Congress announced plans for armed resistance. The British Parliament declared Massachusetts to be in a state of rebellion. The Virginia Provincial Assembly met in St John's church, Richmond, Virginia, and Patrick Henry made his speech, 'Give me liberty, or give me death.'

On 18 April, 700 British troops were sent to seize arms at Concord outside Boston. Revere rode to spread the news ('The Redcoats are coming!') and 77 armed colonists blocked their way. Eight colonists were killed (the 'shot heard round the world') and 4,000 colonial Americans attacked the British troops on their way to Boston, leaving 273 dead or wounded against 90 suffered by the colonists.

The strength of the republican idea in Templarism is demonstrated by the treasonable acts of Benjamin Franklin. Already a Rosicrucian Freemason, he became a Templar Freemason as well in the 1770s. While in England, he had become friendly with his counterpart Sir Francis Dashwood, British Deputy Postmaster General, who was a Jacobite Templar and supporter of Charles Edward Stuart. Franklin stayed at Dashwood's house during the summers of 1772, 1773 and 1774.[40] Through his friends in the postal service he became colonial ambassador to France and a Templar Mason. English Templar MPs raised money for anti-British activities in America and sent it to Franklin in Paris, who sent it on to North America by post or bought arms with it in France.

Franklin returned to America in March 1775, expecting a revolution. On 10 May he was a delegate at the Templars' Second Continental Congress at the State House, Philadelphia. The President was again the Templar Peyton Randolph. When he died he was replaced by John Hancock of the Templar St Andrew's Lodge, Boston.

From the time Franklin joined the Templars in the 1770s, Templar

Freemasonry controlled American politics.[41] First Baconian Rosicrucian Freemasonry, then Scottish/French Templar Freemasonry created opportunities at the lodges for secret meetings to be held which could foment revolution and shaped the Founding (as opposed to the Planting) Fathers.

Of the 56 who signed the Declaration of Independence, nine according to some, 53 according to others, were Freemasons.[42] The first President, George Washington, had been initiated as a Rosicrucian Mason in the lodge at Fredericksburg, Virginia, in 1752 and become a Templar Mason by 1768.[43] By the time he was elected, he was Grand Master of the Templar Alexandria Lodge no. 22 in Virginia, and John Adams was his Vice-President.[44]

In the Boston Tea Party, the Declaration of Independence, the War of Independence, the Templar Constitution of 1787 and, as we shall see, the physical layout of the city of Washington, there is an abundance of evidence that Freemasonry was at work in the founding of the United States and that it rejected the Catholicism, Anglicanism and Puritanism of the very first American Planters. Templarism, like Rosicrucianism, was regarded as a means of securing revolution through secret meetings that would not be betrayed. The Founding Fathers still retained the Planting Fathers' fundamental vision of God, but only just, and used it more as a front or convenient veneer they could hide behind. For, as we shall now see, they were Deists.

CHAPTER 5

ENLIGHTENMENT DEISTS IN NEW ENGLAND

Behind the apparent Christianity of the Planting Fathers which the Founding Fathers of the United States inherited, other secret influences besides Templar Freemasonry shaped the documents the Founding Fathers produced. A very important secret influence was Deism.

Deism, the Enlightenment and Freemasonry

Deism is perceived as growing out of the Enlightenment, that seventeenth-century movement in thought and belief that drew inspiration from Greek philosophy and the scientific revolution. Greek philosophy had first come to western Europe with the Renaissance following the fall of Byzantium (Constantinople) to the Ottomans in 1453 and the salvaging of classical texts from the Byzantine libraries. Socrates' philosophy was extensively read and the reasoning mind was elevated to supreme importance. It was not overlooked that Christianity had originally been hostile to pagan writings, and there was a feeling that, though it now absorbed them, just as Aquinas had made Aristotle part of the Christian outlook, Renaissance Christianity had brought political turmoil to Italy and that Luther's revolt in Germany had brought more discord. Erasmus, for one, was horrified.[1]

Against this background of disenchantment with Christianity, Bacon and Descartes focused on the reasoning mind. In *Novum Organon* (1620), Bacon set out the inductive method of thinking, a new logic that challenged old learning with its *a priori* speculation and abstract thought derived from the concrete data of experience. Descartes offered deduction ('I think, therefore I am'). Galileo invented a more powerful telescope and proved Copernicus' view that the Earth travelled round the sun, demonstrating that Ptolemy's view that the universe travelled round the Earth was wrong. Newton, through empirical observation and calculation, showed that the stars and physical objects obeyed mechanical laws, including gravity. He held that the universe was 'eminently knowable because [it was] completely rational'.[2] His was a 'clockwork universe'. Many of the main Enlightenment thinkers – Bacon, probably Descartes, Newton, Locke, Rousseau and Goethe – were also Freemasons.

With so much new reasoning and observation going on, there was inevitably a fresh look at religion. The role of God as Creator was separated from Christianity and Christ. God, Nature, reason and man were focused on. The idea grew that everyone on Earth had a religious sense, regardless of the particular religion they followed, and that there was a common natural religion. Enlightened religion was essentially the reasoning mind looking at God, and it set out to improve society. The ancient world's view of history as cyclical change – that the Roman Empire rose and fell and was followed by a Dark Age – had been replaced by a view of history as progress towards reason and perfection so long as religious wars could be avoided.[3]

Deism came out of these attitudes. It was a 'belief in the existence of a God, with rejection of revelation; a natural religion' (*Oxford English Dictionary*) and a 'belief in the existence of a supreme being arising from reason rather than revelation' (*Concise Oxford Dictionary*). 'Revelation' is 'the supposed disclosure of knowledge to humankind by a divine or supernatural agency' (*Concise Oxford Dictionary*).

Deism was first seen in the work of Edward Herbert, Lord Herbert of Cherbury, who, in an essay called *De Veritate* ('On Truth'), published in Paris (where he was British ambassador) in 1624, held that instructed reason was the safest guide by which to seek truth.

Lord Herbert asserted that there were five religious ideas that were naturally innate in man and given by God: (1) belief in a supreme being; (2) belief in the need to worship him; (3) belief that the best way of worshipping him was to lead a virtuous life; (4) belief in repentance; (5) belief in the rewards and punishments of the next world. Christ did not feature in these five points. Whatever was contrary to them was contrary to reason and therefore false, in Lord Herbert's view, and he rejected revelation. The Deist God was a First Cause, a transcendent God who created the world but did not intervene in its affairs or its mechanical and unchanging laws and was not immanent or knowable through revelation.

Lord Herbert is known as the 'father of English Deism',[4] but Bacon was behind his ideas. Lord Herbert was a friend of his.[5] He was the elder brother of the poet George Herbert, who wrote one of the 32 Latin elegies on Bacon's death known as *Manes Verulamiani* and worked with Bacon, possibly as one of his scrivenery of 'good pens' ('scholars, lawyers, university wits and poets who acted as secretaries, writers, translators, copyists and cryptographers').[6]

Bacon himself was a churchgoer who often referred to 'God's plenty', 'God's all' and 'God everywhere manifest'.[7] In view of his Freemasonic focus on Solomon's Temple, he would have been interested in George Herbert's *The Temple*. Nevertheless, as we have seen, he was a Freemason who frequently quoted from the Bible. In 1799 he was described as a concealed atheist and in 1926 as 'an unenthusiastic Christian' who looked on the Church of England as 'a branch of the Civil Service'.[8]

Freemasonry is older than Deism and, just as Francis Bacon's work preceded and gave rise to that of his friend Lord Herbert, so Freemasonry preceded and gave rise to Deism. Freemasonry requires belief in a Supreme Being. But, being tolerant, like the Baconian Enlightenment, it accepts members from almost every religion, including all denominations of Christianity, Judaism, Islam and Buddhism, and also Deists.[9] The Grand Orient of France also accepts atheists and agnostics, upholding the principle of 'Liberty, Equality, Fraternity', the credo of the French revolution which it spawned.[10] In non-French Freemasonry this principle is translated as 'Brotherly Love, Relief and Truth' ('Brotherly Love' recalling Penn's Philadelphia). The interaction between Freemasonry and Deism was a two-way process. Freemasonry threw up Deism via Bacon, and Deists – wealthy men of a Deistic rather than a Christian outlook – entered and guided Freemasonry both in Britain and America.[11] (This interaction can be seen in the works of Spinoza and Goethe.)

Freemasonry is secret because its initiatory system of degrees is not revealed to the public.[12] Because of its secrecy, it does not write much about itself, so there are virtually no claims that Deism originated in Freemasonry. However, there is much circumstantial evidence suggesting that this was the case.

The interactive link between Freemasonry and Deism can be understood if we consider why the French king suppressed the Templars in 1312. The trouble was, the Templars were a secret society with initiations and sayings known only to themselves. They rejected the Christian Christ and the cross, altered the Christian Mass, introduced Eastern beliefs and symbols, worshipped the Baphomet, which was represented by a severed head or a skull, allegedly standing for a goat's head said to represent the Devil; they practised homosexuality and formed their own governing instruments so that they were answerable only to their own Grand Masters. Deism and Freemasonic Templarism could therefore make common cause in rejecting Christ. The Freemasons were Deists in acknowledging one Supreme Being amid many religions and denominations. Both British and American Deists could find a home in Freemasonry.

English Deism found resonance in Rosicrucianism. At the Masonic Congress of 1663 it was decided that the Rosicrucians' beliefs should be incorporated into English Freemasonry. Though their beliefs derived from alchemy, the Kabbalah and the occult, Rosicrucians had more sympathy for Christianity than had non-Rosicrucian Freemasons. Rosicrucianism had Eastern connections and Freemasonry now admitted Eastern influences – the *Hermetica*, Tarot, the Kabbalah, Mithraism, Osiris-worship, Pythagoreanism and Essene and Druid influences. Deists were tolerant of all such traditions, all of which revealed the Supreme Being.

Deism developed through the works of the philosophers Thomas Hobbes, Charles Blount, the Earl of Shaftesbury, Anthony Collins, Thomas Woolston, Matthew Tindal, Thomas Morgan, Thomas Chubb and Henry St John, Viscount Bolingbroke.[13] They attacked the orthodox Church establishment and the dissenters' alternative, and they were detached from Catholic, Church-of-England and Protestant fanatics. They denounced religious intolerance because they believed that the core of all religions was the same – and always would be – and so they were also detached from temples, churches and synagogues. The Deist God was gentle, loving and benevolent, an architect who designed and created the universe. (Compare Freemasonry's Great Architect.) Deists were enjoined to be the same. Deists ridiculed biblical prophecy and revelation, regarding Christianity as a burden on natural religion. They asked how Christians could rationally defend revelation.[14]

With the Glorious Revolution of 1688–9 English Deism declined before William III's Rosicrucianism.[15] Deism passed to the Continent, to France, where there was disillusion with Louis XIV. Voltaire took it up and put it in his *Lettres philosophiques* (1728), writing:

> 'The great name Deist, which is not sufficiently revered, is the only name one ought to take. The only gospel one ought to read is the great book of Nature … the only religion that ought to be professed.'[16]

Jean-Jacques Rousseau introduced Deism into his novel *Émile*. He attacked all doctrines and clerical institutions that came between man and God. Other French Deists included the philosopher Pierre Bayle, whose *Dictionnaire historique et critique* was popular with Benjamin Franklin and Thomas Jefferson, and the philosopher Jean Le Rond d'Alembert.[17]

By and large, eighteenth-century French intellectuals preferred atheism to Deism. Deism moved to Germany through the translations of Shaftesbury, and influenced Leibniz. It was championed in Germany by Hermann Reimarus, Gotthold Lessing and Immanuel Kant, and in Holland by Barukh Spinoza.[18]

Christianity fought back against Deist subversion through both the pulpit and the press. Deism and Christianity tussled and, following Newton's work in the 1660s, materialism, the enemy of both, arose. The work of Lucretius was published by a French humanist and then Pierre Gassendi suggested that Epicurus's honesty and inner peace should be seen against a background of atoms and voids. Scepticism increased. John Locke wrote *An Essay Concerning Human Understanding* (1690) and in Scotland David Hume's Deism can be detected in his *Treatise of Human Nature* and *Natural Religion*.

The Scottish Enlightenment

Deism resurfaced in Scotland where, as we have seen, Templar Freemasonry was strong. The Scottish Enlightenment grew out of the Scottish Reformation and John Knox's Calvinist thesis of God's predetermination of man's predestination. The work of sixteenth-century scholars – Hector Boece, John Mair (Major) and George Buchanan, who argued that 'the people have the power to conferre the government on whom they please'[19] – was taken up by Thomas Reid and Dugald Stewart in the eighteenth century.[20]

The Scots had lost their royal court in 1603 when James VI had gone to England as James I, and their parliament in 1707, when union with England had placed them under Westminster, and they had endured failed rebellions against London in 1715 and 1745. They were open to 'thinkers who would be doers' such as David Hume and Adam Smith, whose *An Inquiry into the Nature and Causes of the Wealth of Nations* came out in 1776. They appreciated the common sense of Reid, Paine and Rush, the economic and scientific progress they could take from Adam Smith, James Watt and others, and the role of commerce in a new society made possible by Scottish thinkers.

The Scottish Enlightenment began in Glasgow in 1725 with Francis Hutcheson's *Inquiry into the Originals of the Ideas of Beauty and Virtue* and his essay *The Right to Resistance*. It spread to Glasgow and Edinburgh universities and to the colonies, where Scottish ideas influenced the Founding Fathers. Thomas Jefferson, James Madison and Alexander Hamilton were all taught at school by Scots. Madison was taught by Donald Robertson, who had studied at Aberdeen and Edinburgh universities under the Scottish educator Reverend John Witherspoon. Francis Allison, a pupil of Hutcheson, became a tutor in Maryland in 1735 and later taught three of those who signed the Declaration of Independence. William Small taught Scottish moral philosophy at the College of William and Mary to Jefferson, who also pursued studies at Princeton that were shaped by Witherspoon.

When the Continental Congress wanted a list of books, it appointed a committee chaired by James Madison. The 1783 list included Scottish authors – Hume (who asserted 'a large republic will sustain freedom'), Smith, Ferguson and Miller – most of whose books Madison, Witherspoon and Jefferson had owned.

David Hume, the philosopher of the Scottish Enlightenment, showed how man could have a sound inner centre without being affiliated to a religious tradition. He influenced Jefferson and Madison. Jefferson, believing that reason and not revelation was the path to true religion, was at odds with orthodox Christianity, arguing against original sin, for man's conscience was as 'much a part of man as his leg or arm'.

Scottish sociological historians had grasped that the Industrial Revolution and the new commercial organization of society had made obsolete the old agrarian society. Commerce was not to be treated with suspicion. Hutcheson argued that increased standards of living would make behaviour more virtuous. In Scottish thinking, business generated wealth, and self-interest was a force for public good. The Scottish Enlightenment was known as the 'common sense' school of philosophy.

Scottish thinking also advocated justifiable resistance – revolution of the kind Jefferson wrote into the Declaration of Independence. Jefferson acknowledged that he drew on Scottish and English writings, while Thomas Paine was influenced by the Scottish-educated Benjamin Rush in calling his essay *Common Sense* instead of 'Plain Truth'.

In short, the American Deists were inspired by the Deists of the Scottish Enlightenment. And throughout this Enlightenment thought ran the idea of progress – progress towards a better society, like Bacon's New Atlantis.

The Great Awakening and Deism

Deism spread to America and appealed to many educated Americans. Freemasonry had also spread. The Masonic *Constitutions* of 1723, written by James Anderson, presented Freemasonry as a universal religion. In 1717 non-Jacobite English Freemasonry, which had blocked the accession of the Catholic James II and supported the Rosicrucian William of Orange,[21] triumphantly appealed for an increase in its English membership and, as a result, the Grand Lodge was created following a meeting at the Apple Tree tavern in Covent Garden, London. This lodge structure reached America by 1733, three years after Daniel Cox became the first Grand Master of the North American colonies. At this time the Catholic Church was demonizing Masonic leaders as occultists.

Between *c.*1720 and *c.*1740 there was a religious revival, the 'Great Awakening', which sought to reverse the Enlightenment rationalism and secularization in the American colonies caused by Deism and Freemasonry. It was part of the religious fervour of Pietism and Quietism in western Europe and the evangelical Methodism of John Wesley in England. First and foremost it was an attempt to renew the covenant between God and the chosen people which had inspired the first Protestant settlers. It was also an attempt to combat the rationalist Deism of New England and the formal liturgy of the Dutch Reformed Church. It emphasized 'new birth' in Jesus Christ. It took place among the Dutch Reformed, Congregationalists, Presbyterians, Baptists and some Anglicans, and it called them to evangelical Calvinism. Here lie the roots of the modern American 'born again' evangelism, particularly in the South.

Initially, the leading figure of the Great Awakening was an Anglican priest, George Whitefield. He had been influenced by Wesley and the Calvinists, and he wanted Americans to return to the faith of the Puritan Fathers, including John Cotton. In 1739–40 he toured America preaching to huge crowds in fields. He burst into several parishes without permission and stirred the people up with excessive emotion.

A congregational pastor from Connecticut, Jonathan Edwards, took up the cause. He preached that faith rather than reason achieved salvation. He attacked Deists, describing them as people who had:

> '…wholly cast off the Christian religion…. They deny the whole Christian religion. Indeed they own the being of a God; but they deny that Christ was the son of God, and say he was a mere cheat…. They deny any revealed religion, or any word of God at all; and say that God has given mankind no other light to walk by but their own reason.'[22]

The Great Awakening split Christians into pro- and anti-revival factions across America. It spread Christianity throughout the land and created missions to the native Americans, but by 1750 it was over, and Deism had survived the challenge. In an Age of Reason rather than an Age of Faith, the Founding Fathers of the United States looked to the main Enlightenment figures of Bacon, Newton and Locke, whose portraits can be seen in the parlour in Jefferson's house at Monticello. Jefferson referred to them as 'the three greatest men that have ever lived, without any exception, and as having laid the foundation of those superstructures which have been raised in the Physical and Moral Sciences'.[23]

Deist Founding Fathers

The leading American Deist was, perhaps, Benjamin Franklin, the sage of the colonies and then of the new republic. He had played a leading role in the Great Awakening. As a printer and newspaper publisher, he had printed and published George Whitefield's sermons and journals and had covered the revival in the *Pennsylvania Gazette*. Whitefield also stayed at Franklin's house when he was in Philadelphia. However, Franklin remained a free-thinker and Freemason – and Deist who followed his own reason and would not accept Whitefield's 'new birth'. When, during one of his stays at Franklin's house, Whitefield said that Franklin had made a business offer 'for Christ's sake', Franklin replied: 'Don't let me be mistaken; it was not for Christ's sake, but for your own.'[24]

In 1790, at the age of 84, alarmed by the violence of the French revolution, Franklin wrote to Ezra Stiles, the President of Yale University, who was briefly a Deist before returning to Calvinism, conveying his view of religion in terms that echoed the five beliefs of Lord Herbert of Cherbury:

> 'Here is my creed. I believe in one God, Creator of the universe. That He governs it by His providence. That He ought to be worshipped. That the most acceptable service we render Him is doing good to His other children. That the soul of man is immortal and will be treated with justice in another life respecting its conduct in this. These I take to be the fundamental principles of all sound religion, and I regard them as you do in whatever sect I meet with them.
>
> 'As to Jesus of Nazareth, my opinion [of] whom you particularly desire, I think the system of morals and his religion, as he

left them to us, the best the world ever saw [or] is likely to see; but I apprehend it has received various corrupt changes, and I have, with most of the present Dissenters in England, some doubts about his divinity though it is a question I do not dogmatize upon, having never studied it, and think it needless to busy myself with it now, when I expect soon an opportunity of knowing the truth with less trouble....

'I shall only add, respecting myself, that, having experienced the goodness of that Being in conducting me prosperously through a long life, I have no doubt of its continuance in the next, without the smallest conceit of meriting it.... I have ever let others enjoy their religious sentiments, without reflecting on them for those that appeared to me unsupportable and even absurd. All sects here, and we have a great variety, have experienced by good will in assisting them with subscriptions for building their new places of worship; and, as I never opposed any of their doctrines, I hope to go out of the world in peace with them all.'[25]

Stiles himself was acutely conscious of a shift in religious belief in his own lifetime. His father had 'the old learning', 'the old Logic, Philosophy and Metaphysics' and the truths of the Puritan divines, whereas he himself had 'the new learning' and had read Newtonian science. (Newton's books had been in the Yale library when his father had studied there, but had not found their way onto the students' syllabus.) However, he was concerned that 'Deism has got such Head in this Age of Licentious Liberty'.[26]

As for Franklin, he had turned against the Church in his youth. Believing that Presbyterian dogma kept clergymen in power rather than made men more moral, he 'early absented [himself] from the Public Assemblies of the Sect'.[27] He believed that 'lighthouses are more helpful than churches'.[28] He nevertheless sought moral perfection and identified 13 virtues that would help him attain it.

We can understand Franklin's attitude to Christianity if we consider how American colonists saw the severity of pro-English Anglican Christianity in America. Baptists were arrested in Boston in 1651 and one was whipped. A decade later two Quakers, Robinson and Stevenson, were hanged for resisting banishment, followed, as we have seen, by Mary Dyer (who 'showed neither remorse nor contrition when she spoke after her sentencing').[29] In Virginia colonists had to pay a church tax and it was illegal to challenge any biblical scripture. In Georgia, South and North Carolina, New Jersey and New Hampshire, colonists were compelled to practise the Protestant religion. Any accusation of witchcraft led to the torture and death of the unfortunate accused.

Liberally minded, tolerant Americans, including the Founding Fathers, could best distance themselves from pro-English religious tyranny by being pro-American Freemasonic Deists who championed natural as opposed to institutionalized religion and whose 'Bible' could not be challenged.

The first three Presidents of the United States – George Washington, John Adams and Thomas Jefferson – were Deists, as can be seen from their letters. Jefferson took the view that Jesus, like Socrates, left no writings, and that accounts of what he did were corrupted by his followers. He ascribed to Jesus 'every *human* excellence', as 'he never claimed any other', and rejected all facets of Christianity that included the supernatural and miraculous, that contradicted the laws of Nature or that suggested an angry God, whereas Nature showed a rational Being not given to anger. When he was President in 1819 or 1820 he edited the Bible to focus on Jesus's moral human teachings. This work was called *The Life and Morals of Jesus*. He denied the divinity of Christ, as this was claimed by his disciples, not by Jesus himself, and questioned Christianity's beliefs.[30]

To Jefferson good behaviour was more important than right belief. He urged Peter Carr, his nephew, to judge every fact or opinion with reason and not to depend on the Bible, the Church or ministers: 'Those facts in the Bible which contradict the laws of nature must be examined with more care, and under a variety of faces.'[31] His nephew should base his religious belief on observation. Jefferson wrote quite bluntly:

'It is not to be understood that I am with him [Jesus Christ] in all his doctrines. I am a Materialist; he takes the side of Spiritualist.'[32]

And again:

'No one sees with greater pleasure than myself the progress of reason in its advances towards rational Christianity. When we shall have done away the incomprehensible jargon of the Trinitarian arithmetic, that three are one, and one are three....'[33]

During the 1800 presidential campaign, the Dutch Reformed minister William Linn asserted:

'My objection to [Jefferson's] being promoted to the presidency is founded singly upon his disbelief of the Holy Scriptures; or, in other words, his rejection of the Christian Religion and open profession of Deism.... No professed Deist, be his talents and achievements what they may, ought to be promoted to this place by suffrages of a Christian nation.'[34]

One Federalist voter declared: 'God – and a religious President ... [or] Jefferson – and no God.'[35] He added that Jefferson had 'disbelief of the Holy Scriptures' and was known for his 'rejection of the Christian Religion'.[36] David Daggett, a New Haven lawyer and federalist, wrote in 1800: 'Mr Jefferson never has attended public worship during a residence of several years in New York and Philadelphia.'[37] Baptists disagreed with Jefferson 'that religious liberty should include the right to hold office even for Jews, Mohammedans, Deists, atheists and infidels'.[38]

Previously, John Adams had rejected his Latin schoolteacher Joseph Cleverly, who accepted Puritan precepts as dogma and argued (with bigotry) for doctrinal purity. A parson, debating with Cleverly, said: 'Cleverly! You would be the best Man in the World, if You had no Religion.'[39]

Though often called an atheist, Thomas Paine was also a Deist. In *Common Sense* he argued that the colonists were oppressed not by a bad king but because they were governed by a king. He asserted:

'I do not believe in the creed professed by the Jewish church, by the Roman church, by the Greek church, by the Turkish church, by the Protestant church, nor by any church that I know of.

My own mind is my own church.'[40]

In other words, he followed his reason as a Deist. He also remained independent as regards revelation:

'Each of those churches chose certain books, which they call revelation, or the Word of God. The Jews say that their Word of God was given by God to Moses face to face; the Christians say, that their Word of God came by divine inspiration; and the Turks say, that their Word of God (the *Koran*) was brought by an angel from heaven. Each of those churches accuses the others of unbelief; and for my own part, I disbelieve them all.'[41]

Again, Paine champions Deism:

'There are times when men ... doubt the truth of the Christian Religion; and well they may, for it is too full of conjecture, inconsistency, improbability and irrationality, to afford consolation to the thoughtful man. His reason revolts against his creed. He sees none of its articles are proved, or can be proved.... Here it is that the religion of Deism is superior to the Christian religion. It is free from all those invented and torturing articles that shock our reason or injure our humanity and with which the Christian religion abounds. Its creed is pure, and sublimely simple. It believes in God, and there it rests.... It avoids all presumptuous beliefs and rejects, as fabulous inventions of men, all books pretending to revelation.'[42]

George Washington was a moderate Deist[43] but was perceived as a model Christian. He belonged to the Anglican Church and was a vestryman, yet he relied 'upon a Grand Designer along Deist lines'.[44] Also:

'Washington can be classified as a Deist.... The Supreme Being whose aid he counted upon Washington usually called Providence, Heaven or, to a lesser extent, God.... He also made much use of such stock Deist phrases as Grand Architect, Governor of the Universe, Higher Cause, Great Ruler of Events, Supreme Architect of the Universe, Author of the Universe, Great Creator, Director of Human Events, and Supreme Ruler.'[45]

A Presbyterian minister, Arthur B. Bradford, wrote that his associate Ashbel Green, another Presbyterian minister who had known George Washington personally, 'often said in my hearing, though very sorrowfully of course, that while Washington was very deferential to religion and its ceremonies, like nearly all the founders of the Republic, he was not a Christian, but a Deist'.[46]

Washington certainly had a Deistic belief in Providence. After the American defeat at Germantown in 1777, he wrote: 'We must endeavour to deserve better of Providence and, I am persuaded, she will smile on us.'[47] He kept quiet about – indeed, concealed – his beliefs, however, as Jefferson stated:

'Dr Rush told me (he had it from Asa Green) that when the clergy addressed General Washington on his departure from the government, it was observed in their consultation that he had never, on any occasion, said a word to the public which showed a belief in the Christian religion, and they thought they should so pen their address as to force him at length to disclose publicly whether he was a Christian or not. However, he observed, the old fox was too cunning for them. He answered every article of their address particularly, except that which he passed over without notice.'[48]

The result of his behaviour was that:

'George Washington's conduct convinced most Americans that he was a good Christian, but those possessing first-hand knowledge of his religious convictions had reasons for doubt.'[49]

As the Reverend Doctor Bird Wilson, an Episcopal minister in Albany, New York, stated in a sermon preached in October 1831:

'The founders of our nation were nearly all Infidels, and that of the presidents who had thus far been elected [Washington, Adams, Jefferson, Madison, Monroe, Adams, Jackson] not a one had professed a belief in Christianity.'[50]

Jefferson again suggested that Washington was not Christian:

'I know that Gouverneur Morris, who claimed to be in his secrets and believed himself to be so, has often told me that General Washington believed no more in that system [Christianity] than he did.'[51]

Washington was certainly suspiciously reticent on the subject of Christ:

'Unlike Thomas Jefferson – and Thomas Paine, for that matter – Washington never even got around to recording his belief that Christ was a great ethical teacher. His reticence on the subject was truly remarkable. Washington frequently alluded to Providence in his private correspondence. But the name of Christ, in any correspondence whatsoever, does not appear anywhere in his many letters to friends and associates throughout his life.'[52]

And again:

'[Washington] did not mention Christ or even use the word "God". Following the phraseology of the philosophical Deism he professed, he referred to "the invisible hand which conducts the affairs of men", to "the benign parent of the human race".'[53]

And:

'Washington's religious belief was that of the Enlightenment: Deism. He practically never used the word "God", preferring the more impersonal word "Providence".'[54]

In short: 'Sir, Washington was a Deist.'[55]

It is worth noting that Washington never received communion:

'As pastor of the Episcopal Church, observing that on sacra-
mental Sundays George Washington, immediately after the desk
and pulpit services, went out with the greater part of the congregation – always leaving Mrs Washington with the other
communicants, she invariably being one – I considered it my duty,
in a sermon on public worship, to state the unhappy tendency
of example, particularly of those in elevated stations, who
uniformly turned their backs on the Lord's Supper. I acknowledge the remark was intended for the President; and as such he
received it.... He never afterwards came on the morning of
sacrament Sunday, though at other times he was a constant
attendant in the morning.'[56]

The first bishop of Pennsylvania and bishop of Christ's church, Philadelphia, which Washington attended for some 25 years when in town,
confirms this:

'General Washington never received the communion in the
churches of which I am the parochial minister. Mrs Washington
was an habitual communicant. I have been written to by many
on that point, and have been obliged to answer them as I now
do you.'[57]

Another eyewitness says the same:

'On communion Sundays, he left the church with me after the
blessing and returned home, and we sent the carriage back after
my grandmother.'[58]

Even on his deathbed 'Washington asked for no ritual, uttered no
prayer to Christ, and expressed no wish to be attended by His representatives.'[59] At the end of his life the Reverend Doctor Bird Wilson

judged him to have been Deist:

> 'I have diligently perused every line that Washington ever gave to the public, and I do not find one expression in which he pledges himself as a believer in Christianity. I think anyone who will candidly do as I have done will come to the conclusion that he was a Deist and nothing more.'[60]

A year later he added:

> 'I do not believe that any degree of recollection will bring to my mind any fact which would prove General Washington to have been a believer in the Christian revelation further than as may be hoped from his constant attendance upon Christian worship, in connection with the general reserve of his character.'[61]

Schwartz sums up:

> 'George Washington's belief and practice of Christianity was limited and superficial, because he was not himself a Christian. In the enlightened tradition of his day, he was a devout Deist – just as many of the clergymen who knew him suspected.'[62]

Outwardly, much was made of Washington's Christian piety, but the saintly image was enhanced by spin-doctors of the time. Their idealization was in the manner of a Roman emperor, as can be seen in *The Apotheosis of Washington*, painted in 1800 by David Edwin, in which Washington sits god-like on clouds, deified, while a cherub puts a laurel garland on his head.[63]

The reason the Founding Fathers kept their Deism secret and retained the façade of Christianity was to unify the Catholic, Anglican and Puritan settlers into one new nation-state. They wanted to be sure of having a nation of trusting and passive followers. So religion served a utilitarian, rather than a spiritual, purpose.[64] As Schwartz put it:

'The less pious men of the time saw in religion a necessary and assured support of civil society. Although guided by their own secular traditions they felt that only religion could unite the masses and induce their submission to custom and law.'[65]

To put it more bluntly:

'Sympathizers with Deistic rationalism hesitated to go public because of their fear that dissemination of the new way of thinking would undermine social stability. Many colonial intellectuals attracted to Deism were also suspicious and contemptuous of what they tended to think of as the "mob". They feared that a diminution of the normative and ecclesiastical authority of traditional Christianity would open the floodgates of anarchy. The "common" people, in their estimation, were too boorish and too unlettered to appreciate or profit from a religion founded upon reason and nature, and therefore needed artificial and institutionalized standards to control their behaviour. The Deists thought it better to allow the mob to attain its faith in conventional Christian belief until such time as it was better educated and hence more receptive to the dictates of rational conscience. Until that day arrived, Deism was best confined to the genteel drawing-room and the gentlemen-scholars' study.'[66]

And so the Founding Fathers went to church and paid lip-service to the Christian Light of revelation which the Planting Fathers brought with them in the seventeenth century, although they had a more secularized approach, having been educated in the new learning.

That new learning was steeped in Enlightenment Deism. Jean-Jacques Burlamaqui, in his *Principles of Natural and Political Law*, held that God was the author of natural law and men used their reason to study Nature. That reason then enabled them to infer the existence of God from Nature.[67] James Otis, John Hancock, Joseph Warren and John and Samuel Adams all studied Burlamaqui's political theory at Harvard. The Declaration of Independence (The Unanimous Declaration of the Thirteen United States of America), which Jefferson wrote, avoids mentioning Jesus Christ or Christianity or the New Testament God and instead refers to 'Nature's God'[68] and 'the laws of nature' and 'divine Providence'.

Franklin put the principles of the Newtonian scientific revolution into practice, applying them to the study of lightning. He saw this as a phenomenon to be understood scientifically within the new learning, not as a mystery, as referred to in the old learning. He discovered the true nature of lightning by constructing a kite with a wire protruding a foot above the top, which produced 'Electric Fire' in a thunderstorm. He wrote of his discovery:

> 'It has pleased God in his goodness to mankind at length to discover to them the means of securing their habitations and other buildings from mischief by thunder and lightning.'[69]

John Adams, raised in the old learning, thought Franklin had interfered in God's uses of Nature and that 'the erection of iron points was an impious attempt to rob the Almighty of his thunder'.[70] However, he then encountered Newton and Locke and accepted the Enlightenment's optimistic belief in progress, imagining 'our lives lengthened at pleasure' as a result of the new learning.[71]

It was also through the new learning that Jefferson had a progressive view of the human mind, which was 'perfectible to a degree of which we cannot as yet form any conception'.[72]

It should be noted here that one Christian lobby disputes that the Founding Fathers were influenced by Deism, saying that those who claim that they were Deists take isolated statements out of context. This view, of which H. Wayne House in *The Christian and American Law* is a representative, criticizes Carl Becker's work (1922) on the Declaration of Independence and C. B. MacPherson's *The Political Theory of Possessive Individualism* (1962), which traces twentieth-century rights theory to Jefferson and Madison when (House claims) it should be attributed to John Stuart Mill and Jeremy Bentham.[73]

It should also be noted that the Romantic poets opposed Deism by elevating the imagination above reason. In 1788 Blake headed a short work

There is No Natural Religion and in 1802 he rejected the materialist Newton,[74] writing: 'May God us keep/From Single vision & Newton's sleep!'

In 1820 he would write:

> 'You, O Deists, profess yourselves the Enemies of Christianity, and you are so; you are also the Enemies of the Human Race and of Universal Nature.... Deism is the Worship of the God of this world by means of what you call Natural Religion and Natural Philosophy, and of Natural Morality or Self-Righteousness, the Selfish Virtues of the Natural Heart.'

Whereas Deism arrived at the Supreme Being through reason, the Romantics arrived at the One, the 'Wisdom and Spirit of the universe' (Wordsworth), through revelation, Nature being approached by the imagination, not reason. Hence Blake demonized Urizen ('Your reason') and was on the side of Los (an anagram for Sol, the Light), the principle of revelation.[75]

The Enlightenment had disintegrated towards the end of the eighteenth century. Wesley's emotional Methodism and the feeling of the Romantic movement had challenged religious rationalism. The French revolution, where the goddess Reason had been enthroned on church altars while the guillotine liquidated an entire social class, had shattered the idea that reason promoted tolerance and calm within a society. A revival known as the Second Great Awakening (which was less emotional than the First Great Awakening) had taken place in New England in the 1790s and further eroded the decaying Enlightenment. Soon afterwards the consequences of Napoleon's invasions and wars had shattered the idea of progress.

How Deism and Freemasonry Shaped the Constitution

The Enlightenment and Deism caused the Founding Fathers to question orthodox Christianity. Franklin, Adams, Jefferson, Paine, Madison, Washington and Hamilton did not follow the Bible or submit to clergy in church. They believed in religious liberty so that reason could identify truth.

As individual experience (to evangelicals) and individual reason (to Enlightenment Deists) mattered more than Church doctrine, so it followed that when drawing up the Constitution for the new republic, the American churches had to be kept separate from the State. The truth should not *be* the State as it was for the Puritans. Rather, the secular State should be impartial towards differing religious views, sects and denominations but protect them all.[76] James Madison, the Father of the Constitution, declared: 'Religion and government will both exist in greater purity the less they are mixed together'[77] and Paine wrote of 'the adulterous connection of Church and State'.[78]

When the Founding Fathers came to write the constitution for a 'more perfect Union' in 1787, they had in mind a non-Christian State that would be acceptable to all settlers then alive. So they opted for a government that gave no support to Catholicism, Anglicanism or Puritanism, or to the concept of a 'Citty upon a Hill', and encouraged a marketplace attitude towards religion whereby people could shop around for the religion or sect of their choice. They thought people should be free to follow their own reason as they sought religious truth.

Enough has been said to prove pretty conclusively that the Founding Fathers were Deists who used the Planting Fathers' Christianity as a means of controlling the masses of settlers, just as they used Freemasonry's secret meeting-places as a means of fomenting revolution against the British, as can be seen from the Boston Tea Party. Their noble libertarianism and tolerance in making religion independent of the State came at the zenith of the Enlightenment movement. Their political outlook can be tracked back to the Scottish Enlightenment and Deism, which blended with the legacy of the Freemasonic Scottish Templars. But there was another secret influence on the Founding Fathers' Freemasonic Deism, one that arose from a Freemasonic development in Germany. We shall examine this in the next chapter.

CHAPTER 6

GERMAN ILLUMINATI

The German Illuminati came into existence in 1776. Their leading light was Adam Weishaupt. How they came to influence some of the Founding Fathers is a curious story.

Adam Weishaupt was the son of a Jewish rabbi. He became a Jesuit priest before his reading in his godfather's library convinced him that he was an atheist. He studied in France, where he met Robespierre, later the leader of the French revolution.[1] He graduated in law in 1768 at the Bavarian University of Ingolstadt and then served as a tutor there for four years, during which he met Charles de Lorraine.

Charles de Lorraine, Weishaupt and Rothschild

Charles de Lorraine was the younger brother by four years of François de Lorraine, the Merovingian 'King of Jerusalem', who had married the Austrian Merovingian Empress Maria Theresa von Habsburg in 1735. The period of Frankish rule under the Merovingian dynasty, 476–751, included a bloodline of a 'King of Jerusalem' whose descendants reigned in Jerusalem from 1099 to 1187 and have lived in exile ever since. In 1755 Charles de Lorraine married Maria Theresa's sister Marie-Antoinette and became the commander-in-chief of the Austrian armed forces.

In 1746, following the death of Charles Radclyffe, François appointed Charles de Lorraine Grand Master of the Priory of Sion.[2] This was originally the Order of Sion that was based in a priory in Jerusalem in the 1090s (nearly 900 years before imposters latched on to its long tradition). It founded the Templars to protect the Kingdom of Jerusalem in 1113–15 and became a secret society under a Grand Master. Its centuries-old aim has been to restore the King of Jerusalem. Following Charles de Lorraine's appointment as Grand Master, the court at Vienna became the capital of English Sionist and Rosicrucian Freemasonry.

Charles de Lorraine was an opponent of Frederick II (the Great) of Prussia, a 32nd-degree Templar Freemason who had a great influence on Templarism. In December 1757 the Prussians under Frederick II routed a superior Austrian force under Charles de Lorraine at Leuthen. After this defeat, Maria Theresa relieved Charles de Lorraine of his army command and he retired to Brussels and gathered a court in his palace there, five rooms of which can be visited today.[3]

Despite the defeat at Leuthen, Austria's power increased over the next few years. She had only to occupy France to become the greatest military power in Europe. This meant taking France by force, subversion or marriage. François and Maria Theresa chose marriage and 'to strengthen the alliance between Austria and France' they gave their daughter Marie-Antoinette in marriage to the Bourbon king of France, Louis XVI, in 1770. She became Queen of France in 1774.

The House of Lorraine had already acquired the throne of Austria and the Holy Roman Empire by marriage and was now within a generation of controlling France if a child of Marie-Antoinette's were to succeed Louis as king. But the Lorraines' control of Europe was still threatened by Frederick II of Prussia, who had sensed that Templarism was being developed to topple the French throne. The Templars blamed the French Bourbon king Philippe IV for banning them between 1307 and 1312 and were itching to take revenge on Philippe's Bourbon successor, Louis XVI, and Frederick was now using the Scottish Rite lodges to ally with the Templar opponents of France to destroy the alliance between Austria and France in a bid for the French throne.[4] Having been initiated into Templar Freemasonry in 1738, by 1746 he had founded 14 Templar lodges which he used to make trouble for France. (He was now Head of Templar Freemasonry and had considerable influence over Templar lodges.)

Charles de Lorraine, Grand Master of the Priory of Sion, was determined to block Frederick's designs. Though related by marriage to the Austrian royal family, he had his own agenda: not to wait for France to become Austrian through Marie-Antoinette's children, for Frederick II's Templar lodges might have wrested the French throne by then, but to seize the French throne for Sion and Rosicrucianism, and for Austria, before Frederick II seized it for Templarism. So he set about fomenting a French revolution.

Charles de Lorraine may have met Adam Weishaupt in 1771. In that year Weishaupt is known to have met a Jutland merchant named Kolmer, who initiated him into the Egyptian Rose-Croix (i.e. Rosicrucianism). This Kolmer may have been Charles de Lorraine travelling under an assumed name. Whether they met then or not, Charles de Lorraine selected Weishaupt to found a secret society that would penetrate Templarism and turn its lodges into revolutionary cells. Under Charles de Lorraine, Sion's goal was to overthrow the French Bourbon dynasty and create a democratic republic through a coalition with the Templars. He would then control the successor regime and restore Merovingian rule. He could not replace the Bourbons with the Merovingians from Austria without Templar help and he had to act swiftly before Frederick II. Weishaupt's brief was to unite with the Templars, overthrow the Bourbons in France and shape the Sionist, Baconian New Atlantis in the New World.[5]

During his five-year apprenticeship under Charles de Lorraine from 1771 to 1776,[6] and while teaching law at the university, Weishaupt studied Manichaeism and other pagan religions, the Eleusinian mysteries, Pythagoras, the Kabbalah, the Essenes and the *Major Key of Solomon* and *Lesser Key of Solomon*, which taught him how to conjure demons and perform occult rituals. He rose rapidly. In 1772 he became Professor of Civil Law and in 1773 Professor of Canon Law. In 1775 he became Dean of the Faculty of Law.

In 1773 Weishaupt held a meeting with Mayer Amschel Rothschild (i.e. *Rotschildt* or 'Red Shield', which hung over the door in his ancestors' ghetto house) to discuss world revolution.[7] The Rothschilds were Freemasons. The head of the family, Mayer Amschel, had begun as a clerk in a bank owned by the Oppenheimers and left to take over a business begun by his father in 1750, buying and selling rare coins. In 1769 he had become court agent for the Elector, William IX, Landgrave of Hesse-Kassel. In 1785 William would inherit the largest private fortune in Europe, $40m paid by Great Britain for the use of 16,800 Hessian troops used as mercenaries during the American Revolution. But in 1773 Mayer Amschel was court agent to the ruler of territories in west central Germany, who was able to provide mercenaries and who might be an ally in blocking Frederick II and the Templars.

At this time the Rothschilds were not the richest bankers the world had ever known. They only reached that position by speculating on the Battle of Waterloo, spreading news of an English defeat, buying stock when prices collapsed and then selling it when the market recovered. So at this time Mayer Amschel was open to offers that might advance his wealth. He seems to have been in league with Charles de Lorraine, certainly after 1773, and there are reports that he funded Weishaupt from 1770 to 1776.[8]

In 1774 Weishaupt made contact with a Freemasonic lodge in Munich, but found its members knew too little about pagan mystery religions. Resolved to found his own secret society, he took over the organizational structure of the Jesuits and blended it with the hierarchical structure of Freemasonry. He based his rituals on the Egyptian rites of Ormus, another name for the Priory of Sion, as *ormus* in Latin means 'elm' and recalled the cutting of the elm at Gisors in 1188 to symbolize the Templar breakaway from Sion. Weishaupt's order had three degrees: Novice, Minerval and Illuminated Minerval. (Minerva was the Roman form of Pallas Athena who was adopted by Bacon.)[9]

In the initiation ceremony to the Illuminated Minerval's grade, the initiate entered a room that contained a throne and, on a table, a crown, sceptre and sword. He was told to take them, but if he did he would not be allowed to enter the order. He then went to a room draped in black and a curtain revealed an altar covered with a black cloth, on which lay a red Phrygian cap of the kind used in the mysteries of Mithras. He was told, 'Wear this – it means more than the crown of kings.' Weishaupt based this ritual on the Mithraic mysteries in which the neophyte had to refuse a crown and sword, saying, 'Mithras alone is my crown.'[10]

Weishaupt believed that people could be restored to their pre-Fall perfection if they followed the occult traditions of the pagan mystery schools, which (like the Rosicrucian and Freemasonic traditions) included the ancient wisdom and the original teachings of Jesus. All members of his order had classical names – Weishaupt's was Spartacus – and the months of the year were renamed and the calendar reconstituted so the year began on 21 March. The headquarters was known as the Grand Lodge of the Illuminati, a name that suggested the Illuminated Minervals. In fact, the order was first known as the Order of the Perfectabilists (suggesting the Cathar *Parfaits*) and its name was changed to the Order of the Ancient Illuminated Seers of Bavaria and then to the Order of the Bavarian Illuminati, which soon became 'The Order of the Illuminati'.[11] There were also lodges in Ingolstadt, Heidelberg, Bavaria and Frankfurt.

Weishaupt's Utopianism held that ownership of property forced people to remain in a fixed residence and prevented them from being nomads in Paradise, and that patriotism and love of one's family divided people from the whole human race and prevented universal love between human beings and love of Nature. Weishaupt believed that if property, country and family were eliminated, then mankind would be one happy family in full liberty and equality. He wrote to instruct initiates:

> 'At the moment when men united themselves into nations they ceased to recognize themselves under a common name. Nationalism or National Love took the place of Universal Love. With the division of the Globe and its countries benevolence restricted itself behind boundaries.... It became permissible to despise foreigners, and to deceive and offend them. This virtue was called Patriotism. That man was called a Patriot who, whilst just towards his own people, was unjust to others, who blinded himself to the merits of foreigners and took for perfections the vices of his own country.... Do away with this love of country, and men will once more learn to know and love each other as men, there will be no more partiality, the ties between hearts will unroll and extend.'[12]

This was an embryonic form of Communism, and while (like Communism) the programme had a certain idealistic appeal, the scam was to have a revolution – in France and later in Russia – and inflict a post-revolutionary Communist State on people that would do business with rich 'well-wishers' like Mayer Amschel Rothschild, who would build up their fortunes through inside contacts with the new State. (Weishaupt's Freemasonic programme was later at the core of the Masonic outlook of Communism in the Soviet Union.)

Those lower down the order believed that the Illuminati wanted a one-world government to prevent future wars. Initiates who reached Minerval, the second degree, learned Weishaupt's revolutionary goals:

'(1) abolition of all ordered government; (2) abolition of private property; (3) abolition of inheritance; (4) abolition of patriotism; (5) abolition of all religion; (6) abolition of the family (via abolition of marriage); and (7) creation of a World Government.'[13]

All were to live in a Utopian superstate in which there was no social authority, nationality, private property or religion – no monarchy, Church or land owning, just universal brotherhood. The attack on monarchy came from Charles de Lorraine and masked his plan to wrest the French throne from the Bourbons and replace it with Lorraine rule. The attack on ordered government, private property and inheritance came from Jean-Jacques Rousseau who, like Weishaupt, came under the influence of Charles de Lorraine. It is possible that Charles de Lorraine taught Rousseau and later taught Rousseau's doctrines to Weishaupt.[14] The attack on religion came from Deist Freemasonry. The attack on patriotism, family life, marriage and morality came from the Utopianism of More, Bacon and Hartlib.

Weishaupt instructed that his order should be invisible, like the Rosicrucian Invisible College:

'Secrecy gives greater zest to the whole.... The slightest obser-vation shows that nothing will so much contribute to increased zeal of the members as secret union. The great strength of our Order lies in its concealment, let it never appear in any place in its own name, but always covered by another name, and another occupation. None is fitter than the three lower degrees of Freemasonry; the public is accustomed to it, expects little from it, and therefore takes little notice of it. Next to this, the form of a learned or literary society is best suited to our purpose.... The Order wishes to be secret, and to work in silence for thus it is better secured from the oppression of the ruling powers, and because this secrecy gives a greater zest to the whole.'[15]

Fools were encouraged to be initiates. Weishaupt wrote:

'These good people swell our numbers and fill our money box; set yourselves to work; these gentlemen must be made to nibble at the bait.... But let us beware of telling them our secrets, this sort of people must always be made to believe that the grade they have reached is the last.... One must speak sometimes in one way, sometimes in another, so that our real purpose should remain impenetrable to our inferiors.'[16]

Initiates were deliberately deceived. They were told that the Order of Illuminati represented the highest ideals of the Church, that Christ was an Illuminist, that his secret mission was to restore to people the liberty and equality they lost in the Garden of Eden. Weishaupt told them that Christ despised riches to prepare for the abolition of property ownership and the sharing of all possessions. He wrote to Xavier von Zwack, his close associate:

'The most admirable thing of all is that great Protestant and reformed theologians (Lutherans and Calvinists who belong to our Order) really believe they see in it the true and genuine mind of the Christian religion.... [But] Behold our secret ... in order to destroy all Christianity, all religion, we have pretended to have the sole true religion ... to deliver one day the human race from all religion.'[17]

Weishaupt's choice of name for his order, 'Illuminati', was one aspect of his intention to deceive Christian members. Behind it in their minds were the Spanish Alhumbrados ('Enlightened' or 'Illuminated' Ones), but the name also applied to a fifteenth-century German sect who were Satanists.

The divine Light of God that inspired Dante and the Spanish Alhumbrados was different from the psychic 'Light' the German magicians received from Satan, which they manipulated with their wills. Weishaupt himself was a secret Satanist who lured Christians into his order and wanted recruits to believe they were joining a mystical order.[18]

Weishaupt used women to give the order respectability and to satisfy members' sexual drives. Some women were sent out to compromise and blackmail men in high places. They then faced ruin unless they co-operated with the order.[19]

All initiates were urged to be 'Insinuating Brothers', to act as spies:

> 'Every person shall be made a spy on another and on all around him…. Friends, relations, enemies, those who are indifferent – all without exception shall be the object of inquiries; he shall attempt to discover their strong side and their weak, their passions, their prejudices, their connections, above all, their actions – in a word, the most detailed information about them.'[20]

All Insinuants were to write reports twice a month so that their superiors would know who was to be trusted in each district. Those higher up were let in on the secret that the Illuminati's aim was revolution and anarchy to overthrow civilization and return to Nature – to win power and riches, to undermine secular or religious government and to attain the mastery of the world.[21]

Weishaupt's programme was unveiled on 1 May 1776. Its founding is thought to have generated the annual May Day celebrations among his pagan supporters and 'May-day' as a distress call among anti Weishauptians who deemed the founding of Weishaupt's order a catastrophic day. However, there is an equally strong view that the 'May-day' distress call came from the French *M'aidez*.

Weishaupt's order was funded by the Sionist House of Rothschild and four other Jews.[22] It combined the traditions of the Priory of Sion (the Merovingian Kingship of Jerusalem, Kabbalism, the Egyptian Rose-Croix, the Rosicrucian Invisible College, the scientific research of Boyle's Royal Society, the rationalism of Descartes and Newton, and Rousseau's restatement of the New Atlantis) with the traditions of Templarism (republicanism, the Manichaeism of the Cathars and revenge for the death of Jacques de Molay).[23]

Weishaupt wanted both Sion and the Templars in his new organization, which included the rational Enlightenment, Rousseau's revolt against it and the Manichaean Catharism which had inspired the Templars. The House of Lorraine and the Jacobite Templars could unite on the overthrow of the Bourbon king – the House of Lorraine because it wanted the throne for Sion, and the Templars to avenge Jacques de Molay.

Franklin, Jefferson and the Great Seal of America

On 4 July 1776, the day the Declaration of Independence was adopted, Benjamin Franklin, Thomas Jefferson and John Adams were appointed by the Continental Congress to design the Great Seal of the new United States of America.[24] They were to be assisted by the portrait painter Pierre Eugene du Simitière.[25]

The four were clear that there should be a two-sided seal that would be America's national coat of arms. It would be in the tradition of Edward the Confessor's seal, created during his reign (1042–66). Franklin proposed showing Moses, Pharaoh and a pillar of fire. Jefferson proposed showing the Israelites, a cloud by day and a pillar of fire by night. Adams proposed showing Hercules. Du Simitière proposed a shield divided into six (representing England, Scotland, Ireland, Holland, France and Germany) and the goddess of liberty. Congress rejected the first committee's proposals in January 1777.[26]

We have seen that Benjamin Franklin, having long been a Rosicrucian Sionist, had been sent to Paris as a colonial ambassador to seek military and financial help for the colonies in December 1776.[27] While there he came into contact with the Illuminati, perhaps with Weishaupt himself. Franklin was widely popular, as he embodied the new spirit of revolution in the New World, and his picture was displayed everywhere, on snuff boxes and in broadsheets. It would have been natural for Weishaupt or one of his agents to contact such a popular figure who embodied Illuminati revolutionary principles.

From this meeting Franklin learned the esoteric significance of the number 13 – the thirteenth being the day in October 1307 that the Templar persecution began – and the Illuminati plan for the 13 American colonies which were to become a New World democracy, a philosophical Atlantis.[28] He also saw a sketch of the seal Weishaupt had produced for the Illuminati, which sought to unite Sion and the Templars. The Illuminati Seal's reverse side showed a Templar 13-layered, four-sided pyramid with its capstone missing. Above was a triangle in sun-rays and within it the All-Seeing Eye of Osiris and Sion, which some said represented Weishaupt's spying system. On the bottom layer in Latin was a date, 1776, the year Weishaupt founded the Illuminati. The seal represented the Secret Doctrine of the Ages – the plan to build a new Atlantis in the New World. Weishaupt adopted the reverse side of the seal as the symbol of the Illuminati when he founded it on 1 May 1776.[29]

The esoteric significance of the pyramid was connected with Atlantis. There was a belief that the university of Atlantis, where all arts and sciences originated, was housed in a pyramid with an observatory at the top where the stars could be studied.[30] This university was the prototype of the 'Invisible College' of Sionist Rosicrucianism. The 13 layers of bricks symbolized the 13 colonies that would become a New Atlantis under Sion's watchful (spying?) eye. The 13 letters in *Annuit Coeptis* ('Announcing the Birth') suggested 13 October 1307, when Templarism was first persecuted, and the 13 degrees of Templar initiation.[31]

The obverse side of the seal showed a tufted phoenix resembling an eagle. Only one phoenix is held to exist at any time and it is believed to live for 500 years. It nests in Arabia. It dies by making a nest of aromatic boughs and spices and setting it on fire. A new phoenix is born from its ashes. So the tufted phoenix is a Freemasonic symbol of Atlantis reborn in America. It holds 13 arrows and a 13-leafed plant and above it, in a cloud, are 13 stars. There are 13 letters in the inscription *E Pluribus Unum* ('Out of Many, One' – union, the unification of states and eventually nations).

The Illuminati Seal as a whole suggested the union of Sion (the eye) and Templarism (the pyramid) within the reborn (phoenix) Atlantean university.[32]

Weishaupt had the idea of protecting his new order by infiltrating Templar lodges and concealing it within them. In 1777 he became a Freemason, joining the eclectic Masonic lodge Theodore of Good Counsel in Munich.[33] By the end of 1778 he announced the idea of merging the Illuminati and Freemasonry.[34] By mid-1779 the Munich Masonic lodge was under the influence of the Illuminati. There were now 60 active members of the Illuminati and another thousand people were affiliated.[35]

A further opportunity for infiltration arose when the Duke of Orléans, cousin of Louis XVI, an initiate into Templar Grand-Lodge Freemasonry and a Grand Master in 1771, converted National Freemasonry to Grand Orient Freemasonry in 1773. Grand Orient Freemasonry embraced Utopian socialism and took as its cry 'Liberty, Equality, Fraternity'.[36] In December 1781 an understanding was reached between the Grand Orient Freemasons and the Illuminati and a combined order was adopted. It had three classes: Preparation, Novice, Minerval-and-Illuminatus. As the Illuminati degrees were in the first class, all Masons had to become Illuminati before they could progress.

The Illuminati, now hidden within the Grand Orient, moved to Frankfurt and spread throughout Germany and Austria. They were poised for revolution. By 1782 the Rothschilds were controlling the Frankfurt headquarters of the new order.[37]

In 1778 Franklin, already a Templar, joined the Illuminati lodge *Neuf Soeurs* ('Nine Sisters', i.e. the Muses) and assisted in the initiation of Voltaire, who had been a Sionist Freemason for over 30 years. In due course Franklin became Grand Master of this Illuminati lodge and in 1782 he joined a Templar Freemasonic lodge, the Royal Lodge of Commanders of the Temple West.[38]

Congress was still considering the designs for the Great Seal of America. In 1780 it set up a Second Committee, which consulted Hopkinson, designer of the American flag. He had used an unfinished pyramid on a 1778 50-dollar colonial bank note.[39] In 1781 Franklin seems to have sent back from Paris a copy of the Illuminati's republican doctrine and a replica of the unfinished pyramid and seal. As Thomas Paine met Franklin in Paris in that year and became a Grand Orient Freemason, and therefore a member of the Illuminati, it is likely that *he* took the replica back to the United States for Franklin and delivered it in time to come to the attention of the Third Committee.

The Third Committee, formed on 4 May 1782, commissioned Charles Thomson and William Barton to design the Great Seal of the United States, using the Freemasonic symbolism of the unfinished pyramid surmounted by an eye. Their design for the reverse is now on the one-dollar bill, which shows the Illuminati symbol Weishaupt adopted in 1776. There is also an inscription, *Novo Ordo Seclorum (Seculorum)*, 'New Secular Order' or 'New Order of the Ages'. This was translated by Templar Mason Henry A. Wallace, the US Secretary of Agriculture from 1933 to 1940, who was in charge of presenting the New Deal, as 'the New Deal of the Ages'. In 1933 or 1934 Wallace drew Templar Mason President Roosevelt's attention to the image's New Deal connotations, as a result of which Roosevelt, a descendant of the Illuminatus Clinton Roosevelt, put it on the one-dollar bill. The full Latin text on the reverse thus reads: 'Announcing the Birth of a New Secular Order' (or 'New World Order').

The Templar pyramid suggests there is a plan to build a New Atlantis in a New World and that it is America's spiritual destiny to complete its building. The Utopian pyramid is in fact a world government in which all nations are bricks (point seven in Weishaupt's programme), a new Tower of Babel where all languages will be heard. The Templars will build it under the watchful eye of Sion and it will be complete when the sun-rayed capstone, symbolizing the Merovingian successor to the King of Jerusalem, the work of Sion, is lowered into place.

On the obverse side Thomson drew a phoenix under a cloud of 13 stars,[40] a symbol of Atlantis reborn in America, as we have seen.

In March 1785 the Illuminati were suppressed after incriminating information was supplied to the Elector of Bavaria by someone high in the Illuminati command. On 10 July the Elector received more damaging evidence: the news that an Illuminati initiate, Jacob Lang, who had been sent as an emissary to Silesia, had been struck and killed by lightning on the way.[41] A list of 2,000 members of lodges in seven countries (France, Belgium, Denmark, Sweden, Poland, Hungary and Italy) had been found sewn in his clothes. It could be that the list was planted to give the Elector an excuse to ban the Illuminati. The Elector duly did ban the Illuminati and published the documents, which later appeared in Robison's *Proofs of a Conspiracy*, 1798. Weishaupt took refuge with the Duke of Saxe-Gotha, who was related to the Hanoverian English Royal Family.[42]

The third and final Congress of the Illuminati took place in Frankfurt in 1786. Weishaupt's recommendations of the previous year were adopted:

'(1) Pantheism for the higher degrees, atheism for the lower degrees and the populace; (2) Communism of goods, women and general concerns; (3) the destruction of the Church, and all forms of Christianity, and the removal of all existing human governance to make way for a universal republic in which the utopian ideas of complete liberty from existing social, moral and religious restraint, absolute equality and social fraternity, should reign. When these ends should be attained, but not till then, the secret work of the atheistic Freemasons should cease.'[43]

The Congress decreed the death of Louis XVI and Gustavus III of Sweden.[44] Louis XVI was beheaded in 1793; Gustav was shot and mortally wounded by Captain Jacob Johan Ankarström at the Stockholm opera house in March 1792.

The Grand Orient Templars absorbed Weishaupt's degrees[45] and the Illuminati's activities continued within the Grand Orient and Scottish Rite Templar lodges.

Jefferson and John Adams joined Franklin in France in 1784 to negotiate a treaty with France following the end of the American War of Independence. Franklin returned to America in 1785[46] and Jefferson succeeded him as resident US minister to the French government. He remained in France till 1789 and is reputed to have been initiated into a Templar lodge there and to have met Weishaupt. It is likely that the Templar lodge was Grand Orient, with the Illuminati degrees hidden within it. He thought the French revolution 'so beautiful a revolution'.

So the Illuminati's attitudes were taken back to America by the two ambassadors to France in the 1780s, Franklin (in 1785) and Jefferson (in 1789), hence the gift (in 1885–6) of the Statue of Liberty to the American people from the people of France to symbolize the revolutionary links between America and France.

By 1785 there were 15 Illuminati lodges in the 13 colonies. The Columbian Lodge of the Order of the Illuminati was established in New York City and its members included Clinton Roosevelt, an ancestor of Franklin D. Roosevelt. A lodge in Virginia was identified with Thomas Jefferson.[47] The Illuminati were now entrenched in America, and the men most responsible for bringing them there were Franklin, Jefferson and John Adams.

Why did people join these Masonic orders? What advantages were there for them and what drew Masons to join different groups within Freemasonry? Were Freemasonry's leaders good persuaders, recruiters and organizers? Or did Freemasonry's benign non-Christian philosophy and its appeal to self-interest – secretly aiding fellow brethren – prove irresistibly attractive? We have asked this question before, and the answer remains the same. In the 1780s it was socially desirable to attach oneself to a hierarchical organization in which one could progress and be helped in one's career by influential people who acted as if they were family members. The ambience was free from the extremes of religion, but drew on early cultures, and there was a loyalty among members which meant that political issues could be openly discussed without repercussions from State authorities.

According to J. R. Church, John Adams was the founder of the Masonic lodges in New England, and he fell out with Jefferson, whom he accused of using the lodges that he himself had founded for subversive Illuminati purposes. Three letters by Adams on this matter are in the Wittenburg Square Library in Philadelphia. Some believe that the Illuminati manipulated Franklin, Jefferson and Adams until John Adams realized what was going on.[48] Weishaupt, we have seen, intended to deceive initiates and it is possible that Franklin, Jefferson and John Adams (and Thomas Paine) were all deceived, mistaking a destructive programme for a benevolent one. (It is an interesting question as to whether the Founding Fathers were aware of Weishaupt's Satanism, which led him to take such delight in deceiving Christians.)

Jefferson was certainly naïve about the Illuminati. He criticized Illuminism, but excused Weishaupt:

'Wishaupt [sic] seems to be an enthusiastic philanthropist. He is among those … who believe in the infinite perfectibility of man. He thinks he may in time be rendered so perfect that he will be able to govern himself in every circumstance, so as to injure none, to do all the good he can, to leave government no occasion to exercise their powers over him and, of course, to render political government useless.'[49]

In the same passage he writes of the 'ravings against him of Robison' and believes that Weishaupt's secrecy was due to the 'despot and priests' under whom he lived.

Jefferson's beliefs, like Franklin's, coincided with aspects of Weishaupt's. Both Jefferson and Franklin were rationalists who doubted the value of metaphysics as being 'unamenable to the test of our senses'.[50]

It must be pointed out that though Franklin, Jefferson and John Adams (and Paine) were all Illuminati initiates, they were all initiated *after* the American Revolution and so, strictly speaking, the Illuminati's ideas did not influence the course of the revolution from the Boston Tea Party to the Declaration of Independence, only its aftermath and the constitution. Nevertheless it must also be borne in mind that the Illuminati's ideals were passed down from these three Founding Fathers and that they are still strong today.[51] For example, they are reflected in the current dollar bill, as we have seen. They coloured the legacy of the Founding Fathers by influencing the intellectual climate that produced the constitution and its aftermath, the Freemasonic State that the Founding Fathers drew up to embody independence.

In Part Two we have traced how English Baconian, Sionist, Rosicrucian Freemasonry may have reached Virginia via John Smith and how Templar Freemasonry came to London with James I. It may have been exported to America with the Virginia expedition and was certainly well established by the Boston Tea Party of 1773. We have seen how American Templar Freemasonry triumphed over English Freemasonry (which was associated with colonial rule) and shaped, and was shaped by, Enlightenment Deism, which influenced all the Founding Fathers.

Now we have seen that Illuminatist Freemasonry, a more malign and Satanistic influence deliberately hidden within the Grand Orient by Weishaupt, came to America with the Great Seal. This bears on events in the twentieth and twenty-first centuries, for Weishaupt's programme of world government has guided the world-government thinking of what I call the Syndicate, a network of powerful billionaire families that work in the USA and Europe for the end of all nation-states, and also the Grand-Orient thinking that brought about the creation of the Soviet Union as a stepping-stone to the creation of a world government.

Both the American Templar and Illuminatist strains of Freemasonry lead towards world government, one in a more benign way than the other. We shall now consider how they affected the subsequent history of the United States and what this means for us today.

PART THREE

Consequences of the Founders' Vision

CHAPTER 7

A FREEMASONIC STATE

T he origins of the American constitutional State lie in American constitutional challenges to the British understanding of Parliament's rule in the colonial time. These came after the French and Indian War in 1760, the last of a series of wars that had been fought since 1689 between France and Great Britain, round Indian alliances, for control of the vast colonial territory of North America. Now the French withdrew from America and the native Americans ceased to be a threat; and the Americans and British ceased to be united by a common enemy.[1]

In 1760 the map of North America showed a wide chunk of British control along the east coast from Maine to coastal Georgia, extending 100–200 miles inland, then native-American control of a buffer zone which separated the British from the French interior. In the south, Florida was Spanish. The population of the North American colonies had risen from 4,646 in 1630 to 1.6 million in 1760. There were many well-built towns, a homegrown culture and an economy recovering from the wars. In 1763, under the Paris peace settlement, Britain acquired Canada, Florida and all of the continent east of the Mississippi, a vast swathe to bring under control. On paper, British supremacy in North America was unchallengeable, but the American settlers no longer looked to Britain to protect them from the French, and they had begun to find a voice.

The Freemasonic Drive to Independence in 1776

Writs of Assistance were first issued in 1751. They were general search warrants which helped the British government enforce trade and navigation laws by searching houses for smuggled goods without needing to detail specific houses or goods. In 1761 in Massachusetts, James Otis, a supporter of John Adams, representing Boston merchants, attacked their constitutionality with great elegance. Speaking in the Council Chamber of the State House, he argued on a basis of John Locke's concept of a higher law and maintained that colonists had the right to be represented before being taxed. Nevertheless, the legality of Writs of Assistance was confirmed in England in 1762. They then became a colonial grievance in America and when they were authorized by the Townshend Acts of 1767 they were challenged in court in each of the 13 colonies and refused in eight.[2]

The Parson's Cause case involved Anglican ministers in colonial Virginia. Church ministers were paid in pounds of tobacco until in 1755 and 1758 laws restricted their salaries to currency at twopence per pound of tobacco, when tobacco was selling at sixpence per pound. A royal veto of 1759 encouraged church ministers to sue in court for back pay. In 1763 the Templar Freemason Patrick Henry defended a Hanover County parish against a suit by Reverend James Maury. He attacked interference by the Crown, claiming that the king was a father to his subjects, and restricted damages to one penny. In 1769 an Act was passed in England specifying that tobacco should sell for twopence, and church ministers stopped protesting.[3]

Under the Treaty of Paris of 1763, ending the Seven Years War which affected Europe and the colonies, Britain took possession of Canada, east and west Florida, all territory east of the Mississippi in North America and St Vincent, Tobago and Dominica in the Caribbean. The British Empire in America was thus greatly expanded, but expenditure on it rose from £6.5 million to £14.5 million a year. Most British people felt that the American colonies should help defray this additional expenditure and government officers in London felt the same. Their priority was to preserve British military control in the new territories, especially against the native Americans, who kept up guerrilla attacks until 1765. As such military control had been established for the locals' protection, the British felt that the colonials should pay an increased contribution.

Taxes continued to be a contentious issue. The Sugar Act of 1764 imposed taxes that affected New York's merchants, who traded with the West Indies, and the De Lancey family spoke up for American liberty against the interference of the English Parliament. They also refused to obey the Quartering Act, which required colonists to support imperial soldiers stationed in America. In Pennsylvania, Benjamin Franklin and Joseph Galloway tried to secure the revoking of William Penn's proprietary charter, hoping to replace Penn as owner of the lands. In North and South Carolina Americans defied the authority of British aristocrats, and in Virginia and Maryland there was defiance of the Currency Act of 1764.

In 1765, taxes were introduced on stamps. In several ports there was opposition to collecting this tax – in Boston the Freemason Samuel Adams led the American Sons of Liberty against it and in Virginia Patrick Henry opposed it – and the Stamp Act finally had to be repealed, as London merchants were suffering from the American boycott. The Townshend Duties Act of 1767 then imposed taxes on lead, glass, paint, paper and tea, and all were repealed except the tax on tea. As we have seen, this resulted in the Boston massacre of 1770, when British sentries shot five rioters dead. From then on the Americans were opposed to the British.

After a boom there was a recession. With the East India Company on the verge of bankruptcy, Parliament passed a Tea Act on 10 May 1773 that allowed the company a refund of import duties paid on tea stored in London if it were shipped to America. English-Indian tea could thus undercut Dutch tea, which most Americans drank, as it was cheaper. We have seen that this united American resistance and led to Templars organizing the Boston Tea Party of 17 December 1773.[4]

Six months later, in May 1774, a ship arrived in Boston with details of King George III's retaliation: the four punitive 'Intolerable Acts'.[5] As already related, the Americans retaliated and on 5 September 1774 the First Continental Congress convened at Carpenters' Hall, Philadelphia, to plan action against the British. Its President was a Templar Freemason and the Provincial Grand Master of Virginia, Peyton Randolph. Samuel Adams of the Sons of Liberty attended, together with Templar Freemason Paul Revere.

In February 1775 the Massachusetts Provincial Congress announced plans to resist the British with arms. As already explained, in April 1775 4,000 colonial Americans attacked the British troops at Concord, outside Boston, and afterwards, at Congress's suggestion, several colonial militias prepared for more conflict.

Tracts denying Parliament's power over the colonies were now written by Thomas Jefferson, John Adams, James Wilson and Alexander Hamilton, but they all stopped short of calling for independence. On 19 April 1775 Thomas Paine – whom Franklin had met in England and had sent to Philadelphia in November 1774 to help edit his *Pennsylvania Magazine* – argued in the magazine that America should demand independence, not just less taxation. Franklin had returned from 11 years in England in March 1775 and may have been behind Paine's article – he may have used Paine to say the unsayable. On 10 May Franklin was a delegate at the Second Continental Congress. George Washington, a Virginian Templar Freemason whose Grand Master had been Peyton Randolph, was also a delegate, as was another Templar Freemason from Virginia, Thomas Jefferson. The Second Continental Congress allowed the raising of a continental army.

Then, in December 1775 Paine wrote a pamphlet, *Common Sense*, that called for American independence. He debunked all claims that kings deserve loyalty and wrote, 'We have it in our power to begin the world over again.'[6] It was printed in January 1776 and sold 100,000 copies. Again, it may have been inspired by Franklin, who increasingly seemed to be the key figure in the winning of American independence, having published 126 newspaper articles critical of British policy between 1765 and 1775.[7]

In the following months the colonies were split. New England and Virginia (where Freemasonry was strongest) were prepared to risk independence; the more southern colonies opposed it, fearing uprisings from native Americans, slaves and frontiersmen. Congress issued a call to colonies to organize their own government as states. It seemed as if a break with Great Britain was imminent and in June 1776 a committee was set up to draft a statement of the reasons for this decision. The Freemasons Franklin and Jefferson had met at the second Continental Congress in May 1775 and were both on this committee, as were John Adams, Roger Sherman and Robert Livingstone.

Franklin and Adams had been impressed by the 33-year-old Jefferson's talent and they allowed him to be the main author of the Declaration of Independence. Jefferson drafted the document in two weeks, working in his lodgings, the second-floor parlour of the home of Jacob Graff, a German bricklayer. Although he was writing a State paper, he sought to express the American way of thinking, addressing it 'to the opinions of mankind'. He proclaimed the freedom of the 13 colonies from British rule and made the first formal pronouncement by an organized group of people of the right to government by choice. In accordance with eighteenth-century Deist-Enlightenment political theory, he affirmed the natural rights of man and the doctrine of government by contract (a concept developed by Locke and Rousseau). Congress felt that George III had violated the contract and grievances were listed, followed by the declaration of the right and duty to revolt. Jefferson proclaimed the self-evident truths of man's equality and unalienable right to life, liberty and the pursuit of happiness as well as people's right to alter their government when 'a long train of abuse' reduced them to living 'under absolute despotism'. In the context of the time, this was political innovation of the highest order.

Franklin and Adams made small alterations to the document, and Congress deleted a condemnation of slavery and the slave trade, which would have alienated the Southern states and perhaps prevented them from signing.

The Declaration was handed to President John Hancock on 2 July 1776 and adopted on 4 July 1776 (*see* Appendix V) in the same Council Chamber of the State House where James Otis had argued against the Writs of Assistance, overlooking the square where the Boston massacre had taken place. Its adoption has been commemorated annually as Independence Day, a national holiday, ever since.

The Declaration of Independence was read from the balcony of the Council Chamber of the State House to citizens of Philadelphia assembled in the square below on 8 July 1776 and the Liberty Bell was rung. Cast in 1752 and cracked, the bell was inscribed with a text from Leviticus: 'Proclaim Liberty throughout all the Land unto all the Inhabitants thereof.' The Declaration was signed a month later by 56 signatories.

The Declaration of Independence included the phrase 'Nature's God', as we have seen, meaning that with their reason people could infer from the natural world the existence and nature of God. Its natural and 'unalienable' rights included religion, and there was no reference to any separation between Church and State. This crept in between 1776 and 1787. As we shall see, this separation was not due to independence – a nationalistic desire to eclipse the power of the British Church – but to Freemasonry.

On 2 July, two days before publishing the Declaration, Congress voted for independence. War with the British government was now inevitable. Virtually all – 31 out of 33 – of the military generals under Washington were Templar Freemasons, including Richard Montgomery, David Wooster, Hugh Mercer, Arthur St Clair, Horatio Gates, Israel Putnam, John Dixon, Joseph Frye, William Maxwell and Elias Dayton.[8]

I have dealt with the details of the War of Independence (1775–83) elsewhere.[9] In brief, short of troops, Britain purchased three-fifths of its 30,000 troops from the Landgrave of Hesse and attacked Massachusetts in 1775. There was a British offensive in the northern colonies, notably Massachusetts, throughout 1776 and 1777. American rebels besieged British held Boston, but they were defeated after an abortive invasion of Canada and suffered reverses in New York and Pennsylvania in 1777. The British military leadership was Freemasonic: Sir William Howe, Brigadier-General Augustine Prevost and 34 senior colonels were all Freemasons. The Templar Freemasonic American military leaders captured General Burgoyne at the battle of Saratoga in October 1777 and as a result the French entered the war. The American–French alliance of 1778 turned the tide of the war in favour of the Americans. The French sent 6,000 soldiers as Franklin had requested, and Spain (1779) and the Netherlands (1780) also joined the war on the side of the Americans. Washington, co-ordinating an attack on land with French naval support, with help from the French Templar Freemason Marquis de Lafayette, brilliantly trapped General Cornwallis, commander of the British forces, and forced the surrender of 8,000 men at Yorktown in October 1781. A band played 'The World Turned Upside Down'.

London blamed Templar Freemasonry for the humiliating British defeat, suggesting that Cornwallis, Clinton and the Howe brothers were all Templar Freemasons and had conspired to lose to their fellow

Freemasons. In 1781 General Howe and Admiral Howe were accused by 'Cicero' of betraying their country to Benjamin Franklin.[10]

Under the peace settlement following Cornwallis's surrender, the western boundary of the USA was the Mississippi. Britain retained Canada, Spain received the area from Florida to the Mississippi and everything west of the river. France, the USA's ally, received nothing.

The consequences of the British defeat were clearly visible. From now on the sea war mainly comprised naval battles between Britain and France, Spain and the Netherlands. After 1780, Spanish and Dutch fleets controlled British waters. A peace treaty was signed in Paris in 1783.

The Freemasonic Constitution of 1787

The constitutional arrangements for the newly independent colonies were slow in coming. In mid-1776 Congress had adopted Richard Henry Lee's resolution 'That these United Colonies are, and of right ought to be, free and independent States'. On Lee's proposal, work began on the Articles of Confederation, the first constitution.

The Articles of Confederation were based on Franklin's Albany Plan of 1754, which proposed colonial union (*see* Appendix IV). (As we have seen, the British Board of Trade had convened the Albany Congress to cement the loyalty of the Iroquois League against the French and had not adopted Franklin's plan.) The Articles of Confederation (*see* Appendix VI) were approved on 15 November 1777, after Saratoga. By approving them, the Continental Congress agreed a new system that would be a federation of states, and the confederacy was to be called the United States of America, which would be a 'perpetual union'. Each state was to ratify the Articles of Confederation. This took until March 1781.

There was now a loose association of states held together by the Articles of Confederation, with a weak central government. The new national State did not work. Sovereignty was vested in 13 states that were more concerned with their own local interests than with the national interest. The localizing of sovereignty in the states may have been a reaction against British central authority. In theory, Congress could conduct foreign policy, make war, make military appointments, borrow money and run the postal service. In fact, it had no power to enforce its requests and there was corruption and incompetence too.

The economy was in depression and the national government had inherited a war debt of $60 million. The revolutionary soldiers had not been fully paid. In 1781–2 the victorious general, George Washington, wintered with the Continental Congress in Philadelphia. He made efforts to secure payment for the army, and in 1782 received a letter from Colonel Lewis Nicola urging him to use the army to make himself king. Washington indignantly declined. He seems to have believed that America would become a monarchy and also in the necessity of the principle of monarchy, but kingship contradicted his Templar Freemasonic philosophy, which was republican.[11]

By the end of 1786 government by the Continental Congress had ceased to be effective, although claims by some states to western lands were settled and the Northwest Ordinance established government north of the Ohio river. However, the confederation had given the nation the experience of operating a constitution under a written document and laid the basis for the present form of the US government.

The government of the Continental Congress muddled through for six years until May 1787, when the Constitutional Convention of 55 delegates met in the Pennsylvania State House, Philadelphia (now called Independence Hall). Its aim was 'to render the Constitution of the Federal Government adequate to the exigencies of the Union'.

The concept of federalism had been taken from Freemasonry, in particular the federalism of the Grand Lodge system of Freemasonry, which had been set down in writing in Anderson's *Constitutions* of 1723 (*see* Appendix III), so the fact that the new State was not working amounted to a crisis for the federalist idea and therefore a crisis for Freemasonry.

Federalism had developed in Freemasonry following the meeting of four London lodges of Rosicrucian Freemasons on 24 June 1717 at the Apple Tree tavern in Charles Street, Covent Garden, to form a Grand Lodge. Doctor James Anderson had been one of the seven men present. A Presbyterian minister in London who had been born in Aberdeen, and a freethinker, he had been chosen to draw up a constitution which would dechristianize the Grand Lodge. His new constitution, *Ancient Charges of a Free Mason*, turned Freemasonry into an open organization behind which secret organizations could hide. Freemasonry had declared itself Christian so that the ignorant could be recruited and deceived. Officially, "'Tis now thought more expedient only to oblige [members of the Brotherhood] to that Religion in which all men agree, leaving their particular Opinions to themselves.'[12] And so men of all faiths could attend semi-dechristianized lodges. Prayers in English lodges ended with the name of Christ until 1813, when the Duke of Sussex made English Freemasonry Deistic, completing its dechristianization.[13]

Just as Weishaupt had based the organization of his Order of the Illuminati on the Jesuit structure, so Dr Anderson based his *Constitutions* on the regulations of the Jesuits' Society of Jesus, even to the point of pinching their title. St Ignatius of Loyola (1491–1556) had already written his *Constitutions*, in which he had laid down that his followers should abandon the chanting of the divine offices, physical punishments, penitential dress and chapter government for the more authoritative regime of his order. When he died there were 1,000 Jesuits divided into 12 administrative units called provinces.[14] To Anderson, lodges were like these provincial units and the Grand Lodge like the Order of the Society of Jesus.

By 1787, the Masonic federal system was already operating in the 13 colonies, the states being independent internally but units of the federal government externally. There was a federal union of sovereign states, with a federal government to operate that union, based on internally independent lodges within a federal Grand Lodge. The Articles of Confederation, however, had failed to deliver a national government, sound currency and consistent judicial system. It was therefore natural that patriotic American Freemasons should fall back on the Masonic model to strengthen the growing American nation. This federal structure of independent lodges passed into the US constitution.

Delegates at the Constitutional Convention of 1787 had read the philosophers: Locke, who saw government as a social contract between ruler and ruled; Hume, who regarded republicanism as 'a dangerous novelty'; Adam Smith, who saw a State in terms of the marketplace; and Montesquieu, whose *The Spirit of Laws* analysed the relationship between political and social structures. But they took their three principles from

Freemasonry: the investment of power in a man's office, not in the man; the adoption of a system of checks and balances between executive, legislative and judicial branches of government; and the adoption of the Masonic federal system of organization.

Henry C. Clausen has brought out the parallel between the federal American constitution and the federal Masonic lodge, writing, 'The significance of Freemasonry's influence on the Constitution cannot be overstated'[15] and:

> 'Since the Masonic federal system of organization was the only pattern for effective organization operating in each of the original Thirteen Colonies, it was natural that patriotic Brethren should turn to the organizational base of the Craft for a model. Regardless of the other forces that affected the formation of the Constitution during the Constitution Convention in 1787, the fact remains that the federalism created is identical to the federalism of the Grand Lodge system of Masonic government created in Anderson's *Constitutions* of 1723.'[16]

The 55 delegates at the Constitutional Convention included the Freemasons Benjamin Franklin, now 81, and George Washington (*see* Appendix IX). Washington, who had led the American army against the most powerful nation on Earth, arrived at the convention the day before it opened and was unanimously chosen President. He could not speak in the debates during the next four months, but his aide-de-camp, Governor Edmund Randolph of Virginia, was his mouthpiece. Randolph proposed that there should be an entirely new basis for the constitution rather than an attempt to tinker with the Articles of Confederation, thus it was the Freemason Washington who was behind the move to scrap the old constitution.

Most of the delegates were strong nationalists. Some, led by Washington and Franklin, wanted a limited national authority without any conditions; two (for example, Hamilton) were monarchists; some, notably Gouverneur Morris of Pennsylvania and John Rutledge of South Carolina, were aristocrats who wanted a national government that was as aristocratic as possible; some, led by James Wilson of Pennsylvania and James Madison of Virginia, were democratic nationalists who wanted a popular base. There were nationalists, including Edmund Randolph, who demanded republican principles and a few delegates wanted no increase in national authority at all.

The principle of a national authority was quickly approved, as was the principle that the new government should have executive, legislative and judicial branches. James Madison, who often stayed with Jefferson at Monticello, his house in Virginia, is called the Father of the Constitution as, besides making the most accurate record of the progress of the convention, his Virginia plan provided the framework for debate. It had been endorsed by Washington and was proposed on 29 May by Edmund Randolph as 15 resolutions that would demolish the Articles of Confederation and replace them with a strong national government through the domination of the larger states.

The plan saw Congress as bicameral, with the lower house chosen by election and the upper house picked by the lower house from candidates named by state legislatures. Each house's representation was to be a percentage of the total population (i.e. proportional representation). The smaller states, however, supported the New Jersey plan proposed by William Paterson on 14 June. This advocated a one-house legislature elected by states. Larger states wanted proportional representation, smaller states an equal voice. There was something of an impasse between the two plans and Roger Sherman of Connecticut proposed the 'Connecticut Compromise': proportional representation in the House of Representatives and equal representation in the Senate.[17]

The task of resolving the issue was given to a special committee comprising one member from each state. On 5 July the committee recommended Sherman's plan, but there was another compromise over slavery. Representation in the lower house would be based on the total of the white population plus three-fifths of the slave population. (The Southern delegates wanted the whole of the slave population.)

On 16 July the convention accepted equal representation in the Senate, with the House of Representatives to have proportional representation. By 26 July the delegates had also adopted the basic plan of the constitution, scrapping the Articles of Confederation, creating a charter for a 'more perfect Union' and establishing three branches of government – executive, legislative and judicial – which Washington called 'an indivisible system'.

The convention sent the plan to a committee of detail chaired by John Rutledge of South Carolina. Washington's mouthpiece Edmund Randolph provided a proposed draft of the constitution and gave the committee its brief, 'to insert essential principles only' to connect the constitution 'to times and events', and 'to use simple and precise language and general propositions'.[18] In other words, the constitution was to be confined to broad principles and not cluttered with unnecessary detail.

The committee of detail listed 18 specific powers of Congress, including the power 'to make all laws'. It listed what the states were prohibited from doing: from coining money and making treaties to granting titles of nobility. A charter of government had been achieved in ten days.

The draft constitution went back to the convention and from 6 August to 10 September the delegates debated, proceeding from draft clause to draft clause. The first mention of religion was on 20 August, when Pinckney proposed that 'no religious test or qualification shall ever be annexed to any oath of office under the authority of the US'.[19] (Some delegates may have considered religion to be under state rather than national control.)

The convention then approved the draft constitution and sent it to a committee of style. The penmen there included William Samuel Johnson (the chairman), Gouverneur Morris, Madison, Rufus King and Alexander Hamilton (who served under King). The contribution of Gouverneur Morris of Pennsylvania, a close friend of Washington, was arguably the greatest, as he reworded the preamble to throw attention on the people. Instead of 'We the people of the States of New Hampshire, etc. do ordain, declare and establish the following Constitution for the government of ourselves and our posterity' he wrote:

> 'We the People of the United States, In Order to form a more perfect Union, establish Justice, insure domestic Tranquility, provide for the common defence, promote the general Welfare, and secure the Blessings of Liberty to ourselves and our Posterity do ordain and establish this Constitution for the United States of America.'

Morris thus made the people the source of authority, reflecting the English Revolution of Cromwell.[20] He also introduced ambiguity into the text to make the constitution flexible, and Rufus King, a Freemason, inserted a clause forbidding states to pass a law that impaired or rescinded contractual obligations.[21]

The convention approved the final draft and on 17 September the engrossed constitution was read and adopted (*see* Appendix VI). Washington presided on a low rostrum in the Assembly Room of the State House (Independence Hall), where the Declaration of Independence had been approved. On the top of his chair was a carving of a half-sun with two eyes and a nose and 13 rays like hairs. Above it hung a pyramid-shaped plant. Together they formed a Freemasonic symbol. As the delegates signed the new constitution, Benjamin Franklin declared that the sun on Washington's chair was rising, not setting on the new nation.[22] In all, 39 of the 42 remaining delegates signed and then (according to Washington's diary) 'adjourned to the City Tavern, dined together and took a cordial leave of each other'.[23]

By July 1788 the constitution had been ratified by the nine states required to bring it into law, thanks to Washington's quiet authority. So, having been behind the scrapping of the old constitution, Washington was now behind the ratification of the new one.

A Freemasonic *Coup* on the Colonies

The pro-constitution Federalists who wanted sovereignty to be vested in the nation had battled with the anti-constitution Anti-Federalists, who were on the side of state sovereignty, in each state. The battle had been particularly great in Virginia, where the Freemasons Patrick Henry and Richard Henry Lee had spoken out against the constitution, claiming it was a threat to liberty, that a large standing army was a threat to peace, that the new nation's rulers were being given too much power and that the 'great and mighty president' was little less than a monarch. Madison countered these arguments. Virginian Anti-Federalists wanted a second convention, hoping it would undo the work of the first. They wanted to add a Bill of Rights to the constitution to highlight the rights of all citizens.[24]

It cannot be said, however that the Federalists were Templar Freemasons and the Anti-Federalists not Templar Freemasons. Rather, the Federalists had broken free from British rule and sought to replace it with some central American control to make all America a New Atlantis, whereas the Anti-Federalists had broken free from the British monarch and wanted monarchy-free republican state autonomy for their own state. Both centralist and localist opinions and support for national sovereignty and support for state sovereignty were found within Templarism. But it has to be said that support for national sovereignty was more Templar in outlook, and perhaps in ideology, than support for state sovereignty, and the majority of Freemasons were on the side of national sovereignty. In fact, there is an element of North versus South in the Templar divide, with the issue of slavery colouring Patrick Henry's pro-state view. Southerners demanded liberty from central government to continue to use slaves to run their plantations.

Twentieth-century historians have debated the motives of the Founding Fathers. Following the War of Independence and a brief boom there had been an economic depression with business and commodity prices downward and an unstable, depreciating currency that required businessmen to conduct their transactions in goods rather than coin. Many farmers were in debt and foreclosures in 1786 were at a record high. At least 80,000 and perhaps 200,000 Americans had left for England or Canada during the Revolutionary War and their absence had contributed to the economic malaise. Were the drafters and ratifiers of the constitution affected by deteriorating social and political conditions under the confederation from 1781 to 1787, and were they acting to safeguard their own property interests?[25]

It has to be said that there is no evidence that the Founding Fathers were motivated by personal gain. Many believe that they were concerned to create a political system that would give the central government power to act for the general welfare amid the deteriorating economic conditions. They were, however, Freemasons, and they had used the Masonic model of Anderson's *Constitutions* as the most effective one available. We cannot help asking: to what extent were they acting on behalf of Freemasonry rather than on behalf of their own philanthropic, charitable instincts? It has to be asked: was there a Freemasonic plan to seize control of the former colonies and turn them into a Freemasonic State? Was the convention a conspiracy against state democracy, and is that why there was opposition from the consciences of the Templar Freemasons Patrick Henry and Richard Henry Lee? Did the Constitutional Convention amount to a Freemasonic *coup d'état*? Were the new Federal government, the constitution and the presidency all aspects of a Freemasonic *coup* on the 13 colonies?

Were Freemasonic considerations also behind the choice of the first President? At the time, George Washington had retired to Mount Vernon 'under his vine and fig tree', as he often said, echoing Solomon. He was the only man who could give the presidency prestige in Europe, but he prevaricated and his reluctance made him even more popular. It reminded people of Lucius Quinctius Cincinnatus, who left his farm to become dictator at Rome in 458 BC and to rescue a consular army surrounded by the Aequi. He defeated the enemy in a single day and then returned to his farm. The Founding Fathers had georgic values – in the sense that Virgil's *Georgics* and, long before them, Hesiod's *Works and Days* were about the practicalities of managing estates such as tree-care – as opposed to pastoral values, which represent the idealized view of the town-dweller romanticizing the countryside. Jefferson was also a Founder-Farmer, and Washington's return to his land struck a chord in all the georgics of the time.[26] The electors were chosen in early 1789 and on 4 February George Washington was swept to power, having received every electoral vote. He accepted reluctantly and left Mount Vernon on 16 April. He was inaugurated on 30 April and stood on the balcony of Federal Hall above a cheering crowd. To what extent had he been urged into office by Freemasons?

Certainly many of the Founding Fathers who took part in the War of Independence, the signing of the Declaration of Independence and the drawing up of the Articles of Confederation and the constitution were Freemasons. Below is a list compiled by Ronald E. Heaton:[27]

Arnold, Benedict. General Officer

Baylies, Hodijah. Officer

Bedford, Gunning, Jr. Signer of the Constitution

Biddle, Edward. Signer of Articles of Association

Blair, John. Signer of the Constitution

Brearley, David. Signer of the Constitution

Broom, Jacob. Signer of the Constitution

Carroll, Daniel. Signer of Articles of Confederation and the
    Constitution

Cary, Richard. Officer

Caswell, Richard. Signer of Articles of Association

Clinton, James. General Officer

Dayton, Jonathan. Signer of the Constitution

Dayton, Elias. General Officer

Dickinson, John. Signer of Articles of Association, Confederation,
    and the Constitution

Ellery, William. Signer of Declaration of Independence, and Articles
    of Confederation

Fitzgerald, John. Officer

Franklin, Benjamin. Signer of Declaration, and the Constitution

Frye, Joseph. General Officer

Gilman, Nicholas. Signer of the Constitution

Gist, Mordecai. General Officer

Glover, John. General Officer

Greaton, John. General Officer

Hancock, John. Signer of Declaration, and Articles of Confederation

Hand, Edward. General Officer

Harnett, Cornelius. Signer of Articles of Confederation

Hewes, Joseph. Signer of Declaration, and Articles of Association

Hogun, James. General Officer

Hooper, William. Signer of Declaration, and Articles of Association

Humphreys, Charles. Signer of Articles of Association

Humphreys, David. Officer

King, Rufus. Signer of the Constitution

Knox, Henry. General Officer

Lafayette, Marie-Joseph Paul Yves Roch Gilbert du Motier de.
    General Officer

Laurens, Henry. Signer of Articles of Confederation

Lincoln, Benjamin. General Officer

McHenry, James. Signer of the Constitution, and assistant secretary to Washington

Maxwell, William. General Officer

Mercer, Hugh. General Officer

Montgomery, Richard. General Officer

Muhlenberg, John Peter Gabriel. General Officer

Nixon, John. General Officer

Paine, Robert Treat. Signer of Declaration, and Articles of Association

Palfrey, William. Officer

Parsons, Samuel Holden. General Officer

Paterson, John. General Officer

Paterson, William. Signer of the Constitution

Putnam, Israel. General Officer

Putnam, Rufus. General Officer

Randolph, Edmund. Aide-de-Camp to Washington

Randolph, Peyton. Signer of Articles of Association, first President: of Continental Congress

Roberdeau, Daniel. Signer of Articles of Confederation

St Clair, Arthur. General Officer

Smith, Jonathan Bayard. Signer of Articles of Confederation

Stark, John. General Officer

Steuben, Baron Friedrich Wilhelm August Heinrich Ferdinand von. General Officer

Stockton, Richard. Signer of Declaration

Sullivan, John. Signer of Articles of Association, and General Officer

Sumner, Jethro. General Officer

Thompson, William. General Officer

Varnum, James Mitchell. General Officer

Walker, John. Officer Walton, George. Signer of Declaration

Washington, George. Signer of Articles of Association, and the Constitution, and Commander-in-Chief of the Continental Force

Weedon, George. General Officer

Whipple, William. Signer of Declaration

Williams, Otho Holland. General Officer

Woodford, William. General Officer
Wooster, David. General Officer

This list focuses on the War of Independence and the three documents. It excludes Thomas Jefferson, who was not at the Constitutional Convention as he was in Paris, Samuel and John Adams, Patrick Henry, Richard Henry Lee, Paul Revere and many others who, we have seen, were associated with the independence movement. Which of the Founding Fathers were *not* Freemasons? James Madison? Alexander Hamilton? Both of them were mouthpieces for Washington at different times, regardless of whether they were Freemasons or not.

What can be said with certainty is that the consequence of the constitution was that America became a Freemasonic State. At the time of his election in 1789, the first President, George Washington, was Grand Master of Alexandria Lodge no. 22 in Virginia. His Vice President, John Adams, was also a Freemason. The oath of office was administered by Robert Livingston, Grand Master of New York's Grand Lodge. The Marshall of the day was a Freemason, General Jacob Morton. Washington's escort was General Morgan Lewis, a Freemason. The Bible used for the oath was a Masonic edition from St John's Lodge no. 1 of New York.[28]

Three of Washington's first Cabinet of four were Freemasons: Thomas Jefferson, head of the Department of Foreign Affairs, Edmund Randolph, Attorney General, and Henry Knox, Secretary of War. That left the position of Secretary of the Treasury. Washington had wanted Robert Morris of Philadelphia, the financier of the revolution, but he declined and Washington appointed Alexander Hamilton, his former aide-de-camp.[29] Twenty-four of Washington's major-generals and 30 of his 33 brigadier-generals were Freemasons, so it would be extraordinary if Alexander Hamilton had not been a Freemason.[30]

We have already seen that of the 56 signers of the Declaration of Independence, 53 may have been Master Masons[31] and that the model for the constitution was based on Anderson's *Constitutions*, so the design of the new State was literally Freemasonic, as were its incumbents. In 1789 the first United States dollar bill had a four-sided pyramid based on the Great Seal, suggesting a Freemasonic attempt to stabilize the currency of the new republic.[32]

Looking back on the 1780s, it does seem that the Founding Fathers hijacked the economies of the states for Freemasonry.

Freemasonic Symbolism in Washington, DC

Furthermore, the federal capital was designed along Freemasonic lines. It was to be in 10 square miles ceded to Congress by Maryland and Virginia. The North of the United States was chosen as the South was threatening to break away from the union and Congress had been unable to agree on several proposed sites. In 1790 President Washington chose a marshy swamp as the site and in 1791 he selected Pierre Charles l'Enfant, an engineer in the continental army and a Templar Freemason,[33] to design the new city. The site was called the 'Territory of Columbia'.

Under George Washington's guidance, l'Enfant chose Capitol Hill as the focal point. He proposed rectangular streets with broad avenues like spokes of a wheel. His plan produced octagonal patterns in which the splayed cross used by Masonic Templars could be imagined.[34] L'Enfant was dismissed by Washington in 1792 and his plan underwent changes, but his avenues and vistas remained. What is interesting is that his plan proposed a city of 800,000 inhabitants at a time when the population of the entire United States was less than four times that amount. In other words, he was looking beyond 13 colonies with 3 million inhabitants to 50 states and 500 million inhabitants.[35] Why would he do this if not motivated by the Freemasonic idea of a New Atlantis?

In 1795 the Freemasonic Templar Founding Fathers laid out the streets of Washington to form Masonic symbols: a compass, square, rule, pentagram, pentagon and octagon. Edward Decker describes facing the Capitol from the Mall.[36] If the Capitol is the top of a compass, the left leg is Pennsylvania Avenue and stands on the Jefferson Memorial and the right leg is Maryland Avenue. The square is formed by the intersection of Canal Street and Louisiana Avenue. Behind the Capitol the circular drive and short streets form the head and ears of the 'Goat of Mendes' or 'Goat's Head'. On top of the White House to the north is an inverted five-pointed star or pentagram. The point facing south in occult style is within the intersections of Connecticut and Vermont Avenues to the north with Rhode

Island and Massachusetts to the west and Mount Vernon Square to the east. The centre of the pentagram is 16th Street, where 13 blocks north of the centre of the White House is the Masonic House of the Temple. The Washington Monument is in perfect line to the intersection of the Masonic square stretching from the House of the Temple to the Capitol. Within the hypotenuse of the right-angled triangle are many of the head-quarters of the most powerful government departments, such as the Justice Department, the US Senate and the Internal Revenue Service. The geometry behind Washington, DC, reinforced the Templar symbolism within the Great Seal and the dollar bill.

Furthermore, Freemasonry was behind the new State's most important ceremonies. On 18 September 1793 President George Washington laid the foundation stone of the Capitol building. He wore full Masonic regalia and was surrounded by his brother Masons. It is believed that he used the square and level, and of course the trowel, to lay the stone according to traditional Masonic rites. The *Columbian Mirror and Alexandria Gazette* for 23 September 1793 states:

> 'The President of the United States, the Grand Master *pro tem.*, and the Worshipful Master of No. 22, taking their stand to the east of a large stone, and all the Craft forming a circle westward, stood a short time in solemn order.'[37]

Was the reporting accurate? Did George Washington act as Grand Master during the cornerstone ceremony? If so, the laying of the cornerstone of the Capitol is one of the most important events in the history of American Freemasonry.

All the main Federal buildings from the White House to the Capitol are said to have had a cornerstone and Masonic regalia laid in a Masonic ritual.

When Washington died he was buried at Mount Vernon with full Masonic honours, and members of Alexandria Lodge no. 22 acted as pall-bearers. The George Washington Masonic National Memorial in Alexandria, Virginia, was built by Freemasons between 1923 and 1932 to safeguard the Washington relics in the possession of Alexandria-Washington Lodge no. 22. It is a massive three-tiered pillared building on a classical base with a pyramid top. The 17-foot-3-inch-high heroic statue of Washington as Worshipful Master in the Great Hall and the Washington memorabilia in the George Washington Museum both indicate how central Washington was to Freemasonry in his time.

Freemasonry was also behind Jefferson's architecture. After contributing to Masonic Washington, between 1794 and 1809 Jefferson enlarged Monticello, the house on his 5,000-acre plantation in Virginia, building in Templar designs: octagonal bays in the parlour, the tea-room adjoining the dining-room and the cabinet off his bedroom. The west front beneath the dome reflects the front of the Roman Temple at Nîmes, the first-century Maison Carrée, on which the design of the Virginia State Capitol in Richmond was based in 1785. Ornamental decoration is taken from other Roman buildings: in his bedroom from the frieze of the Temple of *Fortuna Virilis*, in his parlour from the Temple of Jupiter the Thunderer and his Apollo or sun-god frieze in the North Piazza from the Baths of Diocletian. In the parlour, as we have already noted, he had pictures of the Rosicrucian Freemasons Bacon, Newton and Locke, 'the three greatest men that had ever lived'. In the dining-room there was a frieze of rosettes and skulls. The purpose of the octagonal dome and of the columned, pedimented temple on the circular wall beneath it is officially 'unknown', but there is no doubt that this is a Masonic Templar building with Illuminatist embellishments.[38]

Enough has been said to demonstrate the Freemasonic bent of the new republic. To sum up, in the late eighteenth century, American republicanism was Templar. This Templarism was epitomized by George Washington, who was idealized as a symbol of duty, goodness, diffidence, frugality, industry, wisdom, genius and piety. Washington was on a pedestal, but this was a spin-doctored image.[39]

Templar Freemasons now occupied every dominant position in the State. Their plan, to establish a democratic nation in the New World, had been implemented. Can we now really believe that this happened by accident rather than by design? I submit that Washington, Franklin and others had not just borrowed a Freemasonic model (Anderson's *Constitutions*) and acted off their own bat, but were in touch with their lodges and were intentionally creating a Freemasonic State (as happened in revolutionary France).[40] I submit that the constitution intentionally removed sovereignty from the 13 states to a Freemasonry-dominated national central government so that Freemasonry could dominate America in accordance with the Atlantis plan. In short, the Founding Fathers had staged a *coup* against the states.

Freemasonic Law on Religion

This said, we are now in a position to see why the Founding Fathers reversed the Planting Fathers' view on religion, which saw the State as the Church. It was the Founding Fathers' Freemasonry that was behind their attitude to religion.

John Winthrop's *Modell of Christian Charitie* had looked to 'special overruling Providence' and the 'Churches of Christ' for its authority,[41] but the constitution of the Founding Fathers said nothing about religion. It did not mention Christ, or God, or divine guidance, or a godly society, and took its authority from 'the People'. It did not mention God even in a Deist sense, though it was by implication Deist.

William Williams of Connecticut felt that the Founding Fathers had betrayed the Puritan Fathers by failing to establish a Christian nation which could be looked on as a 'City upon a Hill'. He proposed a preamble:

> 'We the people of the United States, in a firm belief of the being and perfections of the one living and true God, the creator and supreme governour of the world, in his universal providence and the authority of his laws; that he will require of all moral agents an account of their conduct; that all rightful powers among men are ordained of, and mediately derived from God....'[42]

But, unlike the Planting Fathers, the Founding Fathers did not intend to create a State within the Church. Asking how the Puritan Fathers were transformed into the Founding Fathers, Frank Lambert says:

> 'The answer lies in the changing meaning of freedom in the concept of freedom of religion.... Religious freedom in the "City

upon a Hill" meant freedom from error, with church and state, though separate, working together to support and protect the one true faith.... The Founding Fathers had a radically different conception of religious freedom. Influenced by the Enlightenment, they had great confidence in the individual's ability to understand the world and its most fundamental laws through the exercise of his or her reason. To them, true religion was not something handed down by a church or contained in the Bible but rather was to be found through rational inquiry.... The framers sought to secure their idea of religious freedom by barring any alliance between church and state.'[43]

By keeping Church and State separate, the Founding Fathers allowed all people from all faiths or no faith free exercise of religion. To James Madison, the note-taker at the convention and the most authoritative voice on the constitution, the constitution protected this freedom by eliminating the government's voice in ecclesiastical matters ('the separation between Religion & Govt in the Constitution of the United States').[44] Following John Witherspoon, a delegate at the Second Continental Congress in 1775 and the only minister to sign the Declaration of Independence, Madison saw America as a haven of religious liberty based on the separation of Church and State. He and Jefferson had already fought for the separation of Church and State in Virginia and a decade-long struggle had resulted in the Virginian Statute for Religious Freedom of 1785.[45] Their task had been helped by the arrival of thousands of dissenters, who had poured in during the previous 40 years, creating a *de facto* marketplace of different religious emphases.

Following the ratification of the constitution, the position of religion in the United States was very different from what it was under the Elizabethan Settlement in England, which ordained 'a national church under royal and parliamentary authority' – a national State Church, the Church of England. Under the Founding Fathers' Settlement, churches were voluntary, comprising individuals who shared particular views, and their right to worship was freely guaranteed, along with their right to attract new members. Ezra Stiles' view that 'the United States was God's American

Israel' and that John Winthrop was 'an American Nehemiah' who founded a society on 'true religion'[46] was not reflected in the constitution.

Two years later, the Virginian Federalists complied with demands for a Bill of Rights. In September 1789 Madison proposed 12 amendments to the constitution, 10 of which were passed in December 1791. These amendments limited the powers of the federal government and guaranteed personal freedom, and are known as the Bill of Rights. The First Amendment embodied their religious settlement: 'Congress shall make no law respecting an establishment of religion, or prohibiting the free exercise thereof....' It meant that the State would stand back from all religious dealings, leaving a marketplace in which all religions and sects could freely compete. Adam Smith in his *Wealth of Nations* (1776) had described religious organizations in the same terms in which he had described commerce. The churches the Planting Fathers established were like trading monopolies, according to Smith: 'The clergy of every established church constitute a great incorporation.'[47] But the State was now separate from the Church.

Many still wonder how a nation so linked to public virtue could establish a national constitution whose text is silent about virtue. There is a view that political rule is not necessary to the unfallen order of Nature – St Augustine's view in *The City of God* – and that a political constitution should leave virtue out (as the *Fundamental Orders* of 1639 did not).[48] The answer can be found in the Founding Fathers' Freemasonry.

The American State was now secular – tolerant towards religious freedom, yes, but secular. There is some evidence, however, that Deists such as Jefferson and Madison were out of step with the American people who were, indeed, still a Christian people. This was due to their Freemasonry, which set them apart from the rank and file Americans, as can be seen from an attitude expressed in the presidential campaign of 1800, when a Dutch Reformed minister, William Linn, praised Jefferson as a public servant but urged voters not to vote for him as President in view of his religious beliefs:

'My objection to his being promoted to the presidency is founded singly upon his disbelief of the Holy Scriptures; or, in other words, his rejection of the Christian Religion and open profession of Deism.... No professed Deist, be his talents and achievements what they may, ought to be promoted to this place by the suffrages of a Christian nation.'[49]

The truth is, Enlightenment Templarism was opposed to Puritanism, to the old Elizabethan feudalism of the first settlers and to the Spanish Catholics – to the Planting Fathers. The Founding Fathers were Freemasons and Deists, and their United States was a Freemasonic State based on reason – tolerant of all religions but supporting none. The Founding Fathers had no time for the Planting Fathers and one aspect of their Freemasonic *coup* was to banish them with silence.

The Elizabethan landed values that accompanied the advent of Anglicanism during the early settlements of the Planting Fathers survived until the Civil War, when, as we shall see, they embraced Freemasonry and received a terrific blow. Today the traditionally Republican, Christian South is a distinctive place and though there are still traces of the Elizabethan outlook in the plantations, the landed values have undergone a change and can never be fully recovered. We shall look at this in the next chapter.

CHAPTER 8

FREEMASONRY'S BATTLE
FOR AMERICA

The Southern states continued to embody the old Elizabethan agrarian ideal brought to Jamestown by Admiral Newport, Bartholomew Gosnold and others in 1607. This was essentially feudal but, as we have seen, in place of aristocracy by birth there was an aristocracy based on ownership of land. The oldest settler families could expect to own 50 acres, certainly from 1618 when the Virginia Company made this offer following Dale's Code.[1] From origins in primitive backwoods communities, farmers, labourers, minor squires, younger sons of minor squires, adventurers and gentlemen of a sort[2] formed a new aristocracy which began to reveal itself about 1700. This new colonial gentry, the Virginians, were a new order of planters who ran their plantations, exported tobacco and depended on their slaves. Nine-tenths of those who would direct the Confederate government in the 1860s during the American Civil War came from such origins – backcountrymen turned planters who were embracing slavery at a time when the rest of the world was giving it up.

The South had grown up with these agrarian values in a different way from the North. With its Elizabethan pedigree, the South had preserved the old values of chivalry and honour. According to Rollin Osterweis in *Romanticism and Nationalism in the Old South*, the Old South 'rested on a tripod – cotton and the plantation system forming one leg, Negro slavery a second. Historians have generally described the third in terms of the chivalric cult.'[3] This chivalric cult, Osterweis shows, was one phase of the

Romantic movement that arrived from English literary Romanticism and made its way across America between the war of 1812 and the Civil War of 1861. It expressed itself in European Romantic nationalism – the 'most conspicuous theme in Southern romanticism' – and made a war for Southern independence 'more than a possibility'.

The European Romantic movement reacted to the intellectual, social and political revolutions of the eighteenth century and attempted to create a new set of values, such as those found in the poems and novels of Sir Walter Scott. It was 'an outgrowth of an agrarian civilization'. The Southern settlers had conquered the wilderness and now sought to escape from reality, from the monotony and boredom of everyday life on the plantations, which fulfilled the role of the medieval manors and provided receptive conditions. The Southern mind was fascinated by horsemen riding about the countryside – a country gentleman should strive to be a chivalrous knight – and took to heart Tennyson's Arthurian *Idylls of the King* (1859). There was a deep romanticism in the South, with its landed sense of being 'other' and its preservation of a way of life it had received in the past. It is crucial to understand this, for this was the climate, the soil, in which Freemasonry flourished in the South during the nineteenth century.

The Southern Jurisdiction Controls the Agrarian South

The Scottish Rite had assisted the post-1787 American national government in developing French republican ideals and its lodges had 32 degrees as opposed to English Freemasonry's three. (This made it more attractive, with a more automatic progression for the less philosophically-minded, and it provided greater opportunities for displaying one's status.) In 1801 nine American Freemasons created the 33rd degree and the Charleston lodge in the South became the Mother Council of the World.

The British meanwhile sent John James Joseph Gourgas to New York to organize clandestine Scottish Rite lodges that would appear to be pro-French but would in fact be pro-English and help Britain's war in America of 1812–14.[4] This is an example of deliberate deception by Freemasonry in the tradition of Weishaupt, to effect certain people's aims.

By 1813 Gourgas had organized five rival lodges, one of which was called the Cerneau Supreme Council of Sovereign Grand Inspectors General of the Thirty-Third Degree. In the summer of 1813 Emanual de la Motta, a Supreme Council member from Charleston, South Carolina, visited New York and discovered these five lodges. After conferring with the Charleston leadership he was told to rectify the situation as discreetly as possible. He reached a territorial agreement with Gourgas whereby from 5 August 1813 the northern area was under the (English) Northern Jurisdiction of Scottish Rite Freemasonry and based in Boston, with Masonic dominion over all the states north and east of the Ohio and Mississippi rivers, while Charleston became the base for the (French) Southern Jurisdiction of Scottish Rite Freemasonry. The Northern Jurisdiction became known as 'the Eastern Establishment'.

Despite having been defeated in the war of 1812–14 and having signed the non aggression treaty of 1814, Britain still hankered to return America to its rule. Through the Scottish Rite lodges of the English obedience in the North, it controlled North-eastern wealth, but could not control the South, as Southern wealth was measured in slaves. If Britain was to have economic control over the South, slavery would have to be abolished. And so a plan was devised to divide America over the slavery issue – in the hope that America could be controlled economically and financially, if not militarily.[5]

Rothschilds Plan an American Central Bank

Central to this plan was the Rothschild family. We have seen that Mayer Amschel Rothschild funded Weishaupt's Order of the Illuminati in the 1770s. He died in 1812, the richest man ever to have lived.[6] He had five sons, who controlled five banks in London, Paris, Frankfurt, Vienna and Naples. Different branches of the family influenced the politics of Britain, France, Germany, Austria and Italy.

The Rothschilds wanted to start a central bank in America. The second Bank of America, created by James Madison in 1816, had collapsed in 1836. Mayer Amschel's grandson Lionel, Nathan's son, and his son James were behind the funding of both North and South in the planned division. The

North was to be annexed to Canada as a British colony via Lionel Rothschild, who was based in London. (It was Lionel who in 1875 would buy the Suez Canal for Disraeli for £4 million from the Khedive Said Pasha, a demonstration of Rothschilds' power at this time.) The South was to be given to Napoleon III of France via James Rothschild, who was based in Paris.[7]

The Rothschilds' funding of the North was via August Belmont (real name August Schoenberg, a cousin of the Seligman family of Frankfurt). He had been sent to America in 1837 to run a bank in New York City and establish himself by buying government bonds. He later became financial adviser to the President. In 1857, a meeting in London convened by Mazzini's Illuminati (*see below*) decided that there should be a conflict between North and South, and Lionel Rothschild used Belmont as an emissary, together with Jay Cooke, the Seligman brothers and Speyer and Co.

James Rothschild controlled the South via the Rothschild agent Judah P. Benjamin of the law firm Slidell, Benjamin and Conrad in Louisiana, who later became Secretary of State for the Confederacy in 1862. His law partner John Slidell (August Belmont's wife's uncle) was the Confederate envoy to France. Slidell's daughter was married to Baron Frederick d'Erlanger in Frankfurt, who was related to the Rothschilds and acted for them. Slidell was the representative of the South who borrowed money from the d'Erlangers to finance the Confederacy.[8]

So Rothschilds controlled the North via August Belmont, later financial adviser to the President, and the South via Judah Benjamin, Secretary of State for the Confederacy, and the Slidell / d'Erlanger family.

Britain Controls the Southern Jurisdiction

In 1851 Giuseppe Mazzini, who had taken over the Illuminati in 1834 and who had links with the British politician Lord Palmerston,[9] began the process of bringing about a civil war by forming revolutionary groups throughout the United States to intensify the debate on slavery. He sent his right-hand man Adriano Lemmi and the Hungarian Louis Kossuth to the USA. They organized 'Young America' lodges (similar to Mazzini's 'Young Italy'),[10] using Cincinnati Lodge no. 133 as their headquarters.[11]

Lemmi eventually returned to London, but Kossuth stayed on, touring

El Adelantado Hernando de Soto,

Plate 1 *(right)* Hernando de Soto (c.1496–1542)

Plate 2 *(below)* René Goulaine de Laudonnière (c.1529–82) and Chief Athore in front of Ribault's Column

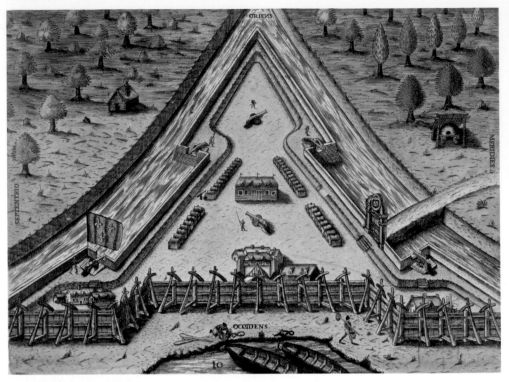

Plate 3 *(above)* Fort Caroline

Plate 4 *(below)* Map depicting the destruction of the Spanish colony of St Augustine in Florida, 7 July 1586, by the English fleet commanded by Sir Francis Drake (1540–96)

Plate 5 *(above)* The arrival of the English in Virginia

Plate 6 *(right)* Sir Thomas Smythe (c.1558–1652)

Plate 7 *(above)* Landing of the first settlers at Jamestown

Plate 8 *(below)* Landing at Jamestown: the founding of the colony of Jamestown, Virginia, by Captain Christopher Newport and 105 of his followers in 1607

Plate 9 *(above)* The first settlers from England giving thanks for their safe arrival at Jamestown, Virginia, in 1607

Plate 10 *(right)* The first day at Jamestown, 14 May 1607

Plate 11 *(left)* The Indian village of Secoton

Plate 12 *(below)* Trading with the Indians at Jamestown

Plate 13 *(above)* Jamestown c.1614

Plate 14 *(below)* Map of Virginia, showing (upper left) a picture of Chief Powhatan by John Smith (1580–1631)

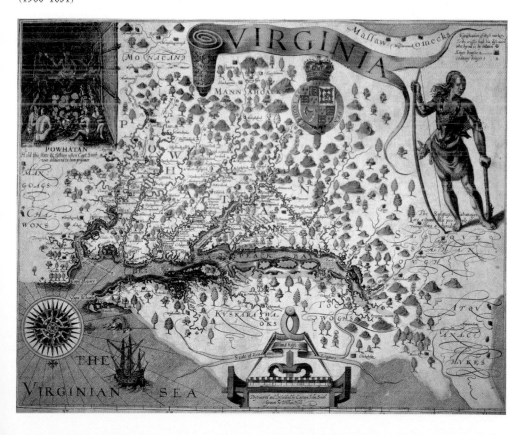

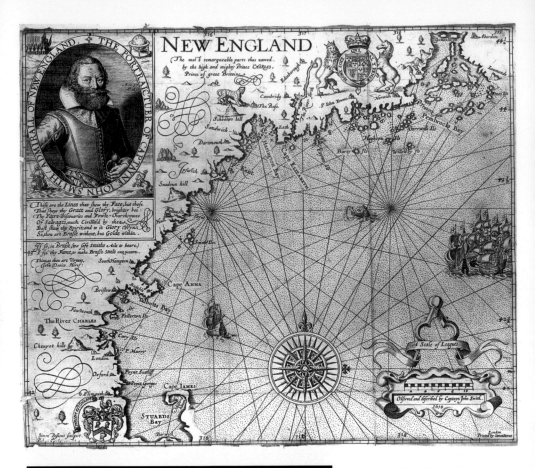

Plate 15 *(above)* Map of the coast of New England, observed and described by Captain John Smith

Plate 16 *(left)* Captain John Smith

Plate 17 *(above)* A description of part of the adventures of Captain John Smith in Virginia

Plate 18 *(below)* Arrival of Lord De La Warr at Jamestown

King Powhatan comands C. Smith to be slayne, his daughter Pokahontas beggs his life his thankfullnes and how he Subiected 39 of their kings reade ŷ hist

MATOAKA ALS REBECCA FILIA POTENTISS PRINC POWHATANI IMP: VIRGINIA.

Matoaks als Rebecka daughter to the mighty Prince Powhatan Emperour of Attanoughskomouck als virginia converted and baptized in the Christian faith, and wife to the wor.ll M.r Joh Rolff

Plate 19 *(above)* Pocahontas (1595–1617), a native American princess, saves Captain John Smith from execution

Plate 20 *(left)* Pocahontas, who was baptised Rebecca in 1613 and married Thomas Rolfe in the same year

Plate 21 (*above*) Map of Plymouth, Massachusetts, 17th century

Plate 22 (*below*) William Penn (1644–1718) receiving the Charter of Pennsylvania from King Charles II of England

Plate 23 *(left)*
Benjamin Franklin
(1706–90)

Plate 24 *(below)*
The Boston Tea
Party, 1773

Plate 25 *(above)* George Washington (1732–99) as a Freemason

Plate 26 *(left)* Thomas Jefferson (1743–1826) writing the Declaration of Independence

Plate 27 *(above)* Adam Weishaupt (1748–1830), founder of the Order of the Illuminati

Plate 28 *(below left)* The Great Seal of the US, *obverse*

Plate 29 *(below)* The Great Seal of the US, *reverse*, which features the 'All-Seeing Eye'

Plate 30 *(above)* The signing of the Constitution of the United States in 1787

Plate 31 *(right)* The inauguration of President George Washington on 30 April 1789 at the Old City Hall, New York

Plate 32 *(below)* Map of Washington (originally drawn 1790–2). Washington was designed by Pierre Charles l'Enfant and laid out in 1795, the streets forming Masonic symbols

Plate 33 *(below right)* Abraham Lincoln (1809–65), 16th President of the United States

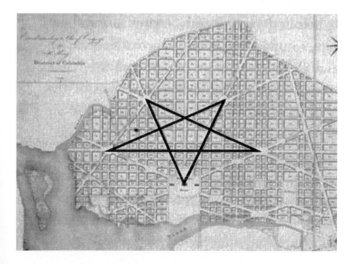

Plate 34 *(above)* The fall of Richmond, Virginia, 2 April 1865

Plate35 *(below)* The 300th anniversary celebration of the founding of Jamestown, 1907

lodges in the United States. When Franklin Pierce became a presidential candidate for the Democrats in 1852, Kossuth offered him his Young America organization if he would agree to make certain appointments in his cabinet – positions Mazzini's Illuminati calculated would have a divisive effect. Pierce was not a Freemason and did not realize the significance of Kossuth and the Young America movement. Mazzini wrote in his diary:

'Kossuth and I are working with the very numerous Germanic element [Young America] in the United States for [Pierce's] election, and under certain conditions which he has accepted. Of these conditions he has already fulfilled enough to give us security that he will carry out the rest.'[12]

Pierce was elected President in 1853 and appointed a combination of Southern planters and Northern businessmen to his cabinet. He appointed Caleb Cushing US Attorney General. Cushing was affiliated to the Northern Jurisdiction of Freemasonry and became the architect of the Civil War. He wrote against slavery and transferred money from the British Freemasonic banker George Peabody to the abolitionists of slavery who were calling for the dissolution of the Union, thereby financing the Southern insurrectionists through London's Freemasonic banks. Peabody hired J. P. Morgan Sr to handle the funds when they arrived in the United States.[13,14]

The Peabody funds in London were handled by Pierce's appointee to the US Consulate, George Sanders. He, though not a Freemason, was a supporter of Freemasonic revolutions and hosted one gathering on 21 February 1854 that included Mazzini, Garibaldi, Kossuth, Arnold Ruge, co-editor of a revolutionary magazine for Young Germany with Marx, Herzen, who initiated Bakunin into Mazzini's Young Russia, and also the next President of the USA, James Buchanan. Five of the eight men present were deeply involved in the coming Civil War. Sanders himself would operate a cross-border spy ring for the Confederacy during the Civil War.

Cushing prepared for British control of the Southern Jurisdiction of Scottish Rite Freemasonry, which had received its constitution from French Freemasonry. He selected Albert Pike, a school principal in his hometown of Newburyport, Massachusetts, to further this cause.[15] Two weeks after Cushing was appointed Attorney General, on 20 March 1853, he sent a message to Pike, who was then living in Little Rock, Arkansas, to go to Charleston and receive the 4th to 32nd Masonic degrees from Albert Gallatin Mackey, who would instruct him further. Pike received the 33rd degree in New Orleans and in 1859 was elected Sovereign Grand Commander of the Supreme Council of the Southern Jurisdiction of Scottish Rite Freemasonry.

The Southern Jurisdiction starts the Civil War

It is important to trace in greater detail how Cushing and Pike began the Civil War.

The Northern Jurisdiction was still under the British spy and 33rd-degree Freemason J. J. J. Gourgas. In 1854 he is said to have helped Killian Van Rensselaer found the Knights of the Golden Circle, in Cincinnati, Ohio.[16] In another view, the Knights were founded by George W. L. Bickley for the Southern Jurisdiction of Freemasonry in 1854.[17] Regardless of who carried out the founding, there is general agreement that the Knights of the Golden Circle were a front to direct an insurrection. The name Golden Circle came from a plan to create a 'slave empire' occupying a circle with Havana at its centre and a radius of 1,200 miles that would include all the Southern states, Mexico, Central America, the northern part of South America and the West Indies. This 'slaveocracy' would produce most of the world's cotton, sugar and tobacco and would rival ancient Rome in power and prestige. By 1858 the Knights had established regalia and initiation ceremonies that would have appealed to Southerners steeped in the novels of Sir Walter Scott.

The Golden Circle immediately absorbed the Freemasons working within Young America and became the Confederacy's military pre-organization. These Arthurian Knights rode west across Ohio, Indiana and Illinois, south to the Gulf of Mexico and east into Maryland and Virginia. As they rode, they opened castles (chapters) and signed up recruits. One castle was opened by John Quitman in Jackson, Mississippi, and another by Albert Pike in New Orleans (through which Mazzini's Illuminati Mafia would enter the USA after the Civil War). The romantic Southern mind and the local cultural conditions were receptive to the ideal of knights riding round the countryside doing good deeds.

Caleb Cushing brought the anti-slavery North and pro-slavery South into collision by encouraging the Pierce Administration to pass the Kansas-Nebraska Act in 1854. According to the Act, Nebraska was to be divided into Kansas and Nebraska and the inhabitants were to decide whether to have slavery. This led to many murders and arson attacks by pro-slavery Missourians and massacres by abolitionists under John Brown. Brown was a Master Mason (in Hudson Lodge no. 68, Hudson, Ohio) from 1824 to 1830 and then renounced Freemasonry. Cushing regarded him as the perfect person to cause an insurrection for Freemasonry as, being an anti-Mason, he would not be under suspicion. During the Pierce Administration Brown joined Mazzini's Young America and was supported financially by the John Jacob Astor Freemasonic interest in Boston and New York. After receiving instructions from Cushing, he set about causing a civil war.[18]

In January 1857 the new President was James Buchanan, a Freemason. The new Sovereign Grand Commander of the Southern Jurisdiction of Scottish Rite Freemasonry was supposed to be John Quitman, but on 17 July 1858 he suddenly died – apparently poisoned.[19] Pike, Cushing's nominee, was elected to take his place and became leader of the Southern secessionists.

Pike now became the most powerful Mason in the world, occupying simultaneously the positions of Grand Master of the Central Directory at Washington, DC, Grand Commander of the Supreme Council at Charleston, South Carolina, and Sovereign Pontiff of Universal Freemasonry.[20] He was also Grand Master of a Luciferian group, the Order of the Palladium (or Sovereign Council of Wisdom) – 'Palladium' coming from the Hindu *pala*, 'phallus'. He was a member of virtually every Supreme Council in the world and received 130 Freemasonic degrees.

Before his accession to these Masonic positions Pike secretly organized the rebellion of the Southern states against the United States, using the Sovereign Jurisdiction of Scottish Rite Freemasonry to conceal his conspiracy.[21] Most of the political and military leadership of the Confederacy was composed of Freemasons under Pike's secret command.

He also controlled the Knights of the Golden Circle.

The Confederate states were seeking to restore their independence and to achieve a position in which each state would be like an independent country – free to choose whether to continue with the slavery that kept the plantations going and not bound by any Union legislation. The very word 'Confederate' recalls the Articles of Confederation preceding the constitution that established the United States and suggests the constitutional arrangement *before* the Union.

President Buchanan appointed to government posts all those who were certain to start a Southern revolt. He made Edward M. Stanton, a Freemason, Attorney General, and Howell Cobb of Georgia, a Freemason, Secretary to the Treasury. In March 1860 Cobb became a 33rd-degree Mason and appointed Pike leader of the secessionists in Georgia and chairman of the convention which organized the Confederacy in Montgomery, Alabama. Buchanan also made John B. Floyd, a Freemason of St John's Lodge no. 36 in Richmond, Virginia, Secretary of War. In 1860 Floyd agreed with South Carolina's Governor William Gift to sell 10,000 US government rifles to South Carolina – arms that went to the secessionist leaders. He was made a brigadier-general in the Confederate army.

Buchanan's Vice-President was John C. Breckinridge of Kentucky, a Freemason. He attended the 1860 Democratic National Convention at Charleston, the headquarters of the Southern Jurisdiction. Caleb Cushing of the Northern Jurisdiction presided over the convention. Under his supervision, the Gulf states delegation walked out – seceded – and formed their own convention. They elected Cushing as chairman and Breckinridge as their candidate for President. On 28 March 1860 Breckinridge received the 33rd degree from Pike.

The Republican party nominated Abraham Lincoln, not a Freemason, as presidential candidate on 18 May 1860. Lincoln won the election in November. It seems that Pike began intriguing the process of secession in earnest as soon as Lincoln was elected.

Officially convinced that its way of life was threatened by Lincoln's appointment, South Carolina, headquarters of the Southern Jurisdiction, was the first state to secede on 20 December 1860. It was followed the same day by Mississippi, whose secessionist organization had been created by Quitman. Buchanan was still serving out his presidential term and his Secretary of War, John Floyd, sent 124 cannons to unfinished forts where they could be seized by insurrectionists – an indirect way of arming the South.

On 22 December Florida seceded from the Union, led by US Senator David Levy Yulee, a Freemason (of Hayward Lodge no. 7, Gainesville, Florida). Alabama seceded on 24 December. On 2 January 1861 Georgia's secession was led by two Freemasons, Howell Cobb, Buchanan's Secretary to the Treasury, and Robert Toombs, who became the Confederacy's First Secretary of State. (He received the 33rd degree after the Civil War.) Louisiana's secession was led by John Slidell and Pierre Soule, both Freemasons who later received the 33rd degree after the Civil War. Thousands of armed paramilitary Knights of the Golden Circle forced the Texas Governor, Sam Houston, a Freemason, to secede in February 1861.[22]

Lincoln was inaugurated on 4 March 1861. When he came to Washington to assume the presidency, General Winfield Scott foiled an attempt by the Knights of the Golden Circle to assassinate him. Lincoln made the mistake of appointing Edwin Stanton, a Freemason, as Secretary of War. Stanton would be involved in the second assassination attempt.

On 12 April 1861 General Beauregard, a Freemason, one of the Knights of the Golden Circle and the brother-in-law of John Slidell, Louisiana's political leader, was ordered to make a surprise attack on US-held Fort Sumter. This began the Civil War.

Four more states, Arkansas, North Carolina, Tennessee and Virginia, now joined the secession. Richmond in Virginia became the Confederacy capital. Eleven Southern states had now seceded from the Union.

The Confederate flag had 13 stars, a Freemasonic number evoking the day the Templars were suppressed, Friday 13th, and indicating to all who saw the flag that the secession of the Southern states was caused by the Knights Templars' Southern Jurisdiction.[23]

Breckinridge was now elected US Senator for Kentucky. At the beginning of the Civil War he defended the South and was expelled from the Senate in December 1861 for entering the Confederate service. The President of the Confederate States, Jefferson Davis, a Freemason, appointed him his Secretary of War.

Lincoln Defeats the Freemasonic Central Bank

Now the Civil War had begun, British Freemasonic financiers who had funded the South's insurrection, notably the Rothschilds, offered Lincoln the same funding if he would authorize them to establish a central bank.[24] Lincoln refused, as it would be interest-bearing money. Instead, he decided that the USA would print its own money, interest-free and debt-free.

To fund the war, the North raised $450 million from the people by selling them bonds, or 'greenbacks'. Issues were in February and March 1862 and March 1863. These were not redeemable until 1865, when three could be exchanged for one in silver. The bonds meant that the Union stayed free from having to raise money from intermediate bankers such as the Rothschilds.

Britain and France, alerted by Rothschilds to the possibility that Lincoln would issue bonds, then sent troops to bring pressure to bear on him: in 1861 Britain sent 8,000 troops to Canada, and French and Spanish troops landed on the coast of Mexico at Veracruz, ostensibly to collect the debts Mexico owed them. On 10 June 1863 the French General Elie-Frederic Forey took Mexico City with 30,000 additional French troops. He then controlled most of the country and the French imposed on Mexico their choice of ruler: Maximilian, the brother of Emperor Joseph I of Austria. The Confederates offered the states of Louisiana and Texas to Napoleon III if he would send troops against the North.

Lincoln was aware that these troop movements were to press him to create a central bank and he asked Russia for help. Alexander II, Tsar of Russia, gave him his support. He sent a large fleet to the ports of New York and San Francisco and placed it under Lincoln's orders.[25] Russia had emancipated the serfs in 1861, and Lincoln, eager to cement the alliance, issued his Emancipation Proclamation to free the slaves on 1 January 1863.

Lincoln's first concern, however, was to protect the Union from the South, not to abolish slavery. He had said on 22 August 1862:

> 'My paramount object in this struggle is to save the Union, and is not either to save or destroy slavery. If I could save the Union without freeing any slave I would do it; and if I could save it by

freeing all the slaves I would do it; and if I could save it by freeing some and leaving others alone, I would also do that.'[26]

Whatever, Lincoln's primary motive, the alliance with Russia worked. Britain and France did not wish to go to war with Russia and withdrew their troops.

The Freemasonic bankers were still trying to achieve a central bank. Their agent sent a letter to leading American financiers and bankers saying that the greenback would put American Masonic bankers out of business.

Lincoln now created bonds with 'a banking basis' to be issued in place of greenbacks. In 1863 Congress passed the National Bank Act and created a federally chartered national bank that had power to issue US banknotes, allowing centralized banking under federal control, which again was not what the Rothschilds wanted. In effect paper money was loaned to the government at interest, supported by debt. This bill was suggested by the Secretary of the Treasury, Salmon P. Chase. David Rockefeller's Chase Manhattan Bank was named after him.

Now fortunes were made by supplying the South with arms, despite the Union blockade. Thomas House, whose father was an agent for the Rothschilds back in England, made a fortune smuggling arms from Britain to Texas. His son, a 33rd-degree Freemason, gave himself the title 'Colonel' and later advised Woodrow Wilson.

The Rothschilds had not achieved their central bank in America. The course of the war, involving great battles and generalship, proved a missed opportunity for them. The charismatic Robert Lee led the South, an Arthur whose Camelot was Richmond, and General Pike fought alongside him as a towering Confederate general. The Knights of the Southern Jurisdiction who protected him kept alive the romantic Arthurian patriotic spirit. But the next four years saw a succession of Southern defeats. New Orleans fell in 1862, Vicksburg in 1863, Atlanta in 1864 and finally Richmond in 1865. The Rothschilds then turned their attention to achieving a central bank in the long term and eventually established the Federal Reserve System near the beginning of the next century.[27]

Freemasons Kill Lincoln

Lincoln had been on the receiving end of the Southern secession. He had stood up to the Freemasons and had defeated them but, like Washington, he was a Deist who was in trouble for not belonging to a church. He once explained why he never joined a church, although he attended Presbyterian services in Springfield and in Washington:

> 'When any church will inscribe over its altar, as its sole qualification for membership, the Saviour's condensed statement of the substance of both Law and Gospel, "Thou shalt love the Lord thy God with all thy heart, and with all thy soul and will all thy mind, and thy neighbor as thyself," that church will I join with all my heart and all my soul.'[28]

The truth is, Lincoln occupied the no man's land between Christianity and Freemasonry.

Nevertheless, Lincoln was hated by Freemasons. He had prevented them from taking over America and from establishing a central bank and had restored the Union. British Freemasonry planned to kill him, using the Knights of the Golden Circle, in particular their member John Wilkes Booth, a 33rd-degree Mason and member of Mazzini's Young America.

Five days after the South's surrender on 9 April 1865, after two unsuccessful attempts at kidnap, the Freemasons were successful in killing Lincoln at Ford's Theatre. After shooting the President, Booth grappled with the theatre's patron, swung himself over the balustrade and leaped from Lincoln's box, shouting 'Sic semper tyrannis! The South is avenged!' He landed heavily on the stage, breaking a bone in the lower part of his left leg, but hobbled out to his horse.

The same evening there was an attempt on the life of Secretary of State William H. Seward and in 1866 an attempt was made to assassinate Alexander II, who had supported Lincoln against the South. Were all three attacks instances of Southern revenge?

Edwin Stanton, the Freemason in Lincoln's Cabinet, was assigned to cover up Masonic involvement in Lincoln's assassination.[29] Afterwards he imposed a military blockade on every road out of Washington except the one Booth took. A Booth lookalike was murdered and his body burned alongside the same road, and by coincidence Stanton personally found it and identified the remains as Booth's. Booth escaped.[30]

In Booth's trunk coded messages were found. The key to the code was discovered in the possession of Judah Benjamin, the Rothschild agent who had fled to England, where he died. Investigations showed that he had given the order for the assassination.

Palmerston, the British Prime Minister from 1859 to 1865 and a 33rd-degree Freemason, was also involved in the assassination plot. He had links with Mazzini – he had persuaded the British Parliament to fund Mazzini's Grand-Orient insurrection in Italy from 1848 to 1865[31] – and was directly implicated according to reporters attending the Indianapolis trial of 2–28 June 1865.[32] Jacob Thompson, former Interior Secretary in the Buchanan Administration, had withdrawn $180,000 from the Bank of Montreal to set the plot in motion.

The exposure of the Knights of the Golden Circle in the trials of 1865 was so emphatic that in 1867 Pike and some ex-Confederate generals set up a military wing, the Ku Klux Klan. The Knights of the Golden Circle then disbanded and passed into the Ku Klux Klan, a secret organization that pressed for racial segregation in the South. The name Ku Klux Klan was allegedly taken from the Greek for 'circle', *kuklos*, which suggested the Golden Circle. Pike referred to it as an 'Order of Southern Brotherhood'.[33] He was arrested for the murder of Lincoln.

In 1974, 18 pages of Booth's diary were found in Stanton's posthumous papers, with the names of 70 people involved in Booth's plan to kidnap Lincoln. The original plan had been that Lincoln, Vice-President Andrew Johnson and Secretary of State Seward would all be kidnapped. The plot was very wide and included Maryland farmers, Confederates including Jefferson Davis (President of the Confederacy), Judah Benjamin (the Confederate Secretary of War and Secretary of State), Northern banking interests including Jay Cooke, and radical Republicans, including three senators. All these groups had clubbed together and used Booth as their front.[34] In fact, the Knights of the Golden Circle had been behind the assassination, which was probably carried out with

Pike's connivance. As a member of Mazzini's Carbonari, Booth was a member of the Illuminati.

Freemasons Control America

Following the assassination there were riots throughout the South and Vice-President Andrew Johnson, a 3rd-degree Freemason and Master Mason who assumed the presidency after Lincoln, believed they were an attempt to incite a new Civil War.[35] Johnson was not a 33rd-degree Mason and so he was unaware of the activities of the 33rd-degree Supreme Council and could not see the hidden hand of Freemasonry in the riots. He was unaware that Jesse James, the legendary bank robber, was a 33rd-degree Mason and member of the Knights of the Golden Circle, and that he had been assigned to rob Northern banks to fund this new civil war. It is believed that he buried $7 billion in gold, money which has never been found.[36]

President Johnson issued the Amnesty Proclamation on 29 May 1865 to reunite the country. All secession laws were to end and slavery was abolished. The proclamation announced that the South would not be responsible for the debt incurred. The Rothschilds, who had heavily funded the South, lost a lot of money.

At the end of the war, Russia submitted a bill for $7.2 million for the services of the Russian fleet. As Congress had not authorized the hiring of the fleet, Johnson could not pay the bill. His Secretary of State William Seward, an anti-Mason, proposed that instead America should buy a worthless territory, Alaska, from the Russians for $7.2 million, in a transaction that became known as 'Seward's Folly', because Alaska was technically worthless. The payment was made in April 1867.

Suspecting him of being implicated in Lincoln's assassination, President Johnson attempted to impeach Stanton for treason against Congress, but failed to win Senate support. Pike was tried and found guilty of treason. However, he was President Johnson's superior as a Freemason and on 1 July 1865 Benjamin B. French, a 33rd-degree Freemason and member of the board of directors of the Supreme Council of the Scottish Rite, wrote a letter to Johnson urging him to pardon him. Others made similar appeals.[37] As a result of this pressure, Johnson pardoned the man most responsible for the Civil War.

Some Congressmen then tried to impeach President Johnson because he had 'pardoned large numbers of public and notorious traitors'.[38] However, three months later, on 20 June 1867, Johnson received a delegation of Scottish Rite officials in his bedroom at the White House and 'received the 4th through the 32nd degrees of the Scottish Rite as an honorarium'.[39] So he received his reward from Freemasonry for pardoning Pike.

As both an English and a Scottish Rite Freemason, Johnson had reunited Freemasonry. It now ruled the United States and was stronger than ever before. The Elizabethan values of the Jamestown planters had fallen along with Richmond, and the churches now provided little religious common ground to Americans as they were disparate voluntary organizations separated from the State.

In 1871 Pike wrote *Morals and Dogma*, a Masonic handbook. He did not reveal in this work or in the 33rd-degree ritual[40] the great secret that 30th–33rd-degree Masons are told – that the god of Freemasonry is Lucifer.[41] But he did reveal it in a letter he put out in 1889 to 23 Freemasonic Supreme Councils, in a dualistic statement which disparaged the Christian God Adonay:

> 'Yes, Lucifer is God, and unfortunately Adonay [Jehovah] is also God. For the eternal law is that there is no light without shade, no beauty without ugliness, no white without black, for the absolute can only exist as two Gods: darkness being necessary to light.... The true and pure philosophic religion is the belief in Lucifer, the equal of Adonay; but Lucifer, God of Light and God of Good, is struggling for humanity against Adonay, the God of Darkness and Evil.'[42]

The Gnostic dualism would not be out of place among Manichaeans or the Manichaean Cathars.

Lucifer, the god Weishaupt had looked to, the god of the world, the flesh, money and revolution, was now blatantly worshipped in Freemasonic lodges but, as in Weishaupt's Illuminati, those lower than 30th-degree were not told.[43]

It was as though Freemasonry had won the Civil War. The unified, federal Freemasonic State would now become even stronger by harnessing the Industrial Revolution in the North and exercise an even greater control over America.

Despite his opposition to Freemasonry, Lincoln is lionized as a hero of American history for crushing the Southern revolt and preserving the Union. Perhaps Freemasonry was behind this hero-worship to cover up the fact that America was now firmly under Freemasonic control.

CHAPTER 9

THE FREEMASONIC STATE TODAY

The story we have followed now brings us to the present day. We have seen that early America was dominated by the Church to such an extent that the State *was* the Church in the early seventeenth century. We have seen that as a result of Freemasonry and Enlightenment Deism the Church was used as a veneer by the Founding Fathers and lost its dominant position, and that under the constitutional settlement of 1787 the State became Masonic and was separated from the Churches, which now had to compete with each other for clients in a commercial setting. We have seen that despite losing the Civil War, Freemasonry retained its formidable hold over the instruments of power in the American State.

The Freemasonry that attracted the Founding Fathers was one of high-minded ideals, but we have noted a deterioration since those early days, perhaps due to the Illuminatist Freemasonic strain that was hidden within the Grand Orient. Since Weishaupt, deception has masked Freemasonry's drive to create a world government and its agenda includes hidden strategies based on Masonic self-interest to a degree that might shock the Founding Fathers if they were to come back and witness them today.

We saw that Freemasons dominated the State machinery in Washington's day, including the offices of the President and the Vice-President, where both men were sworn in on the Masonic Bible, and also state governors, US senators and Congressmen, the military and the judiciary. The same can be said of the twentieth century.

Since Washington many Presidents have been 33rd-degree Masons. The list includes Jefferson (33rd degree); Madison; Monroe (Williamsburgh Lodge no. 6, Virginia); Jackson (Harmony Lodge no. 1, Tennessee); Polk (Columbia Lodge no. 31, Tennessee); Atchison (President for one day) (Platte Lodge no. 56, Missouri); Buchanan (Lodge no. 43, Pennsylvania); Andrew Johnson (1851, Greenville Lodge no. 119, Tennessee, 32nd degree and Grand Master); Garfield (1864, Columbus Lodge no. 20, Ohio); McKinley (1865, Hiram Lodge no. 21, Virginia); Theodore Roosevelt (1901, Matinecock Lodge no. 806, Oyster Bay); Taft (1909, Kilwinning Lodge no. 356, Ohio); Harding (1920, Marion Lodge no. 70, Ohio, 33rd degree); Franklin D. Roosevelt (1911); Truman (1909, Belton Lodge no. 450, 33rd degree and Grand Master); Lyndon Johnson (Entered Apprentice, 1937); and Ford (1951, Columbia Lodge no. 3).[1]

Other Presidents who were not Freemasons still had links with Freemasonry. Abraham Lincoln applied for Freemasonic membership in Tyrian Lodge, Springfield, shortly after he was nominated for the presidency in 1860, but he withdrew because he felt that applying for membership might be construed as a political ruse to obtain votes. He advised the lodge that he would resubmit his application when he ceased to be President. On his death, Tyrian Lodge stated that Lincoln's decision to postpone his application 'lest his motives be misconstrued, is the highest degree honorable to his memory'. Lyndon Johnson was elected to Congress in the year he became an Entered Apprentice, 1937, and was too busy to pursue further Masonic degrees.

Eisenhower was not a Freemason, but had Freemasons serving under him: Sherman Adams, his Chief of Staff, Christian Herter, Secretary of State, Douglas McKay, Secretary of the Interior, and Robert B. Anderson, Secretary of the Treasury.[2] There is no evidence of a link between Freemasonry and John F. Kennedy, Richard Nixon or Jimmy Carter. Ronald Reagan was not a Freemason, but was an honorary member of the Imperial Council of the Shrine (Scottish Rite). He was involved in numerous Shrine and Masonic functions and has been consequently listed as a Freemason. Reagan's honorary membership was presented by the Scottish Rite Grand Master of DC on 11 February 1988.[3]

Although neither George Bush Sr nor George Bush Jr is a Freemason in the strictest sense, both are members of Yale University's Skull and Bones, a secret organization of a Freemasonic nature. Bush Sr is in the Catalogue of Members for 1948, Bush Jr for 1968.[4] Skull and Bones, or the Order, was established at Yale in 1833, three years after Weishaupt died. It was imported from Germany as a chapter of a German secret society and has been linked to the German Illuminati, which is also called 'the Order'.[5] It permits membership to 15 seniors each year, who are photographed with a skull and crossbones, symbol of the Knights Templar. They wear an image of this Templar symbol on their breast for their entire lives to define their Templar allegiance. Some 500–600 Yale graduate members of the Order are reckoned to be still alive. It is possible that Skull and Bones is a front or a cover for an Illuminati organization.

The New World Order is arguably a Freemasonic Templar echo of the Order of Skull and Bones. It is interesting that Bush Sr so frequently spoke about the New World Order before the First Iraq War in 1990. For example, he told a joint session of Congress on 11 September 1990: 'A New World Order can emerge. This is the vision I shared with President Gorbachev in Helsinki.'[6] It is likely that Bush Sr's New World Order is an offshoot of a Freemasonic plan for a world State that was anticipated in the *Novo Ordo Seclorum* on the back of the one-dollar bill in 1933 or 1934, as we have seen.

By the same token it is possible that Bush Jr's regime and the neo-conservative PNAC (Project for the New American Century), which was started in 1997 by Robert Kagan (a US State Department adviser), William Kristol (a US editor) and Richard Perle (then a senior Pentagon adviser), are also the expression of this same plan.

Bill Clinton, who replaced George Bush Sr as President, once joined the Order of DeMolay, a Freemasonic youth group, but claims he did not progress into full Freemasonry after his studies.[7] Clinton studied at Georgetown University under Carroll Quigley, the author of *Tragedy and Hope* (Macmillan, 1966), and became a Rhodes Scholar, receiving special training in the one-world ideology championed by Cecil Rhodes. He then graduated from Yale in 1973. He has been described as an ally of English Freemasonry.[8]

The Masonic Bible from the altar of St John's Lodge no.1 in New York City, a Templar Freemasonic lodge, that was first used during the inauguration of George Washington was later used for the inauguration oaths administered to Warren G. Harding, Dwight D. Eisenhower, Jimmy Carter, George Bush Sr and George Bush Jr. Some believe that these five Presidents have been wrongly described as Freemasons as a result of confusion following their swearing-in on this George Washington Freemasonic Bible. In fact the Masonic Bible is an essential part of the Masonic State, to the extent that it is now normal for non-Freemasons to be sworn in on it. It has an introductory section explaining that Freemasonry is not a Christian fraternity but supports all religions. It states that 'for well over 150 years the destiny of this country has been determined by men who were members of the Masonic Fraternity'.[9]

Certainly many state governors, senators and Congressmen are Freemasons. There is a Grand Lodge in every state. Newt Gingrich and Bob Dole are 33rd-degree Freemasons,[10] as was Barry Goldwater. Jesse Jackson[11] and Ross Perot[12] are also Freemasons.

The modern US military contains Freemasons, most notably General George C. Marshall (of Marshall Aid), Omar Bradley (West Point Lodge no. 877, New York), Mark Clark (1929, Mystic Tie Lodge no. 398, Indianapolis), Douglas MacArthur (1937, Manila Lodge no. 1, Philippines)[13] and more recently it has been reported that Colin Powell is a 33rd-degree Freemason.[14] Marshall and MacArthur were, like President Taft, Freemasons 'at sight'. Still writes, 'That is, they had little idea of what they were getting into.'[15]

The judiciary is also full of Freemasons. From 1935 to 1945 32nd-degree Franklin D. Roosevelt appointed to the Supreme Court a majority of justices who were anti-Christian, pro-communist, radical Freemasons. Several senators spoke out in 1987. Senator Simpson of Wyoming said: 'Forty-one members of the Federal judiciary are presently Masons ... I just say that Masonry in this country is the bedrock.' Senator Thurmond of South Carolina said: 'I guess about half of the members of the Judiciary Committee are members of the Masonic order.'[16]

In the UK there has been a similar pattern. Britain too is a Masonic State. Since 1737 every male monarch has been a Freemason, as has been the head of the Anglican Church.[17] In other words, both Crown and Church have been controlled by Freemasonry. George VI was a devoted Freemason and when Prince Philip of Greece asked him for his daughter's hand in the summer of 1947, he said that Elizabeth's husband would have to be a patron of Freemasonry. Philip promised George that he would join the order. His uncle, Earl Mountbatten, was an anti-Mason, however, and advised Philip not to become one. When George VI died Philip felt honour bound to keep his promise and was initiated at Navy Lodge no. 2612. But he remained at the first level and has snubbed Freemasonry ever since.

Prince Charles has followed Mountbatten's advice and his father's instinct, and the Queen Mother supported him in this. Charles refused to become a Freemason at 21, saying he did not want to join any secret society, but his perhaps nominal announcement that he would reign as 'Defender of Faiths' (that is, all religions including Christianity, Islam and Judaism), rather than as 'Defender of the Faith' was bound to win the approval of Freemasonry, which supports all religions and thereby weakens all religions.

It is interesting that of the non-Freemasonic or semi-Freemasonic royals, Earl Mountbatten was assassinated, and Prince Philip and Prince Charles have had to endure negative press propaganda, including claims about the manner in which Princess Diana was killed. Elizabeth II became Grand Patroness of English Freemasonry soon after her accession.[18]

Sub-Masonic Secret Societies

Out of British Freemasonry came a number of new secret societies in the twentieth century: the Round Table (1909–13), the Royal Institute of International Affairs (RIIA, 1919), the Council on Foreign Relations (CFR, 1921), the Bilderberg Group (1954), the Club of Rome (1968) and the Trilateral Commission (1972). All these offshoots of Freemasonry urged world government.

Membership of these sub-Masonic bodies is vital for politicians wanting to get on in Britain, Europe and America, and especially since the Second World War many Western leaders have been members of one or more of these groups. Since 1945 every US presidential candidate has been a CFR member.[19] President Nixon appointed more than 100 members of the CFR to his administration. Bill Clinton was a member of the CFR, the Bilderberg Group (whose meeting in Baden Baden, Germany, he attended in 1991) and the Trilateral Commission. It is likely that many modern leaders have found it too time-consuming to be members of these new secret sub-Masonic organizations *and* members of Freemasonic lodges.

A network of families and commercial interests has grown up around these sub-Masonic secret organizations, which elsewhere I have called 'the Syndicate'.[20] The US is heavily influenced by the Syndicate, regardless of whether the Republicans or Democrats are in power, and also by these secret organizations. The principle of a Masonic State, in which all the incumbents of all the principal State institutions are Freemasons or members of sub-Masonic secret organizations, remains very strong, although the forms in which its Freemasonry is expressed have evolved into these sub-Masonic entities. Many modern leaders have their immediate roots in these twentieth-century sub-Masonic secret organizations rather than in eighteenth-century Freemasonry, but are no less tied into world Freemasonry. The apparent division at the top of US politics now embodied in the Bush and Clinton dynasties may be a consequence of a variance in emphasis within Freemasonry and its related Syndicate sub-organizations.

Freemasonry in International Relations

The First World War had Freemasonic origins. Gabriel Princip, a Grand-Orient Mason, killed Archduke Ferdinand and precipitated the war, which caused the collapse of the Romanovs in Russia, the Habsburgs in Austro-Hungary and the Ottoman Empire. (The Grand-Orient Templars' aim was to overthrow monarchies and damage the Catholic Great Powers.) Rockefellers funded the Kaiser to build the Berlin-to-Baghdad railway line through the Federal Reserve system so they could drill oil under Ottoman control and wrest Near-Eastern oil from the British. (Churchill signed away British oilfields in Mesopotamia in return for American involvement at the end of the First World War, following the disastrous battle of Verdun in 1916.) The defeat of Kaiser Wilhelm and the general overthrow of aristocracy in favour of socialist and nationalist movements signified that Grand-Orient Freemasonry had achieved its objectives in starting the war.

The Russian revolutions – there were four in all – involved Syndicate families. For example, the 'Rothschilds', the commercial descendants of Mayer Amschel Rothschild, were behind the Socialist International, and Rothschilds' Royal Dutch Co. and Rockefellers' Standard Oil vied for control of the Russian Baku oilfields around 1900. In 1905 'Rockefellers' – the inverted commas round 'Rothschilds' and 'Rockefellers' now denote a particular emphasis of a commercial pattern and make it clear I am not referring to particular individuals – funded Trotsky's abortive 1905 revolution.

With an eye on Baku oil and also the Tsar's wealth, 'Rothschilds' mobilized Lord Milner, a 33rd-degree Mason, and the British Embassy in Moscow to install Kerensky in 1917. 'Rockefellers', taken by surprise, sent Trotsky, who had been living on 'Rockefeller'/Standard Oil property at Constable Hook, Bayonne, New Jersey,[21] with Grand-Orient backing, to liaise with Lenin and implement a plan based on Adam Weishaupt's world-government objectives – to foment revolution in Russia so it would be a platform for world revolution. After his Bolshevik *coup* (financed by $5–6 million given him by the Warburg family, a mere third of their funding),[22] Lenin packed his administration with Freemasons.[23] The plan demanded the overthrow of Church and State, and Lenin, a Grand-Orient Freemason, gave orders for the Tsar and his family to be murdered and closed the Russian Orthodox Church. He turned his Communist regime into a terroristic one-party dictatorship before, as the result of ill health resulting from an attempted assassination, he eventually surrendered power to Stalin.

In 1922 Freemasonry swiftly turned the Soviet Union into a Masonic State by setting up Grand-Orient lodges in Paris to house 'a temporary committee recognized by the Supreme Council of France, which will subsequently become the Supreme Council of the Scottish Rite in Russia'.[24] A new legislative body comprising the people and the republics would come into being. This would be called the 'Supreme Soviet' (or Council) after the 33rd-degree Supreme Council of Freemasonry. It was controlled by a Communist Party hierarchy.[25]

In a fourth revolution Stalin finally replaced Lenin when he died in 1923, and in 1925 he entered into a compact with a Syndicate family, 'Rockefellers', selling them a half-interest in Russia's oilfields, including Baku, in return for funding for his Five-Year Plans.[26] The Freemasonic Syndicate was now effectively running the Soviet Union's economy.

Having backed Stalin to create a world government, the Syndicate families assisted in the funding of Hitler's war machine during the 1930s in the hope that Hitler would establish a Nazi world government. In other words they were backing both sides as a ruse to gain world control. Several American corporations traded with and funded Nazi Germany from 1929 onwards, and there were cross-border links throughout the Second World War. Throughout the war Standard Oil of New Jersey shipped oil to the Nazis through Spain, and the Reichsbank acted as go-between between Hitler and Wall Street, dealing with American banks such as the Schröder Bank of New York.

The buildings intended to cope with this world government can be visited in Nuremberg, which was to be the headquarters of the world: a congress hall based on the design of the Roman Coliseum that was to seat 50,000 representatives, and a stadium gouged out of a lake that was to hold 350,000–450,000 people.

Factions in the Syndicate encouraged Hitler to invade Russia, but when it became clear that he was losing the war they switched their full support to Stalin,[27] whom they had never stopped funding. Encouragingly, Freemasonic plans do not always work. The Freemasonic world government is not as all-powerful as it appears and it does make miscalculations.

Stalin was a Martinist Rosicrucian Freemason.[28] (Martinism was founded in 1754 by a Rosicrucian Spanish Jew, Martines de Pasqually or Martinez Paschalis.) Allied decisions involving General Marshall prevented Montgomery from reaching Berlin first and as a result Stalin spread a Soviet Empire from there that might eventually establish a Communist world government.

Factions within the Syndicate supported Communism as a means of gathering the world into two armed blocs which, at a later date, could be merged (as happened in 1989). They wanted a dialectic of opposites which could advance their commercial agenda, including making loans so that both sides could arm with nuclear missiles in an arms race. They were not, as rich capitalists, proposing to live under Communism. Their support was self-interested. Syndicate families appearing as friends of the Kremlin when they were not resembled Deist Freemasons appearing to be Christian when they were not.

Immediately after the war the Rockefeller family, acting in conjunction with the CFR and the Syndicate, was instrumental in setting up the UN. John D. Rockefeller III donated $8.5 million for the purchase of 18 acres of land in Manhattan on which the UN building was built. (New York City contributed a further $4.25 million.) Nelson Rockefeller reached an agreement with Stalin that the UN would not interfere in Russian affairs.[29]

The Cold War followed immediately after the Second World War. It was called 'cold' because the two sides both had enough atomic weapons to destroy mankind many times over and, as these could not be used in local conflicts, they fought small proxy wars in Asia, Africa and Latin America, while vying also for possession of Europe. The Soviet Union acquired Eastern Europe and the USA defended Western Europe. Some Syndicate families financed the sale of arms to both sides, and fuelled the conflicts in Korea, Suez, Cuba, Vietnam and the four Arab-Israeli wars during the Cold War: in 1948–9, 1956, 1967 and 1973.

The Cold War was profoundly influenced by Freemasons on both sides – effectively an American Freemasonic State and a Soviet Freemasonic State. Throughout, factions within the Syndicate deliberately maintained a flow of arms to both sides.

The Soviet Politburo was run by the Central Committee of the Communist Party of the Soviet Union and the Council of Elders. Thus a speech by Krushchev, quoted in the *Cominform* weekly journal of 11 February 1955, began: 'Comrade deputies, on the instruction of the Central Committee of the CPSU and the Council of Elders, I wish...'[30] This Council of Elders seems to have been the Supreme Council of the Scottish Rite in Russia envisaged in 1922, a Freemasonic body.

Stalin's 1925 oil-for-funding deal with a Syndicate family was strictly a commercial deal that financed his Five-Year Plans, while the Nazis invested heavily in securing Caucasian and Middle-Eastern oil. Because of this deal a faction within the Syndicate had influence over the Communist leadership. This was brought out in August 1964 when Krushchev was dismissed. He had fallen out with Mao and his anti-Maoist policy had affected Soviet–Chinese trade, to the cost of David Rockefeller, who owned the rights to all oil exported from China.[31] Exactly what happened can only be conjectured, but it is known that Krushchev phoned David Rockefeller, who was holding a Bilderberg conference in Leningrad, and implored him to go to Moscow immediately to discuss Soviet–Chinese trade in the Kremlin. A difficult meeting took place at which David Rockefeller's daughter Neva took notes.[32] In October Krushchev was ousted.

Many commentators have observed that David Rockefeller seems to have been impressively able to influence Soviet domestic politics, including the Soviet choice of leadership, perhaps via the Council of the Elders, to protect his oil interests in China. The issue of course concerned more than oil interests – it was about geopolitical control.

Factions within the Syndicate act in accordance with its world strategy and also their corporate interests. These generally coincide, but if there are conflicts of interest then, as we have already observed, the high-minded idealism of the past may give way and self-interest prevail. So it seems that the Syndicate's relationship with the post-Stalin leadership was such that Rockefeller could go to Moscow, demand the replacement of the Russian leader and secure it two months later.[33]

Syndicate family oil links with North Vietnam may have been a factor at the time. The North Vietnamese had been armed by Laurance Rockefeller, General MacArthur's assistant, who sold weapons and munitions from the US stockpile on Okinawa to Ho Chi Minh at the end of the Second World War. Standard Oil had searched for oil off Vietnam from 1950 to 1960, when they located vast oil reserves. A stable Vietnam would allow them to remove the offshore oil and so the link with Ho Chi Minh developed. In November 1964 the Soviet Union promised to help North Vietnam and around this time a Syndicate family set up a huge arms production site in Russia, which is believed to have kept the Viet Cong well supplied with arms. Through the International Basic Economy Corporation and its associated Tower International Inc., headed by a former secretary of John D. Rockefeller I, Cyrus Eaton, and his son, the Syndicate was a major commercial force in the Vietnam area in the 1960s and would anyway command the respectful attention of the Kremlin.[34] Nevertheless, it does seem as if deals were being made between the American and Soviet

Freemasonic States for commercial gain, to which military interests were to some extent subordinated.

At the military level, President Lyndon B. Johnson stepped up the Vietnam War. This had the effect of intensifying one side of the Freemasonic Syndicate's dialectic, that there should be two conflicting blocs which can be put together in a synthesis, as happened when North Vietnam won the war. After the victory, a Syndicate family (as Ho Chi Minh's ally) occupied a special position in relation to the victorious regime and had a clear run to remove the offshore oil in fulfilment of the Syndicate's master plan. The US defeat was a further advance in Freemasonry's plan to convert the USA from a nation-state into a state within an American Union bloc which would eventually be under a forthcoming world government.

It is easier to unify the world if it is divided into two camps. The Cold War had the effect of achieving this division, making it possible to move toward a unifying world government by eliminating the division, as happened with the fall of the Berlin Wall and Communism. Of the two leaders involved at the time, President Gorbachev of the USSR had visited Paris in 1984 and been initiated into French Grand-Orient Templar Freemasonry[35] and US President Ronald Reagan had many links with Freemasons, as we have seen. Though not a Puritan, he brought the Puritan vision to the last months of the Cold War and spoke of America as being a 'city on a hill', using rhetoric that contrasted Christianity and Communism while piling on arms pressure that was too great for the Soviet Union to withstand. (The USA has a tendency to brand its enemies as 'evil': to Reagan the USSR was an 'evil empire' and, more recently, to Bush Jr 'terrorist states' such as Iraq, Iran and North Korea were an 'Axis of Evil'.)

Reagan used Puritan imagery to end the Cold War and his modest throwaway line 'We won the Cold War' does not do justice to the skill he brought to his victory. There is an opinion that only Americans and pro-Americans believe that Reagan and the USA ended the Cold War and that the USA won. This asserts that the real credit should go to Gorbachev, who had the vision of reforming the USSR, using perestroika (restructuring) and glasnost (openness). It may be that he demonstrated (in accordance with his plan) that the Soviet system was incapable of being reformed and opened the way to a foreign capitalist takeover via Yeltsin.

Now that the USSR has been carved up into oil republics and oil is being transported west from the Caspian, it does look as if the Cold War ended because there was a deal between Freemasonic mindsets to advance their commercial interests – that is, the plan was neither Reagan's nor Gorbachev's but the Syndicate's. It is interesting that as early as April/May 1991 the Gorbachev Foundation in the USA was capitalized with $3 million from the Carnegie Endowment for International Peace, the Ford Foundation, the Rockefeller Brothers Fund and the Pew and Mellon Funds. This suggests that Gorbachev was backed by the Syndicate to loosen the union of the USSR and make possible the beginnings of a regional world government in which the USSR would be broken up and Europe would be uncoupled from the USA.[36]

Now Freemasonry's federal plan for a United States of the World is rapidly being implemented. The Free Trade Area of the Americas (FTAA) began in December 1994 and has 34 member States, including the USA. It is the basis for an American Union designed to dominate the Western hemisphere. It is conceived that there will be a United States of Europe, including Russia, a regional United States of the Middle East and a United States of Africa (the African Union began in 2002). There are equivalent bodies in the East: the South Asian Free Trade Area (SAFTA) and a forthcoming Asian Economic Community that will include China, Japan and Korea. The Eastern hemisphere will comprise India, Pakistan, China, Japan, South and South-East Asia, Australia and New Zealand. The Majority World, which includes India and China, seems to be overtaking the West but is already settling into the new structure of Freemasonry's federal plan.

In view of all this, although the final success of the plan is still in doubt, it looks as if a hidden Freemasonry is the most powerful influence in contemporary international relations.

Freemasonry's Christian Veneer

Nevertheless, the Christian tradition remains strong. A recent survey has established that 38 per cent of Americans attend church each week.[37] Both Freemasonic Deists and Christians believe 'In God We Trust', and Christian voters were crucial in sending Bush Jr to the White House for his second term. US support of Israel is mainly right-wing Christian. Bush Jr projects himself as a born-again Christian while happily being inaugurated on the Freemasonic Bible from St John's Lodge, New York, and he has used the theme of Christian values in speaking about Islam and Muslim terrorists.

The idea that Islam is unified against the West is a Western idea. In fact there are various strains in the Muslim world: the USSR-inspired socialists of the 1950s; the Islamic *mujahedin* of the 1970–90s; the anti-Western *jihadists*, including part of al-Qaeda, who want to restore the caliphate and *Sharia* law; and the more moderate Islamic social tribal movements, such as Hamas and part of al-Qaeda, who seek an end to foreign intervention in the Middle East.

The background to the conflict in the Middle East is the Syndicate's alleged ambition to change regimes and impound oil as a world-government resource. The aim seems to be a world-government regional United States of the Middle East, eventually embracing Palestine, Israel, Iraq, Iran, Lebanon and Syria. To some commentators this has seemed to provoke a clash between civilizations, or rather, a clash between factions within the North American and Arab civilizations. Many commentators have observed that, at the time of writing, Sunni Iraq and Shi'ite Lebanese Hizbollah have been dealt with and that Shi'ite Syria and Iran remain to be dealt with. A United States of the Middle East cannot happen without some levelling down of the warlike postures of most of the local states. (Levelling down worked in the First World War and again in the Second World War, when in the course of less than 30 years the mighty warring monarchies of Europe were shattered into today's united European states.)

Throughout this process there has been a covert crusading outlook which Freemasons, eager to seek world government, and Syndicate families, eager to control Middle-Eastern oil, have readily adopted. As in the mid-eighteenth century, the extended Freemasonic tradition is working covertly behind the Christian façade which apparently dominates American life. It may suit Freemasonry's agenda for Christianity and Islam to be opposed – indeed, in conflict – and so the descendants of the Founding Fathers are quite happy to maintain the *status quo*: a Masonic State with a Christian outlook often couched in Deist language, with neutral church services that Deists can attend.

Freemasonry's willingness to shelter behind Christianity conceals a secret which is only revealed to Masons above the 30th degree. As Pike wrote in *Morals and Dogma*, Freemasons believe with Gnostics and Cathars that there are two gods: that Lucifer never fell to Earth but is really the ultimate God and that Jehovah (or Adonay) is the god of the world, a demiurge.[38] Pike, rebelling against the Union at the start of the Civil War, wrote: 'Lucifer, the Sun of the Morning! It is *he* who bears the *Light*... Doubt it not!' And, as already noted, in his instructions to the 'Twenty-three Supreme Councils of the World' on 14 July 1889 he wrote: 'Yes, Lucifer is God, and unfortunately Adonay is also God... Lucifer, God of Light and God of Good, is struggling for humanity against Adonay, the God of Darkness and Evil.'[39] Pike instructs the Sovereign Grand Inspectors-General, 'You may repeat it to the brethren of the 32nd, 31st and 30th degrees.' In other words, Freemasonry shelters its heretical belief in rebellious Lucifer behind Christianity's public worship of Jehovah.

The balance of power between Freemasonic and Christian attitudes can be seen at work in the planning of the 400th anniversary of America's founding, a ceremony at the very heart of American life scheduled to be 'observed' in 2007. (Americans prefer 'observed' to 'celebrated', which is deemed to convey triumphalist feelings that are pejorative towards native Americans.) Back in 1997, America decided that its first founding took place when the first permanent English-speaking settlement at Jamestown was founded in 1607. Floridan supporters of St Augustine, mainly Hispanics and members of a Hispanic popular movement, claim that 1565 was the true start date – the date of the founding of the first permanent settlement in the New World.

It is likely that Bartholomew Gosnold and John Smith brought conflicting ideologies to the New World, perhaps without realizing it: Gosnold the official Anglican Christianity of the royal court and John Smith, perhaps even from the outset rather than in later life, the early Baconian Freemasonry. Gosnold, as we have seen, organized and funded the voyage via his wife's relative Sir Thomas Smythe, and he recruited Smith, who was an underling during the voyage and, indeed, spent from January to June 1607 in the hold in chains. Yet it is John Smith's statue that dominates present-day Jamestown, not Gosnold's, perhaps signalling indirectly that Freemasonry presided over the settlement of Jamestown, having arrived with, and hidden behind, Anglican Christianity.

Today, following the lecture I gave in Richmond, Virginia, in October 1998, Gosnold has his supporters, in particular Dr William Kelso. Nevertheless, the observance of the anniversary has focused on John Smith and Pocahontas – a story of one-world racial harmony – and there have been moves to shift the ceremony from Jamestown to Williamsburg, which did not become the colonial capital until 1700. Visitors to colonial Williamsburg will know that John D. Rockefeller Jr reconstructed the town from 1926 to 1960 at a cost to himself of $68 million and to other members of the Rockefeller family of a further $40 million.

Behind the scenes, Freemasons are in charge of the observation of the anniversary, hence the focus on the probably Freemasonic John Smith at the expense of Gosnold and his Elizabethan outlook. This outlook was finally defeated by Lincoln during the Civil War and is now, like the Dutch Puritan Amish, confined to small enclaves within the USA, notably on plantations that owe their origins to the Elizabethan and early Jacobean adventurers who braved the seas to plant the English flag and settle in the New World.

The real story of the founding of America is that it was planted by Christians and founded constitutionally by Deist Freemasons. What does this tell us about the America of today? What is the story behind Bush Jr's War against Terror? Is he crusading for Christendom against Islamic terrorists in the name of self-defence while easing pressure on Israel? It could be argued that at the same time he is spreading a democratic Masonic State and moving towards a Syndicate-led world government and control of Middle-Eastern oil reserves. It must be pointed out that in his inauguration address for his second term he adopted the Rothschildian Israeli Sharansky's position as stated in *The Case for Democracy: The Power of Freedom to Overcome Tyranny and Terror*. Bush Jr is an oilman like his father and, as a President surrounded by neo-cons, he has close links with Israel, and therefore with the Syndicate.

America is currently the most powerful nation on Earth. Is the American President of the day able to make policy of his own free will or is he pressed behind the scenes to reflect a Freemasonic agenda? This question will be asked of every President in the coming generations. Our investigation of the secret founding of America and America's Masonic State has put us in a position to know the answer.

The Syndicate has its roots in the constitutional founding of America and the Deist Founding Fathers. It seeks a United States of the World that will include the Majority World in regional blocs, a new federal-continental world order in which all nation-states are to become constituent world states. According to this plan, US superpower domination will cease to exist as the USA will become a member state within a regional American Union.

The Syndicate denies that there are larger historical forces in the Majority World (China, India, the Islamic world, Africa, Latin America) which may not want to be in regional blocs and which might be overpowering this agenda. Its control of the world's infrastructure and social movements is so great that it does not believe it can be outflanked and its agenda overwhelmed. It is confident that its plans cannot conceivably be upset by climate change, pandemics, toxic or technological disasters or by new world views.

Nevertheless, world government can be a good thing in the right hands. It can abolish wars, diseases and famines – the very weapons, some would say, being used by the Syndicate to achieve the goal of world government. It can also reverse the Syndicate's commitment to depopulation and a planned reduction of the world's population by as much as a third.[40] A genuinely Universalist world government, acknowledging the common basis of the Divine Light in all religions – which involves restating the tradition of revelation[41] and rejecting Deism's opposition to it – could bring freedom, democracy and a redistribution of resources to all the world's citizens.

There are two New World Orders: one which can be seen as reflecting the vision of all religions, mirroring Heaven and embodied in this genuinely Universalist world government, and one which can be seen as Weishaupt's, mirroring Hell and embodied in a debased world government that powerful self-interested factions have tried to bring in.

I live in hope that a high-minded world government, drawing on the ideals of the Founding Fathers of the United States of America, *can* outflank the Syndicate and overwhelm its agenda. But this will involve rejecting their Deism and also the self-interested machinations of mega-billionaires who aspire to world government in order to control the planet's natural resources for their own gain.

APPENDICES

CONSTITUTIONAL DOCUMENTS

John Winthrop, *A Modell of Christian Charitie*, 1630

Written on board the *Arbella* on the Atlantic Ocean by the Hon. John Winthrop Esqr. In his passage (with a great company of Religious people, of which Christian tribes he was the Brave Leader and famous Governor;) from the Island of Great Brittaine to New-England in the North America. Anno 1630.

CHRISTIAN CHARITIE.

A Modell hereof.

God Almighty in his most holy and wise providence, hath soe disposed of the condition of mankind, as in all times some must be rich, some poore, some high and eminent in power and dignitie; others mean and in submission.

The Reason hereof.

1 *Reas.* First to hold conformity with the rest of his world, being delighted to show forth the glory of his wisdom in the variety and difference of the creatures, and the glory of his power in ordering all these differences for the preservation and good of the whole; and the glory of his greatness,

that as it is the glory of princes to have many officers, soe this great king will have many stewards, Counting himself more honoured in dispensing his gifts to man by man, than if he did it by his owne immediate hands.

2 Reas. Secondly that he might have the more occasion to manifest the work of his Spirit: first upon the wicked in moderating and restraining them: soe that the riche and mighty should not eate upp the poore nor the poore and dispised rise upp against and shake off theire yoake. 2ly In the regenerate, in exerciseing his graces in them, as in the grate ones, theire love, mercy, gentleness, temperance &c., in the poore and inferior sorte, theire faithe, patience, obedience &c.

3 Reas. Thirdly, that every man might have need of others, and from hence they might be all knitt more nearly together in the Bonds of brotherly affection. From hence it appears plainly that noe man is made more honourable than another or more wealthy &c., out of any particular and singular respect to himselfe, but for the glory of his creator and the common good of the creature, man. Therefore God still reserves the propperty of these gifts to himself as Ezek. 16. 17. he there calls wealthe, *his gold and his silver*, and Prov. 3. 9. he claims theire service as his due, *honor the Lord with thy riches* &c. All men being thus (by divine providence) ranked into two sorts, riche and poore; under the first are comprehended all such as are able to live comfortably by their own meanes duely improved; and all others are poore according to the former distribution. There are two rules whereby we are to walk one towards another: Justice and Mercy. These are always distinguished in their act and in their object, yet may they both concurre in the same subject in eache respect; as sometimes there may be an occasion of showing mercy to a rich man in some sudden danger or distresse, and alsoe doeing of meere justice to a poor man in regard of some perticular contract &c. There is likewise a double Lawe by which wee are regulated in our conversation towardes another; in both the former respects, the lawe of nature and the lawe of grace, or the morrall lawe or the lawe of the gospell, to omitt the rule of justice as not propperly belonging to this purpose otherwise than it may fall into consideration in some perticular cases. By the first of these lawes man as he was enabled soe withall is commanded to love his neighbour as himself. Upon this ground stands all the precepts of the morrall lawe, which concernes our dealings with men. To apply this to the works of mercy; this lawe requires two things. First that every man afford his help to another in every want or distresse. Secondly, that hee performe this out of the same affection which makes him carefull of his owne goods, according to that of our Savior, (Math.) *Whatsoever ye would that men should do to you.* This was practised by Abraham and Lot in entertaining the angells and the old man of Gibea. The lawe of Grace or of the Gospell hath some difference from the former; as in these respects, First the lawe of nature was given to man in the estate of innocency; this of the Gospell in the estate of regeneracy. 2ly, the former propounds one man to another, as the same flesh and image of God; this as a brother in Christ allsoe, and in the communion of the same Spirit, and soe teacheth to put a difference between christians and others. *Doe good to all, especially to the household of faith;* upon this ground the Israelites were to putt a difference betwccne the brethren of such as were strangers though not of the Canaanites.

3ly. The Lawe of nature would give no rules for dealing with enemies, for all arc to be considered as friends in the state of innocency, but the Gospell commands love to an enemy. Proofe. *If thine Enemy hunger, feed him; Love your Enemies, doe good to them that hate you.* Math. 5. 44.

This lawe of the Gospell propounds likewise a difference of seasons and occasions. There is a time when a christian must sell all and give to the poor, as they did in the Apostles times. There is a time allsoe when christians (though they give not all yet) must give beyond their abillity, as they of Macedonia, Cor. 2, 6. Likewise community of perills calls for extraordinary liberality, and soe doth community in some speciall service for the churche. Lastly, when there is no other means whereby our christian brother may be relieved in his distress, we must help him beyond our ability rather than tempt God in putting him upon help by miraculous or extraordinary meanes.

This duty of mercy is exercised in the kinds, Giveving, lending and forgiving.

Quest. What rule shall a man observe in giveving in respect of the measure? *Ans.* If the time and occasion be ordinary he is to give out of his abundance. *Let him lay aside as God hath blessed him.* If the time and occasion be extraordinary, he must be ruled by them; taking this withall, that then a man cannot likely doe too much, especially if he may leave himselfe and his family under probable means of comfortable subsistence.

Object. A man must lay upp for posterity, the fathers lay upp for posterity and children, and *he is worse than an infidell that provideth not for his owne.* *Ans.* For the first, it is plaine that it being spoken by way of comparison, it must be meant of the ordinary and usuall course of fathers, and cannot extend to times and occasions extraordinary. For the other place the Apostle speaks against such as walked inordinately, and it is without question, that he is worse than an infidell who through his owne sloathe and voluptuousness shall neglect to provide for his family.

Object. The wise man's Eies are in his head, saith Solomon, *and foreseeth the plague;* therefore he must forecast and lay upp against evill times when hee or his may stand in need of all he can gather.

Ans. This very Argument Solomon useth to persuade to liberallity, Eccle.: *Cast thy bread upon the waters,* and *for thou knowest not what evill may come upon the land.* Luke 26. *Make you friends of the riches of iniquity;* you will ask how this shall be? Very well. For first he that gives to the poore, lends to the lord and he will repay him even in this life an hundredfold to him or his. *The righteous is ever mercifull and lendeth and his seed enjoyeth the blessing;* and besides wee know what advantage it will be to us in the day of account when many such witnesses shall stand forth for us to witnesse the improvement of our tallent. And I would know of those whoe pleade soe much for laying up for time to come, whether they holde that to be Gospell, Math. 16. 19. *Lay not upp for yourselves Treasures upon Earth &c.* If they acknowledge it, what extent will they allowe it? If only to those primitive times, let them consider the reason whereopon our Saviour groundes it. The first is that they are subject to the moathe, the rust, the theife. Secondly, They will steale away the hearte; *where the treasure is there will ye heart be allsoe.* The reasons are of like force at all times. Therefore the exhortation must be generall and perpetuall, withallwayes in respect of the love and affection to riches and in regard of the things themselves when any speciall service for the churche or perticular Distresse of our brother doe call for the use of them; otherwise it is not only lawfull but necessary to lay upp as Joseph did to have ready uppon such occasions, as the Lord (whose stewards wee are of them) shall call for them from us; Christ gives us an Instance of the first, when hee sent his disciples for the Ass, and bidds them answer the owner thus, the Lord hath need of him: soe when the Tabernacle was to be built, he sends to his people to call for their silver and gold, &c; and yeildes noe other reason but that it was for his worke. When Elisha comes to the widow of Sareptah and findes her preparing to make ready her pittance for herselfe and family, he bids her first provide for him, he challengeth first God's parte which she must first give before shee must serve her owne family. All these teache us that the Lord lookes that when hee is pleased to call for his right in any thing wee have, our owne interest wee have, must stand aside till his turne be served. For the other, wee need looke noe further then to that of John 1. *he whoe hath this world's goodes and seeth his brother to neede and shutts upp his compassion from him, how dwelleth the love of God in him,* which comes punctually to this conclusion; if thy brother be in want and thou canst help him, thou needst not make doubt, what thou shouldst doe; if thou lovest God thou must help him.

Quest. What rule must wee observe in lending?

Ans. Thou must observe whether thy brother hath present or probable or possible means of repaying thee, if there be none of those, thou must give him according to his necessity, rather then lend him as he requires; if he hath present means of repaying thee, thou art to look at him not as an act of mercy, but by way of Commerce, wherein thou arte to walk by the rule of justice; but if his means of repaying thee be only probable or possible, then is hee an object of thy mercy, thou must lend him, though there be danger of losing it, Deut. 15. 7. *If any of thy brethren be poore* &c., *thou shalt lend him sufficient.* That men might not shift off this duty by the apparent hazzard, he tells them that though the yeare of Jubile were at hand (when he must remitt it, if hee were not able to repay it before) yet he must lend him and that chearefully. *It may not greive thee to give him* (saith hee) and because some might object, why soe I should soone impoverishe myself and my family, he adds with all thy worke &c; for our Saviour, Math. 5. 42. *From him that would borrow of thee turne not away.*

Quest. What rule must we observe in forgiving?

Ans. Whether thou didst lend by way of commerce or in mercy, if he hath nothing to pay thee, must forgive, (except in cause where thou hast a surety or a lawfull pleadge) Deut. 15. 2. Every seaventh yeare the Creditor was to quitt that which he lent to his brother if he were poore as appears ver. 8. *Save when there shall be no poore with thee.* In all these and like cases, Christ was a generall rule, Math. 7. 22. *Whatsoever ye would that men should doe to you, doe yee the same to them allsoe.*

Quest. What rule must wee observe and walke by in cause of community of perill?

Ans. The same as before, but with more enlargement towards others and lesse respect towards ourselves and our owne right. Hence it was that in the primitive Churche they sold all, had all things in common, neither did any man say that which he possessed was his owne. Likewise in theire returne out of the captivity, because the worke was greate for the restoring of the church and the danger of enemies was common to all, Nehemiah directs the Jews to liberallity and readiness in remitting theire debts to theire brethren, and disposing liberally to such as wanted, and stand not upon their owne dues which they might have demanded of them. Thus did some of our Forefathers in times of persecution in England, and soe did many of the faithful of other churches, whereof wee keepe an honorable remembrance of them; and it is to be observed that both in Scriptures and latter stories of the churches that such as have beene most bountifull to the poore saintes, especially in those extraordinary times and occasions, God hath left them highly commended to posterity, as Zacheus, Cornelius, Dorcas, Bishop Hooper, the Cuttler of Brussells and divers others. Observe againe that the Scripture gives noe caussion to restraine any from being over liberall this way; but all men to the liberall and cherefull practise hereof by the sweeter promises; as to instance one for many, Isaiah 58. 6. *Is not this the fast I have chosen to loose the bonds of wickedness, to take off the heavy burdens, to lett the oppressed go free and to breake every yoake, to deale thy bread to the hungry and to bring the poore that wander into thy house, when thou seest the naked to cover them; and then shall thy light brake forth as the morning and thy healthe shall growe speedily, thy righteousness shall goe before God, and the glory of the Lord shalt embrace thee; then thou shall call and the Lord shall answer thee &c., Ch. 2. 10. If thou power out thy soule to the hungry, then shall thy light spring out in darkness, and the Lord shall guide thee continually, and satisfie thy soule in draught, and make falt thy bones, thou shalt be like a watered garden, and they shalt be of thee that shall build the old wast places &c.* On the contrary most heavy cursses are layed upon such as are straightened towards the Lord and his people, Judg. 5. *Cursse the Meroshe because he came not to help the Lord. Hee whoe shutteth his eares from hearing the cry of the poore, he shall cry and shall not be heard;* Math. 25. *Goe ye curssed into everlasting fire &c. I was hungry and ye fedd mee not,* Cor. 2. 9. 16. He that soweth sparingly shall reape sparingly. Haveing already sett forth the practice of mercy according to the rule of God's lawe, it will be useful to lay open the groundes of it allsoe, being the other parte of the Commandment and that is the affection from which this exercise of mercy must arise, the Apostle tells us that this *love is the fullfilling of the lawe,* not that it is enough to love our brother and soe noe further; but in regard of the excellency of his partes giveing any motion to the other as the soule to the body and the power it hath to sett all the faculties on worke in the outward exercise of this duty; as when wee bid one make the clocke strike, he doth not lay hand on the hammer, which is the immediate instrument of the sound, but setts on worke the first mover or maine wheele; knoweing that will certainely produce the sound which he intends. Soe the way to drawe men to the workes of mercy, is not by force of Argument from the goodness or necessity of the worke; for though this cause may enforce, a rationall minde to some present act of mercy, as is frequent in experience, yet it cannot worke such a habit in a soule, as shall make it prompt upon all occasions to produce the same effect, but by frameing these affections of love in the hearte which will as naturally bring forthe the other, as any cause doth produce the effect.

The deffinition which the Scripture gives us of love is this. *Love is the bond of perfection,* first it is a bond or ligament. 2ly it makes the worke perfect. There is noe body but consists of partes and that which knitts these partes togethei, gives the body its perfection, because it makes eache parte soe contiguous to others as thereby they doe mutually participate with each other, both in strengthe and infirmity, in pleasure and paine. To instance in the most perfect of all bodies; Christ and his Church make one body; the severall partes of this body considered a parte before they were united, were as disproportionate and as much disordering as soe many contrary quallities or elements, but when Christ comes, and by his spirit and love knitts all these partes to himselfe and each to other, it is become the most perfect and best proportioned body in the world, Eph. 4. 16. *Christ, by whome all the body being knitt together by every joint for the furniture thereof, according to the effectuall power which is in the measure of every perfection of partes, a glorious body without spott or wrinkle;* the ligaments hereof being Christ, or his love, for Christ is love, 1 John 4. 8. Soe this definition is right. *Love is the bond of perfection.*

From hence we may frame these conclusions. 1. First of all, true Christians are of one body in Christ, 1 Cor. 12. 12. 13. 17. *Ye are the body of Christ and members of their parte.* All the partes of this body being thus united are made soe contiguous in a speciall relation as they must needes partake of each other's strength and infirmity; joy and sorrowe, weale and woe. 1 Cor. 12. 26. *If one member suffers, all suffer with it, if one be in honor, all rejoyce with it.* 2ly. The ligaments of this body which knitt together are love. 3ly. Noe body can be perfect which wants its proper ligament. 5ly. This sensibleness and sympathy of each other's conditions will necessarily infuse into each parte a native desire and endeavour, to strengthen, defend, preserve and comfort the other. To insist a little on this conclusion being the product of all the former, the truthe hereof will appeare both by precept and patterne. 1 John 3. 10. *Yee ought to lay doune your lives for the brethren.* Gal. 6. 2. *beare ye one another's burthen's and soe fulfill the lawe of Christ.* For patterns wee have that first of our Saviour whoe out of his good will in obedience to his father, becomeing a parte of this body and being knitt with it in the bond of love, found such a native sensibleness of our infirmities and sorrowes as he willingly yielded himselfe to deathe to ease the infirmities of the rest of his body, and soe healed theire sorrowes. From the like sympathy of partes did the Apostles and many thousands of the Saintes lay doune theire lives for Christ. Againe the like wee may see in the members of this body among themselves. 1 Rom. 9. Paule could have been contented to have been separated from Christ, that the Jewes might not be cutt off from the body. It is very observable what hee professeth of his affectionate partaking with every member; *whoe is weake* (saith hee) *and I am not weake? Whoe is offended and I burne not;* and againe, 2 Cor. 7. 13. *Therefore wee are comforted because yee were comforted.* Of Epaphroditus he speaketh, Phil. 2. 30. *that he regarded not his owne life to do him service.* Soe Phebe and others are called *the servants of the churche.* Now it is apparent that they served not for wages, or by constrainte, but out of love.

The like we shall finde in the histories of the churche, in all ages; the sweete sympathie of affections which was in the members of this body one towards another; theire chearfullness in serveing and suffering together; how liberall they were without repineing, harbourers without grudgeing, and helpfull without reproaching; and all from hence, because they had fervent love amongst them; which onely makes the practise of mercy constant and easie.

The next consideration is how this love comes to be wrought. Adam in his first estate was a perfect modell of mankinde in all their generations, and in him this love was perfected in regard of the habit. But Adam, rent himselfe from his Creator, rent all his posterity allsoe one from another; whence it comes that every man is borne with this principle in him to love and seeke himselfe onely, and thus a man continueth till Christ comes and takes possession of the soule and infuseth another principle, love to God and our brother, and this latter haveing continuall supply from Christ, as the head and roote by which he is united, gets the predomining in the soule, soe by little and little expells the former. 1 John 4. 7. *love cometh of God and every one that loveth is borne of God,* soe that this love is the fruite of the new birthe, and none can have it but the new creature. Now when this quallity is thus formed in the soules of men, it workes like the Spirit upon the dric bones. Ezek. 39. *bone came to bone.* It gathers together the scattered bones, or perfect old man Adam, and knitts them into one body againe in Christ, whereby a man is become againe a living soule.

The third consideration is concerning the exercise of this love, which is twofold, inward or outward. The outward hath beene handled in the former preface of this discourse. From unfolding the other wee must take in our way that maxime of philosophy. *Simile simili gaudet,* or like will to like; for as of things which are turned with disaffection to eache other, the ground of it is from a dissimilitude or ariseing from the contrary or different nature of the things themselves; for the ground of love is an apprehension of some resemblance in the things loved to that which affects it. This is the cause why the Lord loves the creature, soe farre as it hathe any of his Image in it; he loves his elect because they are like himselfe, he beholds them in his beloved sonne. So a mother loves her childe, because shee throughly conceives a resemblance of herselfe in it. Thus it is betweene the members of Christ; eache discernes, by the worke of the Spirit, his oune Image and resemblance in another, and therefore cannot but love him as he loves himself. Now when the soule, which is of a sociable nature, findes anything like to itselfe, it is like Adam when Eve was brought to him. She must be one with himselfe. *This is flesh of my flesh* (saith he) *and bone of my bone.* Soe the soule conceives a greate delighte in it; therefore shee desires nearness and familiarity with it. Shee hath a greate propensity to doe it good and receives such content in it, as fearing the miscarriage of her beloved, shee bestowes it in the inmost closett of her heart. Shee will not endure that it shall want any good which shee can give it. If by occasion shee be withdrawne from the company of it, shee is still looking towardes the place where shee left her beloved. If shee heard it groane, shee is with it presently. If shee finde it sadd and disconsolate, shee sighes and moanes with it. Shee hath noe such joy as to see her beloved merry and thriving. If shee see it wronged, shee cannot hear it without passion. Shee setts noe boundes to her affections, nor hath any thought of reward. Shee findes recompense enough in the exercise of her love towardes it. Wee may see this acted to life in Jonathan and David. Jonathan a valiant man endued with the spirit of love, soe soone as he discovered the same spirit in David had presently his hearte knitt to him by this ligament of love; soe that it is said he loved him as his owne soule, he takes soe great pleasure in him, that hee stripps himselfe to adorne his beloved. His father's kingdome was not soe precious to him as his beloved David, David shall have it with all his hearte. Himself desires noe more but that hee may be neare to him to rejoyce in his good. Hee chooseth to converse with him in the wildernesse even to the hazzard of his oune life, rather than with the greate Courtiers in his father's Pallace. When hee sees danger towards him, hee spares neither rare paines nor perill to direct it. When injury was offered his beloved David, hee would not beare it, though from his oune father. And when they must parte for a season onely, they thought theire heartes would have broake for sorrowe, had not theire affections found vent by abundance of teares. Other instances might be brought to showe the nature of this affection; as of Ruthe and Naomi, and many others; but this truthe is cleared enough. If any shall object that it is not possible that love shall he bred or upheld without hope of requitall, it is graunted; but that is not our cause; for this love is alluayes vnder reward. It never gives, but it alluayes receives with advantage; First in regard that among the members of the same body, love and affection are reciprocall in a most equall and sweete kinde of commerce.

2nly. In regard of the pleasure and content that the exercise of love carries with it, as wee may see in the naturall body. The mouth is at all the paines to receive and mince the foode which serves for the nourishment of all the other partes of the body; yet it hath noe cause to complaine; for first the other partes send backe, by severall passages, a due proportion of the same nourishment, in a better forme for the strengthening and comforting the mouthe. 2ly the laboure of the mouthe is accompanied with such pleasure and content as farre exceedes the paines it takes. Soe is it in all the labour of love among Christians. The partie loving, reapes love again, as was showed before, which the soule covetts more then all the wealthe in the world. 3ly. Nothing yeildes more pleasure and content to the soule then when it findes that which it may love fervently; for to love and live beloved is the soule's paradise both here and in heaven. In the State of wedlock there be many comforts to learne out of the troubles of that Condition; but let such as have tryed the most, say if there be any sweetness in that Condition comparable to the exercise of mutuall love.

From the former Considerations arise these Conclusions. 1. First, This love among Christians is a reall thing, not imaginarie. 2ly. This love is as absolutely necessary to the being of the body of Christ, as the sinews and other ligaments of a naturall body are to the being of that body. 3ly. This love is a divine, spirituall, nature; free, active, strong, couragious, permanent; undervaluing all things beneathe its propper object and of all the graces, this makes us nearer to resemble the virtues of our heavenly father. 4thly It rests in the love and wellfare of its beloved. For the full certain knowledge of those truthes concerning the nature, use, and excellency of this grace, that which the holy ghost hath left recorded, 1 Cor. 13, may give full satisfaction, which is needful for every true member of this lovely body of the Lord Jesus, to worke upon theire heartes by prayer, meditation continuall exercise at least of the speciall [influence] of this grace, till Christ be formed in them and they in him, all in eache other, knitt together by this bond of love.

It rests now to make some application of this discourse, by the present designe, which gave the occasion of writing of it. Herein are 4 things to he propounded; *first* the persons, 2ly the worke, 3ly the end, 4thly the meanes. 1. For *the persons*. Wee are a company professing ourselves fellow members of Christ, in which respect only though wee were absent from each other many miles, and had our imployments as farre distant, yet wee ought to account ourselves knitt together by this bond of love, and, live in the exercise of it, if wee would have comforte of our being in Christ. This was notorious in the practise of the Christians in former times; as is testified of the Waldenses, from the mouth of one of the adversaries *Aeneas Sylvius* "mutuo ament pere antequam norunt," they use to love any of theire owne religion even before they were acquainted with them. 2nly for the *worke* wee have in hand. It is by a mutuall consent, through a speciall overvaluing providence and a more than an ordinary approbation of the Churches of Christ, to seeke out a place of cohabitation and Consorteshipp under a due forme of Government both civill and ecclesiasticall. In such cases as this, the care of the publique must oversway all private respects, by which, not only conscience, but meare civill pollicy, dothe binde us. For it is a true rule that particular Estates cannot subsist in the ruin of the publique. 3ly The *end* is to improve our lives to doe more service to the Lord; the comforte and encrease of the body of Christe, whereof we are members; that ourselves and posterity may be the better preserved from the common corruptions of this evill world, to serve the Lord and worke out our Salvation under the power and purity of his holy ordinances. 4thly for the *meanes* whereby this must be effected. They are twofold, a conformity with the worke and end wee aime at. These wee see are extraordinary, therefore wee must not content ourselves with usuall ordinary meanes. Whatsoever wee did, or ought to have, done, when wee lived in England, the same must wee doe, and more allsoe, where wee goe. That which the most in theire churches mainetaine as truthe in profession onely, wee must bring into familiar and constant practise; as in this duty of love, wee must love brotherly without dissimulation, wee must love one another with a pure hearte fervently. Wee must beare one anothers burthens. We must not looke onely on our owne things, but allsoe on the things of our brethren. Neither must wee thinke that the Lord will beare with such faileings at our hands as he dothe from those among whome wee have lived; and that for these 3 Reasons; 1. In regard of the more neare bond of mariage between him and us, wherein hee hath taken us to be his, after a most strickt and peculiar manner, which will make them the more jealous of our love and obedience. Soe he tells the people of Israell, *you onely have I knowne of all the families of the Earthe, therefore will I punishe you for your Transgressions.* 2ly, because *the Lord will be sanctified in them that come neare him.* We know that there were many that corrupted the service of the Lord; some setting upp altars before his owne; others offering both strange fire and strange sacrifices allsoe; yet there came noe fire from heaven, or other sudden judgement upon them, as did upon Nadab and Abihu, whoe yet wee may think did not sinne presumptuously. 3ly When God gives a speciall commission he lookes to have it strictly observed in every article; When he gave Saule a commission to destroy Amaleck, Hee indented with him upon certain articles, and because hee failed in one of the least, and that upon a faire pretense, it lost him the kingdom, which should have beene his reward, if hee had observed his commission. Thus stands the cause betweene God and us. We are entered into Covenant with Him for this worke. Wee have taken out a commission. The Lord hath given us leave to drawe our own articles. Wee have professed to enterprise these and those accounts, upon these and those ends. Wee have hereupon besought Him of favour and blessing. Now if the Lord shall please to heare us, and bring us in peace to the place we desire, then hath hee ratified this covenant and sealed our Commission, and will expect a strict performance of the articles contained in it; but if wee shall neglect the observation of these articles which are the ends wee have propounded, and, dissembling with our God, shall fall to embrace this present world and prosecute our carnall intentions, seeking greate things for ourselves and our posterity, the Lord will surely breake out in wrathe against us; be revenged of such a [sinful] people and make us knowe the price of the breache of such a covenant.

Now the onely way to avoyde this shipwracke, and to provide for our posterity, is to followe the counsell of Micah, *to doe justly, to love mercy, to walk humbly with our God.* For this end, wee must be knitt together, in this worke, as one man. Wee must entertaine each other in brotherly affection. Wee must be willing to abridge ourselves of our superfluities, for the supply of other's necessities. Wee must uphold a familiar commerce together in all meekeness, gentlenes, patience and liberality. Wee must delight in eache other; make other's conditions our oune; rejoice together, mourne together, labour and suffer together, allwayes haveving before our eyes our commission and community in the worke, as members of the same body. Soe shall wee *keepe the unitie of the spirit in the bond of peace*. The Lord will be our God, and delight to dwell among us, as his oune people, and will command a blessing upon us in all our wayes. Soe that wee shall see much more of his wisdome, power, goodness and truthe, than formerly wee have been acquainted with. Wee shall finde that the God of Israell is among us, when ten of us shall be able to resist a thousand of our enemies; when hee shall make us a prayse and glory that men shall say of succeeding plantations, "the Lord make it likely that of *New England*." For wee must consider that wee shall be as a citty upon a hill. The eies of all people are uppon us. Soe that if wee shall deale falsely with our God in this worke wee have undertaken, and soe cause him to withdrawe his present help from us, wee shall be made a story and a by-word through the world. Wee shall open the mouthes of enemies to speake evill of the wayes of God, and all professors for God's sake. Wee shall shame the faces of many of God's worthy servants, and cause theire prayers to be turned into curses upon us till wee be consumed out of the good land whither wee are a goeing.

I shall shutt upp this discourse with that exhortation of Moses, that faithfull servant of the Lord, in his last farewell to Israell, Deut. 30. *Beloved there is now sett before us life and good, Death and evill, in that wee are commanded this day to love the Lord our God, and to love one another, to walke in his wayes and to keepe his Commandements and his Ordinance and his lawes,* and the articles of our Covenant with him, that *wee may live and be multiplied, and that the Lord our God may blesse us in the land whither wee goe to possesse it. But if our heartes shall turne away, soe that wee will not obey, but shall be seduced, and worshipp and serve other Gods,* our pleasure and proffitts, *and serve them;* it is propounded unto us this day, *wee shall surely perishe out of the good land whither wee passe over this vast sea to possesse it;* Therefore lett us choose life that wee, and our seede may live, by obeyeing His voyce and cleaveing to Him, for Hee is our life and our prosperity.

Note
The many references to biblical texts reveal the Puritan mindset in 1630. It must be borne in mind that this document was written on board ship in a pre-dictionary time.

Fundamental Orders of 1639

For as much as it hath pleased Almighty God by the wise disposition of his divine providence so to order and dispose of things that we the Inhabitants and Residents of Windsor, Hartford and Wethersfield are now cohabiting and dwelling in and upon the River of Connectecotte and the lands thereunto adjoining; and well knowing where a people are gathered together the word of God requires that to maintain the peace and union of such a people there should be an orderly and decent Government established according to God, to order and dispose of the affairs of the people at all seasons as occasion shall require; do therefore associate and conjoin ourselves to be as one Public State or Commonwealth; and do for ourselves and our successors and such as shall be adjoined to us at any time hereafter, enter into Combination and Confederation together, to maintain and preserve the liberty and purity of the Gospel of our Lord Jesus which we now profess, as also, the discipline of the Churches, which according to the truth of the said Gospel is now practiced amongst us; as also in our civil affairs to be guided and governed according to such Laws, Rules, Orders and Decrees as shall be made, ordered, and decreed as followeth:

1. It is Ordered, sentenced, and decreed, that there shall be yearly two General Assemblies or Courts, the one the second Thursday in April, the other the second Thursday in September following; the first shall be called the Court of Election, wherein shall be yearly chosen from time to time, so many Magistrates and other public Officers as shall be found requisite: Whereof one to be chosen Governor for the year ensuing and until another be chosen, and no other Magistrate to be chosen for more than one year: provided always there be six chosen besides the Governor, which being chosen and sworn according to an Oath recorded for that purpose, shall have the power to administer justice according to the Laws here established, and for want thereof, according to the Rule of the Word of God; which choice shall be made by all that are admitted freemen and have taken the Oath of Fidelity, and do cohabit within this Jurisdiction having been admitted Inhabitants by the major part of the Town wherein they live or

the major part of such as shall be then present.

2. It is Ordered, sentenced, and decreed, that the election of the aforesaid Magistrates shall be in this manner: every person present and qualified for choice shall bring in (to the person deputed to receive them) one single paper with the name of him written in it whom he desires to have Governor, and that he that hath the greatest number of papers shall be Governor for that year. And the rest of the Magistrates or public officers to be chosen in this manner: the Secretary for the time being shall first read the names of all that are to be put to choice and then shall severally nominate them distinctly, and every one that would have the person nominated to be chosen shall bring in one single paper written upon, and he that would not have him chosen shall bring in a blank; and every one that hath more written papers than blanks shall be a Magistrate for that year; which papers shall be received and told by one or more that shall be then chosen by the court and sworn to be faithful therein; but in case there should not be six chosen as aforesaid, besides the Governor, out of those which are nominated, than he or they which have the most written papers shall be a Magistrate or Magistrates for the ensuing year, to make up the aforesaid number.

3. It is Ordered, sentenced, and decreed, that the Secretary shall not nominate any person, nor shall any person be chosen newly into the Magistracy which was not propounded in some General Court before, to be nominated the next election; and to that end it shall be lawful for each of the Towns aforesaid by their deputies to nominate any two whom they conceive fit to be put to election; and the Court may add so many more as they judge requisite.

4. It is Ordered, sentenced, and decreed, that no person be chosen Governor above once in two years, and that the Governor be always a member of some approved Congregation, and formerly of the Magistracy within this Jurisdiction; and that all the Magistrates, Freemen of this Commonwealth; and that no Magistrate or other public officer shall execute any part of his or their office before they are severally sworn, which shall be done in the face of the court if they be present, and in case of absence by some deputed for that purpose.

5. It is Ordered, sentenced, and decreed, that to the aforesaid Court of

Election the several Towns shall send their deputies, and when the Elections are ended they may proceed in any public service as at other Courts. Also the other General Court in September shall be for making of laws, and any other public occasion, which concerns the good of the Commonwealth.

6. It is Ordered, sentenced, and decreed, that the Governor shall, either by himself or by the Secretary, send out summons to the Constables of every Town for the calling of these two standing Courts one month at least before their several times: And also if the Governor and the greatest part of the Magistrates see cause upon any special occasion to call a General Court, they may give order to the Secretary so to do within fourteen days' warning: And if urgent necessity so required, upon a shorter notice, giving sufficient grounds for it to the deputies when they meet, or else be questioned for the same; And if the Governor and major part of Magistrates shall either neglect or refuse to call the two General standing Courts or either of them, as also at other times when the occasions of the Commonwealth require, the Freemen thereof, or the major part of them, shall petition to them so to do; if then it be either denied or neglected, the said Freemen, or the major part of them, shall have the power to give order to the Constables of the several Towns to do the same, and so may meet together, and choose to themselves a Moderator, and may proceed to do any act of power which any other General Courts may.

7. It is Ordered, sentenced, and decreed, that after there are warrants given out for any of the said General Courts, the Constable or Constables of each Town, shall forthwith give notice distinctly to the inhabitants of the same, in some public assembly or by going or sending from house to house, that at a place and time by him or them limited and set, they meet and assemble themselves together to elect and choose certain deputies to be at the General Court then following to agitate the affairs of the Commonwealth; which said deputies shall be chosen by all that are admitted Inhabitants in the several Towns and have taken the oath of fidelity; provided that none be chosen a Deputy for any General Court which is not a Freeman of this Commonwealth.

The aforesaid deputies shall be chosen in manner following: every person that is present and qualified as before expressed, shall bring the names of such, written in several papers, as they desire to have chosen for that employment, and these three or four, more or less, being the number agreed on to be chosen for that time, that have the greatest number of papers written for them shall be deputies for that Court; whose names shall be endorsed on the back side of the warrant and returned into the Court, with the Constable or Constables' hand unto the same.

8. It is Ordered, sentenced, and decreed, that Windsor, Hartford, and Wethersfield shall have power, each Town, to send four of their Freemen as their deputies to every General Court; and Whatsoever other Town shall be hereafter added to this Jurisdiction, they shall send so many deputies as the Court shall judge meet, a reasonable proportion to the number of Freemen that are in the said Towns being to be attended therein; which deputies shall have the power of the whole Town to give their votes and allowance to all such laws and orders as may be for the public good, and unto which the said Towns are to be bound.

9. It is Ordered, sentenced, and decreed, that the deputies thus chosen shall have power and liberty to appoint a time and a place of meeting together before any General Court, to advise and consult of all such things as may concern the good of the public, as also to examine their own Elections, whether according to the order, and if they or the greatest part of them find any election to be illegal they may seclude such for present from their meeting, and return the same and their reasons to the Court; and if it be proved true, the Court may fine the party or parties so intruding, and the Town, if they see cause, and give out a warrant to go to a new election in a legal way, either in part or in whole. Also the said deputies shall have power to fine any that shall be disorderly at their meetings, or for not coming in due time or place according to appointment; and they may return the said fines into the Court if it be refused to be paid, and the Treasurer to take notice of it, and to escheat or levy the same as he does other fines.

10. It is Ordered, sentenced, and decreed, that every General Court, except such as through neglect of the Governor and the greatest part of the Magistrates the Freemen themselves do call, shall consist of the Governor, or some one chosen to moderate the Court, and four other Magistrates at least, with the major part of the deputies of the several Towns legally chosen; and in case the Freemen, or major part of them, through neglect or refusal of the Governor and major part of the Magistrates, shall

call a Court, it shall consist of the major part of Freemen that are present or their deputiues, with a Moderator chosen by them: In which said General Courts shall consist the supreme power of the Commonwealth, and they only shall have power to make laws or repeal them, to grant levies, to admit of Freemen, dispose of lands undisposed of, to several Towns or persons, and also shall have power to call either Court or Magistrate or any other person whatsoever into question for any misdemeanor, and may for just causes displace or deal otherwise according to the nature of the offense; and also may deal in any other matter that concerns the good of this Commonwealth, except election of Magistrates, which shall be done by the whole body of Freemen.

In which Court the Governor or Moderator shall have power to order the Court, to give liberty of speech, and silence unseasonable and disorderly speakings, to put all things to vote, and in case the vote be equal to have the casting voice. But none of these Courts shall be adjourned or dissolved without the consent of the major part of the Court.

11. It is Ordered, sentenced, and decreed, that when any General Court upon the occasions of the Commonwealth have agreed upon any sum, or sums of money to be levied upon the several Towns within this Jurisdiction, that a committee be chosen to set out and appoint what shall be the proportion of every Town to pay of the said levy, provided the committee be made up of an equal number out of each Town.

14th January 1639 the 11 Orders above said are voted.

Anderson's *Constitutions*, 1723

Ancient Charges of a FREE MASON

The Ancient Records of Lodges beyond the Sea To Be Read At The Making of New Brethren, or When The Master Shall Order It.

THE GENERAL HEADS, viz.:

I *Concerning God and Religion.*

A Mason is oblig'd by his Tenure, to obey the moral law; and if he rightly understands the Art, he will never be a stupid Atheist nor an irreligious Libertine. But though in ancient Times Masons were charg'd in every Country to be of the Religion of that Country or Nation, whatever it was, yet 'tis now thought more expedient only to oblige them to that Religion in which all Men agree, leaving their particular Opinions to themselves; that is, to be good Men and true, or Men of Honour and Honesty, by whatever Denominations or Persuasions they may be distinguish'd; whereby Masonry becomes the Center of Union, and the Means of conciliating true Friendship among Persons that must have remain'd at a perpetual Distance.

II *Of the Civil Magistrates Supreme and Subordinate.*

A Mason is a peaceable Subject to the Civil Powers, wherever he resides or works, and is never to be concern'd in Plots and Conspiracies against the Peace and Welfare of the Nation, nor to behave himself undutifully to inferior Magistrates; for as Masonry hath been always injured by War, Bloodshed, and Confusion, so ancient Kings and Princes have been much dispos'd to encourage the Craftsmen, because of their Peaceableness and Loyalty, whereby they practically answer'd the Cavils of their Adversaries, and promoted the Honour of the Fraternity, who ever flourish'd in Time of Peace. So that if a Brother should be a Rebel against the State he is not to be countenanced in his Rebellion, however he may be pitied as any unhappy Man; and, if convicted of no other Crime though the Loyal Brotherhood must and ought to disown his Rebellion, and give no Umbrage or Ground of political Jealousy to the Government for the time being, they cannot expel him from the Lodge, and his Relation to it remains indefeasible.

III *Of Lodges.*
A Lodge is a place where Masons assemble and work; Hence that Assembly, or duly organized Society of Masons, is call'd a Lodge, and every Brother ought to belong to one, and to be subject to its By-Laws and the General Regulations.

It is either particular or general, and will be best understood by attending it, and by the Regulations of the General or Grand Lodge hereunto annex'd. In ancient Times, no Master or Fellow could be absent from it especially when warned to appear at it, without incurring a sever Censure, until it appear'd to the Master and Wardens that pure Necessity hinder'd him.

The persons admitted Members of a Lodge must be good and true Men, free-born, and of mature and discreet Age, no Bondmen no Women, no immoral or scandalous men, but of good Report.

IV *Of Masters, Wardens, Fellows and Apprentices.*
All preferment among Masons is grounded upon real Worth and personal Merit only; that so the Lords may be well served, the Brethren not put to Shame, nor the Royal Craft despis'd: Therefore no Master or Warden is chosen by Seniority, but for his Merit. It is impossible to describe these things in Writing, and every Brother must attend in his Place, and learn them in a Way peculiar to this Fraternity: Only Candidates may know that no Master should take an Apprentice unless he has Sufficient Employment for him, and unless he be a perfect Youth having no Maim or Defects in his Body that may render him uncapable of learning the Art of serving his Master's Lord, and of being made a Brother, and then a Fellow-Craft in due Time, even after he has served such a Term of Years as the Custom of the Country directs; and that he should be descended of honest Parents; that so, when otherwise qualifi'd he may arrive to the Honour of being the Warden, and then the Master of the Lodge, the Grand Warden, and at length the Grand Master of all the Lodges, according to his Merit.

No Brother can be a Warden until he has pass'd the part of a Fellow-Craft; nor a Master until he has acted as a Warden, nor Grand Warden until he has been Master of a Lodge, nor Grand Master unless he has been a Fellow Craft before his Election, who is also to be nobly born, or a Gentleman of the best Fashion, or some eminent Scholar, or some curious Architect, or other Artist, descended of honest Parents, and who is of similar great Merit in the Opinion of the Lodges.

These Rulers and Governors, supreme and subordinate, of the ancient Lodge, are to be obey'd in their respective Stations by all the Brethren, according to the old Charges and Regulations, with all Humility, Reverence, Love and Alacrity.

V *Of the Management of the Craft in Working.*
All Masons shall work honestly on Working Days, that they may live creditably on Holy Days; and the time appointed by the Law of the Land or confirm'd by Custom shall be observ'd. The most expert of the Fellow-Craftsmen shall be chosen or appointed the Master or Overseer of the Lord's Work; who is to be call'd Master by those that work under him. The Craftsmen are to avoid all ill Language, and to call each other by no dis-obliging Name, but Brother or Fellow; and to behave themselves courteously within and without the Lodge.

The Master, knowing himself to be able of Cunning, shall undertake the Lord's Work as reasonably as possible, and truly dispend his Goods as if they were his own; nor to give more Wages to any Brother or Apprentice than he really may deserve.

Both the Master and the Masons receiving their Wages justly, shall be faithful to the Lord and honestly finish their Work, whether Task or journey; nor put the work to Task that hath been accustomed to Journey.

None shall discover Envy at the Prosperity of a Brother, nor supplant him, or put him out of his Work, if he be capable to finish the same; for no man can finish another's Work so much to the Lord's Profit, unless he be thoroughly acquainted with the Designs and Draughts of him that began it.

When a Fellow-Craftsman is chosen Warden of the Work under the Master, he shall be true both to Master and Fellows, shall carefully oversee the Work in the Master's Absence to the Lord's profit; and his Brethren shall obey him.

All Masons employed shall meekly receive their Wages without Murmuring or Mutiny, and not desert the Master till the Work is finish'd.

A younger Brother shall be instructed in working, to prevent spoiling the Materials for want of Judgment, and for increasing and continuing of brotherly love.

All the Tools used in working shall be approved by the Grand Lodge.

No Labourer shall be employ'd in the proper Work of Masonry; nor shall Free Masons work with those that are not free, without an urgent Necessity; nor shall they teach Labourers and unaccepted Masons as they should teach a Brother or Fellow.

VI *Of Behaviour.*
1. In the Lodge while Constituted.
You are not to hold private Committees, or separate Conversation without Leave from the Master, nor to talk of anything impertinent or unseemly, nor interrupt the Master or Wardens, or any Brother speaking to the Master: Nor behave yourself ludicrously or jestingly while the Lodge is engaged in what is serious and solemn; nor use any unbecoming Language upon any Pretense whatsoever; but to pay due Reverence to your Master, Wardens, and Fellows, and put them to Worship.

If any Complaint be brought, the Brother found guilty shall stand to the Award and Determination of the Lodge, who are the proper and competent Judges of all such Controversies (unless you carry it by Appeal to the Grand Lodge), and to whom they ought to be referr'd, unless a Lord's Work be hinder'd the meanwhile, in which Case a particular Reference may be made; but you must never go to Law about what concerneth Masonry, without an absolute necessity apparent to the Lodge.

2. Behaviour after the Lodge is over and the Brethren not Gone.
You may enjoy yourself with innocent Mirth, treating one another according to Ability, but avoiding all Excess, or forcing any Brother to eat or drink beyond his Inclination, or hindering him from going when his Occasions call him, or doing or saying anything offensive, or that may forbid an easy and free Conversation, for that would blast our Harmony, and defeat

our laudable Purposes. Therefore no private Piques or Quarrels must be brought within the Door of the Lodge, far less any Quarrels about Religion, or Nations, or State Policy, we being only, as Masons, of the Universal Religion above mention'd, we are also of all Nations, Tongues, Kindreds, and Languages, and are resolv'd against all Politics, as what never yet conduct'd to the Welfare of the Lodge, nor ever will.

3. Behaviour when Brethren meet without Strangers, but not in a Lodge Formed.

You are to salute one another in a courteous Manner, as you will be instructed, calling each other Brother, freely giving mutual instruction as shall be thought expedient, without being ever seen or overheard, and without encroaching upon each other, or derogating from that Respect which is due to any Brother, were he not Mason: For though all Masons are as Brethren upon the same Level, yet Masonry takes no Honour from a man that he had before; nay, rather it adds to his Honour, especially if he has deserve well of the Brotherhood, who must give Honour to whom it is due, and avoid ill Manners.

4. Behaviour in presence of Strangers not Masons.

You shall be cautious in your Words and Carriage, that the most penetrating Stranger shall not be able to discover or find out what is not proper to be intimated, and sometimes you shall divert a Discourse, and manage it prudently for the Honour of the worshipful Fraternity.

5. Behaviour at Home, and in your Neighborhood.

You are to act as becomes a moral and wise Man; particularly not to let your Family, Friends and Neighbors know the Concern of the Lodge, &c., but wisely to consult your own Honour, and that of the ancient Brotherhood, for reasons not to be mention'd here You must also consult your Health, by not continuing together too late, or too long from Home, after Lodge Hours are past; and by avoiding of Gluttony or Drunkenness, that your Families be not neglected or injured, nor you disabled from working.

6. Behaviour toward a Strange Brother.

You are cautiously to examine him, in such a Method as Prudence shall direct you, that you may not be impos'd upon by an ignorant, false Pretender, whom you are to reject with contempt and Derision, and beware of giving him any Hints of Knowledge.

But if you discover him to be a true and genuine Brother, you are to respect him accordingly; and if he is in Want, you must relieve him if you can, or else direct him how he may be relieved; you must employ him some days, or else recommend him to be employ'd. But you are not charged to do beyond your ability, only to prefer a poor Brother, that is a good Man and true before any other poor People in the same Circumstance.

Finally, All these Charges you are to observe, and also those that shall be recommended to you in another Way; cultivating Brotherly Love, the Foundation and Cap-stone, the Cement and Glory of this Ancient Fraternity, avoiding all wrangling and quarreling, all Slander and Backbiting, nor permitting others to slander any honest Brother, but defending his Character, and doing him all good Offices, as far as is consistent with your Honour and Safety, and no farther. And if any of them do you Injury you must apply to your own or his Lodge, and from thence you may appeal to the Grand Lodge, at the Quarterly Communication and from thence to the annual Grand Lodge, as has been the ancient laudable Conduct but when the Case cannot be otherwise decided, and patiently listening to the honest and friendly Advice of Master and Fellows when they would prevent your going to Law with Strangers, or would excite you to put a speedy Period to all Lawsuits, so that you may mind the Affair of Masonry with the more Alacrity and Success; but with respect to Brothers or Fellows at Law, the Master and Brethren should kindly offer their Mediation, which ought to be thankfully submitted to by the contending Brethren; and if that submission is impracticable, they must, however, carry on their Process, or Lawsuit, without Wrath and Rancor (not In the common way) saying or doing nothing which may hinder Brotherly Love, and good Offices to be renew'd and continu'd; that all may see the benign Influence of Masonry, as all true Masons have done from the beginning of the World, and wil do to the End of Time.

AMEN, SO MOTE IT BE

APPENDIX IV

Albany Plan of Union, 1754

It is proposed that humble application be made for an act of Parliament of Great Britain, by virtue of which one general government may be formed in America, including all the said colonies, within and under which government each colony may retain its present constitution, except in the particulars wherein a change may be directed by the said act, as hereafter follows.

1. That the said general government be administered by a President-General, to be appointed and supported by the crown; and a Grand Council, to be chosen by the representatives of the people of the several Colonies met in their respective assemblies.

2. That within ... months after the passing such act, the House of Representatives that happen to be sitting within that time, or that shall especially for that purpose convened, may and shall choose members for the Grand Council, in the following proportion, that is to say,

Massachusetts Bay	7
New Hampshire	2
Connecticut	5
Rhode Island	2
New York	4
New Jersey	3
Pennsylvania	6
Maryland	4
Virginia	7
North Carolina	4
South Carolina	4
	48

3. ... who shall meet for the first time at the city of Philadelphia, being called by the President-General as soon as conveniently may be after his appointment.

4. That there shall be a new election of the members of the Grand

Council every three years; and, on the death or resignation of any member, his place should be supplied by a new choice at the next sitting of the Assembly of the Colony he represented.

5. That after the first three years, when the proportion of money arising out of each Colony to the general treasury can be known, the number of members to be chosen for each Colony shall, from time to time, in all ensuing elections, be regulated by that proportion, yet so as that the number to be chosen by any one Province be not more than seven, nor less than two.

6. That the Grand Council shall meet once in every year, and oftener if occasion require, at such time and place as they shall adjourn to at the last preceding meeting, or as they shall be called to meet at by the President-General on any emergency; he having first obtained in writing the consent of seven of the members to such call, and sent duly and timely notice to the whole.

7. That the Grand Council have power to choose their speaker; and shall neither be dissolved, prorogued, nor continued sitting longer than six weeks at one time, without their own consent or the special command of the crown.

8. That the members of the Grand Council shall be allowed for their service ten shillings sterling per diem, during their session and journey to and from the place of meeting; twenty miles to be reckoned a day's journey.

9. That the assent of the President-General be requisite to all acts of the Grand Council, and that it be his office and duty to cause them to be carried into execution.

10. That the President-General, with the advice of the Grand Council, hold or direct all Indian treaties, in which the general interest of the Colonies may be concerned; and make peace or declare war with Indian nations.

11. That they make such laws as they judge necessary for regulating all Indian trade.

12. That they make all purchases from Indians, for the crown, of lands not now within the bounds of particular Colonies, or that shall not be within their bounds when some of them are reduced to more convenient dimensions.

13. That they make new settlements on such purchases, by granting

lands in the King's name, reserving a quitrent to the crown for the use of the general treasury.

14. That they make laws for regulating and governing such new settlements, till the crown shall think fit to form them into particular governments.

15. That they raise and pay soldiers and build forts for the defence of any of the Colonies, and equip vessels of force to guard the coasts and protect the trade on the ocean, lakes, or great rivers; but they shall not impress men in any Colony, without the consent of the Legislature.

16. That for these purposes they have power to make laws, and lay and levy such general duties, imposts, or taxes, as to them shall appear most equal and just (considering the ability and other circumstances of the inhabitants in the several Colonies), and such as may be collected with the least inconvenience to the people; rather discouraging luxury, than loading industry with unnecessary burdens.

17. That they may appoint a General Treasurer and Particular Treasurer in each government when necessary; and, from time to time, may order the sums in the treasuries of each government into the general treasury; or draw on them for special payments, as they find most convenient.

18. Yet no money to issue but by joint orders of the President-General and Grand Council; except where sums have been appropriated to particular purposes, and the President-General is previously empowered by an act to draw such sums.

19. That the general accounts shall be yearly settled and reported to the several Assemblies.

20. That a quorum of the Grand Council, empowered to act with the President-General, do consist of twenty-five members; among whom there shall be one or more from a majority of the Colonies.

21. That the laws made by them for the purposes aforesaid shall not be repugnant, but, as near as may be, agreeable to the laws of England, and shall be transmitted to the King in Council for approbation, as soon as may be after their passing; and if not disapproved within three years after presentation, to remain in force.

22. That, in case of the death of the President-General, the Speaker of the Grand Council for the time being shall succeed, and be vested with the same powers and authorities, to continue till the King's pleasure be known.

23. That all military commission officers, whether for land or sea service, to act under this general constitution, shall be nominated by the President-General; but the approbation of the Grand Council is to be obtained, before they receive their commissions. And all civil officers are to be nominated by the Grand Council, and to receive the President-General's approbation before they officiate.

24. But, in case of vacancy by death or removal of any officer, civil or military, under this constitution, the Governor of the Province in which such vacancy happens may appoint, till the pleasure of the President-General and Grand Council can be known.

25. That the particular military as well as civil establishments in each Colony remain in their present state, the general constitution notwithstanding; and that on sudden emergencies any Colony may defend itself, and lay the accounts of expense thence arising before the President-General and General Council, who may allow and order payment of the same, as far as they judge such accounts just and reasonable.

APPENDIX V

Declaration of Independence, July 4, 1776

When in the course of human events, it becomes necessary for one people to dissolve the political bands which have connected them with another, and to assume among the powers of the earth, the separate and equal station to which the laws of nature and of nature's God entitle them, a decent respect to the opinions of mankind requires that they should declare the causes which impel them to the separation.

We hold these truths to be self-evident:
That all men are created equal; that they are endowed by their Creator with certain unalienable rights; that among these are life, liberty, and the pursuit of happiness; that, to secure these rights, governments are instituted among men, deriving their just powers from the consent of the governed; that whenever any form of government becomes destructive of these ends, it is the right of the people to alter or to abolish it, and to institute new government, laying its foundation on such principles, and organizing its powers in such form, as to them shall seem most likely to effect their safety and happiness. Prudence, indeed, will dictate that governments long established should not be changed for light and transient causes; and accordingly all experience hath shown that mankind are more disposed to suffer, while evils are sufferable than to right themselves by abolishing the forms to which they are accustomed. But when a long train of abuses and usurpations, pursuing invariably the same object, evinces a design to reduce them under absolute despotism, it is their right, it is their duty, to throw off such government, and to provide new guards for their future security. Such has been the patient sufferance of these colonies; and such is now the necessity which constrains them to alter their former systems of government. The history of the present King of Great Britain is a history of repeated injuries and usurpations, all having in direct object the establishment of an absolute tyranny over these states. To prove this, let facts be submitted to a candid world.

He has refused his assent to laws, the most wholesome and necessary for the public good.

He has forbidden his governors to pass laws of immediate and pressing importance, unless suspended in their operation till his assent should be obtained; and, when so suspended, he has utterly neglected to attend to them.

He has refused to pass other laws for the accommodation of large districts of people, unless those people would relinquish the right of representation in the legislature, a right inestimable to them, and formidable to tyrants only.

He has called together legislative bodies at places unusual uncomfortable, and distant from the depository of their public records, for the sole purpose of fatiguing them into compliance with his measures.

He has dissolved representative houses repeatedly, for opposing, with manly firmness, his invasions on the rights of the people.

He has refused for a long time, after such dissolutions, to cause others to be elected; whereby the legislative powers, incapable of annihilation, have returned to the people at large for their exercise; the state remaining, in the mean time, exposed to all the dangers of invasions from without and convulsions within.

He has endeavored to prevent the population of these states; for that purpose obstructing the laws for naturalization of foreigners; refusing to pass others to encourage their migration hither, and raising the conditions of new appropriations of lands.

He has obstructed the administration of justice, by refusing his assent to laws for establishing judiciary powers.

He has made judges dependent on his will alone, for the tenure of their offices, and the amount and payment of their salaries.

He has erected a multitude of new offices, and sent hither swarms of officers to harass our people and eat out their substance.

He has kept among us, in times of peace, standing armies, without the consent of our legislatures.

He has affected to render the military independent of, and superior to, the civil power.

He has combined with others to subject us to a jurisdiction foreign to our Constitution and unacknowledged by our laws, giving his assent to their acts of pretended legislation:

For quartering large bodies of armed troops among us;

For protecting them, by a mock trial, from punishment for any murders which they should commit on the inhabitants of these states;

For cutting off our trade with all parts of the world;

For imposing taxes on us without our consent;

For depriving us, in many cases, of the benefits of trial by jury;

For transporting us beyond seas, to be tried for pretended offenses;

For abolishing the free system of English laws in a neighboring province, establishing therein an arbitrary government, and enlarging its boundaries, so as to render it at once an example and fit instrument for introducing the same absolute rule into these colonies;

For taking away our charters, abolishing our most valuable laws, and altering fundamentally the forms of our governments;

For suspending our own legislatures, and declaring themselves invested with power to legislate for us in all cases whatsoever.

He has abdicated government here, by declaring us out of his protection and waging war against us.

He has plundered our seas, ravaged our coasts, burned our towns, and destroyed the lives of our people.

He is at this time transporting large armies of foreign mercenaries to complete the works of death, desolation, and tyranny already begun with circumstances of cruelty and perfidy scarcely paralleled in the most barbarous ages, and totally unworthy the head of a civilized nation.

He has constrained our fellow-citizens, taken captive on the high seas, to bear arms against their country, to become the executioners of their friends and brethren, or to fall themselves by their hands.

He has excited domestic insurrection among us, and has endeavored to bring on the inhabitants of our frontiers the merciless Indian savages, whose known rule of warfare is an undistinguished destruction of all ages, sexes, and conditions.

In every stage of these oppressions we have petitioned for redress in the most humble terms; our repeated petitions have been answered only by repeated injury. A prince, whose character is thus marked by every act which may define a tyrant, is unfit to be the ruler of a free people.

Nor have we been wanting in our attentions to our British brethren. We have warned them, from time to time, of attempts by their legislature to extend an unwarrantable jurisdiction over us. We have reminded them of the circumstances of our emigration and settlement here. We have appealed to their native justice and magnanimity; and we have conjured them, by the ties of our common kindred, to disavow these usurpations which would inevitably interrupt our connections and correspondence. They too, have been deaf to the voice of justice and of consanguinity. We must, therefore, acquiesce in the necessity which denounces our separation, and hold them as we hold the rest of mankind, enemies in war, in peace friends.

We, therefore, the representatives of the United States of America, in General Congress assembled, appealing to the Supreme Judge of the world for the rectitude of our intentions, do, in the name and by the authority of the good people of these colonies solemnly publish and declare, That these United Colonies are, and of right ought to be, FREE AND INDE-PENDENT STATES; that they are absolved from all allegiance to the British crown and that all political connection between them and the state of Great Britain is, and ought to be, totally dissolved; and that, as free and independent states, they have full power to levy war, conclude peace, contract alliances, establish commerce, and do all other acts and things which independent states may of right do. And for the support of this declaration, with a firm reliance on the protection of Divine Providence, we mutually pledge to each other our lives, our fortunes, and our sacred honor.

[Signed by] John Hancock [President]

New Hampshire
    Josiah Bartlett,
    Wm. Whipplt,
    Matthew Thormton.

Massachusetts Bay
    Saml. Adams,
    John Adams,
    Robt. Treat Paine,
    Elbridge Gerry.

Rhode Island
    Step. Hopkins,
    William Ellery.

Connecticut
    Roger Sherman,
    Sam'el Huntington,
    Wm. Williams,
    Oliver Wolcott.

New York
    Wm. Floyd,
    Phil. Livingston,
    Frans. Lewis,
    Lewis Morris.

New Jersey
    Richd. Stockton,
    Jno. Witherspoon,
    Fras. Hopkinson,
    John Hart,
    Abra. Clark.

Pennsylvania
    Robt. Morris,
    Benjamin Rush,
    Benja. Franklin,
    John Morton,
    Geo. Clymer,
    Jas. Smith,
    Geo. Taylor,
    James Wilson,
    Geo. Ross.

Delaware
    Caesar Rodney,
    Geo. Read,
    Tho. M'kean.

Maryland
    Samuel Chase,
    Wm. Paca,
    Thos. Stone,
    Charles Carroll of Carrollton.

Virginia
    George Wythe,
    Richard Henry Lee,
    Th. Jefferson,
    Benja. Harrison,
    Ths. Nelson, Junr.,
    Francis Lightfoot Lee,
    Carter Braxton.

North Carolina
    Wm. Hooper,
    Joseph Hewes,
    John Penn.

South Carolina
> Edward Rutledge,
> Thos. Hayward, Junr.,
> Thomas Lynch, Junr.,
> Arthur Middleton.

Georgia
> Button Gwinnett,
> Lyman Hall,
> Geo. Walton.

Note

Ferdinand Jefferson, Keeper of the Rolls in the Department of State, at Washington, reports:

> 'The names of the signers are spelt above as in the facsimile of the original, but the punctuation of them is not always the same; neither do the names of the States appear in the facsimile of the original. The names of the signers of each State are grouped together in the facsimile of the original, except the name of Matthew Thornton, which follows that of Oliver Wolcott.'

> Revised Statutes of the United States, second edition, 1878, p.6

The Articles of Confederation, 1781

To all to whom these presents shall come, we the undersigned delegates of the states affixed to our names, send greeting:

Whereas the delegates of the United States of America in Congress assembled, did, on the fifteenth day of November in the year of our Lord seventeen seventy-seven, and in the second year of the Independence of America, agree to Certain Articles of Confederation and perpetual union between the states of New Hampshire, Massachusetts Bay, Rhode Island and Providence Plantations, Connecticut, New York, New Jersey, Pennsylvania, Delaware, Maryland, Virginia, North Carolina, South Carolina and Georgia in the words following, *viz*:

Articles of Confederation and Perpetual Union Between the States of New Hampshire, Massachusetts Bay, Rhode Island and Providence Plantations, Connecticut, New York, New Jersey, Pennsylvania, Delaware, Maryland, Virginia, North Carolina, South Carolina and Georgia.

Article I
The style of this Confederacy shall be "The United States of America."

Article II
Each state retains its sovereignty, freedom and independence, and every power, jurisdiction and right which is not by this Confederation expressly delegated to the United States in Congress assembled.

Article III
The said states hereby severally enter into a firm league of friendship with each other for their common defence, the security of their liberties, and their mutual and general welfare, binding themselves to assist each other against all force offered to, or attacks made upon them, or any of them, on account of religion, sovereignty, trade, or any other pretence whatever.

Article IV
The better to secure and perpetuate mutual friendship and intercourse among

the people of the different States in this Union, the free inhabitants of each of these states, paupers, vagabonds and fugitives from justice excepted, shall be entitled to all privileges and immunities of free citizens in the several states; and the people of each state shall have free ingress and regress to and from any other state, and shall enjoy therein all the privileges of trade and commerce, subject to the same duties, impositions and restrictions as the inhabitants thereof respectively; provided, that such restrictions shall not extend so far as to prevent the removal of property imported into any state, to any other state of which the owner is an inhabitant; provided also, that no imposition, duties or restriction shall be laid by any state on the property of the United States, or either of them.

If any person guilty of or charged with treason, felony, or other high misdemeanor in any state, shall flee from justice, and be found in any of the United States, he shall upon demand of the governor or executive power of the state from which he fled, be delivered up and removed to the state having jurisdiction of his offense.

Full faith and credit shall be given in each of these states to the records, acts and judicial proceedings of the courts and magistrates of every other state.

Article V

For the more convenient management of the general interests of the United States, delegates shall be annually appointed in such manner as the legislature of each state shall direct, to meet in Congress on the first Monday in November, in every year, with a power, reserved to each state, to recall its delegates, or any of them, at any time within the year, and to send others in their stead, for the remainder of the year.

No state shall be represented in Congress by less than two, nor by more than seven members; and no person shall be capable of being a delegate for more than three years in any term of six years; nor shall any person, being a delegate, be capable of holding any office under the United States, for which he, or another for his benefit receives any salary, fees or emolument of any kind.

Each state shall maintain its own delegates in a meeting of the states, and while they act as members of the committee of the states.

In determining questions in the United States, in Congress assembled, each state shall have one vote.

Freedom of speech and debate in Congress shall not be impeached or questioned in any court, or place out of Congress, and the members of Congress shall be protected in their persons from arrests and imprisonments, during the time of their going to and from, and attendance on Congress, except for treason, felony, or breach of the peace.

Article VI

No state without the consent of the United States in Congress assembled, shall send any embassy to, or receive any embassy from, or enter into any conference, agreement, alliance or treaty with any king, prince or state; nor shall any person holding any office of profit or trust under the United States, or any of them, accept of any, present, emolument, office or title of any kind whatever from any king, prince or foreign state; nor shall the United States in Congress assembled, or any of them, grant any title of nobility.

No two or more states shall enter into any treaty, confederation or alliance whatever between them, without the consent of the United States in Congress assembled, specifying accurately the purposes for which the same is to be entered into, and how long it shall continue.

No state shall lay any impost or duties, which may interfere with any stipulations in treaties, entered into by the United States in Congress assembled, with any king, prince or state, in pursuance of any treaties already proposed by Congress to the courts of France and Spain.

No vessels of war shall be kept up in time of peace by any state, except such number only as shall be deemed necessary by the United States in Congress assembled, for the defence of such state, or its trade; nor shall any body of forces be kept up by any state, in time of peace except such number only, as in the judgment of the United States, Congress assembled, shall be deemed requisite to garrison the forts necessary for the defence of such state; but every state shall always keep up a well regulated and disciplined militia, sufficiently armed and accoutered, and shall provide and constantly have ready for use, in public stores, a due number of field pieces and tents, and a proper quantity of arms, ammunition and camp equipage.

No state shall engage in any war without the consent of the United States in Congress assembled, unless such state be actually invaded by enemies, or shall have received certain advice of a resolution being formed by some nation of Indians to invade such state, and the danger is so imminent as not to admit of a delay, till the United States in Congress assembled can be consulted: nor shall any state grant commissions to any ships or vessels of war, nor letters of marque or reprisal, except it be after a declaration of war by the United States in Congress assembled, and then only against the kingdom or state and the subjects thereof, against which war has been so declared, and under such regulations as shall be established by the United States in Congress assembled, unless such state be infested by pirates, in which case vessels of war be fitted out for that occasion, and kept so long as the danger shall continue, or until the United States in Congress assembled shall determine otherwise.

Article VII

When land forces are raised by any state for the common defence, all officers of or under the rank of colonel, shall be appointed by the Legislature of each state respectively by whom such forces shall be raised, or in such manner as such state shall direct, all vacancies shall be filled up by the state which first made the appointment.

Article VIII

All charges of war, and all other expenses that shall be incurred for the common defence or general welfare, and allowed by the United States in Congress assembled, shall be defrayed out of a common treasury, which shall be supplied by the several states, in proportion to the value of all land within each state, granted to or surveyed for any person, as such land and the buildings and improvements thereon shall be estimated according to such mode as the United States in Congress assembled, shall from time to time direct and appoint.

The taxes for paying that proportion shall be laid and levied by the authority and direction of the legislatures of the several states within the time agreed upon by the United States in Congress assembled.

Article IX

The United States in Congress assembled, shall have the sole and exclusive right and power of determining on peace and war except in the cases mentioned in the sixth article; of sending and receiving ambassadors; entering into treaties and alliances; provided that no treaty of commerce shall be made whereby the legislative power of the respective states shall be restrained from imposing such imposts and duties on foreigners, as their own people are subjected to, or from prohibiting the exportation or importation of any species of goods or commodities whatsoever; of establishing rules for deciding in all cases, what captures on land or water shall be legal, and in what manner prizes taken by land or naval forces in the service of the United States shall be divided or appropriated; of granting letters of marque and reprisal in times of peace; appointing courts for the trial of piracies and felonies committed on the high seas and establishing courts for receiving and determining finally appeals in all cases of captures, provided that no member of Congress shall be appointed a judge of any of said courts.

The United States in Congress assembled shall also be the last resort on appeal in all disputes and differences now subsisting or that hereafter may arise between two or more states concerning boundary, jurisdiction or any other cause whatever; which authority shall always be exercised in the manner following. Whenever the legislative or executive authority or lawful agent of any state in controversy with another shall present a petition to Congress, stating the matter in question and praying for a hearing, notice thereof shall be given by order of Congress to the legislative or executive authority of the other state in controversy, and a day assigned for the appearance of the parties by their lawful agents, who shall then be directed to appoint by joint consent commissioners or judges to constitute a court for hearing and determining the matter in question: but if they can not agree, Congress shall name three persons out of each of the United States, and from the list of such persons each party shall alternately strike out one, the petitioners beginning, until the number shall be reduced to thirteen; and from that number not less than seven, nor more than nine names, as Congress shall direct, shall in the presence of Congress be drawn out by lot, and the persons whose names shall be so drawn or any five of them, shall be commissioners or judges, to hear and finally determine the controversy, so always as a major part of the judges who shall hear the cause shall agree in the determination: and if either party shall neglect to attend at the day appointed, without showing reasons, which Congress judge sufficient, or being present shall refuse to strike, the Congress shall proceed to nominate three persons out of each state, and the Secretary of Congress shall strike in behalf of such party absent or refusing; and the judgment and sentence of the court to be appointed, in the manner before prescribed, shall be final and conclusive; and if any of the parties shall refuse to submit to the authority of such court, or to appear or defend their claim or cause, the court shall, nevertheless proceed to pronounce sentence, or judgment, which shall in like manner be final and decisive, the judgment or sentence and other proceeds being in either case transmitted to Congress, and lodged among the acts of Congress for the security of the parties concerned: provided that every commissioner, before he sits in judgment, shall take an oath to be administered by one of the judges of the supreme or superior court of the state where the cause shall be tried, "well and truly to hear and determine the matter in question, according to the best of his judgment without favor, affection, or hope of reward": provided also that no state shall be deprived of territory for the benefit of the United States.

All controversies concerning the private right of soil claimed under different grants of two or more states, whose jurisdiction as they may respect such lands, and the states which passed such grants are adjusted, the said grants or either of them being at the same time claimed to have originated antecedent to such settlement of jurisdiction, shall on the petition of either party to the Congress of the United States, be finally determined as near as may be in the same manner as is before prescribed for deciding disputes respecting territorial jurisdiction between the different states.

The United States in Congress assembled shall also have the sole and exclusive right and power of regulating the alloy and value of coin struck by their own authority, or by that of respective state fixing the standard of weights and measures throughout the United States regulating the trade, and managing all affairs with the Indians, not members of any of the states, provided that the legislative right of state within its own limits be not infringed or violated; establishing and regulating post offices from one state to another, throughout all the United States, and exacting such postage on the papers passing through the same as may be requisite to defray the expenses of the said office; appointing all officers of the land forces, in the service of the United States, excepting regimental officers; appointing all the officers of the naval forces, and commissioning all officers whatever in the service of the United States; making rules for the government and regulation of said land and naval forces, and directing their operations.

The United States in Congress assembled shall have authority to appoint a committee, to sit in the recess of Congress, to be denominated "a Committee of the States," and to consist of one delegate from each state; and to appoint such other committees and civil officers as may be necessary for managing the general affairs of the United States under their direction; to appoint one of their number to preside, provided that no person be allowed to serve in the office of president more than one year in any term of three years; to ascertain the necessary sums of money to be raised for the service of the United States, and to appropriate and apply the same for defraying the public expenses; to borrow money, or emit bills on the credit of the United States, transmitting every half year to the respective states an account of the sums of money so borrowed or emitted; to build and equip a navy; to agree upon the number of land forces, and to make requisitions from each state for its quota, in proportion to the number of white inhabitants in such state; which requisition shall be binding, and thereupon the legislature of each state shall appoint the regimental officers, raise the men and clothe, arm and equip them in a soldierlike manner, at the expense of the United States; and the officers and men so clothed, armed and equipped shall march to the place appointed, and within the time agreed on by the United States in Congress assembled: but if the United States in Congress assembled shall, on consideration of circumstances judge proper that any state should not raise men, or should raise a smaller number than its quota, and that any other state should raise a greater number of men than the quota thereof, such extra number shall be raised, officered, clothed, armed and equipped in the same manner as the quota of such state, unless the legislature of such state shall judge that such extra number can not be safely spared out of the same, in which case they shall raise, officer, clothe, arm and equip as many of such extra number as they judge can be safely spared. And the officers and men so clothed, armed and equipped, shall march to the place appointed, and within the time agreed on by the United States in Congress assembled.

The United States in Congress assembled shall never engage in war, nor grant letters of marque and reprisal in time of peace, nor enter into any treaties or alliances, nor coin money, nor regulate the value thereof, nor ascertain the sums and expenses necessary for the defense and welfare of the United States, or any of them, nor emit bills, nor borrow money on the credit of the United States, nor appropriate money, nor agree upon the number of vessels of war, to be built or purchased, or the number of land or sea forces to be raised, nor appoint a commander-in-chief of the army or navy, unless nine states assent to the same: nor shall a question on any other point, except for adjourning from day to day be determined, unless by the votes of a majority of the United States in Congress assembled.

The Congress of the United States shall have power to adjourn to any time within the year, and to any place within the United States, so that no period of adjournment be for a longer duration than the space of six months; and shall publish the journal of their proceedings monthly, except such parts thereof relating to treaties, alliances or military operations, as in their judgment require secrecy; and the yeas and nays of the delegates of each state on any question shall be entered on the journal, when it is desired by any delegate; and the delegates of a state, or any of them, at his or their request, shall be furnished with transcript of the said journal, except such parts as are above excepted to lay before the legislatures of the several states.

Article X

The Committee of the States, or any nine of them shall be authorized to execute, in the recess of Congress, such of the powers of Congress as the United States in Congress assembled, by the consent of nine states, shall from time to time think expedient to vest them with; provided that no power be delegated to the said committee for the exercise of which, by the

Articles of Confederation, the voice of nine states in the Congress of the United States assembled is requisite.

Article XI

Canada acceding to this Confederation, and joining in the measures of the United States, shall be admitted into, and entitled to all the advantages of this Union: but no other colony shall be admitted into the same, unless such admission be agreed to by nine states.

Article XII

All bills of credit emitted, moneys borrowed and debts contracted by, or under the authority of Congress, before the assembling of the United States, in pursuance of the present Confederation, shall be deemed and considered as a charge against the United States, for payment and satisfaction whereof the said United States and the public faith are hereby solemnly pledged.

Article XIII

Every state shall abide by the determinations of the United States in Congress assembled, on all quesions which by this Confederation are submitted to them. And the Articles of this Confederation shall be inviolably observed by every state, and the Union shall be perpetual; nor shall any alteration at any time hereafter be made in any of them, unless such alteration be agreed to in a Congress of the United States, and be afterwards confirmed by the legislatures of every state.

AND WHEREAS it hath pleased the Great Governor of the world to incline the hearts of the legislatures we respectively represent in Congress, to approve of, and to authorize us to ratify the said Articles of Confederation and perpetual Union. Know ye that we the undersigned delegates, by virtue of the power and authority to us given for that purpose, do by these presents, in the name and in behalf of our respective constituents, fully and entirely ratify and confirm each and every of the said Articles of Confederation and perpetual Union, and all and singular the matters and things therein contained: and we do further solemnly plight and engage the faith of our respective constituents, that they shall abide by the determinations of the United States Congress assembled, on all questions, which by the said Confederation are submitted to them. And that the articles thereof shall be inviolably observed by the states we respectively represent, and that the Union shall be perpetual.

IN WITNESS WHEREOF we have hereunto set our hands in Congress. Done at Philadelphia in the State of Pennsylvania the ninth day of July in the year of our Lord one thousand seven hundred and seventy-eight, and in the third year of the independence of America.

On the part and behalf of New Hampshire.
    Josiah Bartlett   John Wentworth, Junr. August 8th, 1778

On the part and behalf of the State of Massachusetts Bay.
| John Hancock | Francis Dana | Samuel Adams |
| James Lovell | Elbridge Gerry | Samuel Holton |

On the part and behalf of Rhode Island and Providence Plantations.
    William Ellery   John Collins   Henry Marchant

On the part and behalf of Connecticut.
| Roger Sherman | Titus Hosmer | Samuel Huntington |
| Andrew Adams | Oliver Wolcott | |

On the part and behalf of the State of New York.
| Jas. Duane | Wm. Duer | Fra. Lewis |
| Gouv. Morris | | |

On the part and behalf of the State of New Jersey (Novr. 26, 1778.)
    Jno. Witherspoon   Nathl. Scudder

On the part and behalf of the State of Pennsylvania.
| Robt. Morris | William Clingan | Daniael Roberdeau |
| Joseph Reed | Jona. Bayard Smith | 22d July 1778 |

On the part and behalf of the State of Delaware.

Tho. M'Kean	John Dickinson	Nicholas Van Dyke
Feby. 12, 1779	May 5th, 1779	

On the part and behalf of the State of Maryland.

John Hanson	Daniel Carroll	March 1, 1781

On the part and behalf of the State of Virginia.

Richard Henry Lee	Jno. Harvie	John Banister
Francis Lightfoot Lee		Thomas Adams

On the part and behalf of the State of North Carolina.

John Penn	Conrns. Harnett
July 21st, 1778	Jno. Williams

On the part and behalf of the State of South Carolina.

Henry Laurens	Richd. Hutson	William Henry Drayton
Thos. Heyward Junr.		Jno. Mathews

On the part and behalf of the State of Georgia.

Jno. Walton	Edwd. Telfair	24th July, 1778
Edwd. Langworthy		

Note

The implementing and ratification of these Articles took from November 1777 to March 1781.

The Federal Constitution, 1787

Preamble

We the People of the United States, in Order to form a more perfect Union, establish Justice, insure domestic Tranquility, provide for the common defence, promote the general Welfare, and secure the Blessings of Liberty to ourselves and our Posterity, do ordain and establish this Constitution for the United States of America.

Article I

Section 1

All legislative Powers herein granted shall be vested in a Congress of the United States, which shall consist of a Senate and House of Representatives.

Section 2

The House of Representatives shall be composed of Members chosen every second Year by the People of the several States, and the Electors in each State shall have the Qualifications requisite for Electors of the most numerous Branch of the State Legislature.

No Person shall be a Representative who shall not have attained to the Age of twenty-five Years, and been seven Years a Citizen of the United States, and who shall not, when elected, be an inhabitant of that State in which he shall be chosen.

Representatives and direct Taxes shall be apportioned among the several States which may be included within this Union, according to their respective Numbers, (which shall be determined by adding to the whole Number of free Persons, including those bound to Service for a Term of Years, and excluding Indians not taxed, three fifths of all other Persons.)[1] The actual Enumeration shall be made within three Years after the first Meeting of the Congress of the United States, and within every subsequent Term of ten Years, in such Manner as they shall by Law direct. The Number of Representatives shall not exceed one for every thirty

Thousand, but each State shall have at Least one Representative; and until such enumeration shall be made, the State of New Hampshire shall be entitled to chuse three, Massachusetts eight, Rhode-Island and Providence Plantations one, Connecticut five, New-York six, New Jersey four, Pennsylvania eight, Delaware one, Maryland six, Virginia ten, North Carolina five, South Carolina five, and Georgia three.

When vacancies happen in the Representation from any State, the Executive Authority thereof shall issue Writs of Election to fill such Vacancies.

The House of Representatives shall chuse their Speaker and other Officers; and shall have the sole Power of Impeachment.

Section 3

The Senate of the United States shall be composed of two Senators from each State, (chosen by the Legislature thereof,)[2] for six Years; and each Senator shall have one Vote.

Immediately after they shall be assembled in Consequence of the first Election, they shall be divided as equally as may be into three Classes. The Seats of the Senators of the first Class shall be vacated at the Expiration of the second Year, of the second Class at the Expiration of the fourth Year, and of the third Class at the Expiration of the sixth Year, so that one third may be chosen every second Year; (and if Vacancies happen by Resignation, or otherwise, during the Recess of the Legislature of any State, the Executive thereof may make temporary Appointments until the next Meeting of the Legislature, which shall then fill such Vacancies.)[3]

No Person shall be a Senator who shall not have attained to the Age of thirty Years, and been nine Years a Citizen of the United States, and who shall not, when elected, be an Inhabitant of that State for which he shall be chosen.

The Vice President of the United States shall be President of the Senate, but shall have no Vote, unless they be equally divided.

The Senate shall chuse their other Officers, and also a President pro tempore, in the Absence of the Vice President, or when he shall exercise the

Office of President of the United States.

The Senate shall have the sole Power to try all Impeachments. When sitting for that Purpose, they shall be on Oath or Affirmation. When the President of the United States is tried, the Chief Justice shall preside: and no Person shall be convicted without the Concurrence of two thirds of the Members present.

Judgment in Cases of Impeachment shall not extend further than to removal from Office, and disqualification to hold and enjoy any Office of honor, Trust or Profit under the United States: but the Party convicted shall nevertheless be liable and subject to Indictment, Trial, Judgment and Punishment, according to Law.

Section 4

The Times, Places and Manner of holding Elections for Senators and Representatives shall be prescribed in each State by the Legislature thereof; but the Congress may at any time by Law make or alter such Regulations, except as to the Places of chusing Senators.

(The Congress shall assemble at least once in every Year, and such Meeting shall be on the first Monday in December, unless they shall by Law appoint a different Day.)[4]

Section 5

Each House shall be the Judge of the Elections, Returns and Qualifications of its own Members, and a Majority of each shall constitute a Quorum to do Business; but a smaller Number may adjourn from day to day, and may be authorized to compel the Attendance of absent Members, in such Manner, and under such Penalties as each House may provide.

Each House may determine the Rules of its Proceedings, punish its Members for disorderly Behaviour, and, with the Concurrence of two thirds, expel a Member.

Each House shall keep a Journal of its Proceedings, and from time to time publish the same, excepting such Parts as may in their Judgment require Secrecy; and the Yeas and Nays of the Members of either House on any question shall, at the Desire of one fifth of those Present, be entered on the Journal.

Neither House, during the Session of Congress, shall, without the Consent of the other, adjourn for more than three days, nor to any other Place than that in which the two Houses shall be sitting.

Section 6

The Senators and Representatives shall receive a Compensation for their Services, to be ascertained by Law, and paid out of the Treasury of the United States. They shall in all Cases, except Treason, Felony and Breach of the Peace, be privileged from Arrest during their Attendance at the Session of their respective Houses, and in going to and returning from the same; and for any Speech or Debate in either House, they shall not be questioned in any other Place.

No Senator or Representative shall, during the Time for which he was elected, be appointed to any civil Office under the Authority of the United States, which shall have been created, or the Emoluments where-of shall have been encreased during such time; and no Person holding any Office under the United States, shall be a Member of either House during his Continuance in Office.

Section 7

All bills for raising Revenue shall originate in the House of Representatives; but the Senate may propose or concur with Amendments as on other Bills.

Every Bill which shall have passed the House of Representatives and the Senate, shall, before it become a Law, be presented to the President of the United States. If he approve he shall sign it, but if not he shall return it, with his Objections to that House in which it shall have originated, who shall enter the Objections at large on their Journal, and proceed to reconsider it. If after such Reconsideration two thirds of that House shall agree to pass the Bill, it shall be sent, together with the Objections, to the other House, by which it shall likewise be reconsidered, and if approved by two thirds of that House, it shall become a Law. But in all such Cases the Votes of both Houses shall be determined by Yeas and Nays, and the

Names of the Persons voting for and against the Bill shall be entered on the Journal of each House respectively. If any Bill shall not be returned by the President within ten Days (Sundays excepted) after it shall have been presented to him, the Same shall be a Law, in like Manner as if he had signed it, unless the Congress by their Adjournment prevent its Return, in which Case it shall not be a Law.

Every Order, Resolution, or Vote to which the Concurrence of the Senate and House of Representatives may be necessary (except on a question of Adjournment) shall be presented to the President of the United States; and before the Same shall take Effect, shall be approved by him, or being ills-approved by him, shall be repassed by two thirds of the Senate and House of Representatives, according to the Rules and Limitations prescribed in the Case of a Bill.

Section 8

The Congress shall have Power To lay and collect Taxes, Duties, Imposts and Excises, to pay the Debts and provide for the common Defence and general Welfare of the United States; but all Duties, Imposts and Excises shall be uniform throughout the United States;

To borrow Money on the credit of the United States;

To regulate Commerce with foreign Nations, and among the several States, and with the Indian Tribes;

To establish an uniform Rule of Naturalization, and uniform Laws on the subject of Bankruptcies throughout the United States;

To coin Money, regulate the Value thereof, and of foreign Coin, and fix the Standard of Weights and Measures;

To provide for the Punishment of counterfeiting the Securities and current Coin of the United States;

To establish Post Offices and post Roads;

To promote the Progress of Science and useful Arts, by securing for limited Times to Authors and Inventors the exclusive Right to their respective Writings and Discoveries;

To constitute Tribunals inferior to the supreme Court;

To define and punish Piracies and Felonies committed on the high Seas, and Offences against the Law of Nations;

To declare War, grant Letters of Marque and Reprisal, and make Rules concerning Captures on Land and Water;

To raise and support Armies, but no Appropriation of Money to that Use shall be for a longer Term than two Years;

To provide and maintain a Navy;

To make Rules for the Government and Regulation of the land and naval Forces;

To provide for calling forth the Militia to execute the Laws of the Union, suppress Insurrections and repel Invasions;

To provide for organizing, arming, and disciplining, the Militia, and for governing such Part of them as may be employed in the Service of the United States, reserving to the States respectively, the Appointment of the Officers, and the Authority of training the Militia according to the discipline prescribed by Congress;

To exercise exclusive Legislation in all Cases whatsoever, over such District (not exceeding ten Miles square) as may, by Cession of particular States, and the Acceptance of Congress, become the Seat of the Government of the United States, and to exercise like Authority over all Places purchased by the Consent of the Legislature of the State in which the Same shall be, for the Erection of Forts, Magazines, Arsenals, dock-Yards, and other needful Buildings; – And

To make all Laws which shall be necessary and proper for carrying into Execution the foregoing Powers, and all other Powers vested by this Constitution in the Government of the United States, or in any Department or Officer thereof.

Section 9

The Migration or Importation of such Persons as any of the States now existing shall think proper to admit, shall not be prohibited by the Congress prior to the Year one thousand eight hundred and eight, but a Tax or duty may be imposed on such Importation, not exceeding ten dollars for each Person.

The Privilege of the Writ of Habeas Corpus shall not be suspended, unless when in Cases of Rebellion or Invasion the public safety may require it.

No Bill of Attainder or *ex post facto* Law shall be passed.

No Capitation, or other direct, Tax shall be laid, unless in Proportion to the Census or Enumeration herein before directed to be taken.[5]

No Tax or Duty shall be laid on Articles exported from any State.

No Preference shall be given by any Regulation of Commerce or Revenue to the Ports of one State over those of another; nor shall Vessels bound to, or from, one State, be obliged to enter, clear, or pay Duties in another.

No money shall be drawn from the Treasury, but in Consequence of Appropriations made by Law; and a regular Statement and Account of the Receipts and Expenditures of all public Money shall be published from time to time.

No Title of Nobility shall be granted by the United States: And no Person holding any Office of Profit or Trust under them, shall, without the Consent of the Congress, accept of any present, Emolument, Office, or Title, of any kind whatever, from any King, Prince, or foreign State.

Section 10

No State shall enter into any Treaty, Alliance, or Confederation; grant Letters of Marque and Reprisal; coin Money; emit Bills of Credit; make any Thing but gold and silver Coin a Tender in Payment of Debts; pass any Bill of Attainder, *ex post facto* Law, or Law impairing the Obligation of Contracts, or grant any Title of Nobility.

No State shall, without the Consent of the Congress, lay any Imposts or Duties on Imports or Exports, except what may be absolutely necessary for executing its inspection laws; and the net Produce of all Duties and Imposts, laid by any State on Imports or Exports, shall be for the Use of the Treasury of the United States; and all such Laws shall be subject to the Revision and Control of the Congress.

No State shall, without the Consent of Congress, lay any Duty of Tonnage, keep Troops, or Ships of War in time of Peace, enter into any Agreement or Compact with another State, or with a foreign Power, or engage in War, unless actually invaded, or in such imminent Danger as will not admit of delay.

Article II

Section 1

The executive Power shall be vested in a President of the United States of America. He shall hold his Office during the Term of four Years, and, together with the Vice President, chosen for the same Term, be elected, as follows

Each State shall appoint, in such Manner as the Legislature thereof may direct, a Number of Electors, equal to the whole Number of Senators and Representatives to which the State may be entitled in the Congress: but no Senator or Representative, or Person holding an Office of Trust or Profit under the United States, shall be appointed an Elector.

(The Electors shall meet in their respective States, and vote by Ballot for two Persons, of whom one at least shall not be an Inhabitant of the same State with themselves. And they shall make a List of all the Persons voted for, and of the Number of Votes for each; which list they shall sign and certify, and transmit sealed to the Seat of the Government of the United States, directed to the President of the Senate. The President of the Senate shall, in the Presence of the Senate and House of Representatives, open all the Certificates, and the Votes shall then be counted. The person having the greatest Number of Votes shall be the President, if such Number be a Majority of the whole Number of Electors appointed; and if there be more than one who have such Majority, and have an equal Number of Votes, then the House of Representatives shall immediately chuse by Ballot one of them for President; and if no Person have a Majority, then from the five highest on the List the said House shall in like Manner chuse the President. But in chusing the President, the Votes shall be taken by States, the Representation from each State having one Vote; A quorum for this purpose shall consist of a Member or Members from two thirds of the States, and a Majority of all the States shall be necessary to a Choice. In every Case, after the Choice of the President, the Person having the greatest Number of Votes of the Electors shall be the Vice President. But if there should remain two or more who have equal

Votes, the Senate shall chuse from them by Ballot the Vice President.)[6]

The Congress may determine the Time of chusing the Electors, and the Day on which they shall give their Votes; which Day shall be the same throughout the United States.

No Person except a natural born Citizen, or a Citizen of the United States, at the time of the Adoption of this Constitution, shall be eligible to the Office of President; neither shall any Person be eligible to that Office who shall not have attained to the Age of thirty five Years, and been fourteen Years a Resident within the United States.

In Case of the Removal of the President from Office, or of his Death, Resignation, or Inability to discharge the Powers and Duties of the said Office,[7] the Same shall devolve on the Vice President, and the Congress may by Law provide for the Case of Removal, Death, Resignation or Inability, both of the President and Vice President, declaring what Officer shall then act as President, and such Officer shall act accordingly, until the Disability be removed, or a President shall be elected.

The President shall, at stated Times, receive for his Services, a Compensation, which shall neither be encreased nor diminished during the Period for which he shall have been elected, and he shall not receive within that Period any other Emolument from the United States, or any of them.

Before he enter on the Execution of his Office, he shall take the following Oath or Affirmation: "I do solemnly swear (or affirm) that I will faithfully execute the Office of President of the United States, and will to the best of my Ability, preserve, protect and defend the Constitution of the United States."

Section 2

The President shall be Commander in Chief of the Army and Navy of the United States, and of the Militia of the several States, when called into the actual Service of the United States; he may require the Opinion, in writing, of the principal Officer in each of the executive Departments, upon any Subject relating to the Duties of their respective Offices, and he shall have Power to grant Reprieves and Pardons for Offenses against the

United States, except in Cases of Impeachment.

He shall have Power, by and with the Advice and Consent of the Senate, to make Treaties, provided two thirds of the Senators present concur; and he shall nominate, and by and with the Advice and Consent of the Senate, shall appoint Ambassadors, other public Ministers and Consuls, Judges of the supreme Court, and all other Officers of the United States, whose Appointments are not herein otherwise provided for, and which shall be established by Law: but the Congress may by Law vest the Appointment of such inferior Officers, as they think proper, in the President alone, in the Courts of Law, or in the Heads of Departments.

The President shall have Power to fill up all Vacancies that may happen during the Recess of the Senate, by granting Commissions which shall expire at the End of their next Session.

Section 3

He shall from time to time give to the Congress Information of the State of the Union, and recommend to their Consideration such Measures as he shall judge necessary and expedient; he may, on extraordinary Occasions, convene both Houses, or either of them, and in Case of Disagreement between them, with Respect to the Time of Adjournment, he may adjourn them to such Time as he shall think proper; he shall receive Ambassadors and other public Ministers; he shall take Care that the Laws be faithfully executed, and shall Commission all Officers of the United States.

Section 4

The President, Vice President and all civil Officers of the United States, shall be removed from Office on Impeachment for, and Conviction of, Treason, Bribery, or other high Crimes and Misdemeanors.

Article III

Section 1

The judicial Power of the United States, shall be vested in one supreme Court, and in such inferior Courts as the Congress may from time to time ordain and establish. The Judges, both of the supreme and inferior

Courts, shall hold their Offices during good Behaviour, and shall, at stated Times, receive for their Services, a Compensation, which shall not be diminished during their Continuance in Office.

Section 2

The judicial Power shall extend to all Cases, in Law and Equity, arising under this Constitution, the Laws of the United States, and Treaties made, or which shall be made, under their authority; – to all Cases affecting Ambassadors, other public Ministers and Consuls; – to all Cases of admiralty and maritime Jurisdiction; – to Controversies to which the United States shall be a Party; – to Controversies between two or more States; – between a State and Citizens of another State;[8] – between Citizens of different States, – between Citizens of the same State claiming Lands under Grants of different States, and between a State, or the Citizens thereof, and foreign States, Citizens or Subjects.

In all cases affecting Ambassadors, other public Ministers and Consuls, and those in which a State shall be Party, the supreme Court shall have original Jurisdiction. In all the other Cases before mentioned, the supreme Court shall have appellate Jurisdiction, both as to Law and Fact, with such Exceptions, and under such Regulations as the Congress shall make.

The Trial of all Crimes, except in Cases of Impeachment, shall be by Jury; and such Trial shall be held in the State where the said Crimes shall have been committed; but when not committed within any State, the Trial shall be at such Place or Places as the Congress may by law have directed.

Section 3

Treason against the United States, shall consist only in levying War against them, or in adhering to their Enemies, giving them Aid and Comfort. No Person shall be convicted of Treason unless on the Testimony of two Witnesses to the same overt Act, or on Confession in open Court.

The Congress shall have Power to declare the Punishment of Treason, but no Attainder of Treason shall work Corruption of Blood, or

Forfeiture except during the Life of the Person attainted.

Article IV
Section 1
Full Faith and Credit shall be given in each State to the public Acts, Records, and judicial Proceedings of every other State. And the Congress may by general Laws prescribe the Manner in which such Acts, Records and Proceedings shall be proved, and the Effect thereof.

Section 2
The Citizens of each State shall be entitled to all Privileges and Immunities of Citizens in the several States.

A Person charged in any State with Treason, Felony, or other Crime, who shall flee from Justice, and be found in another State, shall on Demand of the executive Authority of the State from which he fled, be delivered up, to be removed to the State having Jurisdiction of the Crime.

(No Person held to Service or Labour in one State, under the Laws thereof, escaping into another, shall, in Consequence of any Law or Regulation therein, be discharged from such Service or Labour, but shall be delivered up on Claim of the Party to whom such Service or Labour may be due.)[9]

Section 3
New States may be admitted by the Congress into this Union; but no new State shall be formed or erected within the Jurisdiction of any other State; nor any State be formed by the Junction of two or more States, or Parts of States, without the Consent of the Legislatures of the States concerned as well as of the Congress.

The Congress shall have Power to dispose of and make all needful Rules and Regulations respecting the Territory or other Property belonging to the United States; and nothing in this Constitution shall be so construed as to Prejudice any Claims of the United States, or of any particular State.

Section 4

The United States shall guarantee to every State in this Union a Republican Form of Government, and shall protect each of them against Invasion; and on Application of the Legislature, or of the Executive (when the Legislature cannot be convened) against domestic Violence.

Article V

The Congress, whenever two thirds of both Houses shall deem it neces sary, shall propose Amendments to this Constitution, or, on the Application of the Legislatures of two thirds of the several States, shall call a Convention for proposing Amendments, which, in either Case, shall be valid to all Intents and Purposes, as Part of this Constitution, when ratified by the Legislatures of three fourths of the several States, or by Conventions in three fourths thereof, as the one or the otherMode of Ratification may be proposed by the Congress; Provided that no Amendment which may be made prior to the Year One thousand eight hundred and eight shall in any Manner affect the first and fourth Clauses in the Ninth Section of the first Article; and that no State, without its Consent, shall be deprived of its equal Suffrage in the Senate.

Article VI

All Debts contracted and Engagements entered into, before the Adoption of this Constitution, shall be as valid against the United States under this Constitution, as under the Confederation.

This Constitution, and the Laws of the United States which shall be made in Pursuance thereof; and all Treaties made, or which shall be made, under the Authority of the United States, shall be the supreme Law of the Land; and the Judges in every State shall be bound thereby, any Thing in the Constitution or Laws of any State to the Contrary notwithstanding.

The Senators and Representatives before mentioned, and the Members of the several State Legislatures, and all executive and judicial Officers, both of the United States and of the several States, shall be bound by Oath or Affirmation, to support this Constitution; but no religious Test shall ever be required as a Qualification to any Office or public Trust under the United States.

Article VII

The Ratification of the Conventions of nine States, shall be sufficient for the Establishment of this Constitution between the States so ratifying the Same.

Done in Convention by the Unanimous Consent of the States present the Seventeenth Day of September in the Year of our Lord one thousand seven hundred and Eighty seven and of the Independence of the United States of America the Twelfth.

In witness whereof We have hereunto subscribed our Names.

G. Washington, *President and deputy from Virginia; Attest* William Jackson, *Secretary; Delaware:* Geo. Read, Gunning Bedford, Jr., John Dickinson, Richard Bassett, Jaco. Broom; *Maryland:* James McHenry, Daniel of St Thomas Jenifer, Daniel Carroll; *Virginia:* John Blair, James Madison, Jr.; *North Carolina:* Wm. Blount, Richd. Dobbs Spaight, Hu Williamson; *South Carolina:* J. Rutledge, Charles Cotesworth Pinckney, Charles Pinckney, Pierce Butler; *Georgia:* William Few, Abr. Baldwin; *New Hampshire:* John Langdon, Nicholas Gilman; *Massachusetts:* Nathaniel Gorham, Rufus King; *Connecticut:* Wm. Saml. Johnson, Roger Sherman; *New York:* Alexander Hamilton; *New Jersey:* Wil. Livingston, David Brearley, Wm. Paterson, Jona. Dayton; *Pennsylvania:* B. Franklin, Thomas Mifflin, Robt. Morris, Geo. Clymer, Thos. FitzSimons, Jared Ingersoll, James Wilson, Gouv. Morris.

The Bill of Rights, 15 December 1791

Amendment I

Congress shall make no law respecting an establishment of religion, or prohibiting the free exercise thereof; or abridging the freedom of speech, or of the press; or the right of the people peaceably to assemble, and to petition the Government for a redress of grievances.

Amendment II

A well regulated Militia, being necessary to the security of a free State, the right of the people to keep and bear Arms, shall not be infringed.

Amendment III

No Soldier shall, in time of peace be quartered in any house, without the consent of the Owner, nor in time of war, but in a manner to be prescribed by law.

Amendment IV

The right of the people to be secure in their persons, houses, papers, and effects, against unreasonable searches and seizures, shall not be violated, and no Warrants shall issue, but upon probable cause, supported by Oath or affirmation, and particularly describing the place to be searched, and the persons or things to be seized.

Amendment V

No person shall be held to answer for a capital, or otherwise infamous crime, unless on a presentment or indictment of a Grand Jury, except in cases arising in the land or naval forces, or in the Militia, when in actual service in time of War or public danger; nor shall any person be subject for the same offense to be twice put in jeopardy of life or limb; nor shall be compelled in any criminal case to be a witness against himself, nor be deprived of life, liberty, or property, without due process of law; nor shall private property be taken for public use, without just compensation.

Amendment VI

In all criminal prosecutions, the accused shall enjoy the right to a speedy and public trial, by an impartial jury of the State and district wherein the crime shall have been committed, which district shall have been previously ascertained by law, and to be informed of the nature and cause of the accusation; to be confronted with the witnesses against him; to have compulsory process for obtaining witnesses in his favour, and to have the Assistance of Counsel for his defense.

Amendment VII

In Suits at common law, where the value in controversy shall exceed twenty dollars, the right of trial by jury shall be preserved, and no fact tried by a jury, shall be otherwise re-examined in any Court of the United States, than according to the rules of the common law.

Amendment VIII

Excessive bail shall not be required, nor excessive fines imposed, nor cruel and unusual punishments inflicted.

Amendment IX

The enumeration in the Constitution, of certain rights, shall not be construed to deny or disparage others retained by the people.

Amendment X

The powers not delegated to the United States by the Constitution, nor prohibited by it to the States, are reserved to the States respectively, or to the people.

Later Amendments
Amendment XI (8 January 1798)

The judicial power of the United States shall not be construed to extend to any suit in law or equity, commenced or prosecuted against one of the United States by Citizens of another State, or by Citizens or Subjects of any Foreign State.

Amendment XII (25 September 1804)

The Electors shall meet in their respective states, and vote by ballot for President and Vice-President, one of whom, at least, shall not be an inhabitant of the same state with themselves; they shall name in their ballots the person voted for as President, and in distinct ballots the person voted for as Vice-President, and they shall make distinct lists of all persons voted for as President, and of all persons voted for as Vice-President, and of the number of votes for each, which lists they shall sign and certify, and transmit sealed to the seat of the government of the United States, directed to the President of the Senate;

- The President of the Senate shall, in the presence of the Senate and House of Representatives, open all the certificates and the votes shall then be counted;
- The person having the greatest number of votes for President, shall be the President, if such number be a majority of the whole number of Electors appointed; and if no person have such majority, then from the persons having the highest numbers not exceeding three on the list of those voted for as President, the House of Representatives shall choose immediately, by ballot, the President. But in choosing the President, the votes shall be taken by states, the representation from each state having one vote; a quorum for this purpose shall consist of a member or members from two-thirds of the states, and a majority of all the states shall be necessary to a choice. (And if the House of Representatives snail not choose a President whenever the right of choice shall devolve upon them, before the fourth day of March next following, then the Vice-President shall act as President, as in the case of the death or other constitutional disability of the President.)[10] The person having the greatest number of votes as Vice-President, shall be the Vice-President, if such number be a majority of the whole number of Electors appointed, and if no person have a majority, then from the two highest numbers on the list, the Senate shall choose the Vice-President; a quorum for the purpose shall consist of two-thirds of the whole number of Senators, and a majority of the whole number shall be necessary to a choice. But no person

constitutionally ineligible to the office of President shall be eligible to that of Vice-President of the United States.

Amendment XIII (18 December 1865)

Section 1

Neither slavery nor involuntary servitude, except as a punishment for crime whereof the party shall have been duly convicted, shall exist within the United States, or any place subject to their jurisdiction.

Section 2

Congress shall have power to enforce this article by appropriate legislation.

Amendment XIV (28 July 1868)

Section 1

All persons born or naturalized in the United States, and subject to the jurisdiction thereof, are citizens of the United States and of the State wherein they reside. No State shall make or enforce any law which shall abridge the privileges or immunities of citizens of the United States; nor shall any State deprive any person of life, liberty, or property, without due process of law; nor deny to any person within its jurisdiction the equal protection of the laws.

Section 2

Representatives shall be apportioned among the several States according to their respective numbers, counting the whole number of persons in each State, excluding Indians not taxed. But when the right to vote at any election for the choice of electors for President and Vice President of the United States, Representatives in Congress, the Executive and Judicial officers of a State, or the members of the Legislature thereof, is denied to any of the male inhabitants of such State, being twenty-one years of age, and citizens of the United States, or in any way abridged, except for participation in rebellion, or other crime, the basis of representation therein shall be reduced in the proportion which the number of such male citizens shall bear to the whole number of male citizens twenty-one years of age in such State.

Section 3

No person shall be a Senator or Representative in Congress, or elector of President and Vice President, or hold any office, civil or military, under the United States, or under any State, who, having previously taken an oath, as a member of Congress, or as an officer of the United States, or as a member of any State legislature, or as an executive or judicial officer of any State, to support the Constitution of the United States, shall have engaged in insurrection or rebellion against the same, or given aid and comfort to the enemies thereof. But Congress may by a vote of two-thirds of each House, remove such disability.

Section 4

The validity of the public debt of the United States, authorized by law, including debts incurred for payment of pensions and bounties for services in suppressing insurrection or rebellion, shall not be questioned. But neither the United States nor any State shall assume or pay any debt or obligation, incurred in aid of insurrection or rebellion against the United States, or any claim for the loss or emancipation of any slave; but all such debts, obligations, and claims shall be held illegal and void.

Section 5

The Congress shall have power to enforce, by appropriate legislation, the provisions of this article.

Amendment XV (30 March 1870)

Section 1

The right of citizens of the United States to vote shall not be denied or abridged by the United States or by any State on account of race, color, or previous condition of servitude.

Section 2

The Congress shall have power to enforce this article by appropriate legislation.

Amendment XVI (25 February 1913)

The Congress shall have power to lay and collect taxes on incomes, from whatever source derived, without apportionment among the several States, and without regard to any census or enumeration.

Amendment XVII (31 May 1913)

The Senate of the United States shall be composed of two Senators from each State, elected by the people thereof, for six years; and each Senator shall have one vote. The electors in each State shall have the qualifications requisite for electors of the most numerous branch of the State legislatures.

When vacancies happen in the representation of any State in the Senate, the executive authority of such State shall issue writs of election to fill such vacancies: *Provided,* That the legislature of any State may empower the executive thereof to make temporary appointments until the people fill the vacancies by election as the legislature may direct.

This amendment shall not be so construed as to affect the election or term of any Senator chosen before it becomes valid as part of the Constitution.

Amendment XVIII (29 January 1919)

Section 1

After one year from the ratification of this article the manufacture, sale, or transportation of intoxicating liquors within, the importation thereof into, or the exportation thereof from the United States and all territory subject to the jurisdiction thereof for beverage purposes is hereby prohibited.

Section 2

The Congress and the several States shall have concurrent power to enforce this article by appropriate legislation.

Section 3

This article shall be inoperative unless it shall have been ratified as an amendment to the Constitution by the legislatures of the several States, as provided in the Constitution, within seven years from the date of the submission hereof to the States by the Congress.)[11]

Amendment XIX (26 August 1920)

The right of citizens of the United States to vote shall not be denied or abridged by the United States or by any State on account of sex.

Congress shall have power to enforce this article by appropriate legislation.

Amendment XX (6 February 1933)

Section 1

The terms of the President and Vice President shall end at noon on the 20th day of January, and the terms of Senators and Representatives at noon on the 3d day of January, of the years in which such terms would have ended if this article had not been ratified; and the terms of their successors shall then begin.

Section 2

The Congress shall assemble at least once in every year, and such meeting shall begin at noon on the 3d day of January, unless they shall by law appoint a different day.

Section 3

If, at the time fixed for the beginning of the term of the President, the President elect shall have died, the Vice President elect shall become President. If a President shall not have been chosen before the time fixed for the beginning of his term, or if the President elect shall have failed to qualify, then the Vice President elect shall act as President until a President shall have qualified; and the Congress may by law provide for the case wherein neither a President elect nor a Vice President elect shall have qualified, declaring who shall then act as President, or the manner in which one who is to act shall be selected, and such person shall act accordingly until a President or Vice President shall have qualified.

Section 4

The Congress may by law provide for the case of the death of any of the persons from whom the House of Representatives may choose a President whenever the right of choice shall have devolved upon them, and for the case of the death of any of the persons from whom the Senate may choose a Vice President whenever the right of choice shall have devolved upon them.

Section 5

Sections 1 and 2 shall take effect on the 15th day of October following the ratification of this article.

Section 6

This article shall be inoperative unless it shall have been ratified as an amendment to the Constitution by the legislatures of three-fourths of the several States within seven years from the date of its submission.

Amendment XXI (5 December 1933)

Section 1

The eighteenth article of amendment to the Constitution of the United States is hereby repealed.

Section 2

The transportation or importation into any State, Territory, or possession of the United States for delivery to use therein of intoxicating liquors, in violation of the laws thereof, is hereby prohibited.

Section 3

This article shall be inoperative unless it shall have been ratified as an amendment to the Constitution by conventions in the several States, as provided in the Constitution, within seven years from the date of the submission hereof to the States by the Congress.

Amendment XXII (26 February 1951)

Section 1

No person shall be elected to the office of the President more than twice, and no person who has held the office of President, or acted as President, for more than two years of a term to which some other person was elected President shall be elected to the office of the President more than once. But this Article shall not apply to any person holding the office of President when this Article was proposed by the Congress, and shall not prevent any person who may be holding the office of President, or acting as President, during the term within which this Article becomes operative from holding the office of President or acting as President during the remainder of such term.

Section 2

This article shall be inoperative unless it shall have been ratified as an amendment to the Constitution by the legislatures of three-fourths of the several States within seven years from the date of its submission to the States by the Congress.

Amendment XXIII (29 March 1961)

Section 1

The district constituting the seat of the United States shall appoint in such manner as the Congress may direct:

A number of electors of President and Vice President equal to the whole number of Senators and Representatives in Congress to which the District would be entitled if it were a State, but in no event more than the least populous State; they shall be in addition to those appointed by the States, but they shall be considered, for the purposes of the election of President and Vice President, to be electors appointed by a State; and they shall meet in the District and perform such duties as provided by the twelfth article of amendment.

Section 2

The Congress shall have power to enforce this article by appropriate legislation.

Amendment XXIV (23 January 1964)

Section 1

The right of citizens of the United States to vote in any primary or other election for President or Vice President, for electors for President or Vice President, or for Senator or Representative in Congress, shall not be denied or abridged by the United States or any State by reason of failure to pay any poll tax or other tax.

Section 2

The Congress shall have power to enforce this article by appropriate legislation.

Amendment XXV (10 February 1967)

Section 1

In case of the removal of the President from office or of his death or resignation, the Vice President shall become President.

Section 2

Whenever there is a vacancy in the office of the Vice President, the President shall nominate a Vice President who shall take office upon confirmation by a majority vote of both Houses of Congress.

Section 3

Whenever the President transmits to the President *pro tempore* of the Senate and the Speaker of the House of Representatives his written declaration that he is unable to discharge the powers and duties of his office, and until he transmits to them a written declaration to the contrary, such powers and duties shall be discharged by the Vice President as Acting President.

Section 4

Whenever the Vice President and a majority of either the principal officers of the executive departments or of such other body as Congress may by law provide, transmit to the President *pro tempore* of the Senate and the Speaker of the House of Representatives their written declaration that the President is unable to discharge the powers and duties of his office, the Vice President shall immediately assume the powers and duties of the office as Acting President.

Thereafter, when the President transmits to the President *pro tempore* of the Senate and the Speaker of the House of Representatives his written declaration that no inability exists, he shall resume the powers and duties of his office unless the Vice President and a majority of either the principal officers of the executive department or of such other body as Congress may by law provide, transmit within four days to the President *pro tempore* of the Senate and the Speaker of the House of Representatives their written declaration that the President is unable to discharge the powers and duties of his office. Thereupon Congress shall decide the issue, assembling within forty-eight hours for that purpose if not in session. If the Congress, within twenty-one days after receipt of the latter written declaration, or, if Congress is not in session, within twenty-one days after Congress is required to assemble, determines by two-thirds vote of both Houses that the President is unable to discharge the powers and duties of his office, the Vice President shall continue to discharge the same as Acting President; otherwise, the President shall resume the powers and duties of his office.

Amendment XXVI (1 July 1971)

Section 1
The right of citizens of the United States, who are eighteen years of age or older, to vote shall not be denied or abridged by the United States or by any State on account of age.

Section 2
The Congress shall have power to enforce this article by appropriate legislation.

George Washington's Masonic Record, 1752–99

(Evidence for Washington's Freemasonry based on Allen E. Roberts, *George Washington: Master Mason*.)

Fredericksburg Lodge no. 4, Virginia: initiated on November 4, 1752; passed on March 3, 1753.

Raised to the Sublime Degree of Master Mason on 4 August 1753; remained a member until his death in 1799.

Attended the meeting of 1 September 1753, before leaving for Fort Le Boeuf with a letter from Governor Dinwiddie to the French commander.

Attended the meeting of 4 January 1755, prior to which he had been serving as Lieutenant Colonel and then Colonel of a Virginia regiment; shortly after this meeting he was commissioned Commander-in-Chief of the Virginia forces to protect the frontier against Indians and French troops.

Conventions for the formation of the Grand Lodge of Virginia were held from 6 May 1777 to 30 October 1778, when a Grand Master was installed; during the Convention of 23 June 1777, the reprint of the minutes states: 'This convention beg leave to recommend to their constituents and to the other Lodges in this State, His Excellency General George Washington as a proper person to fill the office of Grand Master of the same...' No record exists stating whether he was asked, and if he was, why he refused.

Philadelphia, Pennsylvania, on 28 December 1778, met with the Freemasons there and participated in the St John's Day activities.

American Union Lodge celebrated St John the Baptist's Day on 24 June 1779, at West Point, New York, and Washington attended the Lodge and participated in the activities.

Washington Lodge was an offshoot of the meeting of 24 June, as several of those attending desired to continue their Masonic activity after American Union Lodge moved; only in this sense can Washington be considered to have visited the Lodge named in his honour.

American Union Lodge met at Morristown, New Jersey, on 15 December 1779, and during this meeting Washington was proposed for General Grand Master.

Grand Lodge of Pennsylvania met on 20 December 1779, and it proposed Washington for General Grand Master of the United States.

American Union Lodge celebrated St John the Evangelist's Day on 27 December 1779, at Morristown, and Washington participated.

Grand Lodge of Pennsylvania again proposed Washington for General Grand Master on 13 January 1780.

Acknowledged the gift of an elaborate apron from Watson and Cassoul on 10 August 1782.

American Union Lodge celebrated St John's Day on 24 June 1782, at West Point, NY, and Washington was present.

Solomon's Lodge no. 1 of Poughkeepsie, New York, met on 27 December 1782, and recorded Washington as being present.

Alexandria Lodge no. 39 of Virginia, but chartered by Pennsylvania, met on 24 June 1784, and Washington was an invited guest; during the meeting he was elected to honorary membership.

General Lafayette presented Washington with an apron made by the Marquis' wife in 1784.

William Ramsay, one of the oldest residents of Alexandria, was buried with Masonic rites on 12 February 1785, and Washington participated as a Master Mason.

Alexandria Lodge no. 39 asked for and received a charter from the Grand Lodge of Virginia, becoming no. 22; it had requested that George Washington be named Worshipful Master in the new charter; his name appeared the first of four brothers named, thereby appointing him the Worshipful Master on 28 April 1788.

Alexandria Lodge no. 22 re-elected Washington unanimously as its Worshipful Master on 20 December 1788. He is said to have been present on 27 December and PGM (Va.) Charles H. Callahan believes the officers were installed on that date.

Inaugurated President of the United States on 30 April 1789, taking the oath of office on the Holy Bible of St John's Lodge no. 1 of New

York City, the oath being administered by Grand Master Robert R. Livingston, Chancellor of New York, immediately after which, Washington bent and kissed the Bible.

Freemasons of New Bern, North Carolina, welcomed Washington on 15 April 1791, and he answered their address in writing.

Grand Master Mordecai Gist of South Carolina welcomed his old friend to Charleston in May 1791 and Washington answered Gist's written address of welcome with a letter.

Grand Master George Houstoun of Georgia greeted Washington in Savannah on 12 May 1791 and his address was also answered in writing by the President.

The Grand Lodge of Pennsylvania sent an address to the President on 27 December 1791, which Washington acknowledged in writing.

The Grand Lodge of Massachusetts in 1792 dedicated its first *Constitutions* to Washington, and he acknowledged the honour with a highly Masonic letter.

The Grand Lodge of Maryland, by invitation, laid the cornerstone of the United States Capitol on 18 September 1793, and Washington officiated as the President of the United States, and as a Past Master of Alexandria Lodge, which also had an honoured place in the program.

The portrait for which Washington sat, and which was painted by William Williams of Philadelphia, showing him clothed as an officer and wearing the jewel of a Worshipful Master, was received by Alexandria Lodge in 1794.

The Grand Lodge of Pennsylvania on 27 December 1796, delivered a letter to 'the Great Master Workman, our Illustrious Br. Washington', which Washington answered in his own handwriting.

Alexandria Lodge no. 22 had Washington in attendance on 1 April 1797, at which time a letter from its only Past Master (under a Virginia charter) was read.

The *Proceedings* of the Grand Lodge of Massachusetts for 12 June 1797, has a copy of an address sent to Washington congratulating him on his good works, the letter being signed by its Grand Master, Paul Revere; it was answered at some length by Washington.

Grand Master William Belton of Maryland presented Washington with a copy of the *Maryland Ahiman Rezon* of 1797 on 7 November and Washington acknowledged the gift in writing.

Alexandria Lodge no. 22 conducted the Masonic funeral ceremonies for its Past Master, George Washington, at the vault at Mount Vernon on 18 December 1799.

HISTORY OF FREEMASONRY / SECRET ORGANIZATIONS

ENGLISH (SIONIST)

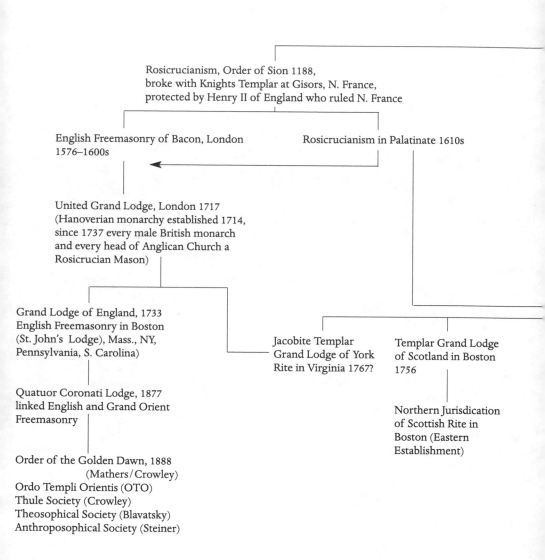

Rosicrucianism, Order of Sion 1188,
broke with Knights Templar at Gisors, N. France,
protected by Henry II of England who ruled N. France

English Freemasonry of Bacon, London
1576–1600s

Rosicrucianism in Palatinate 1610s

United Grand Lodge, London 1717
(Hanoverian monarchy established 1714,
since 1737 every male British monarch
and every head of Anglican Church a
Rosicrucian Mason)

Grand Lodge of England, 1733
English Freemasonry in Boston
(St. John's Lodge), Mass., NY,
Pennsylvania, S. Carolina)

Jacobite Templar
Grand Lodge of York
Rite in Virginia 1767?

Templar Grand Lodge
of Scotland in Boston
1756

Quatuor Coronati Lodge, 1877
linked English and Grand Orient
Freemasonry

Northern Jurisdiction
of Scottish Rite in
Boston (Eastern
Establishment)

Order of the Golden Dawn, 1888
                  (Mathers / Crowley)
Ordo Templi Orientis (OTO)
Thule Society (Crowley)
Theosophical Society (Blavatsky)
Anthroposophical Society (Steiner)

In: GB, Canada, N.E. US, the Far East, Hong Kong, Australia & S. Africa;
deist, pro-rich, right wing; pro-corporate socialism;
UNIVERSAL MONARCHY

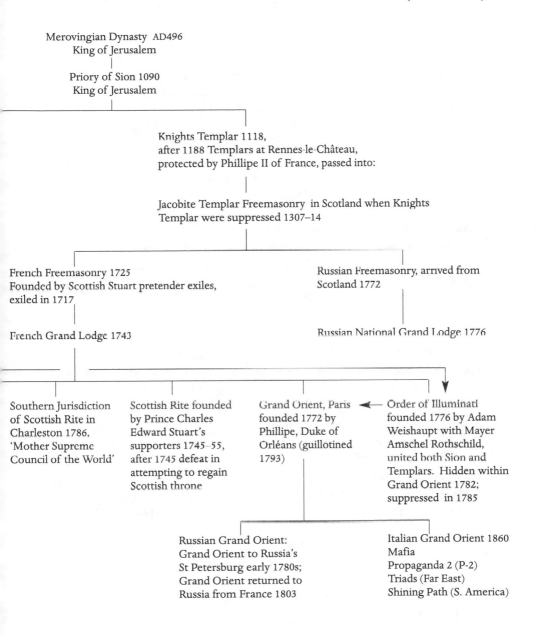

Merovingian Dynasty AD496
King of Jerusalem

Priory of Sion 1090
King of Jerusalem

Knights Templar 1118,
after 1188 Templars at Rennes-le-Château,
protected by Phillipe II of France, passed into:

Jacobite Templar Freemasonry in Scotland when Knights
Templar were suppressed 1307–14

French Freemasonry 1725
Founded by Scottish Stuart pretender exiles,
exiled in 1717

Russian Freemasonry, arrived from
Scotland 1772

French Grand Lodge 1743

Russian National Grand Lodge 1776

Southern Jurisdiction
of Scottish Rite in
Charleston 1786,
'Mother Supreme
Council of the World'

Scottish Rite founded
by Prince Charles
Edward Stuart's
supporters 1745–55,
after 1745 defeat in
attempting to regain
Scottish throne

Grand Orient, Paris
founded 1772 by
Phillipe, Duke of
Orléans (guillotined
1793)

Order of Illuminati
founded 1776 by Adam
Weishaupt with Mayer
Amschel Rothschild,
united both Sion and
Templars. Hidden within
Grand Orient 1782;
suppressed in 1785

Russian Grand Orient:
Grand Orient to Russia's
St Petersburg early 1780s;
Grand Orient returned to
Russia from France 1803

Italian Grand Orient 1860
Mafia
Propaganda 2 (P-2)
Triads (Far East)
Shining Path (S. America)

In: Continent of Europe, S. & W. US, ex-USSR, Philippines, Latin & S. America, Africa including S. Africa;
atheist, pro-poor, left wing; pro-unions and communism;
UNIVERSAL REPUBLIC

NOTES AND SOURCES

References to the *Encyclopaedia Britannica* are to the fifteenth edition, which I believe is more widely available and accessible in libraries than any other edition. In any interpretative study of specific historical events there must be an authoritative standard work where basic facts such as dates and town names can be checked, and the *Encyclopaedia Britannica* serves such a role admirably.

Epigraph

1. Quoted in Mustafa El-Amin, *Freemasonry, Ancient Egypt and the Islamic Destiny*, New Mind Productions, Jersey City, NJ, 1988, p.10

Introduction: Skeleton of a Planting Father

1. Kenneth Haas, an ex-professor to whom I am indebted for a day's intense discussion on the Southern mind as we toured Civil War sites, a focus he will recognize in chapter 8.
2. *See* http://www.sci-tech-today.com/story.xhtml?story_id=12000041xlco

Chapter 1: English Separatists in Plymouth, Puritans in Massachusetts

1. *Encyclopaedia Britannica*, 15.305
2. Charles Norman, *Discoverers of America*, Thomas Y. Crowell, 1968, pp.273–4
3. Quoted in Arthur Quinn, *A New World*, Faber and Faber, 1984, p.86
4. *Ibid.*
5. *Ibid.*, pp.86–7
6. *Ibid.*, p.88, quoting a polemicist
7. Norman, *op. cit.*, p.273
8. Quinn, *op. cit.*, pp.90–91
9. Norman, *op. cit.*, pp.275–6. Bradford: 'Two were chosen and sent into England (at the charge of the rest) to solicit this matter, who found the Virginia Company very desirous to have them go thither, and willing to grant them a patent with as ample privileges as they had or could grant to any.' (The Virginia Company of London was the previous name of the Council for New England.)
10. Norman, *op. cit.*, p.276
11. Quinn, *op. cit.*, p.94
12. *Ibid.*, pp.93–5
13. *Ibid.*, pp.95–6, quoting Bradford. *See* John A. Doyle, *History of the Plimouth Plantation Containing an Account of the Voyage of the 'Mayflower' written by William Bradford*, Ward and Downey, London; Houghton, Mifflin Co., Boston, 1896

14. *Ibid.*, quoting Bradford and therefore the 1620 Julian calendar. The *Encyclopaedia Britannica* gives the date in our calendar as 15 August.

15. Charles Norman, *Discoverers of America*, Thomas Y. Crowell, 1968, p.276

16. *Ibid.*, *also* Arthur Quinn, *A New World*, Faber and Faber, 1984, p.94

17. Norman, *op. cit.*, p.276, quoting Bradford; *see* note 13

18. *Ibid.*, *also* Quinn, *op. cit.*, pp.94–5

19. Quinn, *op. cit.*, p.95

20. Bradford, quoted in Norman, *op. cit.*, p.276

21. *Ibid.*, p.277

22. *Ibid.*

23. *See* http://pilgrims.net/plymouth/history/mayflower.html *also* http://teacher.scholastic.com/researchpools/researchstarters/plymouth for the *Mayflower* Compact. For 'just and equal laws' *see Encyclopaedia Britannica*, 11.591.

24. Bradford, quoted in Charles Norman, *Discoverers of America*, Thomas Y. Crowell, 1968, pp.277–8ff, where details in the following paragraphs can be found.

25. *Ibid.*, p.283

26. Quinn, *op. cit.*, p.97

27. Charles Norman, *Discoverers of America*, Thomas Y. Crowell, 1968, p.284

28. Quoted *ibid.*, pp.285–6

29. *See ibid.*, chapter 10, for New Netherland

30. Quoted *ibid.*, p.291

31. Arthur Quinn, *A New World*, Faber and Faber, 1984, p.114

32. Quoted in Norman, *op. cit.*, pp.292–3

33. *See* http://en.wikipedia.org/wiki/massachusetts_Bay_Colony for the Dorchester Company, Massachusetts Bay Company and Cambridge Agreement

34. *Encyclopaedia Britannica*, 15.307, 'Puritanism'

35. *Ibid.*

36. Quoted in Francis J. Bremer, *John Winthrop: America's Forgotten Founding Father*, Oxford University Press, 2003, p.179. For the 700 settlers, see the website in note 33.

37. For example Darrett Rutman in *Winthrop's Boston: A Portrait of a Puritan Town, 1630–1649*, Norton, 1965

38. William Wilkinson, quoted in William Hunt, *The Puritan Moment: The Coming of Revolution in an English County*, Harvard University Press, 1983, p.87. For this and the remaining notes in this paragraph, *see* Bremer, *op. cit.*, p.181.

39. Richard Rogers, *Certaine Sermons Preached and Penned by Richard Rogers, 1612*, letter to the 'Christian Reader'

40. William Ames, preface to Paul Baynes, *The Diocesan's Tryall*, 1621
41. Nicholas Bownde, prefatory letter in John More, *Three Godly and Fruitful Sermons*, 1594
42. Bezaleel Carter, *The Wise King and Learned Judge*, 1618, p.73.
43. Samuel Clarke, *Lives of Sundry Eminent Persons*, 1683, p.106
44. *Encyclopaedia Britannica*, 15.307
45. Frank Lambert, *The Founding Fathers and the Place of Religion in America*, Princeton University Press, 2003, pp.73–4
46. *See* http://en.wikipedia.org/wiki/massachusetts_Bay_Colony for the Massachusetts General Court, and Bremer, *op. cit.*, p.209, for the 116 freemen admitted in May 1631
47. *Ibid.*
48. *Encyclopaedia Britannica*, 5.9
49. *Ibid.*, 19.891
50. *See* http://en.wikipedia.org/wiki/Connecticut_Colony and Francis J. Bremer, *John Winthrop: America's Forgotten Founding Father*, Oxford University Press, 2003, p.257
51. *See* http://en.wikipedia.org/wiki/Fundamental_Orders_of_Connecticut
52. 'The Fundamental Orders of Connecticut, January 14, 1639' in *Documents of American History*, ed. Henry S. Commager, New York, 1963, seventh ed., pp.23–4, quoted in Lambert, *op. cit.*, p.1. *See* Appendix I.
53. *Ibid.*
54. *See* http://en.wikipedia.org/wiki/massachusetts_Bay_Colony
55. For an estimated population of American colonies 1610–1780, *see* http://web.mala.bc.ca/davies/H320/population.colonies.htm
56. Quoted in *Encyclopaedia Britannica*, 14.24
57. Quoted in David Ballance, *The Buds of Virtue: The Story of Chigwell School*, James and James, 2000, p.33
58. *See Encyclopaedia Britannica*, 14.23–5 for Penn's life
59. Arthur Quinn, *A New World*, Faber and Faber, 1984, pp.337–8
60. Frank Lambert, *The Founding Fathers and the Place of Religion in America*, Princeton University Press, 2003, pp.100–102. For 'holy experiment', *see* note 61.
61. Quoted in Quinn, *op. cit.*, p.339
62. Cited in Edwin Bronner, *William Penn's "Holy Experiment": The Founding of Pennsylvania, 1681–1701*, New York, 1962, p.6, quoted in Lambert, *op. cit.*, p.102
63. Quoted in Lambert, *op. cit.*, p.106
64. *Ibid.*, p.108
65. *Ibid.*, pp.344–6
66. *Ibid.*, pp.108–9

67. Quoted in Quinn, *op. cit.*, p.341
68. *Ibid.*, pp.370–7

Chapter 2: English Anglicans in Virginia and Chesapeake Bay

1. *Encyclopaedia Britannica*, 18.947 and 4.937–9; Nicholas Hagger, *The Secret History of the West*, O Books, 2005, pp.63–4
2. *Encyclopaedia Britannica*, 18.937; Hagger, *op. cit.*, pp.60–61, 64–5
3. *See* Lee Miller, *Roanoke: Solving the Mystery of England's Lost Colony*, Jonathan Cape, 2000, and Hagger, *op. cit.*, p.65
4. Warner F. Gookin, *Bartholomew Gosnold: Discoverer and Planter*, Archon Books, 1963, p.51
5. William Strachey, *The Historie of Travell into Virginia Britania*, eds Louis B. Wright and Virginia Freund, Hakluyt Society, second ser., CIII, 1953, pp.150–51, quoted *ibid.*, p.64
6. Sir Francis Bacon was descended from John Bacon's son Robert, and Bartholomew Gosnold from John Bacon's son Thomas via Dorothy Bacon's marriage to Anthony Gosnold, his father, and via Thomas's first wife Anne Doggett, who became the second wife of Robert Gosnold I, his great-grandfather.
7. *See* Lincoln A. Dexter, *The Gosnold Discoveries ... in the north part of Virginia, 1602 ... according to the Relations by Gabriel Archer and John Brereton*, RFD, Brookfield, Mass., p.15: 'Archer states, "The said captain ... accompanied with 32 persons..." while Brereton reports 32, "in all, two and thirty persons".' Archer's total is 33.
8. Quoted in Gookin, *op. cit.*, p.55
9. *See* Dexter, *op. cit.*, for details of Gosnold's 1602 voyage
10. *Ibid.*, p.1: 'It is clear that Raleigh confiscated the cargo from the voyage. However, an agent for him may have sanctioned the venture.'
11. Charles Norman, *Discoverers of America*, Thomas Y. Crowell, 1968, pp.216–17
12. Everett Hale, *Prospero's Island*
13. Bartholomew Gosnold's wife Mary's grandmother was the second wife of Sir Andrew Judd(e), whose first wife was the grandmother of Sir Thomas Smythe.
14. Jocelyn Wingfield, *Virginia's True Founder: Edward-Maria Wingfield and His Times, 1550–c.1640*, The Wingfield Family Society, 1993, p.148
15. *Ibid.*, p.156 (patent) and p.157 (headed Council)
16. For the Virginia Company's Christian mission, *see* Frank Lambert, *The Founding Fathers and the Place of Religion in America*, Princeton University Press, 2003, pp.22, 46. For a view of Virginia's first planters as being profit-driven, *see* Edmund S. Morgan, *American Slavery, American Freedom: The Ordeal of Colonial Virginia*, New York: W. W. Norton & Co. Ltd, 1975.

17. For Smythe's involvement, *see* Warner F. Gookin, *Bartholomew Gosnold: Discoverer and Planter*, Archon Books, 1963, pp.200–201

18. The figure of 108 was put forward by Dr William Kelso, the archaeologist who discovered Jamestown, in conversation with me. Wingfield, *op. cit.*, p.200, reckons there were 154 men and 5 boys, including 43 sailors.

19. Quoted in Gookin, *op. cit.*, p.202

20. John Smith, *The Generall Historie of Virginia, New-England and the Summer Isles*, 1624, bk 3, ch. 1, reissued by The World Publishing Company, Library of Congress Catalog Number 66-22546, also John Smith, *Works*, The English Scholar's Library, 1884, pp.89–90

21. For Smythe's leadership of the East India Company and Virginia Company, *see* A. L. Rowse, *Shakespeare's Southampton: Patron of Virginia*, Macmillan, 1965, p.242: 'The East India Company was along with the Virginia Company under Sir Thomas Smythe's leadership.' *See* Gookin, *op. cit.*, p.206, for Smythe's role in the organizing of the voyage. The Muscovy Company was behind earlier voyages after the 1550s, and consulted Dr John Dee. The company was behind Frobisher's voyages. For historical reasons it was natural that Smythe's Muscovy Company should back the First Virginia Company's voyage.

22. The Earl of Essex took Bartholomew Gosnold on the Cadiz and Azores expeditions of 1596 and 1597, on the second of which the Earl of Southampton commanded Essex's ship, the *Garland*, and to Ireland and privateering in 1599, when they captured a ship that was probably Spanish. Robert Gosnold III became Secretary and Master of Requests to Essex in 1599. *See* Diarmaid MacCulloch, *Suffolk and the Tudors*.

23. The account of the voyage to the New World and the Jamestown Settlement has been taken from many sources, including Gookin, *op. cit.*; Charles Norman, *Discoverers of America*, Thomas Y. Crowell, 1968; Wingfield, *op. cit.*; Noël Hume, *The Virginia Adventure, Roanoke to James Towne: An Archaeological and Historical Odyssey*, Alfred Knopf, 1998; Arthur Quinn, *A New World*, Faber and Faber, 1984; David A. Price, *Love and Hate in Jamestown*, Faber and Faber, 2003; and archives formerly at Otley Hall.

24. Gookin, *op. cit.*, p.210

25. Jocelyn Wingfield, *Virginia's True Founder: Edward-Maria Wingfield and His Times, 1550–c.1640*, The Wingfield Family Society, 1993, p.177

26. The London Council of Virginia had appointed the following colonists to act as a Council in Virginia: Christopher Newport, Edward-Maria Wingfield, Bartholomew Gosnold, John Smith, John Ratcliffe, John Martin and George Kendall. All were captains. *See* Gookin, *op. cit.*, p.211.

27. This was explained to me almost in these words by Tad Thompson, owner of the Tuckahoe Plantation, where Jefferson was educated in an outbuilding by the river James, as we had drinks under his portrait of Nell Gwyn on 18 October 1998.

28. Bruce S. Thornton, 'Founders as Farmers: The Greek Georgic Tradition and the Founders' in Gary L. Gregg II, ed., *Vital Remnants: America's Founding and the Western Tradition*, ISI Books, 1999, p.33

29. Jocelyn Wingfield, *op. cit.*, pp.206–207

30. For the voyage of Popham and Gilbert, *see* Norman, *op. cit.*, pp.245–8

31. George Percy, *Observations*, quoted *ibid.*, pp.236–7

32. Warner F. Gookin, *Bartholomew Gosnold: Discoverer and Planter*, Archon Books, 1963, p.211: 'Wingfield thereupon refused to swear Smith in as a Councillor.'

33. However, much of the material has been corroborated by contemporary sources researched by Bradford Smith, *Captain John Smith: His Life and Legend*, Lippincott, 1953.

34. John Smith, *A True Relation*, 1608, quoted in Charles Norman, *Discoverers of America*, Thomas Y. Crowell, 1968, p.237

35. John Smith, *The Generall Historie of Virginia, New-England and the Summer Isles*, 1624, reissued by The World Publishing Company, bk 3, ch. 2, p.45

36. Noël Hume, *The Virginia Adventure, Roanoke to James Towne: An Archaeological and Historical Odyssey*, Alfred Knopf, 1998, p.162

37. Quoted in Norman, *op. cit.*, p.238. For the death of Kendall, *see also* Hume, *op. cit.*, pp.162–3.

38. Philip L. Barbour, ed., *The Jamestown Voyages*, vol. I, Cambridge University Press, 1969, p.156

39. Hume, *op. cit.*, pp.171–5, reconciles Smith's conflicting accounts of this whole episode.

40. Quoted in Edward Wright Haile, ed., *Jamestown Narratives: Eyewitness Accounts of the Virginia Colony, 1607–1617*, RoundHouse, 1998, pp.861–2

41. Smith, *Generall Historie*, *op. cit.*, pp.46–8

42. Jocelyn Wingfield, *Virginia's True Founder: Edward-Maria Wingfield and His Times, 1550–c.1640*, The Wingfield Family Society, 1993, p.246

43. Hume, *op. cit.*, pp.181–3

44. Quoted in Frank Lambert, *The Founding Fathers and the Place of Religion in America*, Princeton University Press, 2003, p.21

45. Hume, *op. cit.*, pp.192–206

46. *Ibid.*, pp.206–207

47. John Smith, *The Generall Historie of Virginia, New-England and the Summer Isles*, 1624, reissued by The World Publishing Company, bk 3, ch. 2, p.66

48. Noël Hume, *The Virginia Adventure, Roanoke to James Towne: An Archaeological and Historical Odyssey*, Alfred Knopf, 1998, p.209

49. According to Pedro de Zúñiga, Philip III of Spain's ambassador in London, Sir Walter Raleigh was guiding the company by writing memos from the Tower, one of which came into his hands. *Ibid*, p.215

50. Nell Marion Nugent, *Cavaliers and Pioneers: Abstracts of Virginia Land Patents and Grants, 1623–1666*, Genealogical Publishing Co., 1983, p.240

51. Hume, *op. cit.*, p.214

52. *Ibid.*, pp.218–20

53. *Ibid.*, pp.222–5

54. *Ibid.*, pp.226–7

55. *Ibid.*, pp.228–37

56. Quoted *ibid.*, p.241

57. *Ibid*, pp.245–8

58. John Smith, *The Generall Historie of Virginia, New-England and the Summer Isles*, 1624, reissued by The World Publishing Company, bk 3, ch. 2, p.92

59. Quoted in Noël Hume, *The Virginia Adventure, Roanoke to James Towne: An Archaeological and Historical Odyssey*, Alfred Knopf, 1998, p.251

60. Letter from Ratcliffe to Secretary of State, Lord Salisbury, quoted *ibid.*

61. *Ibid.*, pp.255–6

62. *Ibid.*, p.256

63. *Ibid.*, p.258

64. *Ibid.*, p.260

65. *Ibid.*, pp.261–4

66. *Ibid.*, p.282

67. Frank Lambert, *The Founding Fathers and the Place of Religion in America*, Princeton University Press, 2003, p.50

68. Hume, *op. cit.*, p.270

69. Alexander Whitaker, *News from Virginia. The Lost Flocke Triumphant*, 1610, in Alexander Brown, *The Genesis of the United States*, Boston, 1890, p.23, quoted in Lambert, *op. cit.*, p.49

70. William Crashaw, *A Sermon Preached in London Before the right honourable Lord La Warre, Lord Gouernor and Captaine Generall of Virginea*, London, 1610, quoted in Lambert, *op. cit.*, p.49

71. William Strachey, *For the Colony in Virginea Britannia: Lawes Divine, Morall and Martiall*, 1612, ed. David Flaherty, reprinted Charlottesville, 1969, p.9, quoted *ibid.*, p.51

72. Lambert, *op. cit.*, p.51

73. *Ibid.*, p.58

74. *Ibid.*, p.46

75. Noël Hume, *The Virginia Adventure, Roanoke to James Towne: An Archaeological and Historical Odyssey*, Alfred Knopf, 1998, pp.284–6

76. *Ibid.*, pp.287–8

77. *Ibid.*, pp.289–90

78. *Ibid.*, pp.290–94

79. *Ibid.*, pp.297–8

80. *Ibid.*, p.300

81. *Ibid.*, pp.305–22

82. *Ibid.*, pp.324–5

83. *Ibid.*, p.326

84. For the quotations, *see* Hamor, *A True Discourse of the Present Estate of Virginia, and the successe of the affaires there till the 18 of June, 1615*, reprinted Virginia State Library, Richmond, 1957, p.4, quoted *ibid.*, p.327

85. *Ibid.*, pp.328–30

86. *Ibid.*, pp.335–48

87. Philip L. Barbour, *The Complete Works of Captain John Smith (1580–1631)*, vol. II, University of North Carolina Press, 1986, p.262, quoted *ibid.*, p.353

88. *Encyclopaedia Britannica*, 18.947

89. Noël Hume, *The Virginia Adventure, Roanoke to James Towne: An Archaeological and Historical Odyssey*, Alfred Knopf, 1998, p.373

90. Frank Lambert, *The Founding Fathers and the Place of Religion in America*, Princeton University Press, 2003, p.53

91. *Ibid.*, p.72

Chapter 3: Spanish Catholics in Florida

1. Gentleman of Elvas, quoted in Charles Norman, *Discoverers of America*, Thomas Y. Crowell, 1968, p.63

2. Quoted *ibid.*, p.57

3. *Ibid.*, p.58

4. *Ibid.*, p.71

5. *Ibid.*, p.74

6. *Ibid.*, p.81

7. *Ibid.*, p.88

8. *Ibid.*, p.139

9. De Laudonnière, *A Notable History*, translated by Hakluyt, quoted *ibid.*, pp.140–41

10. Quoted in a letter from Avilés to Philip II, 11 September 1565

11. Quoted in Charles Norman, *Discoverers of America*, Thomas Y. Crowell, 1968, p.152

12. *Ibid.*

13. *Ibid.*, p.153

14. *Ibid.*

15. *Ibid.*

16. The existence of the 1418 map was reported in the London *Times* of 14 January 2006.

17. *See* Gavin Menzies, *1421: The Year China Discovered the World*, Bantam Books, 2002, pp.80–83, for Zheng He's return and Zhu Di's death

18. In Tim Wallace-Murphy and Marilyn Hopkins, *Templars in America from the Crusades to the New World*, Weiser Books, 2004

19. Charles C. Mann, *Ancient Americans: Rewriting the History of the New World*, Granta Books, 2005, p.172

Chapter 4: Freemasons in Virginia and Massachusetts

1. Manly P. Hall, *America's Assignment with Destiny*, The Philosophical Research Society, 1951, pp.59–60

2. *See* Nicholas Hagger, *The Secret History of the West*, O Books, 2005, Appendix 6, for a full history of Septimania

3. Hall, *op. cit.*, pp.59–60

4. *See* Hagger, *op. cit.*, pp.80–81

5. According to A. L. Rowse, *Shakespeare's Southampton: Patron of Virginia*, Macmillan, 1965, pp.210, 214, Southampton danced with Princess Elizabeth on New Year's night 1611 and attended the state reception for Frederick V in October 1612.

6. *The Letters of John Chamberlain*, ed. N. E. McClure

7. *See* Frances A. Yates, *The Rosicrucian Enlightenment*, Routledge and Kegan Paul, 1972, pp.1–9, for full details of the wedding

8. Charlotte Stopes, *The Third Earl of Southampton*, Cambridge University Press, 1922, pp.361–2

9. My local research has established that the Thick Tower by the English Palace, built in 1533 and remodelled by Frederick V in 1619, was reshaped to be a replica of the Globe Theatre, and that performances of Shakespeare's plays took place there.

10. Yates, *op. cit.*, p.90

11. N. B. Cockburn, *The Bacon Shakespeare Question: The Baconian Theory Made Sane*, Biddles, 1998, p.242

12. Quoted in Manly P. Hall, *America's Assignment with Destiny*, The Philosophical Research Society, 1951, pp.69–70

13. Quoted *ibid.*, pp.65–6

14. For example by J. A. C. Chandler in *Library of Southern Literature*, Neale Publishing Company, New York, 1906

15. George V. Tudhope, *Freemasonry Came to America with Captain John Smith in 1607*, pamphlet, n.d., p.1

16. The first Grand Lodge, an association of lodges, was founded in England in 1717. Grand Lodges were subsequently founded in other countries accepting Freemasonry. The first American Grand Lodge was founded in 1723.

17. For the earlier dating of *New Atlantis*, *see* Peter Dawkins, *The Shakespeare Enigma*, Polair, 2004, pp.278–80 (though he wrongly states that the expedition to settle Jamestown was commanded by Captain John Smith).

18. Nicholas Hagger, *The Secret History of the West*, O Books, 2005, p.95; Frances Yates, *The Rosicrucian Enlightenment*, Routledge and Kegan Paul, 1972, pp.125–9.

19. This Nathaniel Bacon was older than the leader of Bacon's Rebellion, the Nathaniel Bacon who was born in 1647 and died in 1676. There is a slab marker in Bruton parish church, Williamsburg, to a Nathaniel Bacon who was born about 1620 and died in 1692 aged 72. If this was the man who brought the missing Bacon papers to the New World in 1635, then he can only have been about 13 when he made the journey.

20. For claims regarding the Bruton vault and Rockefeller Restoration's obstruction of Marie Bauer Hall's detective work based on emblems in George Wither's *Anagrams* (1635) – no doubt because she wanted to dig near existing tombs and her evidence did not convince them – and for her discovery of the first brick church's foundations to the north-west of the present church, *see* Marie Bauer Hall, *Foundations Unearthed*, Veritas Press, pp.23, 37. The slab marker in the Bruton parish church refers to a Nathaniel Bacon who is actually buried several miles east, near the York river at the Ringfield plantation: 'Here lyeth interred y body of Nathaniel Bacon esq whose descent was from the ancient house of y Bacons (one of which was Chancellor Bacon & Lord Verulam) who was Auditour of Virginia and President of y honourable council of ?? & Comander in Chief for the County of York having been of the Council for above 40 years & having always discharged?? In which he served with great ?? & loyalty to his Princ.? Who departed this life y 16 of March 1692 in y 73 year of his age.'

21. Tudhope, *op. cit.*, p.7

22. *See* Hagger, *op. cit.*, p.122–4

23. *Ibid.*, p.112

24. Michael Baigent and Richard Leigh, *The Temple and the Lodge*, Arcade, 1989, pp.201–203

25. *Ibid.*, pp.202, 233, and John Daniel, *Scarlet and the Beast*, vol. I, JKI Publishing, 1995, p.686

26. Daniel, *op. cit.* vol. I, p.166. For points in the above three paragraphs, *see* Hagger, *op. cit.*, pp.237–40

27. Daniel, *op. cit.*, vol. I, p.686

28. Robert Hieronimus, *America's Secret Destiny*, Destiny Books, 1989, p.39. *See* fig. 6 in Hieroniumus for an illustration of this Rosicrucian code.

29. Baigent and Leigh, *op. cit.*, p.201

30. *Ibid.*, pp.34–37, 74, 95

31. *Ibid.*, p.121

32. Nicholas Hagger, *The Secret History of the West*, O Books, 2005, pp.78–9
33. There is a monument to John Gosnold IV and his wife Winifred Windsor in Otley parish church.
34. For the Jacobite manoeuvres, *see* Hagger, *op. cit.*, pp.228–30
35. *Ibid.*, pp.230–31
36. Michael Baigent, Richard Leigh and Henry Lincoln, *The Holy Blood and the Holy Grail*, Corgi Books, 1982, p.149
37. John Daniel, *Scarlet and the Beast*, vol. I, JKI Publishing, 1995, p.684
38. Michael Baigent and Richard Leigh, *The Temple and the Lodge*, Arcade, 1989, pp.221–5; Hagger, *op. cit.*, pp.241–5
39. Charles Dahne, *The Complete Guide to Boston's Freedom Trail*
40. John Daniel, *Scarlet and the Beast*, vol. I, JKI Publishing, 1995, pp.686–7
41. *Ibid.*, p.692
42. Author and Freemason Paul Bessel maintains that only nine were Freemasons (http://bessel.org/declmas.htmp.61). William T. Still, *New World Order: The Ancient Plan of Secret Societies*, Huntingdon House, Lafayette, LA, 1990, states that 53 of the 56 were Freemasons according to the 1951 Masonic Edition of the *Holy Bible*.
43. *Ibid.*, p.60; *see also* Allen E. Roberts, *G. Washington: Master Mason*, Macoy Publishing and Masonic Supply Co., 1976
44. Daniel, *op. cit.*, vol. I, p.692

Chapter 5: Enlightenment Deists in New England

1. *See Encyclopaedia Britannica*, 6.887–8, for the Enlightenment
2. Quoted in Frank Lambert, *The Founding Fathers and the Place of Religion in America*, Princeton University Press, 2003, p.166
3. The historian Edward Gibbon was Deist (despite having been a Roman Catholic convert) in blaming both Christianity and barbarism for the fall of the civilized Roman Empire in the first volume of *The History of the Decline and Fall of the Roman Empire*, which appeared in 1776. However, he was not Deist in seeing Byzantine history as a decline from the intellectual and political freedoms of Rome's Golden Age rather than as Enlightenment progress beyond the Roman time.
4. *Encyclopaedia Britannica*, IV, 1041
5. Nieves Matthews, *Francis Bacon: The History of a Character Assassination*, Yale University Press, 1996, p.11
6. Peter Dawkins, *The Shakespeare Enigma*, Polair, 2004, p.288
7. Matthews, *op. cit.*, p.412
8. Quoted *ibid.*, p.412
9. *See* http://www.irelandinformationguide.com/Freemasonry
10. *See* Nicholas Hagger, *The Secret History of the West*, O Books, 2005

11. R. L. Worthy, *The Founders' Façade: Christianity, Democracy, Freemasonry, and the Founding of America*, KornerStone Books, 2004, p.51

12. *See* http://www.irelandinformationguide.com/Freemasonry

13. *Encyclopaedia Britannica*, 5.562

14. *Ibid.*, 6.887

15. *See* Hagger, *op. cit.*, ch.3

16. Quoted in Worthy, *op. cit.*, p.12

17. *Encyclopaedia Britannica*, 5.563

18. Worthy, *op. cit.*, p.12

19. Quoted in Robert W. Galvin, *What the Scottish Enlightenment Taught Our Founding Fathers*, Rowman and Littlefield, 2002, p.57

20. *Ibid.*, p.70

21. *See* Nicholas Hagger, *The Secret History of the West*, O Books, 2005, ch.3

22. Jonathan Edwards, *A History of the Work of Redemption*, 1773, pp.281–2, quoted in Frank Lambert, *The Founding Fathers and the Place of Religion in America*, Princeton University Press, 2003, p.160

23. Quoted *ibid.*, p.161

24. *Ibid.*, p.159

25. Carl Van Doren, *Benjamin Franklin*, Viking Press, New York, 1938; reprinted Penguin Books, 1991, pp.777–8, quoted in James Srodes, *Franklin: The Essential Founding Father*, Regnery Publishing, 2002, pp.386–7

26. Quoted in Lambert, *op. cit.*, p.163

27. *Ibid.*, p.173

28. Quoted in R. L. Worthy, *The Founders' Façade: Christianity, Democracy, Freemasonry, and the Founding of America*, KornerStone Books, 2004, p.17

29. For the description of Mary Dyer's hanging, *see The Chronicle of America*, p.71, quoted *ibid.*, p.9

30. Merrill D. Peterson, ed., *Thomas Jefferson: A Reference Biography*, Scribner's, 1986, pp.490–94

31. Jefferson, letter to Peter Carr, 1787, quoted in Edwin S. Gaustad, *Sworn on the Altar of God: A Religious Biography of Thomas Jefferson*, Eerdmans, 1996, p.33

32. Quoted in Worthy, *op. cit.*, p.24

33. *Ibid.*, p.15

34. Quoted in Frank Lambert, *The Founding Fathers and the Place of Religion in America*, Princeton University Press, 2003, p.265

35. Gaustad, *op. cit.*, p.92

36. Lambert, *op. cit.*, p.277

37. *Ibid.*

38. William G. McLoughlin, *Soul Liberty: The Baptists' Struggle in New England, 1630–1833*, University Press of New England, Hanover, NH, 1991, pp.267–8, quoted *ibid.*, p.286

39. Lester Cappon, ed., *The Adams–Jefferson Letters: The Complete Correspondence between Thomas Jefferson and Abigail and John Adams*, 2 vols., 2:509, quoted ibid., pp.174–5

40. Thomas Paine, *The Age of Reason, Being an Investigation of True and Fabulous Theology*, 1794; reprint New York, n.d., pp.6–8

41. *Ibid.*

42. Thomas Paine, *Of the Religion of Deism Compared with the Christian Religion*, quoted in R. L. Worthy, *The Founders' Façade: Christianity, Democracy, Freemasonry, and the Founding of America*, KornerStone Books, 2004, p.13

43. Lambert, *op. cit.*, p.272

44. Paul F. Boller, Jr, *Washington and Religion*, S.M.U. Press, 1963, p.92

45. *Ibid.*, pp.8–11, 14–18, 93–4

46. *Ibid.*, p.82

47. Quoted in http://www.deism.com/washington.htm

48. *The Works of Thomas Jefferson*, ed. Paul Leicester Ford, 12 vols, 1904–5, vol. IV, p.572

49. Barry Schwartz, *George Washington: The Making of an American Symbol*, The Free Press, 1987, p.170

50. Quoted in John E. Remsberg, *Six Historic Americans*, The Truth Seeker Company, 1906

51. Ford, *op. cit.*, vol. IV, p.572; Jefferson's private journal, February 1800

52. Boller, *op. cit.*, pp.74–5

53. James Thomas Flexner, *George Washington and the New Nation, 1783–1793*, Little, Brown, 1969, p.184

54. James Thomas Flexner, *George Washington: Anguish and Farewell, 1793–1799*, Little, Brown, 1972, p.490

55. The Reverend Doctor Abercrombie, rector of the church Washington had attended with his wife, to the Reverend Bird Wilson, an Episcopal minister in Albany, New York, quoted in Remsberg, *op. cit.*

56. The Reverend Doctor James Abercrombie, letter to a friend, 1833, in Sprague's *Annals of the American Pulpit*, vol. V, p.394, quoted in Franklin Steiner, *The Religious Beliefs of our Presidents*, Prometheus Books, 1995, pp.25–6

57. The Right Reverend William White, letter to Colonel Mercer of Fredericksberg, Virginia, 15 August 1835, quoted ibid., p.27

58. George Custis, letter to Mr Sparks, 26 February 1833, in *Sparks's Washington*, p.521, quoted ibid., p.29

59. Quoted in R. L. Worthy, *The Founders' Façade: Christianity, Democracy, Freemasonry, and the Founding of America*, KornerStone Books, 2004, p.17

60. The Reverend Doctor Bird Wilson in an interview with Mr Robert Dale Owen, 13 November 1831, quoted in Steiner, *op. cit.*, p.27

61. The Reverend Doctor Bird Wilson, letter to the Reverend P. C. C. Parker, 31 December 1832, in Reverend Bird Wilson, *Memoir of Bishop White*, pp.189–91; quoted *ibid.*, p.28

62. Barry Schwartz, *George Washington: The Making of an American Symbol*, The Free Press, 1987, quoted in Worthy, *op. cit.*, p.18

63. Nicholas Hagger, *The Secret History of the West*, O Books, 2005, p.267

64. Worthy, *op. cit.* p.19

65. Schwartz, *op. cit.*, p.173

66. K. Walters, *Rational Infidels: The American Deists*, Longwood, 1992, pp.6, 8–9; *see also* K. Walters, *The American Deist: Voices of Reason and Dissent in the Early Republic*, University of Kansas, 1992

67. Jean-Jacques Burlamaqui, *The Principles of Natural and Political Law*, 3rd edition, 2 vols, London, 1784, 1:1–12, quoted in Frank Lambert, *The Founding Fathers and the Place of Religion in America*, Princeton University Press, 2003, p.167

68. *Ibid.*

69. Kenneth Silverman, *Benjamin Franklin*, TP212–15, quoted *ibid.*, p.169

70. Quoted *ibid.*

71. *Ibid.*, p.171

72. Quoted in Lambert, *op. cit.*, p.171

73. H. Wayne House, *The Christian and American Law*, Jon Kregel Publications, 1998, pp.49–51

74. Newton spent the last 30 years of his life researching into alchemy and revelation.

75. On a personal note, whereas Deist Freemasonry rejects revelation – the disclosure of knowledge from a divine or supernatural source – in favour of reason, I have endeavoured to blend reason and revelation in my works. Using reason, I have restated the tradition of revelation in *The Light of Civilization* in the course of endeavouring to show that revealed vision inspires civilizations to grow. The One (to move away from the specifically Christian terminology of God) is both transcendent and immanent, and knowable through revelation as Light and as a living presence within Nature, and it is approached by a deeper part of the psyche than the reason. I have included all religions in my Universalist study of history, as would Deists, but have focused on the core of man's being rather than his useful but limited reason.

76. Lambert, *op. cit.*, pp.161–2

77. L. Eigen and J. Siegel, *The Macmillan Dictionary of Political Quotations*, Macmillan, 1993, p.613

78. Quoted in R. L. Worthy, *The Founders' Façade: Christianity, Democracy, Freemasonry, and the Founding of America*, KornerStone Books, 2004, p.23

Chapter 6: German Illuminati

1. David Allen Rivera, *Final Warning: A History of the New World Order*, Rivera Enterprises, 1984, p.5; Nicholas Hagger, *The Secret History of the West*, O Books, 2005, p.289

2. Michael Baigent, Richard Leigh and Henry Lincoln, *The Holy Blood and the Holy Grail*, Corgi Books, 1982, p.133

3. The Palais de Charles de Lorraine is above the Bibliothèque Royale in Brussels. It has three wings, but only the right-hand wing belongs to the original palace. Five rooms in it are open to the public.

4. John Daniel, *Scarlet and the Beast*, vol. I, JKI Publishing, 1995, p.142; Hagger, *op. cit.*, pp.231–2

5. Daniel, *op. cit.*, vol. I, p.149; Hagger, *op. cit.*, pp.233–5

6. William Guy Carr, *The Conspiracy to Destroy All Existing Governments and Religions*, published privately, Canada, 1959, p.1

7. Neal Wilgus, *The Illuminoids*, Pocket Books, 1979, p.154; Hagger, *op. cit.*, p.289

8. Carr, *op. cit.*, p.5; Hagger, *op. cit.*, p.289

9. *Ibid.*, p.290

10. Michael Howard, *The Occult Conspiracy: Secret Societies – Their Influence and Power in World History*, Destiny Books, 1989, p.63

11. David Allen Rivera, *Final Warning: A History of the New World Order*, Rivera Enterprises, 1984, p.6

12. Adam Weishaupt, *Nachtrag ... Originale Schriften (des Illuminaten Ordens)*, Zweite Abteilung, p.65, quoted in Nesta Webster, *World Revolution*, Constable, 1921, p.10. *See also* Hagger, *The Secret History of the West*, O Books, 2005, pp.219–22

13. Salem Kirban, *Satan's Angels Exposed*, Grapevine Books Distributors, 1980; Nesta Webster, *op. cit.*, p.22

14. Hagger, *op. cit.*, p.288

15. Nesta Webster, *op. cit.*, pp.1–2; Hagger, *op. cit.*, pp.294–5

16. Rivera, *op. cit.*, p.8

17. *Ibid.*, p.8

18. *Ibid.*, pp.6–7

19. Webster, *op. cit.*, p.15

20. *Ibid.*, p.16

21. David Allen Rivera, *Final Warning: A History of the New World Order*, Rivera Enterprises, 1984, p.8

22. Nicholas Hagger, *The Secret History of the West*, O Books, 2005, p.294

23. *Ibid.*, pp.293–4

24. Raymond E. Capt, *Our Great Seal: The Symbols of our Heritage and our Destiny*, Artisan Sales, 1979, p.11, quoted in John Daniel, *Scarlet and the Beast*, vol. I, JKI Publishing, 1995, p.708

25. *Ibid*; Robert Hieronimus, *America's Secret Destiny*, Destiny Books, 1989, pp.48–56 and 63–92; Daniel, *op. cit.*, vol. I, p.709; William T. Still, *New World Order: The Ancient Plan of Secret Societies*, Huntingdon House, Lafayette, LA, 1990, pp.65–8

26. Hagger, *op. cit.*, pp.254–5

27. For Franklin's meeting with the Illuminati/Weishaupt, *see* Daniel, *op. cit.*, vol. I, pp.166, 686

28. For 13/philosophical Atlantis, *see ibid.*, pp.167, 686

29. William Guy Carr, *The Conspiracy to Destroy All Existing Governments and Religions*, Canada, 1959, p.xiii

30. Still, *op. cit.*, p.41; Daniel, *op. cit.*, vol. I, p.679

31. *Ibid.*, pp.167–8, 684–5; Hagger, *op. cit.*, pp.256–7

32. Daniel, *op. cit.* vol. I, p.708

33. Nesta Webster, *World Revolution*, Constable, 1921, p.17; Daniel, *op. cit.*, vol. I, p.148. *See also* Nicholas Hagger, *The Secret History of the West*, O Books, 2005, p.293

34. Webster, *op. cit.*, p.17; David Allen Rivera, *Final Warning: A History of the New World Order*, Rivera Enterprises, 1984, p.7

35. *Ibid.*, p.8

36. Saint-Martin, *Des Erreurs et de la Vérité*, 1775

37. Rivera, *op. cit.*, p.10

38. John Daniel, *Scarlet and the Beast*, vol. I, JKI Publishing, 1995, pp.687–8

39. Hagger, *op. cit.*, p.255

40. *Ibid.*

41. Nesta Webster, *Secret Societies and Subversive Movements*, Christian Book Club of America, 1925, p.235; Daniel, *op. cit.*, pp.263–4

42. Rivera, *op. cit.*, pp.20–21

43. George E. Dillon, *Grand Orient Freemasonry Unmasked as the Secret Power Behind Communism*, Sons of Liberty, 1885, p.46

44. Nesta Webster, *World Revolution*, Constable, 1921, p.20

45. Daniel, *op. cit.*, p.264

46. James Srodes, *Franklin: The Essential Founding Father*, Regnery Publishing, 2002, p.371; Daniel, *op. cit.*, pp.166, 688

47. Salem Kirban, *Satan's Angels Exposed*, Grapevine Books Distributors, p.151, quoted in Daniel, *op. cit.*, p.165

48. J. R. Church, *Guardians of the Grail*, pp.163–4, quoted *ibid.*, pp.165–6

49. V. Stauffer, *New England and the Bavarian Illuminati*, Columbia University Press, 1918, p.312

50. Quoted in Robert Hieronimus, *America's Secret Destiny*, Destiny Books, 1989, p.38

51. *See* Nicholas Hagger, *The Syndicate*, O Books, 2004, for the impact of Illuminati ideas on the present American government.

Chapter 7: A Freemasonic State

1. *Encyclopaedia Britannica*, 18.954. For the population figures in the next paragraph, *see* http://web.mala.bc.ca/davies/H320/population.colonies.htm

2. *Encyclopaedia Britannica*, x.763

3. *Ibid.*, vii.772

4. *See* Nicholas Hagger, *The Secret History of the West*, O Books, 2005, pp.241–5

5. *Encyclopaedia Britannica*, v.399

6. Quoted in James Srodes, *Franklin: The Essential Founding Father*, Regnery Publishing, 2002, p.273

7. Hagger, *op. cit.*, p.245

8. John Daniel, *Scarlet and the Beast*, vol. I, JKI Publishing, 1995, p.690

9. Hagger, *op. cit.*, pp.247–54

10. *See A Letter from Cicero to the Right Hon. Lord Viscount Howe*, London, 1781, quoted in Michael Baigent and Richard Leigh, *The Temple and the Lodge*, Arcade, 1989, p.236. *See also* Hagger, *op. cit.*, p253.

11. For Washington and Cromwell declining kingship, *see* Hagger, *op. cit.*, chs 2, 4

12. Stephen Knight, *The Brotherhood: The Secret World of the Freemasons*, Stein and Day, 1984, p.27, quoted in Daniel, *op. cit.*, p.112. For Anderson, *see ibid.*, pp.112–13 also http://freemasonry.bcy.ca/history/anderson_constitutions.html

13. Daniel, *op. cit.* p.113

14. For the Jesuit structure, *see Encyclopaedia Britannica*, 11.167

15. Henry C. Clausen, *Masons Who Helped Shape Our Nation*, Washington, 1976, pp.14–16

16. *Ibid.*, p.82

17. Richard B. Morris, *The Framing of the Federal Constitution, Handbook 103*, Division of Publications, National Park Service, US Department of the Interior, 1986, pp.53–7

18. For the Committee of Detail, *see ibid.*, p.64

19. Frank Lambert, *The Founding Fathers and the Place of Religion in America*, Princeton University Press, 2003, p.251

20. Morris, *op. cit.*, pp.64–5

21. In the English Revolution John Cook, Solicitor for the Commonwealth, indicted Charles I, the British king, on 22 June 1649 in the name of the people through the Commons.

22. For a picture of the Freemasonic rising sun, *see ibid.*, pp.10–11

23. *Ibid.*, p.68

24. *Ibid.*, pp.68–75

25. *See ibid.*, p.111. For deteriorating social conditions, *see* John Fiske, *The Critical Period of American History, 1783–1789* (Houghton Mifflin, 1897) and the challenge to Fiske by Merrill Jensen in *The New Nation: A History of the United States During the Confederation, 1781–1789* (Vintage Books, 1950). *See also* Richard B. Morris, *The American Revolution Reconsidered* (Harper & Row, 1967). For the personal property interests of the Founding Fathers, *see* Charles A. Beard, *An Economic Interpretation of the Constitution* (1913; reprinted Macmillan, 1935) and for a challenge to Beard *see* Robert E. Brown, *Charles Beard and the Constitution* (W. W. Norton & Co., 1965) and Forrest McDonald, *We the People: The Economic Origins of the Constitution* (University of Chicago Press, 1958). For the progress of the convention, *see* Robert L. Schuyler, *The Constitution of the United States: An Historical Survey of Its Formation* (Macmillan, 1923), Carl Van Doren, *The Great Rehearsal: The Story of the Making and Ratifying of the Constitution of the United States* (Viking Press, 1948) and Clinton Rossiter, *1787: The Grand Convention* (Macmillan, 1966).

26. Gary L. Gregg II, ed., *Vital Remnants: America's Founding and the Western Tradition*, ISI Books, 1999, pp.33ff

27. The list was compiled for the Masonic Service Association of the United States. Ronald E. Heaton also wrote *Masonic Membership of the Founding Fathers* M.S.A., 1974. Researchers for the American Lodge of Research reported in 1935 that of the 14,000 American officers of all grades listed by revolutionary authorities, 2,018 were Freemasons, with 218 Masonic lodges being represented among them.

28. Michael Baigent and Richard Leigh, *The Temple and the Lodge*, Arcade, 1989, p.261; John Daniel, *Scarlet and the Beast*, vol. I, JKI Publishing, 1995, p.692

29. Allen E. Roberts, *Washington: Master Mason*, Macoy Pub. and Masonic Supply Co., 1976, pp.126–7

30. *See* the 1951 Masonic Edition of the Holy Bible

31. William T. Still, *New World Order: The Ancient Plan of Secret Societies*, Huntingdon House, Lafayette, LA, 1990, p.61. Freemason Manly Hall says 51 ('all but five') in *America's Assignment with Destiny*. *See* ch, 4, note 42 for the view that only nine were Freemasons. The Philosophical Research Society, 1951, pp.96–7, quoted *ibid.*, p.61.

32. Baigent and Leigh, *op. cit.*, p.261

33. Daniel, *op. cit.*, p.926, which lists l'Enfant as 'FM'.

34. Baigent and Leigh, *op. cit.*, p.262

35. *Encyclopaedia Britannica*, 19.623

36. Edward Decker, 'Freemasonry: Satan's Door to America?' in *Free the Masons Ministries* newsletter, n.d., quoted in Daniel, *op. cit.*, p.707

37. Quoted in Roberts, *op. cit.*, pp.136–7

38. This paragraph is based on books on Monticello on sale at the house. *See also* Hagger, *The Secret History of the West*, O Books, 2005, pp.266–7

39. *See* Barry Schwartz, *George Washington: The Making of an American Symbol*, The Free Press, 1987

40. In France, by 1794, there were 6,800 Jacobin Clubs totalling half a million members, all former Grand Orient Freemasons, taught revolution by the Illuminati. *See* Hagger, *op. cit.*, p.281

41. Quoted in Frank Lambert, *The Founding Fathers and the Place of Religion in America*, Princeton University Press, 2003, p.237

42. Philip B. Kurland and Ralph Lerner, *The Founders' Constitution*, 4 vols, University of Chicago Press, 1987, vol. IV, p.643, quoted *ibid.*, p.236

43. *Ibid.*, p.3

44. *Ibid.*, p.4

45. *Ibid.*, p.244

46. Ezra Stiles, *The United States Elevated to Glory and Honour. A Sermon Preached before His Excellency Jonathan Trumbull, Governor and Commander in Chief, And the honourable The General Assembly of the State of Connecticut Convened at Hartford at the Anniversary Election May 8th, 1783*, New Haven, 1783, pp.7, 53

47. R. H. Campbell and A. S. Skinner, eds, *An Inquiry into the Nature and Causes of the Wealth of Nations by Adam Smith*, vol. II, Liberty Fund, Indianapolis, 1981, p.797, quoted in Lambert, *op. cit.*, p.9

48. Gary L. Gregg II, ed., *Vital Remnants: America's Founding and the Western Tradition*, ISI Books, 1999, pp.108, 135

49. William Linn, *Serious Considerations on the Election of a President: Addressed to the Citizens of the United States*, New York, 1800, pp.4, 20, 28, quoted in Lambert, *op. cit.*, p.265

Chapter 8: Freemasonry's Battle for America

1. *Encyclopaedia Britannica*, 18.947

2. W. J. Cash, *The Mind of the South*, Alfred Knopf, 1941, p.6

3. Rollin G. Osterweis, *Romanticism and Nationalism in the Old South*, Louisiana State University Press, 1949, pp.vii. For other points in this paragraph, *see* pp.vii, 14, 16, 17

4. John Daniel, *Scarlet and the Beast*, vol. I, JKI Publishing, 1995, p.388, quoting Anton Chaitkin, *Treason in America*, New Benjamin Frankin House, 1984, p.161

5. Daniel, *op. cit.*, pp.388–9

6. Nicholas Hagger, *The Syndicate*, O Books, 2004, p.8

7. William R. Denslow, *10,000 Famous Freemasons*, vol. IV, Missouri Lodge of Research, 1961, p.74, quoted in Daniel, *op. cit.*, vol. III, p.63, and David

Allen Rivera, *Final Warning: A History of the New World Order*, Rivera Enterprises, 1984, p.40

8. *Ibid.*, pp.40–41; William T. Still, *New World Order: The Ancient Plan of Secret Societies*, Huntingdon House, Lafayette, LA, 1990, p.148

9. Nicholas Hagger, *The Secret History of the West*, O Books, 2005, pp.367, 373

10. *Ibid.*, p.368

11. Edith Starr Miller, *Occult Theocrasy*, 1933, Christian Book Club of America, 1980, pp.254–5, quoted in Daniel, *op. cit.*, vol. III, p.64

12. Quoted *ibid.*, pp.64–5; Chaitkin, *op. cit.*, p.217

13. Daniel, *op. cit.*, p.65

14. In 1869 Morgan would go to London, would become the agent for N. M. Rothschilds in the United States and would eventually become involved in the financing of the British armaments in the First World War, which was also Freemasonic in conception. Ralph A. Epperson, *The Unseen Hand*, Publius Press, 1985, p.165; Hagger, *The Syndicate*, *op. cit.*, pp.18–19

15. John Daniel, *Scarlet and the Beast*, vol. III, JKI Publishing, 1995, p.66

16. Anton Chaitkin, *Treason in America*, New Benjamin Frankin House, 1984, p.234, cited *ibid.*, p.67

17. Rollin G. Osterweis, *Romanticism and Nationalism in the Old South*, Louisiana State University Press, 1949, pp.179–80; Rivera, *op. cit.*, p.40

18. Daniel, *op. cit.*, vol. III, p.68

19. William R. Denslow, *10,000 Famous Freemasons*, vol. IV, Missouri Lodge of Research, 1961, p.3, quoted in Daniel, *op. cit.*, vol. I, p.68

20. Miller, *op. cit.*, p.221, quoted in Daniel, *op. cit.*, vol. I, p.387

21. Daniel, *op. cit.*, vol. I, p.387

22. *Ibid.*, vol. III, p.69

23. *Ibid.*, p.70

24. *Ibid.*

25. Lincoln's alliance with Russia and the Masonic opposition to him were a precursor to the alliance between the US and Russia during the Second World War.

26. *Encyclopaedia Britannica*, 10.989

27. *See* Nicholas Hagger, *The Syndicate*, O Books, 2004, pp.10–12, for Rothschild's creation of the Federal Reserve System

28. Quoted in *Encyclopaedia Britannica*, 10.986

29. John Daniel, *Scarlet and the Beast*, vol. III, JKI Publishing, 1995, p.75

30. *Ibid*; *see also* Ralph A. Epperson, *The Unseen Hand*, Publius Press, 1985

31. *Ibid.*, vol. I, p.334

32. *Ibid.*, vol. III, pp.76 and 186, note 6 on an official document recorded by Benn Pittman, *The Indianapolis Treason Trial, 1865; Official Report – A Western Conspiracy in the Aid of the Southern Rebellion*, Indianapolis, 1865.

Original documents relating to Lincoln's assassination remain locked in the Defense Department's archives and cannot be shown to researchers.

33. *Ibid.*, p.76

34. David Allen Rivera, *Final Warning: A History of the New World Order*, Rivera Enterprises, 1984, p.42

35. Epperson, *op. cit.*, p.162

36. *Ibid.*, pp.162–3

37. Paul A. Fisher, *Behind the Lodge Door*, Shield, p.209, quoted in Daniel, *op. cit.*, vol. I, p.390

38. *Ibid.*

39. *Ibid.*

40. *See: Secret Ritual of the Thirty-third and Last Degree, Sovereign Grand Inspector General of the Ancient and Accepted Scottish Rite of Freemasonry*

41. *See* Nicholas Hagger, *The Syndicate*, O Books, 2004, Epilogue

42. John Daniel, *Scarlet and the Beast*, vol. I, JKI Publishing, 1995, pp.387, 393–4; Rivera, *op. cit.*, p.36; Nicholas Hagger, *The Secret History of the West*, O Books, 2005, pp.383–4

43. William T. Still, *New World Order: The Ancient Plan of Secret Societies*, Huntingdon House, Lafayette, LA, 1990, pp.31–3, 124

Chapter 9: The Freemasonic State today

1. David Allen Rivera, *Final Warning: A History of the New World Order*, Rivera Enterprises, 1984, *also* http://www.theamericanpresidency.us/masons.htm

2. http://en.wikipedia.org/wiki/User:Hipocrite/Freemasonry

3. http://www.bessel.org/reagan.htm. Stephen Knight listed Reagan as a Freemason (*The Brotherhood*, Stein and Day, 1984, p.34). Harold V. B. Voorhis, *The Story of the Scottish Rite of Freemasonry*, Macoy Publishing, Richmond, 1965, p.56, claims that Reagan progressed from the 32nd to 33rd degree during his presidency, but this may have been an honorary presentation.

4. Antony C. Sutton, *Two Faces of George Bush*, Veritas Publishing Company, 1988, p.17

5. Antony C. Sutton, *The Secret Cult of the Order*, Veritas Publishing Company, 1983, pp.34–7

6. *Point of View* radio broadcast, Larry Abraham interviewed by Marlin Maddox, Dallas, Texas, 11 February 1991, quoted in John Daniel, *Scarlet and the Beast*, vol. I, JKI Publishing, 1995, pp.705, 893

7. Bill Clinton, *My Life*, Alfred A. Knopf, 2004, pp.44–5

8. Daniel, *op. cit.*, vol. I, p.801

9. Rivera, *op. cit.*, p.15

10. http://www.geocities.com/endtimedeception/famous.htm?200619

11. *Ibid.*

12. Christopher Bollyn in *American Free Press*, 16 and 23 December 2002

13. http://freemasonry.dcy.ca/textfiles/famous.html

14. http://www.geocities.com/endtimedeception/famous. htm?200619

15. William T. Still, *New World Order: The Ancient Plan of Secret Societies*, Huntingdon House, Lafayette, LA, 1990, p.109

16. John Daniel, *Scarlet and the Beast*, vol. I, JKI Publishing, 1995, p.44

17. *Ibid.*, pp.33–4

18. Still, *op. cit.*, p.117, quoting Knight, *op. cit.*, pp.211–13

19. David Allen Rivera, *Final Warning: A History of the New World Order*, Rivera Enterprises, 1984, p.92

20. *See* Nicholas Hagger, *The Syndicate*, O Books, 2004, chapter 3, for accounts of all the new secret organizations mentioned in the previous paragraph

21. *See ibid.*, pp.20–21 and p.364, note 77, for full details

22. *Ibid.*, p.21 and p.364, note 78

23. Nicholas Hagger, *The Secret History of the West*, O Books, 2005, p.446; Daniel, *op. cit.*, p.506

24. *Ibid.*, p.513

25. *Ibid.*, p.514

26. Hagger (2004), p.22; Emanuel M. Josephson, *Rockefeller "Internationalist"*, Chedney Press, 1952, pp.204–31, particularly p.212; Emanuel M. Josephson, *The Truth About Rockefeller, Public Enemy No. 1*, Chedney Press, 1964, pp.44, 133

27. Hagger (2005), pp.50–63

28. Michael Baigent, Richard Leigh and Henry Lincoln, *The Messianic Legacy*, Corgi Books, 1987, p.187; John Daniel, *Scarlet and the Beast*, vol. I, JKI Publishing, 1995, pp.572–3

29. Hagger (2004), pp.67–8

30. John Cotter, *A Study in Syncretism*, Canadian Intelligence Publications, 1979, p.105

31. *See* Nicholas Hagger, *The Syndicate*, O Books, 2004, pp.76–7 and p.392, note 62, for 'Rockefellers'' monopolistic supply of kerosene for Chinese lamps until the 1930s via the ruling Soong family

32. Emanuel M. Josephson, *The "Federal" Reserve Conspiracy and Rockefeller*, Chedney Press, 1968, p.292; Gary Allen with Larry Abraham, *None Dare Call It Conspiracy*, Concord Press, 1972, p.107. *See* Hagger (2004), p.394, note 67, for full details.

33. Hagger (2004), p.77

34. *Ibid.*, pp.77–8

35. Daniel, *op. cit.*, pp.518–19

36. *See* Hagger (2004), pp.107–9 and p.403, note 45, for full details of the Gorbachev Foundation, and chapter 4 for the details in the next paragraph
37. *See* http://abcnews.go.com/sections/us/DailyNews/church_poll020301.html
38. Albert Pike, *Morals and Dogma*, 1871, p.321; David Allen Rivera, *Final Warning: A History of the New World Order*, Rivera Enterprises, 1984, pp.16–17
39. Quoted in William T. Still, *New World Order: The Ancient Plan of Secret Societies*, Huntingdon House, Lafayette, LA, 1990, p.124, who gives sources: Edith Starr Miller, *Occult Theocrasy*, 1933, Christian Book Club of America, 1980, pp.220–21, quoting A. C. De La Rive, 'Instructions' issued by Gen. Albert Pike on 14 July 1889 to the 23 Supreme Councils of the world as recorded in *La Femme et l'Enfant dans la Franc-Maconnerie Universelle*, p.588
40. *See* Hagger (2004), pp.267–74
41. *See* Nicholas Hagger, *The Light of Civilization*, O Books, 2006

Appendices

1. Superseded by the Fourteenth Amendment
2. Superseded by the Seventeenth Amendment
3. Modified by the Seventeenth Amendment
4. Superseded by the Twentieth Amendment
5. Modified by the Sixteenth Amendment
6. Superseded by the Twelfth Amendment
7. Modified by the Twenty-fifth Amendment
8. Modified by the Eleventh Amendment
9. Superseded by the Thirteenth Amendment
10. Superseded by the Twentieth Amendment
11. Superseded by the Twenty-first Amendment

BIBLIOGRAPHY

Allen, Gary, with Abraham, Larry, *None Dare Call It Conspiracy*, Concord Press, 1972

Baigent, Michael, Leigh, Richard, and Lincoln, Henry, *The Holy Blood and the Holy Grail*, Corgi Books, 1982

—, *The Messianic Legacy*, Corgi Books, 1987

Baigent, Michael, and Leigh, Richard, *The Temple and the Lodge*, Arcade, 1989

Ballance, David, *The Buds of Virtue: The Story of Chigwell School*, James and James, 2000

Barbour, Philip L., *The Complete Works of Captain John Smith*, (1580–1631), 3 vols, University of North Carolina Press, 1986

—, ed., *The Jamestown Voyages, Under the First Charter, 1606–1609*, 2 vols, Hakluyt Society, Cambridge University Press, 1969

Boller, Paul F., Jr, *Washington and Religion*, SMU Press, 1963

Bremer, Francis J., *John Winthrop: America's Forgotten Founding Father*, Oxford University Press, 2003

Bronner, Edwin, *William Penn's "Holy Experiment": The Founding of Pennsylvania, 1681–1701*, Temple University Publications, 1962

Brown, Alexander, *The Genesis of the United States*, Boston, 1890

Campbell, R. H., and Skinner, A. S., eds, *An Inquiry into the Nature and Causes of the Wealth of Nations* by Adam Smith, 2 vols, Liberty Fund, 1981

Cappon, Lester, ed., *The Adams–Jefferson Letters: The Complete Correspondence between Thomas Jefferson and Abigail and John Adams*, 2 vols, University of North Carolina Press, 1959

Capt, Raymond E., *Our Great Seal: The Symbols of our Heritage and our Destiny*, Artisan Sales, 1979

Carr, William Guy, *The Conspiracy to Destroy All Existing Governments and Religions*, published privately, Canada, 1959

Cash, W. J., *The Mind of the South*, Alfred Knopf, 1941; Thames and Hudson, 1971

Chaitkin, Anton, *Treason in America*, 2nd ed., New Benjamin Franklin House, 1984

Chandler, J. A. C., *Library of Southern Literature*, Neale Publishing Company, 1906

Church, J. R., *Guardians of the Grail*, Prophecy Publications, 1989

Clausen, Henry C., *Masons Who Helped Shape Our Nation*, Washington, 1976

Clinton, Bill, *My Life*, Alfred A. Knopf, 2004

Cockburn, N. B., *The Bacon Shakespeare Question: The Baconian Theory Made Sane*, Biddles, 1998

Cotter, John, *A Study in Syncretism*, Canadian Intelligence Publications, 1979

Daniel, John, *Scarlet and the Beast*, 3 vols, JKI Publishing, 1995

Dawkins, Peter, *The Shakespeare Enigma*, Polair, 2004

Denslow, William R., *10,000 Famous Freemasons*, 4 vols, Missouri Lodge of Research, 1957–1961

Dexter, Lincoln A., comp. and ed., *The Gosnold Discoveries... in the north part of Virginia, 1602... according to the Relations by Gabriel Archer and John Brereton*, RFD, Brookfield, MA, 1982

Dillon, George E., *Grand Orient Freemasonry Unmasked as the Secret Power Behind Communism*, Sons of Liberty, 1885

Doyle, John A., *History of the Plimouth Plantation Containing an Account of the Voyage of the 'Mayflower' written by William Bradford*, Ward and Downey; Houghton, Mifflin Co., 1896

Edwards, Jonathan, *A History of the Work of Redemption*, Philadelphia, 1773

Eigen, L., and Siegel, J., *The Macmillan Dictionary of Political Quotations*, Macmillan, 1993

El-Amin, Mustafa, *Freemasonry, Ancient Egypt and the Islamic Destiny*, New Mind Productions, 1988

Epperson, Ralph A., *The Unseen Hand*, Publius Press, 1985

Fisher, Paul A., *Behind the Lodge Door*, Shield, 1988

Flexner, James Thomas, *George Washington and the New Nation, 1783–1793*, Little, Brown, 1969

—, *George Washington: Anguish and Farewell, 1793–1799*, Little, Brown, 1972

Galvin, Robert W., *What the Scottish Enlightenment Taught Our Founding Fathers*, Rowman & Littlefield, 2002

Gaustad, Edwin S., *Sworn on the Altar of God: A Religious Biography of Thomas Jefferson*, Eerdmans, 1996

Gookin, Warner F., *Bartholomew Gosnold, Discoverer and Planter*, with footnotes and a concluding part by Philip L. Barbour, Archon Books, 1963

Gregg II, Gary L., *Vital Remnants: America's Founding and the Western Tradition*, ISI Books, 1999

Hagger, Nicholas, *The Syndicate*, O Books, 2004

—, *The Secret History of the West*, O Books, 2005

Haile, Edward Wright, ed., *Jamestown Narratives: Eyewitness Accounts of the Virginia Colony, 1607–1617*, RoundHouse, 1998

Hale, Edward Everett, *Discussions of the Drama: Prospero's Island*, Dramatic Museum of Columbia University, 1919

Hall, Manly P., *America's Assignment with Destiny*, The Philosophical Research Society, 1951

Hall, Marie Bauer, *Foundations Unearthed*, Veritas Press, 1940; 1974

Heaton, Ronald E., *Masonic Membership of the Founding Fathers*, MSA, 1974

Hieronimus, Robert, *America's Secret Destiny*, Destiny Books, 1989

History of the American Revolution, Highlights of the Important Battles and Documents of Freedom, Historical Documents Co., 1993

House, H. Wayne, *The Christian and American Law*, Kregel Publications, 1998

Howard, Michael, *The Occult Conspiracy: Secret Societies – Their Influence and Power in World History*, Destiny Books, 1989

Hume, Ivor Noël, *The Virginia Adventure, Roanoke to James Towne: An Archaeological and Historical Odyssey*, Alfred Knopf, 1998

Hunt, William, *The Puritan Moment: The Coming of Revolution in an English County*, Harvard University Press, 1983

Josephson, Emanuel M., *Rockefeller "Internationalist": The Man who Misrules the World*, Chedney Press, 1952

—, *The Truth About Rockefeller, Public Enemy No. 1*, Chedney Press, 1964

—, *The "Federal" Reserve Conspiracy and Rockefeller*, Chedney Press, 1968

Kirban, Salem, *Satan's Angels Exposed*, Grapevine Book Distributors, 1980

Knight, Stephen, *The Brotherhood: The Secret World of the Freemasons*, Stein and Day, 1984

Kurland, Philip B., and Lerner, Ralph, *The Founders' Constitution*, 4 vols, University of Chicago Press, 1987

Lambert, Frank, *The Founding Fathers and the Place of Religion in America*, Princeton University Press, 2003

MacCulloch, Diarmaid, *Suffolk and the Tudors: Politics and Religion in an English County, 1500–1600*, Oxford University Press, 1986

Mann, Charles C., *Ancient Americans: Rewriting the History of the New World*, Granta Books, 2005

Matthews, Nieves, *Francis Bacon: The History of a Character Assassination*, Yale University Press, 1996

McClure, N. E., *The Letters of John Chamberlain*, 2 vols, Philadelphia, 1939

McLoughlin, William G., *Soul Liberty: The Baptists' Struggle in New England, 1630–1833*, University Press of New England, 1991

Menzies, Gavin, *1421: The Year China Discovered the World*, Bantam Books, 2002, 2003

Miller, Edith Starr, *Occult Theocrasy*, 1933; Christian Book Club of America, 1980

Miller, Lee, *Roanoke: Solving the Mystery of England's Lost Colony*, Jonathan Cape, 2000

Morgan, Edmund S., *American Slavery, American Freedom: The Ordeal of Colonial Virginia*, W. W. Norton & Co. Ltd, 1975

Morris, Richard B., *The Framing of the Federal Constitution, Handbook 103*, Division of Publications, National Park Service, US Department of the Interior, 1986

Norman, Charles, *Discoverers of America*, Thomas Y. Crowell, 1968

Nugent, Nell Marion, *Cavaliers and Pioneers: Abstracts of Virginia Land Patents and Grants, 1623–1666*, Genealogical Publishing Co., 1983

Osterweis, Rollin G., *Romanticism and Nationalism in the Old South*, Louisiana State University Press, 1949, 1967

Peterson, Merrill D., ed., *Thomas Jefferson: A Reference Biography*, Scribner's, 1986

Pike, Albert, *Morals and Dogma of the Ancient and Accepted Scottish Rite of Freemasonry, Prepared for the Supreme Council of the Thirty-Third Degree for the Southern Jurisdiction of the United States and Published by its Authority*, Washington, DC, 1871; L. H. Jenkins Inc., 1964

Price, David A., *Love and Hate in Jamestown: John Smith, Pocahontas and the Heart of a New Nation*, Faber and Faber, 2003

Quinn, Arthur, *A New World: An Epic of Colonial America from the Founding of Jamestown to the Fall of Quebec*, Faber and Faber, 1994

Remsberg, John E., *Six Historic Americans*, The Truth Seeker Company, 1906

Rivera, David Allen, *Final Warning: A History of the New World Order*, Rivera Enterprises, 1984, 1994

Roberts, Allen E., *G. Washington: Master Mason*, Macoy Pub. and Masonic Supply Co., 1976

Robison, John, *Proofs of a Conspiracy*, Americanist Classic, 1798; 1967

Rowse, A. L., *Shakespeare's Southampton: Patron of Virginia*, Macmillan, 1965

Rutman, Darrett, *Winthrop's Boston: A Portrait of a Puritan Town, 1630–1649*, W. W. Norton, 1965

Schwartz, Barry, *George Washington: The Making of an American Symbol*, The Free Press, 1987

Secret Ritual of the Thirty-third and Last Degree, Sovereign Grand Inspector General of the Ancient and Accepted Scottish Rite of Freemasonry, Kessinger Publishing, n.d.

Smith, Bradford, *Captain John Smith: His Life and Legend*, Lippincott, 1953

Smith, John, *The Generall Historie of Virginia, New-England and the Summer Isles*, 1624, facsimile reissued by The World Publishing Company

—, *Works: Capt. John Smith, Works*, ed. Edward Arber, The English Scholar's Library, 1884

Srodes, James, *Franklin: The Essential Founding Father*, Regnery Publishing, 2002

Stauffer, V., *New England and the Bavarian Illuminati*, Columbia University Press, 1918

Steiner, Franklin, *The Religious Beliefs of our Presidents*, Prometheus Books, 1995

Still, William T., *New World Order: The Ancient Plan of Secret Societies*, Huntingdon House, 1990

Stopes, Charlotte, *The Third Earl of Southampton*, Cambridge University Press, 1922

Strachey, William, *The Historie of Travell into Virginia Britania*, ed. Louis B. Wright and Virginia Freund, Hakluyt Society, 1953

Sutton, Antony C., *The Secret Cult of the Order*, Veritas Publishing Company, 1983

—, *Two Faces of George Bush*, Veritas Publishing Company, 1988

Tudhope, George V., *Freemasonry Came to America with Captain John Smith in 1607*, pamphlet, n.d.

Van Doren, Carl, *Benjamin Franklin*, Viking Press, 1938; reprinted Penguin Books, 1991

Voorhis, Harold V. B., *The Story of the Scottish Rite of Freemasonry*, Macoy Publishing, 1965

Wallace-Murphy, Tim, and Hopkins, Marilyn, *Templars in America from the Crusades to the New World*, Weiser Books, 2004

Walters, K., *Rational Infidels: The American Deists*, Longwood, 1992

—, *The American Deist: Voices of Reason and Dissent in the Early Republic*, University of Kansas, 1992

Webster, Nesta H., *World Revolution*, Constable, 1921

—, *Secret Societies and Subversive Movements*, Christian Book Club of America, 1925

Wilgus, Neal, *The Illuminoids*, Pocket Books, 1979

Wingfield, Jocelyn, *Virginia's True Founder: Edward-Maria Wingfield and His Times, 1550–c.1614*, The Wingfield Family Society, 1993

Worthy, R. L., *The Founders' Façade: Christianity, Democracy, Freemasonry, and the Founding of America*, KornerStone Books, 2004

Yates, Frances A., *The Rosicrucian Enlightenment*, Routledge and Kegan Paul, 1972, reprinted 1998

INDEX

A

'AA' seal 90-1
'Accepted' Masons 87
Act of Succession 102
Act of Supremacy 3
Act of Uniformity 55
Adams, John 104, 140,
    147, 149, 150
    Deism 117, 118, 124,
    125, 126
    Freemasonry 106,
    163
    and Great Seal 99,
    136
    and Illuminati 141
Adams, Samuel 104,
    105, 124, 148, 163
Adams, Sherman 188
Adonay (Jehovah) 185,
    200
Africa 27, 61, 74, 198
al-Qaeda 199
Alabama 66, 178, 179
Alaska 184
Albany Congress 98,
    152
Albany Plan of Union
    98, 152, 231-4
Albert, Captain 72
alchemy 110
Alexander II of Russia
    180, 182
Alhumbrados 134, 135
Alimamu 69-70
Allison, Francis 112

All-Seeing Eye 92, 137
American central bank
    Lincoln defeats 1801
    Rothschilds' plan
    173-4
American Civil War
    xii, 131, 142, 170, 171,
    172, 180-1, 186, 201
    Southern
    Jurisdiction starts
    176-9
American Constitution
    xii, 37, 94, 106, 152-8,
    168, 253-66
    Deist and Masonic
    influences 126-7
    Puritan influences 9,
    21
    see also Bill of Rights
American Declaration
    of Independence 94,
    99, 106, 112, 113,
    124-5, 136, 142, 150-
    1, 158, 163, 168, 235-
    41
American Revolution/
    War of
    Independence 105-6,
    140, 147-52, 159, 160,
    163
Ameryk, Rickard 28
Ames, William 16
Amnesty Proclamation
    184
Amos 4

Amsterdam 3, 4
Añasco, Juan de 70
Anderson, James
    Constitutions 96, 99,
    113, 153-4, 159, 163,
    166, 225-30
Anderson, Robert B.
    188
Andreae, Johann
    Valentin 88-9, 91, 96
Anglican Church see
    Church of England
Anglicanism 106, 127,
    170, 200, 201
    severity 116-17
Anglicans 62, 80, 99,
    123
    Great Awakening
    114
    in Jamestown 33-8,
    62
    in Virginia 52-62, 147
Anglo-Iroquois
    alliance 98, 152
Ankarström, Jacob
    Johan 140
Anne, Queen 26, 59,
    102
Anne of Denmark 43
Annie 12
Anti-Federalists 158-9
Apalache 67
Appomattoc Indians
    57
Appomattoc river 57

apron, Masonic 93
Aquinas, Thomas 107
Arbella 16, 17
Archer, Gabriel 31, 32, 36, 37, 45, 50, 51, 52, 53
Argall, Samuel 49, 55, 56, 57-8, 59-60
Arguin 27
Aristotle 107
Arkansas 66, 176, 179
Arkansas river 70
Armadas 29
Arminianism 5
Arminius, Jacobus 5
Arthur, King 29
Articles of Confederation 98, 152, 154, 156, 178, 242-52
Astor, John Jacob 177
Atchison, David Rice 188
Atlanta 181
Atlantis 87, 137, 167
Aubrey, John 22
Augustine, St 169
Australia 79
Australian Aborigines 80
Austria 128-30, 138, 173
Autiamque 70
Avilés, Pedro Menéndez de 74-8
Azores 30, 56

B

Bacon, Anthony 85
Bacon, Francis 31, 35-6, 109, 115, 131, 133, 166
and English

Freemasonry 85-9, 97
and John Smith 90-3
The Marriage of the Thames and the Rhine 8
New Atlantis 32, 91, 94, 95, 98, 100, 113
Novum Organum 107-8
Baffin Island 29
Baigent, Michael *The Temple and the Lodge* 99
Baku oilfields 193
Bakunin, Mikhail 175
Bank of America 173
Bannockburn, battle of 100
Baphomet 110
Baptists 116, 118
Barlowe, Arthur 29
Barre, Captain 72
Barrow, Henry 3
Barton, William 139
Bavaria 132
Bayle, Pierre 111
Beaumont, Francis 88
Beauregard, General 179
Becker, Carl 125
Belcher, Jonathon 97
Belgium 139
Belmont, August (August Schoenberg) 174
Benjamin, Judah P. 174, 183
Bentham, Jeremy 125
Bering Strait 80
Bermuda 50, 55, 56
Bermuda City 57
Bible *see* King James Bible; Masonic Bible

Bickley, George W. L. 176
Bilderberg Group 191, 196
Bill of Rights 158, 169, 267-77
Bimini 64
Blackerby, Katherine xiv
Blake, William 125-6
Blessing 50
Blount, Charles 110
Blount, Henry (Nathaniel Bacon) 95
Boece, Hector 113
Booth, John Wilkes 182-3, 184
Boston, Lincolnshire 15
Boston, Massachusetts 17, 19, 21, 116, 147, 148, 151, 173, 177
massacre 103, 150
St Andrew's Lodge 103, 104, 105
St John's Lodge 97, 103
Boston Tea Party 103-4, 106, 127, 142, 148
Bourbons 129, 130, 133, 136
Bownde, Nicholas 16
Bradford, Arthur B. 120
Bradford, Dorothy 11
Bradford, William 3, 4, 5, 6-7, 8, 11, 12, 13, 21
Bradley, Omar 190
Brazil 28, 29
Breckinridge, John C. 178, 179
Brereton, John 31, 32
Brewster, William 4

Bristol sailors 28, 80
Britain/UK 80
  and American Civil
    War 173, 174, 180,
    181
  American grievances
    103, 147-8
  American
    independence
    149-52
  American
    possessions 146,
    147-8
  American resistance
    84, 103-5, 148-9
  American War
    (1812-14) 172, 173
  French and Indian
    War 146
  funds Mazzini's
    insurrection 183
  Hessian troops
    130-1, 151
  Masonic State 150-1
  naval battles 152
  plans to remove
    Penn 25-6
  and Scottish Rite
    Freemasonry in
    America 172, 175-6
  Writs of Assistance
    147
British Board of Trade
  98, 152
British Freemasonry
  180, 182, 191
Brooke, Lord 19
Brown, John 177
Bruno, Giordano 93-4
Brussels 129
Bruton 96
Buchanan, George 112
Buchanan, James 175,
  177, 178, 179

Buck, Richard 59
Buddhism 109
Burghley, Lord 101
Burgoyne, General 151
Burlamaqui, Jean-
  Jacques 124
Bush Jr, George 188-9,
  190, 197, 198-9, 201
Bush Sr, George 188-9,
  190
Byzantium
  (Constantinople) 107

C
'C' 91
Cabot, John 28, 29, 63
Cabral, Pedro Álvares
  28
Cale 67
California 78
Callicut, William 48
Calvin, John 2
Calvinism 3, 112, 114,
  115
Cambridge Agreement
  15
Canada 31, 71, 151,
  159, 180
  British control 146,
    147, 152, 174
  French exploration
    80
  St Clair exploration
    80
Canassatego 98
Cape Ann 14-15
Cape Breton Island 29
Cape Cod xiii, 8-10, 12,
  31, 52, 55
Cape of Good Hope 4,
  27
Capitol Hill 164-5
Carbonari 184

Caribbean 28, 56, 58
Carr, Peter 117
Carter, Bezaleel 16
Carter, Jimmy 188, 190
Cartier, Jacques 80
Cartwright, Thomas
  15
Carver, John 5, 9, 12
Casqui 70
Castillo de San Marcos
  78
Cathars 86, 132, 136,
  185, 200
Catholicism 64, 70, 78,
  106, 127
  English opposition
    93-4, 96
  Masonic leaders
    demonized 113
  Masonic rejection
    106
Catholics 41, 50, 55,
  81, 99, 110, 123, 170
  excluded from
    English succession
    102
  in Florida and the
    South 63-71
  Mary I 86
  Queen Anne's
    detestation 26
Cecil, Robert, Earl of
  Salisbury 35, 41, 51,
  101, 103
Cecilites 35, 36, 42
Cendoya, Manuel de 78
Central America 176
Cerneau Supreme
  Council 173
Chamberlain, John 88
Charles, Prince of
  Wales 191
Charles I of England
  15, 101, 102, 93

Charles II of England
21, 23, 102
Charles V of Spain 66
Charles IX of France
72
Charles de Lorraine,
128-30, 131, 133
Charles Fort 72
Charles river 14, 15, 17
Charleston 173, 176,
177, 178
Mother Council of
the World lodge
172
Charlestown 17
Chase, Salmon P. 181
Chase Manhattan
Bank 181
Chesapeake Bay 29,
46, 61
Chiaha 68
Chicaça 69
Chickahominy Indians
42-4, 48, 55-6, 59
Chickahominy river 42
Chickasaw Indians 69
Chigwell Grammar
School 22-3
China 28
American
exploration 78-9
Soviet-Chinese trade
195-6
chivalric cult 171-2
Christ see Jesus Christ
Christianity
'city on a hill' 16-17,
167, 197
Deist attitude 111,
117-18, 126-7
Enlightenment
disenchantment
107, 113
Freemasonry and

109, 110, 154,
198-203
Fundamental Orders
of Connecticut
20-1
and the Great
Awakening 114
inflicted on native
Americans 67, 68,
70, 71, 78, 114
pro-English Anglican
severity 116-17
questioned by
Founding fathers
126-7
Rosicrucian
sympathy 110
slave-holder 61
Virginia Company's
propagation aims
35, 57, 61-2
Christianization of the
Indies 63
Christians 17, 24, 31,
69
Illuminati deception
134, 135, 141
right-wing 14
Chubb, Thomas 110
Church, J. R. 141
Church
as basis of civil
commonwealth
15-16
Deist attack 110
Franklin's
antagonism 116
as instrument of
State 54
and round-Earth
heresy 28, 92, 94
separation from
State 127, 151, 168,
169, 187

unity with State 14,
15, 20-1, 26, 127,
167, 187
Church of England
(Anglican Church)
xvi, 33, 36, 37, 55,
80, 109, 110, 119,
168, 190-1
Separatists 2-3, 15
Church of Rome 2
Churchill, Winston
192
Cincinnati Lodge
no. 133 174
Clark, Mark 190
Clausen, Henry C. 155
Cleverly, Joseph 118
Clinton, Bill 189, 191-2
Clinton, James 151
Club of Rome 191
Cobb, Howell 178, 179
Coça 68
Colchester 16
Cold War 195-8
Coligoa 70
Collins, Anthony 110
Cologne 85
Columbia 65
Columbus,
Christopher 28, 36,
63, 79, 80
Committee of
Corespondents 104
Communism 132-3,
193, 194, 197
compass, Masonic 92,
93, 164
Concord 105, 149
Concord 31, 32
Confederacy 171, 174,
175, 176, 177-8, 179,
180, 181
Confederation of New
England 21

Congress
  bicamerality 156
  creates federal bank
    181
  federal capital ceded
    to 164
  and the Great Seal
    138
  specific powers 157
Connecticut 18-21, 26,
  114, 167
Connecticut
  Compromise 156
Constitution see
  American
  Constitution
Constitutional
  Convention 153-8,
  160, 163
Constitutions and
  Canons 3
Continental Congress
  112, 136, 152-3
Conventicle Act 23
Cook, James 79
Cooke, Jay 174, 183
Cope, John 102
Copernicus 94, 108
Cornwallis, General
  151, 152
Cornwell, Patricia xv
Cotton, Edward 22-3
Cotton, John 15, 16,
  18, 114
Council for New
  England 5, 8, 18-19,
  60
Council of Elders 195,
  196
Council of Virginia see
  Virginia Council
Council on Foreign
  Relations (CFR) 191,
  195

Cox, Daniel 113
Crashaw, William 54
Creek Indians 67
Cromwell, Oliver 96,
  158
Cuba 28, 63, 64, 65, 66,
  71, 72
Culloden, battle of 102
Cumberland, Duke of
  102
Currency Act 148
Cushing, Caleb 175,
  176, 177, 178
Cushman, Robert 4

D

Daggett, David 118
d'Ailly, Pierre 28
Dale, Thomas 56-7, 58,
  59
Dale's Code 56, 171
d'Alembert, Jean le
  Rond 111
Dante 135
Dashwood, Francis
  105
Davis, Jefferson 179,
  183
Dayton, Elias 151
de Champlain, Samuel
  80-1
De La Warr, Lord 48,
  49, 51, 53, 54-5, 56,
  57
de Lancey family 148
de Laudonnière, René
  72-4, 75
de Rasières, Isaak 13
de Soto, Hernando
  65-71
de Vaca, Cabeza 65-6
Decker, Edward 164
Dee, John 29, 89, 103

Deism 107-11, 167,
  169-70, 182, 199, 202
  and the Constitution
    126-7
  Founding Fathers
    115-26, 142, 187,
    202, 203
  and the Great
    Awakening 113-15
  Scotland 112-13
Deist Freemasonry xii,
  109-10, 133, 154, 198,
  201
Delaware Indians 24-5
Delaware river 23, 24
Deliverance 50, 53, 54
Democratic National
  Convention 178
Democrats 175, 192
d'Erlanger, Frederick
  174
Dermer, Captain 11
Descartes 107-8
Diamond 50
Diana, Princess 191
Discoverer 32
Discovery 36, 41, 54, 55
Disraeli, Benjamin 174
Dixon, John 151
DNA testing xvi, xvii
Dole, Bon 190
dollar bill 139, 163,
  165, 189
Dorchester (Matapan)
  12
Dorchester Company
  14
Dover, New
  Hampshire 12
Drake, Francis 29, 78,
  92, 100
Drayton, Michael 36
Druids 110
Drummond, William 92

Du Simitière, Pierre
Eugene 136
Dudley, Thomas 18
Dutch Amish 201
Dutch Brazil 4
Dutch Reformed
Church 114, 118, 169
Dutch settlers
Connecticut trading
posts 18
New Netherland
12-13
repelled from
Connecticut river
19
Dutch West India
Company 13
Dyer, Mary 19, 24, 117

E
E Pluribus Unum 137
East India Company
33, 34, 104, 148
East Indies 28, 33
East Jersey 22
Eaton, Cyrus 196
Edward II of England
100
Edward the Confessor
136
Edwards, Jonathan 114
Edwin, David 123
Egypt 85
Eisenhower, Dwight
D. 188, 190
El Mina 27
Eleusinian mysteries
130
Elizabeth I of England
2, 29, 35, 37, 54, 101
Elizabeth II of
England 191
'Elizabeth Island' 31-2

Elizabethan era xiv, 37,
87, 103
values 61, 170, 171,
185, 201
Elizabethan
Settlement 168
Elizabethan State 99-
100
Emancipation
Proclamation 180
Emery, Thomas 42, 45
Endicott, John 14-15,
17
*Endless Rise and Fall of
Civilization, The*
(Hagger) xiii
England 10, 12, 25, 28,
30, 41, 48, 51, 55, 56,
72, 85, 90, 98, 136,
149, 159, 183
agrarian system 37
American claims and
possessions xii, 63,
78, 80
American
exploration xi, 29-
30, 74
Anglo-Iroquois
alliance 98, 152
anti-Spanish
paranoia 86-7
Bacon supports
colonization 89
Catholicism threat
93-4
class system 34, 84
Crown grants,
patents and
charters 12, 15, 17-
18, 18-19, 20, 23,
33, 39
Deism 108-9, 110,
111
Elizabethan

Settlement 168
Inquisition 86
Israel analogy 95,
101
Methodism 114
Pilgrim's journey 6-8
Pocahontas' visit 43,
59
Reformation 2-3
religious persecution
14, 15, 18, 22, 23,
30
Romanticism 172
union with Scotland
112
Writs of Assistance
confirmed 147
English (Rosicrucian)
Freemasonry 85-9,
103, 110, 129, 153-4,
172, 189, 191, 200
in America 95-100,
106, 142, 185, 200
Bacon and 85-9
John Smith and 90-4,
99, 200
and Templarism 101
English settlers
Cape Cod landing 8-
10
Jamestown 33-8
Massachusetts 14-22
New Plymouth 11-
14
Pennsylvania 22-6
Roanoke 29-30
Virginia 30-2, 39-52,
52-62
Enlightenment 125,
126, 142, 187
Freemasonry and
Deism 107-11
Epicurus 111
Epistle to the Hebrews 6

Erasmus 107
Essenes 110, 130
Essex, Earl of 30, 31, 38, 85
Essex rebellion 31, 33
Essexites 35, 94
Exeter, New Hampshire 12

F

Falcon 50, 72
Farrar Island 57
Fawkes, Guy *see* Guy Fawkes plot
Federal Reserve System 181
federalism 99, 153-5
Federalists 158-9, 169
Fenwick, George 19
Ferdinand, Archduke 192
Ferdinand II of Bohemia 96
Ferdinand of Spain 28, 63
Ferguson, Adam 112
Fiennes, William, Viscount Saye and Sele 19
Fire and the Stones, The (Hagger) xiii
First Amendment 169
First Continental Congress 105, 148
First Iraq War 189
First Virginia Company *see* Virginia Company of London
First World War 192, 199
Florida 29, 31, 44, 179, 200

British control 78, 146, 147
French settlement attempts 29, 71-8
Spanish control 78, 146
Spanish exploration 44, 63-4, 64-6
Spanish settlement 74-8, 200
Floyd, John B. 178, 179
Ford, Gerald 188
Ford's Theatre 182
Forey, Elie-Frederic 180
Fort Algernon 52-3, 55
Fort Caroline 73-6
Fort Orange (Albany) 13
Fort San Felipe (Fort St Philip) 78
Fort San Mateo (Fort St Matthew) 78
Fort Sumter 179
Fortune 12
Founding Fathers 2, 21, 202
attitude to religion 167-8
Deist 107, 115-26, 142, 202
Enlightenment influences 114-15
Freemasonry 81, 97, 103, 106, 159-63, 166-7, 169, 170, 187
and Illuminati 128, 141-2
Masonic design of Washington 164
motives 159-60
Scottish Enlightenment

influences 112
Fountain of Youth 64
Fountain of Youth Archaeological Park 64
Fox, George 22, 23
Fra Rosi Crosse Society 87, 91
France 23, 72, 73, 98, 105, 128, 136, 139, 167, 173
and American Civil War 174, 180, 181
American expeditions xi, 29, 80-1
American revolutionary links 140
and American War of Independence 151, 152
Anglo-Iroquois alliance against 98, 152
Bacon's visits 85-6, 87, 88
Deism 111
designs on Austria 129-30
Grand Orient 109
Jewish Golden Age 86
Knights Templar persecuted 100, 110
Queen Anne's War 25-6
Stuart sympathies 102
Templarism 102, 103
see also French revolution; French settlers

Francis I of France 80
François de Lorraine
128, 129
Frankfurt 132, 140,
173, 174
Franklin, Benjamin
97-9, 155
Albany Plan of
Union 98, 152
and American
independence 148,
149, 150
Deism 111, 115-16,
126
Freemasonry 98,
105, 138, 166-7
and Great Seal 99,
138-9
and the Illuminati
136-7, 138, 140,
141, 142
lightning studies 98,
125
Frederick II (the Great)
129-30, 131
Frederick V, Elector
Palatinate 88, 89, 96,
101
Fredericksburg Lodge
106
Free Trade Area of the
Americas (FRAA)
198
Freemason 97
Freemasonry
advantages in joining
141
and American
Constitution 126-
7, 153-5, 158
and American law
on religion 167-70
and Christianity 109,
110, 154, 198-203

coup on the colonies
158-64
Deist xii, 109-10,
133, 154, 198, 201
drive for American
independence
147-52
factions amongst
settlers 37, 38, 40,
41, 42, 45, 47, 61
and federalism 153-5
flourishing in the
South 172
history 282-3
hold over America
84-106
in international
relations 192-8
reunited 185
sub-Masonic secret
societies 191-2
symbolism in
Washington, DC
164-7
see also English
(Rosicrucian)
Freemasonry;
Masonic States;
Templar
Freemasonry /
Templarism
Freemasons
American Presidents
188-90
central bank plan
defeated 180-1
control America
184-6
Enlightenment 108
Founding Fathers 81,
97, 103, 106, 159-
63, 166-7, 169, 170,
187
kill Lincoln 182-4

Rothschilds 130
start American Civil
War 176-9
UK royal family
190-1
US judiciary 190
US military 190
in Virginia and
Massachusetts 34,
95-100, 102-6
French, Benjamin B.
184
French and Indian War
103, 146
French settlers 63
failure in Brazil 29
failure in Florida 29,
71-8
repulsed by Dutch
12
French revolution 109,
115, 126, 128, 130,
132, 140, 167
Frobisher, Martin 29
Frye, Joseph 151
Fundamental Orders
(1639) 20-1, 220-4

G

Gage, General 104
Galileo 94, 108
Galloway, Joseph 148
Gama, Vasco da xii, 27
Garfield, James 188
Garibaldi 175
Gassendi, Pierre 111
Gates, Horatio 151
Gates, Thomas 49, 50,
53-4, 54-5, 56, 57, 58
gauge, Masonic 92, 93
Genesis 77
George III of England
103, 148, 150

George VI of England
190-1
George Washington
Masonic National
Memorial 165-6
George Washington
Museum 166
Georgia 66, 117, 146,
178, 179
German Illuminati
128, 131-6, 189
Germany 107, 136,
138, 173, 189, 191
Deism 111
Freemasonry 88, 90,
103
Nazi 194
Rosicrucianism 88-9
Gift, William 178
Gift of God 39
Gilbert, Humphrey 29,
30, 32, 89
Gilbert, John 39
Gilbert, Raleigh 39
Gilbert-Hayes patent
32
Gilmore, Governor xv
Gilmore, Roxane xv
Gingrich, Newt 190
Glass House 47, 49
Glorious Revolution
111, 158
Gnostic Dualism 185,
200
Godspeed 36, 38
Goethe 108, 109
Goldwater, Barry 190
Gondomar, Count 92
Gorbachev, Mikhail
189, 197, 198
Gorges, Ferdinando 52
Gosnold,
Bartholomew xiii-
xiv, xviii, 38, 39, 94,

95, 101, 200-1
1602 voyage xiii, 30-
2, 89
founding of
Jamestown xiii, 33-
8, 89, 171
skeleton found xvi-
xvii
Gosnold III, Robert
xvii, 31, 32, 38
Gosnold IV, John 101
Gosnold V, Robert xvii
Gosnold, Anthony 49
Gourgas, John James
Joseph 172-3, 176
Graff, Jacob 150
Grail legend 86
Grajales, Francisco
Lopez Mendoza 78
Grand Lodge of
England 113, 153
Grand Lodge of the
Illuminati 132
Grand Lodge of York
103
Grand Lodge system
99, 153
Grand-Orient
Freemasonry 183,
192, 193, 197
Illuminati
infiltration 138,
140, 143, 187
Grand Orient of
France 109
Great Architect 111
Great Awakening 113-
15
Great Fire 34
Great Seal 99, 136-9,
143, 163, 165
Greek philosophy 107
Green, Ashbel 120
greenbacks 180, 181

Greenwood, John 3
Grenville, Richard 29
Guanahami 28
Gulf of Mexico 176
Gulf of St Lawrence
29, 80
Gustavus III of
Sweden 140
Guy Fawkes plot 33, 50

H

Hakluyt, Richard 30,
31, 32, 44, 74
Hale, Everett 32
Hall, Manly P. 85
Hamilton, Alexander
112, 126, 149, 155,
157, 163
Hamor, Ralph 58, 59
Hampton Court
Conference 3
Hampton, New
Hampshire 12
Hancock, John 103,
105, 124, 150
Harding, Warren G.
188, 190
Harrison, James 24
Harsnett, Archbishop
22
Hartford, Connecticut
20
Hartlib, Samuel 96, 97,
133
Havana 66, 176
Hawkins, John 29, 74
Hayes, Edward 32
Treatise 30, 31
Heaton, Ronald E. 160
Hebrews 3, 4
Heidelberg 132
Heidelberg castle 88,
89, 95

Henri IV of France 85
Henrico, Virginia 57
Henry VIII 2
Henry, Patrick 103,
    105, 147, 148, 158,
    159, 160, 163
Henry, Prince of
    Wales 57
Herbert, Edward 115
    De Veritae 108-9
Herbert, George 109
Hermetica 110
Hermeticism 88
Herter, Christian 188
Herzen, Alexander 175
Hesiod *Work and Days*
    160
Hiram Abiff 100
Hispanics 200
Hitler 194
Ho Chi Minh 196, 197
Hobart, Henry 89
Hobbes, Thomas 110
Holy Blood and the Holy
    Grail, The 86
Holy Land 100
Holy Roman Empire
    129
Hooke, Thomas 18, 19
Hopewell Indians 80
Hopkinson, Francis
    138
Hosea 4
Hoskins, Stephen 11
House, Thomas 181
House of
    Representatives 156
Houston, Sam 179
Howe, Richard 151-2
Howe, William 151-2
Hudson, Henry 5
Hudson river 5, 8
Hume, David 111, 112,
    113, 154

Hungary 34, 90, 139
Hunt, Captain 11
Hunt, Robert 37, 40,
    45
Hutcheson, Francis
    112, 113
Hutchinson, Anne 19

I

Iapazaws 57
Ignatius of Loyola 154
Illinois 176
Illuminati 128, 131-6,
    136-42, 173, 186, 187,
    189
    Mazzini's 174, 175,
    176-7, 184
Independence Day 150
India 27, 28, 38
Indiana 176
Industrial Revolution
    37, 113, 186
Ingolstadt 132
Inner Light 22
Intolerable Acts 148
Invisible College 96,
    133, 137
Ipswich 32
Ireland 23, 136
Irish Templar Jacobites
    102-3
Iroquois League 98,
    152
Isabella 72, 73
Isabella of Spain 28, 63
Isaiah 28
Islam 109, 199
Israel 85, 199, 201
Italy 107, 139, 173, 183

J

Jackson, Andrew 78,
    188
Jackson, Jesse 190
Jacobites 102
Jacques de Molay 86,
    100, 101, 103
James, Jesse 184
James I of England (VI
    of Scotland) 3, 33,
    35, 36, 38, 39, 43, 54,
    57, 59, 61-2, 88, 92,
    93, 112
    brings Templarism
        to England 34, 47,
        62, 101, 142
James II 21-2, 23, 25,
    102, 113
James river 36, 42, 49,
    50, 57
Jamestown xiii, xiv-xv,
    36-8, 89, 93, 94, 95,
    101, 171, 200-1
    decline 52-60
    founding 36-8
    survival 39-52
Jamestown Fort xiv-xv
Jefferson, Thomas 96,
    115, 136, 149, 156
    authors Declaration
        of Independence
        99, 124-5, 150
    Deism 111, 117-18,
        125, 126, 169-70
    Founder-Farmer 160
    Freemasonry 163,
        166, 188
    and Great Seal 99, 136
    and Illuminati 140,
        141-2
    Monticello
        architecture 166
    Rosicrucianism 99
    Scottish

Enlightenment
influence 112, 113
on Washington's
Christianity 120,
121
Jehovah (Adonay) 185,
200
Jermyn, Robert 16
Jerusalem 86, 128-9
Jesuits 78, 128, 131, 154
Jesus Christ 15, 70, 67,
114, 154
Deist view 109, 115-
16, 117
Illuminist attitude
131, 134
Masonic rejection
110, 154
Washington's
reticence 121
Jewish Golden Age 86
Jewish Kabbalists 86
Jews 85, 135
John and Francis 45, 47,
48
Johnson, Andrew 183,
184-5, 188
Johnson, Lyndon B.
188, 197
Johnson, William
Samuel 157
Jones, Christopher 6, 7
Jonson, Ben 92
Judaism 109
Judd, Anthony 29, 33

K

Kabbalah 86, 88, 110,
130
Kagan, Robert 189
Kansas 71
Kansas-Nebraska Act
177

Kant, Immanuel 111
'kay' cipher 91
Kecoughtan Indians 55
Keith, William 97
Kelso, William xiv-xv,
xvi-xvii, 201
Kendall, George (John
Sicklemore) 40-1,
41-2
Kennedy, John F. 188
Kentucky 178, 179
Kerensky, Alexander
193
Khedive Said Pasha
174
King, Rufus 157, 158
King James Bible 77,
90, 91, 100
King of Jerusalem 128,
129, 139
Knights of the Golden
Circle 176, 178, 179,
182, 183, 184
Knights of the Helmet
91
Knights Templar (Poor
Knights of Christ
and the Temple of
Solomon) 86, 87,
100, 110, 128-9, 189
Knights Templar
degree 103
Knox, Henry 163
Knox, John 112
Kolmer (Jutland
merchant) 130
Kossuth, Louis 174-5
Kristol, William 189
Krushchev, Nikita
195-6
Ku Klux Klan 183

L

Labrador 64
Lachère (cannibalism
victim) 72
Lafayette, Marquis de
151
Lambert, Frank 170-1
Lang, Jacob 139
Languedoc 86
Laud, William 15
Lee, Richard Henry
103, 152, 158, 160,
163
Lee, Robert 181
Leibniz 111
Leiden (Leyden) 4-5
Leigh, Richard The
Temple and the Lodge
99
Lemmi, Adriano 174
l'Enfant, Pierre
Charles 164
Lenin 193
Lesser Key of Solomon
130
Lessing, Gotthold 111
Lewis, Morgan 163
Lewkenor, Edward 16
liberalism 85
Liberty Bell 150
Light 90, 135, 200
light-dark scroll seal
90, 91, 92, 93
Light of Civilization,
The (Hagger) xiii
Lincoln, Abraham 178,
179, 186, 188, 201
defeats American
central bank 180-1
killed by Freemasons
182-4
Linn, William 118,
169-70
Lion 50

Little Breton 72
Little James 12
Liu Gang 79
Livingston, Robert 163
Livingstone, Robert 149
Locke, John 108, 111, 115, 125, 147, 150, 154, 166
lodge system 88, 113
Loe, Thomas 23
London 3, 33, 54, 98, 112, 148, 173, 174
  Templar Freemasonry imported 34, 47, 100, 101, 142
London Adventurers 5, 60
Long Island Sound 19
Long Room Club 104
Lorraine, House of 129, 133, 136
'lost word', Masonic 90
Louis XIV of France 102, 111
Louis XVI of France 129, 138, 140
Louisiana 67, 174, 179, 180
Lucifer 185-6, 200
Lucius Quinctius Cincinnatus 160
Lucretius 111
Ludlow, Roger 20
Luther, Martin 2, 107
Lutherans 74-5

M

MacArthur, Douglas 190, 196
Mackey, Albert Gallatin 176

MacPherson, C. B. 125
Madeira 27, 28
Madison, James 125, 173
  and Bill of Rights 169
  and the Constitution 155-6, 157, 158, 168
  Deism 126, 127
  Freemasonry 163, 188
  Scottish Enlightenment influence 112, 113
Magellan, Ferdinand 28-9, 79
Magnel, Francis 41
Maine 22, 146
Mair (Major), John 113
Maison Carrée 166
Major Key of Solomon 130
Majority World 198, 202
Maldonado, Francisco 69
Manhattan 5, 13, 195
Manichaeism 130, 185
Mao 195
Maquaes Indians (Mohawks) 13
Marco Polo 28
Maria Theresa von Hapsburg, 128, 129
Marie-Antoinette 128, 129
Marshall, George C. 190, 194
Martha's Vineyard xiii, 22, 31
Martin, Edward xvi, xvii
Martin, John 40, 50, 51, 52

Martinism 194
Marx, Karl 175
Mary and John 39, 49
Mary I of England 86
Maryland 25, 98, 112, 148, 164, 176, 183
Mason, John 20
Masonic Bible 163, 187, 189-90, 199
Masonic Congress (1663) 110
Masonic House of the Temple 165
Masonic States
  Soviet Union 193-4, 195, 196-7
  UK 150-1
  United States xii, 163, 166-7, 170, 187-90, 192, 195, 196-7, 201-2
Massachusetts 2, 14-22, 26, 97, 147, 151, 176
  Freemasons 97, 103-5
  Puritan settlers 2, 14-22, 26
  Separatist settlers 11-14
Massachusetts Bay Company 15, 17-18
Massachusetts General Court 18, 19
Massachusetts Provincial Congress 105, 149
Massasoit 11-12
Master Masons 88, 163, 177, 184
Matanzas 76
materialism 111
Mather, Cotton 17
Matthew, gospel 16
maul, Masonic 93

Maury, James 147
Mavila 68-9
Maximilian of Austria 180
Maxwell, William 151
May, Cornelius 12
'May-day' 135
Mayflower xii, 2, 5, 6, 7, 8, 10, 11, 12, 27, 33, 34, 60, 62, 96
Mayflower Compact 9
Maykan Indians (Mohicans) 13
Mazzini, Giuseppe 174, 175, 177, 182, 183
  Illuminati 174, 175, 176-7, 184
McKay, Douglas 188
McKinley, William 188
medieval stonemasons 85
Menzies, Gavin 79
Meras, Solis de 77
Mercer, Hugh 151
Merovingians 128, 130, 135, 139
Merrimack river 12, 14, 15
Methodism 114, 126
Mexico 64, 65, 71, 176, 180
Mexico City 180
Mi'kmaq Indians 80
Middle East 199, 201
Milford Haven 32
Millenary Petition 3
Miller, Eugene 112
Milner, Lord 193
Minerva 131
Mississippi 66, 176, 179
Mississippi Indians 80
Mississippi river 65, 70, 71, 146, 152, 173

Mithraism 110, 131
Mithras 131
Mohegan Indians 20
Monacan Indians 50
Monroe, James 188
Montesqieu Spirit of Laws 154
Montgomery, Bernard 194
Montgomery, Richard 151
Monticello 156, 166
Montreal 80
Montségur 86
More, Thomas 133
Morgan Sr, J. P. 175
Morgan, Thomas 110
Morris, Gouverneur 155, 157-8
Morris, Robert 163
Morton, Jacob 163
Motta, Emanuel de la 173
Mount Vernon 160, 165-6
Mountbatten, Earl 191
Munich 138
Muscovy Company 29, 33, 34, 90
Muslims 85, 86, 199

N

Nansemond Indians 48, 52
Nantasket 12
Nantucket 22
Naples 173
Napoleon 126
Napoleon III 174, 180
Narbonne 86
Narrangaset Indians 20
Narváez, Pánfilo de 64-5, 66

National Bank Act 181
native Americans xi, 19, 92, 93, 146, 147, 200
  American South 65, 67-8, 68-9, 70, 71
  Anglo-Iroquois alliance 98, 152
  Cape Cod 9-10
  discovery of America 80
  'Elizabeth Island' 31-2
  Florida 44, 63, 65, 65, 66, 71, 72, 73, 75, 76
  infliction of Christianity 67, 68, 70, 71, 78, 114
  Jamestown 36-7, 37-8, 40
  land purchase from 20, 25
  New Netherland 13
  New Plymouth 11-12, 13, 14
  Pequot War 20
  Roanoke 43
  Shackamaxon treaty 24-5
  strict deportment imposed 14
  Virginia 40, 42-6, 47-9, 50-1, 52-3, 55-6, 56-7, 57-9, 60, 61
Navarre 85-6, 87
Nazis 194, 195
Nebraska 177
Negative Confessions 3
Netherlands/Holland 13, 136
  and American War of Independence 151

controls British
    waters 152
defeat Britain in
    West Indies 23
Deism 111
New World
    investment 5
Puritan exiles in 3-8
Rosicrucianism 96
see also Dutch
    settlers
Nevis 36
New Amsterdam 4, 18
New Atlantis 62, 87,
    97, 102, 130, 137,
    139, 159, 164 see also
    Bacon, Francis
New Deal 139
New England 2, 89
    Enlightenment
        Deists 113-27
    Masonic lodges 141
    naming 52
    Puritan settlement 8,
        11-22, 26
    Second Great
        Awakening 126
    wants independence
        149
New England
    Company 14, 15
New Hampshire 12,
    21, 117
New Haven 20
New Jersey 97, 117,
    194
New Jersey plan 156
New Mexico 71
New Netherland 13
    renamed New York
        21-2
New Orleans 176, 181
New Plymouth xiii, 2,
    11-14, 18, 26, 60, 92,

94, 97
    unified with
        Massachusetts Bay
        21, 22
New World Order xii,
    139, 189, 202
    two visions 202
New York 21-2, 97, 104,
    148, 151, 177, 180
    Grand Lodge 163
    Scottish Rite lodge
        172-3
    St John's Lodge no. 1
        163, 189-90, 199
New York City 174,
    194, 195
    Colombian Lodge of
        the Order of the
        Illuminati 141
Newfoundland 29, 74
Newgate 23
Newport, Christopher
    35, 36, 37, 45-6, 47-8,
    55, 61, 101, 171
Newton 108, 111, 115,
    116, 125, 126, 166
Nicola, Lewis 153
Nieu Nederlandt 12
Niña 63
Nixon, Richard 188,
    191
Nombre de Dios
    (Name of God) 78
Non-conformists 3, 15,
    18
North (Northern
    States)
    collision with South
        177-8
    defeats South 180-1
    Rothschild control
        173-4
    Southern secession
        178-9

North America
    British control 146
    Christian missions
        78
    civilization xiii
    Dutch settlements 4
    early colonization
        attempts 29-30
    early exploration 29
    English claim 63
    Spanish claim 64
    see also Florida;
        Massachusetts;
        New England;
        Virginia
North Carolina 29, 66,
    117, 148, 179
North Vietnam 196-7
north-west passage 29
Northern Jurisdiction
    see Scottish Rite
    Freemasonry
Northwest Ordinance
    153
Nova Scotia 22, 29, 39
Novo Ordo Seclorum
    139, 189
Nuremberg 194

O

Ochuse 69
Ohio 176, 177
Ohio river 153, 173
Oklahoma 66
one-world ideology 98,
    94, 102, 189 see also
    world government
    agenda
Opechancanough 48-9
Oppenheimers 130
Order of DeMolay 189
Order of Perfectabilists
    132 see also

Illuminati
Order of the Knights
of the Helmet 87
Order of the Knights
Temple 100
Order of the
Palladium 177
Orléans, Duke of 138
Ormus 131
Ortiz, Juan 44, 66-7,
69, 70
Osiris 137
Osterweis, Rollin 171-2
Otis, James 124, 147,
150
Otley xv, 30, 32, 34
Otley Hall xiii, xv, xvi,
xvii, xviii, 31
Ottoman Empire 107,
192
Outina 73
Oxford, 17th Earl 31

P
Pacaha 70
Paine, Thomas 112,
149
Common Sense 113,
118-19, 149
Deism 118-19, 126
and the Illuminati
138-9, 141
Palatinate of the Rhine
88, 95
Pallas Athena 87, 131
Palmerston, Lord 174,
183
Pamet river 9
Pamunkey river 42
Pan 90
Panama 65
Paris 136, 163, 173,
174, 193, 197

Paris Peace Treaty 146,
147
Parson's Cause case
147
Paspahegh Indians 36,
46, 49, 55-6
Pasqually, Martines de
(Martinez Paschalis)
194
Patawomeke Indians
56, 57
Paterson, William 156
Patience 50, 53, 54, 55
Paulet, Amias 85
Peabody, George 175
Pedro 70
Pemaquid Indians 11
Pemaquid river 39
Penn No Cross, No
Crown 23
Penn, William 22-6, 98,
148
Pennsylvania 24-6, 97,
98, 122, 148, 151, 155
Pennsylvania Gazette
115
Pennsylvania Magazine
149
Penny, John 3
pentagram, Masonic
164-5
Pequot War 20
Percy, George 34, 48,
50, 52, 53, 55-6, 57
Percy, John
Observations 39-40
Perkins, William 16
Perle, Richard 189
Perot, Ross 190
Peru 65
Philadelphia 24, 25, 97,
104, 105, 115, 122,
141, 149, 150, 153,
163

Philanthropia 88
Philip II of Spain 3, 75,
76, 77, 85
Philip III of Spain 93
Philip, Prince 191
Philippe IV of France
129
Philippines 28
phoenix 137, 139
Phoenix 46, 47
Pierce, Franklin 175,
177
Pietism 114
Pike, Albert 175-6,
177-8, 181, 183, 184-5
Morals and Dogma
185, 200
Pilgrims
Cape Cod landing
8-10
journey to England
6-8
in Leiden 5-6
New Plymouth 11-
14
origin of term 6
Saints and Strangers
5-6
pillars, Masonic 87, 92,
93
Pinckney, Charles 157
Pine, Tom 98
Pinta 63
Piscataqua river 12
Plan of Union 98
Plantin, Christopher
92
Planting Fathers 21,
62, 106, 107, 124,
127, 167, 169, 170
Plato 87
Plus Ultra 92
Plymouth, England 2,
7, 49, 74

Plymouth,
  Massachusetts *see*
  New Plymouth
Plymouth Rock 10
PNAC (Project for the
  New American
  Century) 189
Pocahontas 43-4, 46,
  48, 49, 57-9, 66, 94,
  201
Point Sayebrooke 19
Poland 139
Polk, James Knox 188
Ponce de Léon, Juan
  63-4
Popham, George 39
Port Royal 72-3
Porto Santo 27
Portsmouth, New
  Hampshire 12
Portugal 27
  American
    exploration 27-8,
    80
Potomac river 46
Powell, Captain 56
Powell, Colin 190
Powhatan 42-4, 45-6,
  47-8, 49, 50, 52-3, 55,
  57-8, 58-9
Powhatan Indians 30,
  51
Presbyterianism 15,
  116, 182
Presbyterians 120, 153
Prevost, Augustine 151
Princip, Gabriel 192
Pring, Martin 32
Priory of Sion 128,
  129, 130, 131, 135,
  136, 137, 139
Protestantism 100, 117
  Navarre 85, 86
Protestants 81, 110

French attempt to
  settle North
  America 71-8
German 88
Providence 31
Provincetown 8, 10
Prussians 129
Ptolemy 108
Puerto Rico 63, 64
Puritanism 22, 26, 94,
  118, 127
  Cold War vision 197
  Masonic opposition
    94, 106, 170
  and Rosicrucianism
    96-7
Puritans 2-3, 26, 27, 33,
  62, 81, 99, 123
  and Church-State
    unity 14, 15, 20-1,
    26, 127
  flight to the
    Netherlands 3-8
  in Massachusetts
    14-22
  revivalism 114
Putnam, Israel 151
pyramid 137, 138, 139
Pythagoras 130
Pythagoreanism 110

Q

Quakers 19
  Penn's 'holy
    experiment' 22-6
  persecution 116-17
Quapaw Plains Indians
  70
Quartering Act 148
Quebec 80, 81
Queen Anne's War
  25-6
Quietism 114

Quigate 70
Quigley, Carroll
  Tragedy and Hope 189
Quitman, John 176,
  177, 179
Quiz-quiz 70

R

Radclyffe, Charles 102,
  128
Raleigh, Walter 29, 30,
  32, 33, 35, 47, 89, 92,
  99
  *The History of the
    World* 92, 100
Randolph, Edmund
  155, 156, 157, 163
Randolph, Peyton 105,
  148, 149
Ratcliffe, John 36, 40,
  41, 45, 46-7, 50, 51,
  52-3
Read, James 41
Reagan, Ronald 188,
  197
Reformation 2-3
Reid, Thomas 112
Reimarus, Hermann
  111
religion xii
  and the Constitution
    157, 168-9
  Deist view 110-11
  dissenters
    persecuted 19,
    116-17
  Dutch toleration 4
  emphasis in
    plantings xii, 31,
    33
  Enlightened 108
  Franklin's view
    115-16

Freemasonic law on 167-70
Fundamental Orders of Connecticut 20-1
Great Awakening 113-15
magistrates right to interfere 20
pluralism 23-4, 25, 55
uniformity imposed 54-5
utilitarian purpose 123-4
Winthrop's covenant 16-17
Renaissance 89, 107
Rensselaer, Killian Van 176
republicanism 153, 154, 159, 166, 172
Republicans 178, 192, 193
Restoration 23
'revelation' 108, 126, 202
Revere, Paul 103, 104, 105, 148, 163
Rhode Island 19, 20, 22
Rhodes, Cecil 189
Ribaut, Jean 71-2, 74, 75, 76-8
Richmond, Virginia xiii, 166, 178, 179, 181, 185, 201
Roanoke Island 29-30, 43, 89
Robert I (the Bruce) 100
Robertson, Donald 112
Robespierre 128
Robinson (Quaker)

116-17
Robinson, John 5, 7, 42, 45
Robison, John 142
  Proofs of a Conspiracy 139-40
Rockefeller, David 181, 195-6
Rockefeller, Laurance 196
Rockefeller III, John D. 195
Rockefeller Jr, John D. 201
Rockefeller, Nelson 195
Rockefeller family 192, 193, 195, 201
Roger, Richard 16
Rolfe, John 58-9, 94
Roman Church 93, 94, 96
Roman Empire 108
Romantic movement 125-6, 172
Rome 102
Rome, ancient xiii, 160, 176
Roosevelt, Clinton 139, 141
Roosevelt, Franklin D. 139, 141, 188, 190
Roosevelt, Theodore 188
Rosenkreutz, Christina 88
Rosi Crosse Society 87-8, 91
Rosicrucian College 87-8, 97
Rosicrucian Manifestos 88
Rosicrucian Freemasons 166

Rosicrucianism 87-9, 95, 96, 98, 99, 130, 137
  and Deism 110, 111
  and Puritanism 96-7
  see also English (Rosicrucian) Freemasonry
Rosslyn 79, 80, 100
Rothschild, James 173, 174
Rothschild, Lionel 173, 174
Rothschild, Mayer Amschel 130-1, 132, 135, 173, 193
Rothschild family 130-1, 138, 184, 193
  American central bank plan 173-4, 180, 181
Round Table 191
Rousseau, Jean-Jacques 108, 111, 133, 135-6, 150
Royal Institute of International Affairs (RIIA) 191
Royal Lodge of Commanders of the Temple West 138
Royal Society 96, 98
Rufin, Guillaume 72
Ruge, Arnold 175
Rush, Benjamin 112, 113
Russia 33, 90, 192, 196, 198
  sells Alaska 184
  supports Lincoln 180, 181
  see also Soviet Union/USSR
Russian Orthodox

Church 193
Russian revolutions
132, 193-4
Rutledge, John 155,
157

S

Sagadahoc (Kennebec)
39
Saints 5-6, 8, 14
Salem (Naumkeag) 12,
15, 17
Salomon de Caus 89,
95
Samoset 11
San Diego 78
San Domingo
(Hispaniola) 28
San Francisco 92, 180
San Pelayo 75
San Salvador 63
San Salvador 75
San Vincente, Captain
77
Sanders, George 175
Santa Maria 63
Saratoga, battle of 151,
152
Satanism 134-5, 141,
143
Saxe-Gotha, Duke of
140
Schliemann, Heinrich
xv
Schröder Bank 194
Schuylkill river 24
Schwartz, Barry 123-4
Scotland 136
Deism 111, 112-13
Jacobite rebellions
102
Templar (Jacobite)
Freemasonry 34,

62, 100, 103, 112
Scott, Walter 172, 176
Scott, Winfield 179
Scottish
Enlightenment 112-
13, 127
Scottish Rite
Freemasonry 102-3,
129, 140, 172, 184,
185, 188, 195
Northern
Jurisdiction 173,
175, 176, 178
Southern
Jurisdiction 173,
175-6, 177, 178,
179, 181
Scottish Templar
(Jacobite)
Freemasons 102-3
Scrivener, Matthew 49
*Sea Venture (Sea
Adventure)* 49-50, 53
seals 90-2, 96 *see also*
Great Seal
Second Book of Esdras
28
Second Committee
138
Second Continental
Congress 105, 149-
50, 168
Second Great
Awakening 126
Second World War
194, 196, 199
Secret Doctrine 87, 95,
98, 137
Seligman family 174
Senate 156
Separatists xii-xiii, 2-3,
5, 9, 14, 15, 27, 33,
84, 92
Septimania 86

Seven Years War 147
Seward, William 182,
183, 184
Seward's Folly 184
Shackamaxon 25
Shaftesbury, Earl of
110, 111
Shakespeare, William
100
First Folio 91
Masonic connections
91, 94
Othello 88
Southampton's
patronage 31, 60,
88
Tempest 29, 32, 50,
88, 95
Twelfth Night 14
Venus and Adonis 91
Sharansky, Israeli *Case
for Democracy* 201
Sherman, Roger 149,
156
Sicklemore, John *see*
Kendall, George
Sierra Leone 27
Simpson, Senator 190
Skene, John 97
Skull and Bones 188-9
slave trade 61, 74, 150
slavery 150, 156, 159,
171
abolition 184
and Civil War 173,
174, 175, 177, 178,
180-1
'slave empire' plan
176
Slidell, John 174, 179
Small, William 112
Smith, Adam 154
Wealth of Nations
112, 169

Smith, John xiii-xiv, 34, 36, 37, 38, 53, 100
A Description of New England 52, 89, 93
Freemasonry 90-4, 99, 142, 200-1
Generall Historie 43-4, 48, 49, 51, 52, 90, 93
and Jamestown's survival 40-52
A New and Accurat Map of the World 93
and Pocahontas 57, 59, 66
Proceedings 47, 48, 49, 51
A True New Relation 43, 47, 90
True Travels 52
Smythe, Thomas 33, 34, 35, 38, 49, 90, 101, 200
Socialist International 193
Socrates 107, 117
Solomon 85, 160
Somers, George 50, 53, 55
Sons of Liberty 104, 105, 148
Soule, Pierre 179
South (American South/Southern States)
'born again' evangelism 114
Britain wants control 173
chivalric cult 171-2
de Soto in 66-71
defeat 181
Knights of the

Golden Circle recruitment 176-7
landed values 170, 171
rebellion 177-8
riots 184
Rothschild control 173-4
secession 178-9
and slavery 61, 156, 159, 171, 176, 177
Southern Jurisdiction control 172-3
South America 28, 29, 58, 176
Dutch settlements 4
Spanish claims and possessions 29, 63, 65
South Asian Free Trade Area (SAFTA) 198
South Carolina 66, 67-8, 78, 97, 117, 148, 155, 157, 173, 177, 178, 190
Southampton, Earl of 31, 33, 52, 60, 88
Southern Jurisdiction *see* Scottish Rite Freemasonry
Soviet Union/USSR 86-7, 133, 143, 193-8
Masonic State 193-4, 195, 196-7
Spain 65, 73, 194
alleged spies 41
and American Civil War 180
American claims and possessions 29, 63, 64, 65, 75, 78, 146, 152

American 'discovery' 28, 80
American domination resisted 30, 63, 86, 99-100
American exploration ix, 63-71
and American War of Independence 151
Bacon's opposition 85-7
controls British waters 152
Dutch independence 3
Jewish Golden Age 86
native American slaves 11
Spanish Alhumbrados 134, 135
Spanish Armada 2, 30, 86, 93
Spanish settlers 63, 99, 170
Florida 74-8
Spanish Inquisition 86
'Spanish Main' 65
Sparke, John the Younger 74
Sparkes (English emissary) 58
Speedwell 6, 7, 32
Spelman, Henry 51, 52
Speyer and Co 174
Spice Islands (Indonesia) 4
Spinoza, Barukh 109, 111
square, Masonic 164
St Lawrence river 81

St Augustine, Florida
64, 71, 72, 75, 78, 200
St Clair, Arthur 151
St Clair, Henry 79-80
St John, Henry,
Viscount
Bolingbroke 110
St Johns river 71, 72, 73,
74
Stage Point 14
Stalin 193-4, 195
Stamp Act 98, 148
Standard Oil 194, 196
Standish, Miles 9
Stanton, Edward M.
178, 179, 182-3
Statue of Liberty 140
Stevenson (Quaker)
116-17
Stewart, Dugald 112
Stiles, Ezra 115, 116,
168-9
Stow, John *Annales of*
England 34-5
Strachey, William 53,
55, 56, 61
Historie of Travail into
Virginia Britania 31,
89
Lawes Divine, Morall
and Martiall 55, 56
True Repertory 50, 55,
95
Strangers 5-6, 8-9, 14, 18
Stuart, Charles Edward
102-3, 105
Stuart, Elizabeth 88, 96,
101
Stuart, Francis Edward
102
Stuart Mill, John 125
Stuarts 100, 102
Suez Canal 174
Sugar Act 148

Supreme Being 109,
110, 119-20, 126
Supreme Soviet 193
Susan Constant 36
Sussex, Duke of 154
Suwannee river 67
Swallow 50
Sweden 139, 140
Syndicate 143, 192,
193-8, 199, 201, 202

T

Taft, William 190
Tampa Bay 44, 64-5, 66
tarot 110
Tascaluça Indians 68-9
taxation 103, 148
Tea Act 104, 148
Templar Freemasonry /
Templarism 100-6,
136
and American War of
Independence
151-2
and Boston Tea Party
103-4, 148
and design of
Washington 164-5
Founding Fathers
127, 170
Frederick II and 129,
130, 131
Illuminati infiltration
130, 136, 137-8, 140
James I brings to
England 34, 47, 62,
101, 142
Monticello designs
166
and republicanism
105, 153, 166
in Scotland 34, 62,
100, 103, 112

St Clairs 79, 80
State domination
105-6, 166-7
support for national
sovereignty 159,
160
Temple of Solomon
(Temple of
Jerusalem) 86, 87,
109
Tennessee 66, 179
Tennyson *Idylls of the*
King 172
Texas 65, 66, 71, 179,
180, 181
Thanksgiving Day 12,
18
Theodore of Good
Council 138
Third Committee 139
thirteen, significance
137, 179
Thomason, Charles
139
Thompson, Jacob 183
Thurmond, Senator
190
Thutmose III 85
Tilney, Elizabeth
Gosnold xvi
Timucuan Indians 64
Tindal, Matthew 110
Tisquantum (Squanto)
11
Toledo 86
Toombs, Robert 179
Toscanelli, Paolo
27-8
Tower of London 23,
33, 92
Townshend Acts 147,
148
Trilateral Commission
191, 192

Trinity 76
Trotsky, Leon 193
Truman, Harry 188
Tudhope, George 90, 91
Tudors 91
Tulla 70
Tyrian Lodge 188

U

UK *see* Britain/UK
Ulalah 44
United Nations (UN) 195
United States
  400th anniversary of founding xiii, 38, 200
  advanced civilization xi
  beginning of democratic tradition 18
  Christianity and Freemasonry 198-201
  Cold War 195-8
  early confederacy 152-3
  Freemasonic religious law 167-70
  Freemasons control 184-6
  Masonic State xii, 163, 166-7, 170, 187-90, 192, 195, 196-7, 201-2
  sub-Masonic secret societies 191-2
  Syndicate influence 192
  Vietnam War 197
  see also American

Constitution; American Declaration of Independence; Founding Fathers; Great Seal
United States of the World xii, 198, 202
Unity 50
Utopianism 24, 32, 87, 89, 95, 132, 133

V

Vázquez de Coronado, Francisco 71
Venezuela 29, 65
Veracruz 180
Verdun, battle of 192
Vespucci, Amerigo 28, 63
Vicksburg 181
Vienna 129, 173
Vietnam 196-7
Vikings 28, 80
Virgil Georgics 37, 160
Virginia, xvi 5, 86, 98, 148, 156, 164, 176, 179
  Alexandria Lodge no. 22 106, 163, 165-6
  Anglicans in 27, 31-2, 33-62, 147
  colonial gentry 171
  Federalists vs. Anti-Federalists 158
  Fredericksburg Lodge 106
  Freemasons in 95-6, 99, 101, 103, 142
  Hagger's lecture xiii-xiv, 201
  Illuminati 141

  Jesuit missionaries 78
  Parson's Cause case 147
  religious compulsion 117
  St John's Lodge no. 36 178
  wants independence 149
Virginia 50, 54
Virginia Company of London 33, 34, 35, 36, 39, 47-8, 49, 51, 56, 57, 59, 60-1, 89, 94, 101, 171
Virginia Company of Plymouth 39, 51-2, 60
Virginia Council 34, 35, 36, 37, 40, 47, 54, 89, 95
Virginia plan 156
Virginia Provincial Assembly 105
Virginian Statute for Religious Freedom 168
Visigoths 86
Voltaire 25, 111, 139

W

Wainman, Ferdinando 55
Waldo, Richard 49
Wall Street 194
Wallace, Henry A. 139
Walloons 12-13
Walsingham 30
Wampanoag Indians 11-12
Wapen van Amsterdam 13

War against Terror 201
Ward, Nathaniel 18
Warraskoyack Indians
56
Warren, Joseph 104,
124
Warren, Rhode Island
(Sowams) 11
Warwick, Earl of 18-19
Washington, DC
164-7, 177, 179
Washington, George
187
  and American
    independence 149,
    151, 153
  and the Constitution
    155, 156, 157, 158
  death and relics
    165-6
  Deism 117, 119-23,
    126, 182
  and design of
    Washington, DC
    164
  and Freemasonic
    State 166-7
  Freemasonry 106,
    149, 153, 163, 165-
    6, 278-81
  inauguration 160,
    163, 189-90
  lays Capitol
    foundation stone
    165
  return to the land
    160
Washington
  Monument 165
Waterloo, Battle of
  131
Watt, James 112
Wayne House, W. 125
Weishaupt, Adam 128,

130-6, 137-8, 139,
  140, 141-2, 143, 154,
  172, 173, 185, 187,
  189, 193
Werowocomoco 48
Wesley, John 114, 126
West Indies 23, 28, 65,
  74, 148, 176
West Jersey 22
West, Francis 48, 50-1,
  52
Westminster Abbey 91
Weston, Thomas 5-6,
  7, 12
Wethersfield 20
Weymouth, Captain
  17
Whigs 23
Whitaker, Alexander
  54, 59
White, John 29-30
White, Susannah 12,
  14
White House 164, 165,
  185
White Oak Swamp 42
Whitefield, George
  114, 115
Whitney Choice of
  Emblems 87, 92
Wiffin, Richard 49
Wilhelm, Kaiser 192
Wilkins, John 96
William II 25
William III (William of
  Orange) 25, 102,
  111, 113
William IX of Hesse-
  Kassel 130
Williams, Roger 18, 20
Williams, William 167
Williamsburg 201
Wilson, Bird 120-1,
  122-3

Wilson, James 149, 155
Wilson, Woodrow 181
Windsor 20
Wingfield, Edward-
  Maria 34, 35, 36, 37,
  40-1, 61, 101
Winslow, Edward 4,
  11, 12
Winthrop Jr, John 19
Winthrop Sr, John
  15-18, 19-20, 21, 23,
  169
  A Modell of Christian
    Charitie 16, 167,
    205-19
Witherspoon, John
  112, 168
Woolston, Thomas
  110
Wooster, David 151
world government
  agenda 133, 139, 143,
  187, 191, 193, 197,
  199, 201, 202-3
Wowinchopunck 49,
  56
Writs of Assistance
  147, 150

Y

Yale University 188-9
Yeardley, Governor 59-
  60
Yeltsin, Boris 197
York 85
York Rite 103
Yorktown 151
Young America 174,
  175, 176, 177, 182
Young Germany 175
Young Russia 175
Yule, David Levy 179
Yupaha 67-8